Gas and oil in Northeast Asia

Research by the Energy and Environmental Programme is supported by generous contributions of finance and technical advice from the following organizations:

Ashland Oil • British Nuclear Fuels • British Gas
British Petroleum • Department of Trade and Industry
Eastern Group • Enron Europe • Enterprise Oil
Esso • LASMO • Mitsubishi Fuels • National Grid
National Power • Nuclear Electric • PowerGen
Saudi Aramco • Shell • Statoil • Texaco
Tokyo Electric Power Co

Additional support is received for specific research projects from the following:

Commission of the European Communities • Department of Environment (UK) • ENEL • Energy Technology Support Unit • German Environment Ministry • Hydro-Quebec Imatran Voima Oy • London Electricity • Rolls Royce Industrial Power • Siemens • Southern Electric • Tennessee Valley Authority • Swiss Environment Ministry

Gas and oil in Northeast Asia

Policies, Projects and Prospects

Keun Wook Paik

THE ROYAL INSTITUTE OF INTERNATIONAL AFFAIRS
Energy and Environmental Programme

First published in Great Britain in 1995 by
Royal Institute of International Affairs, 10 St James's Square, London SW1Y 4LE
(Charity Registration No. 208 223)

Distributed in North America by
The Brookings Institution, 1775 Massachusetts Avenue NW,
Washington DC 20036-2188

A catalogue record for this book is available from the British Library.

Paperback: ISBN 0-905031-94-6
Hardback: ISBN 0-899658-09-2

The Royal Institute of International Affairs is an independent body which promotes the rigorous study of international questions and does not express opinions of its own. The opinions expressed in this publication are the responsibility of the author.

Typeset by Koinonia, Manchester.
Printed and bound by The Chameleon Press, Wandsworth, London.
Cover by Visible Edge.
Cover illustration by Harry Brockway.

To my mother with respect,

and to Soo-Hyun with love.

Contents

Maps

Figures

Tables

Preface

With its huge population, explosive economic growth and correspondingly growing energy demand, Northeast Asia is a region of great importance and growing global interest for all those concerned with energy and related issues. Within its vast land area there are also extensive fossil fuel resources. But the region's immense diversity in politics, stages of economic development, and location of the major energy resources make development of these resources a complex international political, financial and industrial issue.

Gas and oil in Northeast Asia offers the most extensive and detailed analysis of these issues yet published. Dr Paik is uniquely qualified to conduct such research, having spent many years working on the region using source material in Russian, Chinese, Japanese and Korean. The book's origins lie in Dr Paik's PhD thesis on the topic, and we are most fortunate indeed that Dr Paik expressed interest in developing that work and taking it through all the stages required to turn it into a book of this nature.

Dr Paik's thesis research was generously supported by the University of Aberdeen, the British Council in Korea and by BP Seoul. We are most grateful to them, and to Clive Archer, Alexander Kemp, Jonathan Stern and to David Rose for helping to supervise Dr Paik's thesis work and its subsequent development at Aberdeen University Petroleum and Economic Consultants (AUPEC). We are also most grateful to BP Exploration and the Palmco Corporation for providing additional support, and I would add my thanks to Dr Paik's for all the others involved in the huge task of developing a book such as this. Most of all, of course, all of us on the Energy and Environmental Programme are grateful to Dr Paik himself for his dedication and commitment to bringing this project to such a successful conclusion.

November 1995

Dr Michael Grubb
Head, Energy and
Environmental Programme

Acknowledgments

I am grateful to all those people who have contributed to the preparation of this study. My thanks go first to Michael Grubb, John Mitchell and Jonathan P. Stern of the Energy and Environmental Programme at the Royal Institute of International Affairs. They provided me with the chance to draw to a conclusion my ten years of research. Special thanks are also due to Clive Archer at Aberdeen University whose guidance broadened my insight.

I would particularly like to thank Alexander G. Kemp and David Rose at Aberdeen University Petroleum and Economic Consultants. Without their full and strong support, this study would not have been possible. My thanks are also due to Hoesung Lee, Jeong-Shik Shin and Gyoo-Jeong Jeon of the Korea Energy Economics Institute. They invited me to join the Sakha gas project study and this provided a valuable opportunity to gather useful materials. My thanks should be extended to Masaru Hirata and Kengo Asakura of the National Pipeline Research Society of Japan. They invited me to the Tokyo Conference early this year, which provided me with useful materials for this study.

This work owes much to the helpful comments and suggestions made by members of the study group convened by the Energy and Environmental Programme. My special thanks are due to Michael J. Bradshaw for his helpful comments. Many thanks to Richard L. Grant. Robert E. Ebel, Tatsu Kambara, David Rose and Alexander G. Kemp who had the patience to read the final draft and made invaluable suggestions. Finally I am greatly indebted to Jane Chapman at Chatham House who has endured all the difficulties of bringing this publication together, and Judith Ravenscroft who did a splendid editing job.

October 1995 Keun-Wook Paik

Summary and conclusions

In recent years Northeast Asia has experienced an explosive economic growth, with a concomitant increase in energy – and particularly in oil – demand, with growth rates amongst the highest in the world. The dilemma facing the region is how to maintain its economic growth with a stable oil and gas supply in the coming decades.

Within the region overall, there are substantial fossil fuel resources, but they are unevenly located. Most are far from the major centres of population and economic – and hence energy – growth; the major deposits are in Russian Asia and remote areas of China (including disputed offshore areas), whereas demand comes mainly from southern/eastern China and the smaller 'tiger' economies of the Pacific rim. Given the complex politics of the region, this makes the exploitation of fossil fuel resources a complex technological, economic and industrial issue, with potent implications for international relations

The uneven distribution of oil and gas resources among the Northeast Asian countries indicates that common benefits can be derived from cooperation in oil and gas development. Russian Asia and China, with huge oil and gas reserves, need capital, technology and equipment for exploration and development; while Japan, Taiwan and South Korea, with capital, technology and equipment, need to diversify their energy supplies.

Historically, energy has been a source of competition in the region. But the changing political environment in recent years is encouraging cooperation in oil and gas development, despite the legacies of the Cold War that remain. The remote location and relatively small scale of proven oil resources in the region's frontier areas will limit their role and that of multilateral cooperation in oil development. In contrast, natural gas resources are very large and offer the prospect of making an important regional contribution involving multilateral cooperation.

Gas offers the best combination of low emissions and a high potential for substitution for oil in the industrial sector, and is ideal for the region's energy balance and environmental concerns. But the role of gas is currently underestimated. Its share in the region's energy mix is far below the world average, despite the fact that the region dominates the world trade in liquefied natural gas (LNG).

Currently, natural gas in the region is almost all supplied from distant sources (particularly the Middle East and southeast Asia) via LNG. Projected continued expansion of gas use from these sources raises concerns both about cost and about security. In contrast, resources within the region could be transported via pipeline, including a subsea pipeline to Japan and South Korea. Pipelines offer potentially greater volumes at lower long-run economic and environmental costs than LNG, and allow additional diversification of sources. The most promising possibility for the future therefore lies in Russian Asia's gas development.

Four major frontier oil and gas resource regions exist, at different stages of consideration or development. Sakhalin alone has four projects, of which the Sakhalin-II project is ready for development. Sakhalin-I will be ready once preparatory work is complete. Sakhalin-III and IV are in the early stages of comprehensive exploration. Both the Sakha republic and the Irkutsk region's gas projects are undergoing feasibility studies for development. Part of China's Tarim Basin is already under development, but most of the Basin needs comprehensive exploration. In short, a lot of studies have been undertaken, but not much is yet happening in project development.

Given China's galloping energy demand, the Tarim Basin and offshore development cannot meet China's needs, let alone those of the region, at least until a string of super-giant oil and gas discoveries are made.

In contrast, Russian Asian projects could make a considerable regional contribution. The merit of Sakhalin-I and II lies in their relative geographical proximity to the Northeast Asian market, and that of the Irkutsk project in its relatively easy conditions for pipeline construction, with extensions to neighbouring countries. The Sakha project has a relatively large export capacity. However, overall these projects are big, complex and remote, requiring considerable investment recouped over long periods. Furthermore, delivering the gas by pipeline would require development of an extensive pipeline system crossing several political boundaries, with the output shared amongst the different participating countries. For these reasons - and because much of the capital and technology required for such development lies outside Russian Asia itself – such developments would at least benefit from, and may both require and themselves promote, multilateral cooperation. Indeed successful implementation could also ease political tensions, and consequently promote regional peace and security.

In addition to the sheer scale of investment required, however, difficult political obstacles and other uncertainties stand in the way. The worst concern specific political disputes. For example, the unresolved territorial dispute between Russia and Japan is still hampering Japan's active participation in Russian Asian development, and disputes over the Spratly islands may foreshadow difficulties over still-disputed boundaries through the East China Sea and Yellow Sea. The possibility of other projects proceeding in preference to those in Russian Asia poses a second problem. For instance, China and Japan's approach to introduce Turkmenistan gas into the Northeast Asian market may distract from Russian gas development. These factors confirm the overall difficulty of regional countries realizing multilateral benefits from big projects, rather than engaging in political competition to attract investment on a bilateral basis.

Besides this, a number of grass-roots LNG projects, like Indonesia's Natuna project and the US Alaska project, aiming at supplying LNG to the Northeast Asian market, could compete with the Russian gas. But the benefits of tapping the massive Russian resources outweigh the burden of long-distance pipeline costs. Other projects appear either unrealistic or insufficiently promising to justify delaying the strategic development of Russian gas.

Because of the complexity of the region's frontier projects, with the need for cooperation to maximize benefits, and the obstacles posed by political disputes, development is likely to proceed in an effective way only if a multilateral framework is established. Fortunately, regional countries are beginning to recognize the need for cooperation in promoting early development of frontier energy resources. Northeast Asia will witness the beginnings of partial multilateral cooperation in the region's frontier energy development by the end of the next decade, and a long-distance gas pipeline grid is likely to be developed over the same period.

The sequence of development of the region's frontier projects will be as follows: Sakhalin-II will proceed first, followed by the Irkutsk project. Then Sakhalin-I will go ahead. All these projects will start between 1996 and 1998. At the end of this decade, the Sakha project will be developed because of its connection with the Irkutsk project.

Multilateral cooperation will accelerate the region's long-delayed frontier energy development. The establishment of a multilateral government–industry forum could hasten the way forward. So what is really needed for the region is a Northeast Asian Energy Forum (NAEF) whose resolutions are binding or official. Regional environmental regimes are already emerging: establishment of a Northeast Asia energy consortium, based on Siberia's gas resources, was proposed by the Northeast Asian Economic Forum in early 1995. The establishment of NAEF is not such a remote reality.

Once NAEF is established, it could tackle issues such as binding investment protection, transit of energy supplies, environmental protection, development of energy security installations, dispute-settlement procedures and increased energy security throughout Northeast Asia. Like the European Energy Charter Treaty, NAEF could provide institutional comfort for potential investors in the event of political problems.

In conclusion, Northeast Asia's energy resources, and particularly gas resources, offer huge potential benefits. Early development of these resources will provide the region with economic and energy security, and environmental, and potentially political, benefits. Multilateral cooperation is essential for the early realization of oil and gas development: will the region accept the concept of multilateral cooperation for its frontier gas development? If so, when and in what form? Northeast Asia stands at a crossroads.

Chapter 1

The energy scene in Northeast Asia

1.1 Introduction

This study is concerned with energy in Northeast Asia: in China, Japan, North and South Korea, Taiwan, Mongolia and Russian Asia.[1] This geographical focus is determined by a figurative economic watershed that orients the region's political, economic and military outputs towards Northeast Asia rather than westwards. The key features of the region that bear upon the issues in this book are its vast size, an explosive growth in its energy demand, and the scale and location of its energy resources.

Northeast Asia is a huge region – at nearly 20 million sq. km the land area, dominated by China and Russian Asia, is equivalent to that of the United States and Canada combined (see Map 1.1).[2] In recent years it has also been a region of huge economic growth, with an increase in energy – and particularly oil – demand. Growth rates average around 8%. Within the region overall, there are substantial fossil resources, but they are far from evenly located.

This study concentrates on the extensive gas and lesser oil resources, and the issues raised by efforts to tap them. The defining feature of these resources is that most are located far from the major centres of population and economic – and hence

[1] This definition could be regarded as controversial because it includes Russian East Siberia (RES) and the Russian Far East (RFE) in the category of Northeast Asia. It does not, however, constitute a totally new approach. Allan Whiting, using the term 'East Asian Siberia' rather than the conventional 'Soviet Far East', argued that the term 'East Asian Siberia' denoted the criterion of relevance to East Asia with implications for China, Korea and Japan. See Allan Whiting, *Siberian Development and East Asia: Threat or Promise?*, Stanford University Press, Stanford, 1981, pp. 14–18.

[2] Of the seven countries, the largest is China, extending 5,200 km from east to west and 5,500 km from north to south, with 9.6 million sq. km. The second largest is Russian Asia, composed of RES (1.55 million sq. km) and the RFE (6.22 million sq. km). Despite the region's size, the populations of RES and the RFE as of 1989 are merely 5.24 and 7.95 million respectively. The total size of other Northeast Asian countries is only 2.2 million sq. km, a combination of Mongolia (1.567 million sq. km), the Korean peninsula (0.22 million sq. km), Taiwan (0.036 million sq. km) and Japan (0.378 million sq. km).

Map 1.1: Northeast Asia

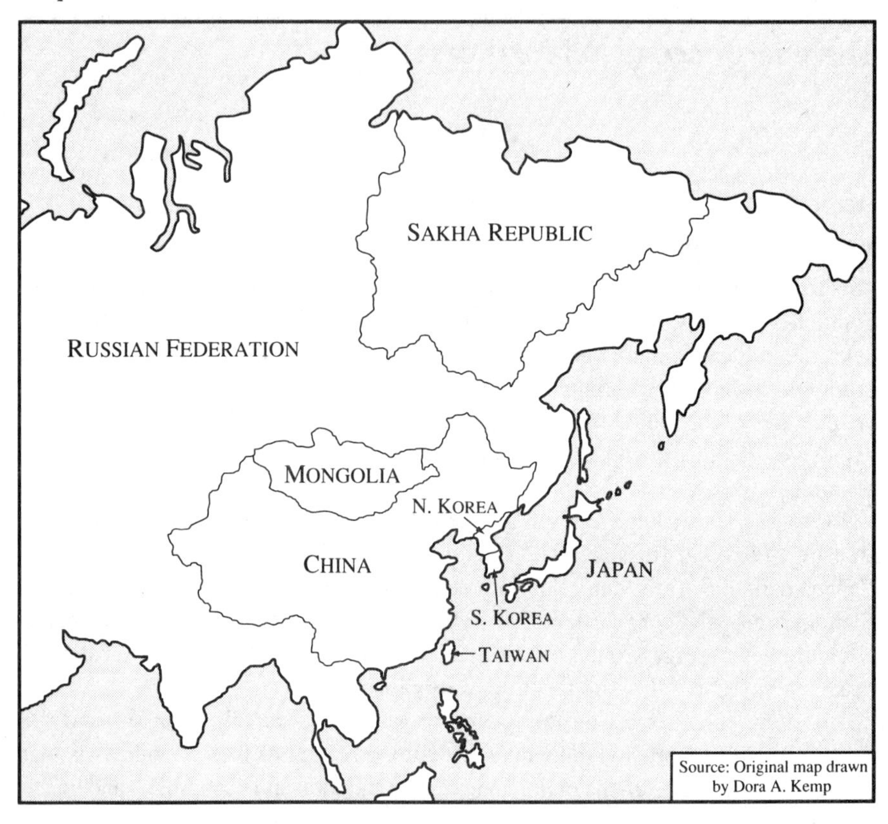

Source: Original map drawn by Dora A. Kemp

energy – growth; the major deposits are in Russian Asia and China (including disputed offshore areas), whereas demand growth is concentrated in southern/eastern China and the smaller 'tiger' economies of the Pacific rim. Given the complex politics of the region, the exploitation of these resources is not merely a complex technological, economic and industrial issue, but also a potent issue in international relations.

This study draws together an immense amount of technical information on the resources, industries and projects involved, and seeks to address the following questions:

- Will the region's major energy resources be developed, and if so how and over what timescale? Which major projects seem most likely to proceed or most deserve government backing? What kind of investments may be required, and how can such technical and financial resources best be mobilized? What is the appropriate and likely relationship between government and industry?

- To what extent will development of these resources depend upon resolution of political disputes in the region? Will efforts to develop them contribute to the political stability of the region, or is there a risk that competition for available resources may exacerbate regional conflicts, and if so, how can policy encourage the former rather than the latter? Will this require regional, rather than just bilateral, energy cooperation, and if so along what lines, and how likely is this to be realized?
- Given the limitations on the known reserves and their development prospects, to what extent can the region's energy needs be met internally, and to what extent is the region likely to draw ever more expansively on global energy markets? Does the region's dependence on energy imports pose a threat to its economic development, or to the stability of the global market; and to what extent would development of the region's resources help to address either of these problems?

This is a complex set of questions, few of which have been examined seriously before. It is not possible to develop definitive answers, but this study provides many clues and contains much of the information required to address the questions, and to evaluate the region's gas and oil prospects.

This first chapter sets out the background to the region, and the study. It starts by touching on the problems and prospects for the region's energy demands. Then the region's resources, and the situation and importance of energy in Russia and China will be discussed. Finally, it will explore the possibility of multilateral cooperation for the region's frontier gas and oil projects.

1.2 Energy demand: problems and prospects

1.2.1 Oil imports

The Asia–Pacific region's energy demand has grown explosively in parallel with its rapid economic growth. For example, during 1971–91, East Asia's GDP growth exceeded 7%, and total primary energy demand expanded at an average annual rate of 6.6%. This was a faster rate of growth than that experienced in any other region and resulted in East Asia's share of global energy demand doubling to 4.6%. The region accounted for about 9% of total world incremental energy demand.[3]

---

[3] Here, East Asian countries are Brunei, Hong Kong, Indonesia, Kampuchea, Laos, Malaysia, Myanmar, North Korea, Papua New Guinea, Philippines, Singapore, the Republic of Korea, Taiwan, Thailand, Vietnam and the Pacific Islands. The IEA study did not put Japan and China in this definition. It dealt with Japan as an OECD Pacific country, and China separately. See International Energy Agency, *World Energy Outlook*, 1994 edn., IEA, Paris, 1994, pp. 143–5.

Figure 1.1: Primary energy consumption in Northeast Asia: 1983 vs. 1993

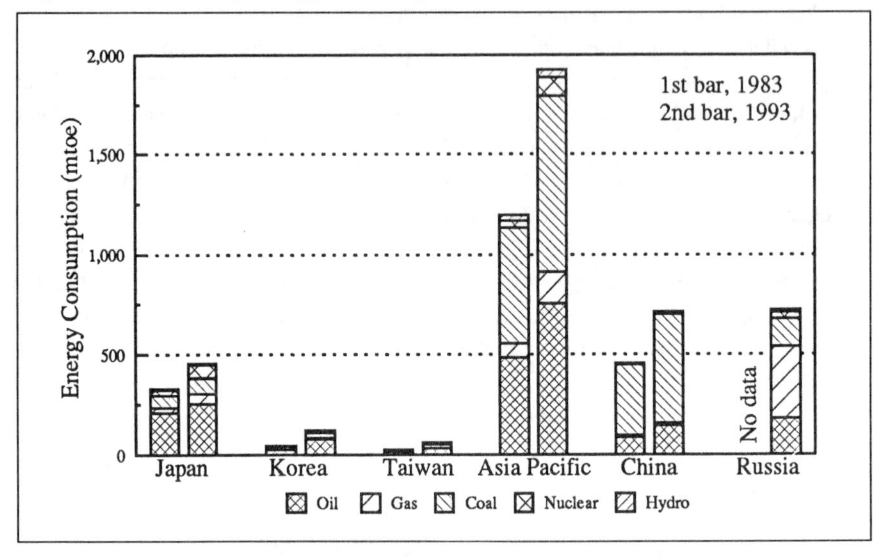

Note: 1. Asia–Pacific total includes China, and comparable data for Russia (as distinct from the USSR) not available for 1983. Here Northeast Asia includes all of Russia, not just Russian Asia.
Souce: BP Statistical Review of World Energy, June 1994.

In particular, Northeast Asian countries, like Japan, South Korea, Taiwan and China, were major constituents in energy-demand growth. As shown in Figure 1.2, primary energy consumption by these four Northeast Asian countries in 1993 recorded roughly 1,352 million tonnes of oil equivalent (mtoe), equivalent to 70.2% of consumption the Asia–Pacific region and 17.3% of the world total. During 1983–93, the increase in the world's primary energy consumption was 1,372.9 mtoe, of which 36% (497.2 mtoe) was by these four countries. The average annual growth rates of primary energy consumption by Japan, South Korea and Taiwan during 1987–92 were 3.9%, 11.9% and 8.0% respectively. The figures for oil-demand growth rates, in particular, were 4.3%, 19.9% and 8.4% respectively.

This sort of galloping energy demand is the result of growing industrialization, expanding transportation systems and the rapidly increasing demand for electricity. The growth in energy demand seems likely to continue in the coming years, but raises a series of questions as to the balance of energy supply and demand in the region.

The most important questions relate to oil. According to a study on the Asia–Pacific energy outlook to 2010 by the East–West Center, demand for oil products in the region will grow by an average of 4.1%, from 14.9 mb/d in 1993 to 19.8 mb/d in

2000. In the first decade of the next century, demand will grow by 3% annually and reach 26.6 mb/d.[4] Much of this demand seems to be coming from Northeast Asia, particularly China.

However, the Asia–Pacific region's crude-oil production is expected to remain unchanged for the rest of the decade after reaching 6.9 mb/d in the mid-1990s and then to decline to 6.7 mb/d by 2010. In other words, the region's crude-oil production will be unable to satisfy regional demand, and the gap between supply and demand will widen rapidly. Consequently, crude-oil imports from outside the Asia–Pacific region will represent two-thirds of its consumption by 2000 and three-quarters by 2010. Of the region's crude-oil imports, it is projected that the Middle East will contribute 87% in 2000 and 95% in 2010.[5]

1.2.2 Oil concerns

This is an alarming forecast. A study by the International Energy Agency (IEA), predicting that the Middle East plus Venezuela would take a leading position in the world's oil supply in 2010, confirmed that this forecast is not groundless. According to the IEA's oil demand and supply projection, as shown in Table 1.1, in the decade between 2000 and 2010 oil supplies from the Middle East Gulf and Venezuela are forecast to rise from 31 mb/d to 45.4 mb/d; while OECD production declines from 15.2 mb/d to 14.2 mb/d. Meanwhile world oil demand will rise to 94 mb/d by 2010 from 67 mb/d in 1991, an increase of 40%. Of this increase, the demand from the OECD countries will take up some 7 mb/d, from 38 mb/d in 1991 to 45 mb/d in 2010, an increase of 18%.

However, the pace of oil-demand growth will be set by a group of non-OECD countries outside the former Soviet Union and Central and Eastern Europe, which will see oil demand doubling during the 1991–2010 period, from 18.9 mb/d to 38.5 mb/d. This phenomenal demand growth is primarily attributable to rapid economic growth in a number of Asian countries, led by China.

The IEA study confirms the important role of the Middle East as a major oil-supply source in the coming decade. Melvin A. Conant, former editor of *Geopolitics of Energy*, put the implication of the IEA study this way: 'the Middle East Gulf is even more certain to be the cockpit of oil rivalry which will not be resolved through free market practices'.[6] According to a paper prepared for the World Petroleum

[4] Fereidun Fesharaki, Allen L. Clark and Duangjai Intarapravich, eds, *Pacific Energy Outlook: Strategies and Policy Imperative to 2010*, East–West Center, Occasional Paper 1, March 1995, p. 40.

[5] Ibid.

[6] Melvin A. Conant, 'The Geopolitics of Oil', *Geopolitics of Energy*, 1 July 1994, p. 8.

Table 1.1: World oil demand and supply outlook (mb/d)

	1991	2000	2005	2010
Total world demand	66.9	77.3	84.6	93.9
OECD	38.3	42.8	44.2	45.1
FSU/CEE	9.6	7.7	8.6	10
ROW	18.9	26.5	31.5	38.5
Stock Changes	0.2	0.3	0.3	0.3
Total world supply	66.9	77.3	84.6	93.9
OECD	16.2	15.2	14.5	14.2
FSU/CEE	10.7	8.3	9.3	10.3
ROW (ex. ME & Venezuela)	18.6	21.1	21.5	22.1
Middle East & Venezuela	20.1	31	37.5	45.4
Processing gains	1.4	1.7	1.8	1.9

Key: FSU = former Soviet Union; CEE = Central and Eastern Europe; ROW = the rest of the world.
Source: International Energy Agency, OECD, *World Energy Outlook 1994*, IEA, OECD, Paris, 1994, p. 45.

Conference by S.A. Al-Fathi, head of OPEC's energy studies department in Vienna, OPEC's share of world oil production is expected to be 43.1% in 1995 and rise to 52.8% in 2010.[7] This is the highest its share of the market has risen since the 1970s oil crises, leading to obvious fears, either of oil shocks induced by short-term crises or establishment of an effective cartel. This prediction of OPEC's commanding position in world oil production in the next decade is a real warning to the Asia–Pacific region, which will become more and more dependent on Middle East oil.

If no steps are taken to reduce the share of oil in the energy structure, Northeast Asia's heavy dependence on Middle East oil imports can only continue. (During the period 1990–2, Japan, South Korea and Taiwan's dependence on Middle East oil was measured as 72–5%, 74–5%, and 79–80% of total consumption respectively.[8])

[7] The paper estimated that demand for OPEC oil is likely to be 35 mb/d in 2000 when world demand is 72.45 mb/d if oil prices remain constant in real terms ($17/bbl in 1993). After 2000, an increase in real oil prices to $24/bbl in 2010 is likely. At that time, world oil demand will be 79.17 mb/d, and OPEC will be supplying 41.77 mb/d. See *Oil and Gas Journal*, 6 June 1994, p. 34.

[8] Petroleum Association of Japan (PAJ), *Petroleum Association of Japan Annual Review 1992*, PAJ, Tokyo, 1993, p. 7; Korea Petroleum Association (KPA), *The Petroleum Industry in Korea 1993*, KPA, Seoul, 1993, p. 7; Energy Commission, Ministry of Economic Affairs, *The Energy Situation in Taiwan, Republic of China 1992*, EC, MEA, Taipei, 1993.

Furthermore, China too is expected to be a massive Middle East oil importer in the coming years.

During the next decade, competition among the regional countries to secure crude-oil sources could provide the Middle East with a strong price-control leverage. According to the IEA's oil-price forecast to 2010, the crude-oil price, currently hovering below $20, will rise steadily to $28 by 2005 and then remain constant to the end of the outlook period.[9] If the crude-oil price is around $25–30 during the next decade and an effective cartel by oil-producing countries in the Middle East is re-established, Northeast Asian countries would have no choice but to accept the oil price set by the cartel. The point is that their heavy dependence on Middle East oil does not provide them with any bargaining power. This could place a serious burden on the Northeast Asian economy.

Security of supply will be another burden on Northeast Asia arising from the region's heavy dependence on Middle East oil. The continuing potential for crises in the Gulf, like Iraq's invasion of Kuwait in 1990, poses a potential threat to the region's stable oil supply. Repeats of this sort of crisis in the future will only expose the vulnerability of the Middle East oil supply to Northeast Asia.

So too will the long-running dispute about sovereignty over the Spratly Islands in the South China Sea, as strategically vital sea lanes, linking the Indian and Pacific oceans via the Malacca straits, run close by the disputed islands. A quarter of the world's maritime trade, including almost 70% of Japan's oil supplies, passes through the Spratly Islands, and any serious military confrontation in the South China Sea caused by the Spratly dispute could seriously affect the security of oil supplies (see Chapter 5, section 2), not least to Northeast Asian countries, which have no mechanism for handling such a situation.

For this reason Northeast Asian countries have tried to diversify their oil-supply sources and are trying to reduce considerably the share of oil in their energy mix and to increase the roles of other major energy sources.

1.2.3 Regional energy needs

Northeast Asia's energy needs are extending far beyond oil. With the introduction of new technologies, the demand for other major energy sources that could replace oil in industry, heating and electricity generation is growing very rapidly, and this trend seems set to continue. Demand for clean energy is also on the increase due to the region's environmental problems, including poor local air quality, acid rain and CO_2 emissions.

Coal is Northeast Asia's most abundant fossil-fuel resource, and it will remain the

[9] Here, $20 and $28 refer to constant 1993 US dollars.

main energy source in the coming years. However, coal is a major contributor to environmental pollution. China, the world's leading producer and consumer of coal, is responsible for about two-thirds of the Asia–Pacific region's sulphur oxide emissions. Coal is being challenged, therefore, by cleaner alternatives, like natural gas, nuclear power and hydropower. In Northeast Asia, only Japan can afford the universal adoption of clean-coal technologies.[10] China is expected to depend primarily on low-sulphur coal to reduce environmental problems for the time being, and its universal adoption of clean coal technologies is surely so far in the future that it would Northeast Asia cannot expect a substantial improvement in the region's environment for some time to come.

Nuclear energy is an important energy source in Northeast Asia. Despite its burdensome cost countries prefer the nuclear option because of its relative self-sufficiency. In 1993 Japan accounted for roughly 70% of all nuclear generation in the Asia–Pacific region, while nuclear generation in South Korea and Taiwan amounted to 40% and 33% respectively of each country's total energy generation. However, public resistance to nuclear energy on account of safety problems is a big constraint on development. It is uncertain whether the three countries' ambitious plans to increase the share of nuclear power in the energy mix will be realized. For example, the Japanese government is forecasting about 70 GW of nuclear capacity in 2010, but Japan may not achieve that level because of public resistance, a declining economic growth rate and demand that will probably be dampened by energy conservation.[11]

Natural gas has become popular in Northeast Asia, particularly among the power-generating utilities, which prefer gas because of security of supply, minimal price volatility and its environment-friendly qualities. (The Japanese utilities prefer nuclear and also coal, but are forced into gas because of environmental pressures.) With the development of a gas distribution system, gas use is expected to expand, but the absence of the regional pipeline grid is still a limitation.

1.2.4 The role of gas

Northeast Asian countries are very conscious of the region's energy-balance and environmental issues. It is no surprise that Japan, South Korea and Taiwan are aiming at substantially reducing the share of oil and increasing the shares of other energy sources, like natural gas and nuclear energy, in their future energy consumptions.

Predictions for Japan's long-term energy supply, as shown in Table 1.2(a), indicate a decrease in the share of oil, from almost 58% in 1992 to 48% in 2010, and an

[10] Fesharaki, Clark and Intarapravich, eds, *Pacific Energy Outlook* (op. cit., n. 4), p. 69.
[11] Ibid., p. 86.

Table 1.2(a): Japan: long-term energy-supply outlook

	1992 (actual)		2000		2010	
Energy source	Quantity	(%)	Quantity	(%)	Quantity	(%)
Oil[1] (mkl)[2]	315	(58.2)	306	(52.9)	303	(47.7)
Natural gas (mt)	40.7	(10.6)	53.0	(12.9)	58.0	(12.8)
Coal (mt)	116.3	(16.1)	130.0	(16.4)	134.0	(15.4)
Nuclear (bkWh)[3]	223	(10)	310	(12.3)	480	(16.9)
Geothermal (mkl)	0.6	(0.1)	1.0	(0.2)	3.8	(0.6)
Hydro (conventional: bkWh)	79	(3.8)	86	(3.4)	105	(3.7)
New energy sources[4] (mkl)	6.7	(1.2)	12.1	(2.0)	19.1	(3.0)
Total Supply (mkl)	541	100	582	100	635	100

Notes:
1 Includes oil sand and oil shale.
2 Million kilolitres.
3 Billion kilowatt hours.
4 Includes solar energy, alcohol fuels, factory pulp waste, firewood, and others.
Source: Ministry of International Trade and Industry (MITI), 1994.

Table 1.2(b) South Korea: long-term energy-supply outlook

	1992 (actual)		2000		2010	
Energy source	Quantity	(%)	Quantity	(%)	Quantity	(%)
Oil (mbl)	356.3	(53.8)	714.0	(55.9)	902.6	(52)
Natural gas (mt)	2.3	(3.2)	9.6	(7)	18.9	(9.7)
Coal (mt)	43.4	(26.2)	63.7	(22.4)	78.4	(20.1)
Nuclear (GWh)	52900	(14.2)	95600	(13.4)	193000	(19)
Hydro (GWh)	6400	(1.7)	3800	(0.5)	4500	(0.4)
New energy sources (mtoe)	0.8	(0.9)	1.4	(0.8)	3.4	(1.3)
Total supply (mtoe)	93.2	(100)	177.7	(100)	253.3	(100)

Source: Korea Energy Economics Institute, *Outlook for Energy Demand and National Energy Policy toward the 21st Century*, KEEI, Seoul, 1992.

Table 1.2(c): Taiwan: long-term energy-supply outlook (mkloe[1])

	1992 (Actual)		2000		2010		1992-2010
Energy source	Quantity	(%)	Quantity	(%)	Quantity	(%)	Annual growth rate (%)
Oil	33.5	(53)	38.3	(45)	47.6	(39)	2.3
Natural gas	3.3	(5)	9.4	(11)	19.8	(16)	9.9
Coal	16.1	(26)	25.1	(29)	30.9	(26)	4.5
Nuclear power	8.4	(13)	10.5	(12)	16.7	(14)	3.4
Hydropower	2.1	(3)	2.2	(3)	3.2	(3)	4.4
New energy	0.1	(0.2)	0.5	(1)	2.5	(2)	18.5
Total supply	63.4	(100)	86.0	(100)	120.7	(100)	3.9
Indigenous	3.2	(5)	4.5	(5)	7.1	(6)	5.2
Imported	60.2	(95)	81.5	(95)	113.6	(94)	3.9

Note: [1]mkloe: million kilolitres oil equivalent.
Source: Energy Commission, Ministry of Economic Affairs, *The Energy Situation in Taiwan, Republic of China*, EC, MEA, Taipei, 1993.

increase in the roles of nuclear energy, and other non-fossil fuels (geothermal, hydro, and new energy sources), from 15% in 1992 to 24% in 2010. As for South Korea, as shown in Table 1.2(b), its long-term energy-supply outlook envisages the strengthened roles of natural gas (from 3% in 1990 to 10% in 2010) and nuclear power (from 14% in 1990 to 19% in 2010). As far as oil is concerned, the forecast is fairly cautious, putting its share in 2010 at 52%. Taiwan took the most ambitious and environment-oriented approach. Its forecast, as shown in Table 1.2(c), puts the share of oil in 2010 as low as 39%, and that of natural gas as high as 16%.

The three countries' forecasts share common features: a reduction of oil's importance as a main energy source and strengthened roles for natural gas and nuclear energy. So far as oil is concerned, however, it is questionable whether Japan and Taiwan could reduce their share to 39–48% in 2010. In a study of ways of harmonizing Japan's economic growth with its efforts for global environmental preservation and energy supply–demand balance, Kazuya Fujime, associate director for research of the Japan Institute of Energy Economics, argued that Japan's oil share will hover at 50% in 2010, unless environment-oriented policies are taken seriously.[12]

Another point that should be questioned is the projection on combined shares of

[12] Kazuya Fujime, 'Post-Earth Summit Long-Term Energy Supply–Demand Outlook and Japan's Responses', *Energy in Japan* 120 (March 1993), pp. 1–24.

natural gas and nuclear energy in 2010, from 17–21% to 29–30%. Here an interesting finding is that the share of nuclear energy is somewhat higher than that of gas. This confirms that the three countries are placing more emphasis on nuclear energy than on gas. However, it is not certain whether nuclear energy can meet the three countries' high expectations, given strong public resistance.

The projected shares of natural gas by Japan and South Korea (only Taiwan projected natural gas at 16% and nuclear energy at 14%) look quite conservative. The three countries have taken the lion's share in global LNG trade (for example, in 1994 they imported a total of 50 mt of LNG, accounting for 76% of world LNG trade),[13] and the scale is expected to rise substantially during the next decade if a number of grass-roots projects are developed. Even so, it would not seriously affect the region's total energy mix.

It is not an exaggeration to say that the potential role of gas in Northeast Asia is being considerably underestimated. As a clean energy source, natural gas is not only important in supporting economic development but also effective in replacing oil. From a long-term perspective, there is great potential for a rapid expansion of gas in the region. If a pan-regional gas grid, whose main players (as participants as well as beneficiaries) would be all the regional countries, including Russia, China, North and South Korea, Japan and presumably Taiwan and the United States (due to its firm position in the region), were to be established early in the next decade, a total reshaping of Japan's and South Korea's and presumably Taiwan's energy-supply structure could be possible. The distribution of energy resources in Northeast Asia strongly supports the increased role of gas in the region in the coming years.

1.3 Resources

Northeast Asia is endowed with a variety of natural resources. However, though abundant, these are unevenly distributed in the region, mainly concentrated in mostly remote regions of Russia and China. Besides the great potential reserves of oil, gas and coal, Russian Asia is the main producing region of diamond, gold and tin, and China boasts of its status as the world's largest producer of antimony, rare earth metals, tin, tungsten and barytes.[14] The primary concern of this study is with the deposits of fossil fuels – notably gas and oil.

---

[13] In 1994 a total of world LNG trade recorded 65.4 million tonnes, of which Japan imported 42.07 mt, South Korea 5.93mt, and Taiwan 1.95 mt. See 'World LNG Trade: Australia in Focus', a report prepared by Department of Resources Development, Government of Western Australia, June 1995, p. 7.

[14] James P. Dorian, *Minerals, Energy and Economic Development in China*, Clarendon Press, Oxford, 1994, p. 92 (Table 4.1); James P. Dorian, Pavel A. Minakir and Vitaly T. Borisvich,

Table 1.3: Energy reserves and production, 1993

	Oil R & P			Gas R & P			Coal R & P		
Country	Oil R (bt)	Oil P (mb/d)	R/P	Gas R (tcf[1])	Gas P (tcf/y)	R/P	Coal R (bt)	Coal P (mtoe)	R/P
China	3.2	2.9	21.9	59	547.1	*	114.5	558.4	
India	0.8	0.6	28.6	25.4	568.9	49.4	62.5	123.4	
Indonesia	0.8	1.5	10.8	64.4	1704.1	33.1	32.1		
Malaysia	0.6	0.6	17.8	76.7	734.6	85.1	-		
Australia	0.2	0.5	9.2	19.6	855.7	22.5	90.9	118.6	
Brunei	0.2	0.2	21.5	14	308.5	40.1	-		
Vietnam	0.1	0.1	11.5	-	-	-	-		
Japan	+	-	9.2	-	-	-	0.8	4.8	
S. Korea	-	-	-	-	-	-	0.2	5	
Taiwan	-	-	-	-	-	-	0.1		
Asia-Pacific	6	6.8	17.6	354.5	6097.9	53	303.9	873.2	171
Middle East	89.6	19.28	95.1	1581	7920.7	*	0.2	0.9	
World	136.7	65.075	43.1	5016	76219	64.9	1039	2133.1	236

Key: + = less than 0.05; * = over 100 years; R&P means reserves and production respectively.
Note: [1]Trillion cubic feet.
Source: *BP Statistical Review of World Energy*, June 1994.

In the global context, the oil and gas resources of the Asia–Pacific region are relatively poor. As shown in Table 1.3, as of 1993 proven oil reserves are around 6 billion tonnes, equivalent to only 4.4% of the world total. (For a comparison of oil-reserves classification by the United States, the CIS and China, see Table 1.4.) China alone accounted for 53% of the region's oil reserves. In 1993, oil production in the Asia–Pacific region was 6.8 mb/d (accounting for 10.4% of the world total). Its reserves-to-production (R/P) ratio of roughly 18 years is far less than the world average of 43 years and the Middle East average of 95 years.

As for natural-gas reserves, 7.1% of proven world reserves (354.5 tcf) is located in the Asia–Pacific region. However, the region's R/P ratio is around 76 years due to the relatively small extent of exploitation. Gas production in 1993 was 6,098 tcf, 8% of the world total. The region is far less extensively explored than others, and

eds, *CIS Energy and Minerals Development: Prospects, Problems and Opportunities for International Cooperation*, Kluwer Academic Publishers, Dordrecht, 1993.

Table 1.4: Different concepts of oil-reserves classification: a comparison of the United States, the CIS and China

US	CIS	China
Proved (measured)	A + B + C1 (partly)	Class I *Tanming Chuliang*
Probable (indicated)	C1 (partly)	Class II *Kongzhi Chuliang*
Possible (inferred)	C1 + C2 (partly	Class III *Yuce Chuliang*
Hypothetical (undiscovered)	C2 + D1 (partly)	IV Qianzai *Ziyuanliang*
Speculative (undiscovered)	D2	V Tuice *Ziyuanliang*

Note: Some sources quote *Kongzhi Chuliang* as proved reserves and *Tanming Chuliang* as probable reserves.
Source: Wu Choucheng, 'Petroleum Resources Evaluation in China and a Unique System Approach', *Acta Petrolei Sinica* 10:4 (1989), p. 4.

most exploration has focused on oil; further finds seem likely, following the pattern set elsewhere.

Coal reserves are relatively rich. As of 1993, the region has a total of 304 bt of proved coal reserves (anthracite and bituminous, 171 bt; sub-bituminous and lignite, 133 bt). China has the largest reserves in the region, with 114.5 bt. In 1993 the region's coal production was 873.2 mtoe, of which almost two-thirds was produced by China. Based on the heat content (in terms of oil-equivalent), the Asia–Pacific region features the world's largest coal producer and consumer (China), largest coal importer (Japan) and largest coal exporter (Australia).[15]

But coal is also very unevenly distributed, both within and between countries. The difficulty of transporting coal, combined with the inappropriateness of coal as a fuel for many purposes (especially transport and urban heating) and its relatively greater environmental impact, pose important limitations. For these and other reasons, demand for oil and gas has been expanding dramatically, raising ever more urgently

[15] Fereidun Fesharaki, Kang Wu and Shiva Pezeshki, 'The Supply and Demand Outlook for Energy in the Asia–Pacific Region', East–West Centre, Honolulu, February 1994, p. 7.

Table 1.5: Uneven distribution of production factors among Northeast Asian countries

	Oil & gas	Coal & minerals	Labour	Capital	Technology	Management expertise
Russia	VR	VR	VP	VP	S	S
China	R	VR	VR	VP	S	S
Taiwan	S	S	S	R	R	R
N. Korea	A	R	R	VP	VP	VP
S. Korea	A	S	S	R	R	R
Japan	VP	S	S	VR	VR	VR

Key: VR = very rich; R = rich; S = short; VP = very poor; A = absent.
Source: Keun-Wook Paik , 'Towards a Northeast Asian energy charter', *Energy Policy*, May 1992, p. 442.

the profile of energy issues in the region, and the wider questions that these trends raise.

In Northeast Asia, this uneven distribution of energy resources becomes more conspicuous. The region's energy-resources distribution is shown schematically in Table 1.5. As far as oil and gas reserves are concerned, Japan, South Korea and Taiwan have almost none to speak of. In contrast, there are five frontier oil and gas areas in China and Russian Asia: the East China Sea and Xinjiang Province including the Tarim Basin in China, and Sakhalin island offshore, the Republic of Sakha, and the Irkutsk region in Russian Asia.

According to an interim summary report on a study of energy resources in East Siberia[16] and the Russian Far East (RFE), prepared by the Northern Regions Centre in February 1993 and submitted to Japan's Ministry of Foreign Affairs, proven oil reserves in East Siberia and the RFE are around 640 mt, split almost equally between the two. For natural gas, the figure is around 2.5 tcm, with two-thirds of this in the RFE. Ultimate recoverable oil reserves in both the RFE and East Siberia are equally 8.9 bt, and gas figures are as much as 56 tcm (RFE: 43%; East Siberia: 57%).[17]

As for China, it is very difficult to get the exact figures on the country's frontier oil and gas reserves. For example, the widely quoted figures for the Tarim Basin's oil and gas reserves are 19.8 billion tonnes and 8.4 tcm respectively.[18] In short, both

[16] Here, 'East Siberia' is much bigger than this study's definition of RES. As well as RES, it comprises Krasnoyarsk Kray, Taymyr and Evenki Autonomous Okrug.
[17] An unpublished report prepared by Northern Regions Centre, Tokyo, 1993.
[18] *China OGP* 3:1 (1 January 1995), p. 3.

Russia and China have relatively huge gas and oil reserves. It will be pointless to discuss the region's oil and gas development in the coming years without a proper understanding of the two countries' oil and gas factors.

1.4 Energy in Russia and China

In terms of the scale of energy reserves, production, consumption and exports, both Russia and China have been and are energy superpowers (though, as far as export is concerned, China is losing this status). However, both countries currently face difficulties in developing their energy resources, especially in maintaining their present oil-production levels and allocating their oil for export.[19] The success or failure of the oil and gas industries will play an important role in accelerating or retarding the process of reform in Russia and the implementation of a socialist market economy in China.

More importantly, the success or failure of Russia's and China's oil and gas industries is no longer, following the end of the Cold War, of concern only to themselves. The changing political environment in the region does not allow Northeast Asian countries such as Japan, South Korea and Taiwan to remain detached from the problems of both Russia's and China's oil and gas industries.

Currently both the RFE and China are suffering from an energy shortage. In the case of the RFE, the shortage was caused by delays in oil and gas development despite huge reserves. In the early 1990s, annual Sakhalin crude production totalled less than 2 mt, but the RFE's oil demand hovered at around 20 mt/year. In other words, a substantial amount of oil had to be imported to meet the region's oil demand (see Chapter 3 for further discussion). In 1991 natural-gas production was 3.4 bcm, up from 1.8 bcm in 1985, but was still insufficient to meet local energy demands. As of 1991, the shares of Far East oil and gas production in total Russian oil and gas output were merely 0.4% and 0.5% respectively.[20]

In China, energy shortage is becoming a real hindrance to its galloping economy. According to the Ministry of Energy Resources, energy production in 1992 recorded 1,056 mt of standard coal, only 13 mt more than in 1991.[21] China's coal,

---

[19] China's crude-oil export is projected to fall to almost zero by 2005 from 0.2 mb/d in 2000. See James P. Dorian, *Energy in China: Foreign investment opportunities, trends and legislation*, Pearson Professional Ltd., London, 1995, p. 51.

[20] E. Khartukov and F. Fesharaki, 'Russian Far East: Energy Review and Outlook to 2000', *Energy Advisory* 105, East–West Center, Honolulu, 15 September 1992, p. 4, Table 2.

[21] For example, the electricity-generating capacity increased by 10.85% in 1992, but GNP grew by 12%, and industry output increased by 18%. See *Beijing Review*, 4–10 January 1993, pp. 5–6.

accounting for about three-quarters of its total energy consumption, seems unlikely to alleviate the country's burden of energy shortage. China plans to increase coal production from 1.14 bt in 1993 to 1.4 bt in 2000, but China's coal demand in 2000 is expected to exceed 1.5 bt, even in conservative estimations.

The result of Chinese oil policy during the past two decades is not so encouraging either. China's onshore production has succeeded in maximizing production in the eastern region at the expense of the rapid depletion of workable reserves. In 1993 China's crude-oil production totalled 144 mt.[22] It is a substantial increase compared with 30.7 mt in 1970, but the production increase during 1989–93 was merely 6.4 mt (137.6 mt in 1989). After ten years of effort to find major discoveries in China's offshore basins, it has found little success despite opening most of the offshore areas to foreign participation. In 1993 total offshore production amounted to a mere 4.6 mt,[23] or 3.2% of China's total output. Chinese offshore production is expected to peak at around 12 mt in 1997 and then decline gradually to a more maintainable 8–10 mt by 2007.[24]

Considering that China's requirements have been growing by 7% annually over the past few years, the recent stagnation in oil production has become a real burden. In 1993 oil imports reached a fairly high level for the first time.[25] Wu and Li, at the programme on Resources, East–West Centre, estimated that China's oil demand would grow at an average rate of about 7% during 1992–2000, and would reach 4.4 mb/d in 2000. Taking all possibilities into consideration, they also estimated that, by the year 2000 China's oil production would range from 3.1 mb/d as a low estimate to 3.4 mb/d as a high estimate, depending on how successful the Chinese government is in mobilizing domestic and foreign investment. In either case, the gap between domestic production and oil demand is expected to widen by the end of the century,[26] with China importing more than 50 mt per year (1 million b/d).

Energy shortage is common to both countries but in the RFE it is likely to be a short-term phenomenon and, with total demand currently not exceeding 25 mtoe, not a serious problem. Once the Sakhalin offshore development is undertaken, the region's energy shortage will probably be settled quite easily. By contrast, China seems very unlikely to be free of energy shortage in the foreseeable future. A

---

[22] *BP Statistical Review of World Energy 1994*.

[23] *China Petroleum Investment Guide*, China Feature and AP Energy Business Publications, Singapore, 1994, p. 107.

[24] Ibid., p. 96.

[25] Crude-oil export and import recorded 19.4 mt and 15.7 mt respectively, while oil-product figures were 4.6 mt and 17.5 mt. See *China OGP* 2:8 (15 April 1994), p. 4.

[26] Kang Wu and Bingsheng Li, 'Energy Development in China: A Policy Perspective', paper presented at the IAEE's 17th Annual International Conference, Stavanger, 25–27 May 1994.

crucial point for foreign investors is that in China they may be asked to invest in energy resources for internal consumption, whereas in Russia they will be investing principally in export-oriented projects.

The two countries share another common characteristic. As both countries are in dire need of capital, they cannot afford to channel huge amounts of investment to frontier oil and gas development. Highly advanced technology and equipment from western countries are desperately needed to develop oil and gas reserves located in environmentally harsh areas. As a result Russia and China are taking a very positive stance towards international cooperation in their oil and gas policies in the 1990s.

Their urgent need for oil and gas development has provoked competition between the two countries for foreign investment and technology. The situation in the 1990s will be totally different from the 1970s, when China succeeded in manipulating regional power politics to affect its oil policy favourably (see Chapter 5). Even though China has hurriedly opened its frontier onshore and offshore areas to distract Japan and South Korea from Russian Asia, it remains to be seen whether and how far this move will succeed in influencing foreign investors yearning to secure a bridgehead for future business opportunities in Northeast Asia. Two important factors should be considered seriously by foreign investors, especially from Japan and South Korea.

The first relates to the investment climate. In the short term, China seems to be in a better position than Russia to attract foreign investment, because of a much more stable political and economic environment. China's experience with foreign companies in offshore development over the past ten years has given it an advantage. Until Russian energy laws and regulations applicable to foreign investments are sufficiently developed and stabilized, and the many problems associated with the division of authority between federal and local governments are settled, an uncertain investment environment will act unfavourably on Russia's efforts to attract foreign investment. China will take full advantage of the opportunity offered by the relative instability of its competitor.

The second factor concerns the availability of oil and gas exports. In the long term, the strength of Russian Asia's gas development lies in the fact that the region's proved gas reserves are big enough to satisfy regional consumption and allow exports to neighbouring countries, like China (especially its Northeastern provinces), North and South Korea and Japan. Even some oil exports from Russian Asia to neighbouring countries are conceivable if gas replaces oil as a main source in the region's energy consumption. As for China, its galloping energy consumption seems unlikely to allow the country to allocate developed oil and gas from its far western frontier for export even after the Tarim Basin's full-scale development is implemented, unless the Basin's reserves reach a very high level (see Chapter 7).

1.5 The need for regional cooperation

No country in Northeast Asia is free of energy problems. Despite the different nature of the problems in each country, none would challenge the importance of the region's frontier oil and gas development. The uneven distribution of oil and gas resources paradoxically indicates that mutual benefits can be derived from cooperation in oil and gas development among the countries concerned. Russian Asia and China with huge oil and gas reserves certainly need capital, technology and equipment for their exploration and development; while Japan, Taiwan and South Korea, with capital, technology and equipment, need to lessen their heavy dependence on Middle East oil and diversify their energy supplies. In other words, space for multilateral energy cooperation exists in Northeast Asia.

The strongest possibility for cooperation lies in the natural gas industry rather than the oil industry. The possibility that China can use its oil and gas resources for multilateral energy cooperation is slight (unless oil and gas discoveries are made in the East China Sea, which looks unlikely). As for the RFE's oil resources, the scale of proven reserves is not big enough. But even though the region's frontier oil development can make only a limited contribution to supply, its development will still remain economically very important, particularly for those that own the oil, but also as a way of diversifying the region's oil-supply sources. However, gas reserves in RES and the RFE are huge enough to cover domestic demand as well as exports to neighbouring countries. In short, Russian Asia's gas resources could provide a base for multilateral energy cooperation in the region.

The ideal way to make all countries in Northeast Asia the beneficiaries of multilateral energy cooperation would be to establish a pan-regional gas-pipeline grid. At present, the region is depending on railways and shipping deliveries for energy trade. Considering that both Russia's and China' poor transportation systems make even their domestic oil and gas deliveries from producing areas to consuming ones very difficult, a large-scale gas trade seems unlikely to be handled by the current regional transportation system. In particular both countries' massive oil and gas resources located in remote and environmentally harsh areas cannot be developed without a proper delivery system.

A number of pipeline-grid proposals have been made since the early 1990s, like the former Soviet Union's Vostok plan, Japan's Energy Community plan and China's Energy Silk Route project, aimed at introducing a new delivery system (see Chapters 6 and 7). The point of a pipeline-grid is to make the development economics of frontier oil and gas in the region comparable to those of frontier oil and gas projects elsewhere in the world. The benefits would not only be economic. Because of the strategic importance that energy, especially oil, has had, the benefits from a pan-regional pipeline grid would be political as well. The grid could help to overcome political difficulties arising from mutual mistrust among formerly hostile neighbours. On the other hand, it could exacerbate them if the approach towards establishment of the grid is handled badly.

1.6 Conclusion

The complex nature of both Russian Asia's and China's oil and gas industries has implications for neighbouring countries heavily dependent on Middle East oil. All the countries that make up Northeast Asia have reason to consider very seriously the economic and political costs and benefits of cooperation in developing Russian Asia's and China's frontier oil and gas projects. The most important point is that the development of these projects will bring about a significant change in the region's energy structure.

Having sketched out why energy is so important to the region, and the nature of some of the important issues involved, the rest of this book examines the prospects for development of the region's energy resources over the next 10–20 years. Will resources be adequately developed? Will development contribute to the region's stability, or could competition over access to resources and infrastructure actually be a flashpoint for conflict, and how can policy minimize the danger of this?

This book seeks to develop insights into these and other questions. To this end, Chapter 2 will touch on the political context for energy developments in Northeast Asia. Chapters 3 and 4 will examine Russia's and China's oil and gas production industries respectively. After reviewing the goals of Russian and Chinese oil and gas policies in Northeast Asia in Chapter 5, Chapter 6 will explore importers, especially Japan and South Korea, and their policies towards Russia's and China's oil and gas development. The region's major projects will be fully analysed in Chapter 7, and finally Chapter 8 will bring together the previous analyses to look at the energy and investment implications for Northeast Asia – and perhaps its wider export potential – for the first couple of decades in the next century.

Ultimately, this study could provide some ideas on the following issues: the implications of frontier oil and gas development for the region's energy balance and flow and the way these may interact with and depend upon the development of regional politics (as well as energy demand); the possibilities for an energy regime integrating all the regional countries in Northeast Asia, and how and when it might emerge.

Chapter 2

The political context for energy developments

The interplay of energy economics and politics is of central importance, both in understanding the current situation in Northeast Asia and in projecting how it could develop. In the context of huge energy projects, this perspective is particularly important because of the strategic element and the need for international cooperation to assemble the financial and other resources for development.

This chapter explains the history of the most important international relationships and how they have affected the evolution of energy cooperation. The most important relationships – those that will determine whether and how certain projects go ahead – are: *Japanese–Russian*, reflecting an historical distrust and centred specifically on the dispute over the Kurile Islands; *Japanese–Chinese*, centred on strengthened economic relations now that the dispute over the Senkaku Islands is dormant; *North–South Korean*, focused on their changing relations with Russia and China; *Taiwanese–Chinese*, highlighting their respective stances towards reunification and touching on improved Taiwanese–Russian relations; and *superpower relations* in the region's changing environment.

This chapter examines each in turn, focusing on how development of the political relationship has interacted with energy developments and which political issues are likely to affect future developments. In addition, the impact of the end of the Cold War has had an important influence on the politics of the region and this is examined in the final section.

Obviously, there are other dimensions: notably, the complementary as well as competitive Japanese–Korean relationship, and the recently substantially improved Sino-Russian relationship could also affect the region's energy relationships. In practice, however, they are unlikely to play a central role, but could exercise an indirect influence on Northeast Asia's energy projects.

2.1 Japanese–Russian relations and the Kurile Islands dispute

2.1.1 The Kurile Islands dispute

The territorial problem between the former Soviet Union (Russia) and Japan has been and is a complex of legal, political, strategic and economic issues which have become the symbol of the failure of Soviet (Russian)–Japanese relations to recover from their post-Second World War condition.[1] Due to the long-standing and bitter territorial dispute over the Kurile Islands, Soviet dreams of transforming Sakhalin island into a major hydrocarbon-producing centre (originally proposed as early as 1966, when the first meeting of the Japanese–Soviet Economic Cooperation Committee was held), and of exporting West Siberian oil and the East Siberian gas to Japan (the so-called Tyumen oil project and Yakutia gas project, proposed during the second half of the 1960s), have long been frustrated.[2] These projects have been discussed over the past 25 years, and none has progressed significantly. This confirms that there remains a residue of the Cold War in Northeast Asia.

The territories in question – Etorofu, Kunashiri, Shikotan and Habomai – are claimed by both Japan and the FSU (see Map 2.1). The disputed territories were occupied by the Soviets after the end of the Second World War. The Soviet Union promised to return Habomai and the Shikotan islands on signing of a formal peace treaty with Japan, under the terms of the peace agreement concluded between the two countries in 1956. However, the promise was not kept due to Soviet domestic opposition to territorial concessions.

It was on the occasion of the visit in December 1988 of Foreign Minister Shevardnadze to Tokyo that the Soviet Union formally acknowledged the existence of the territorial question for the first time. An agreement was reached to establish working groups to discuss the conclusion of a peace treaty.[3] The Soviets' acknowledgment of the territorial issue itself was a small gift brought by Gorbachev's

---

[1] For details of the territorial problem, see Graham Allison, Hiroshi Kimura and Konstantin Sarkisov, eds, *Beyond Cold War to Trilateral Cooperation in the Asia–Pacific Region: Scenarios for New Relationships Between Japan, Russia, and the United States*, Harvard University Press, Cambridge, 1992; David Rees, *The Soviet Seizure of the Kuriles*, Praeger, New York, 1985; Young C. Kim, *Japanese–Soviet Relations: Interaction of Politics, Economics and National Security*, Sage Publications, London, 1974, pp. 17–53; Rajan Menon, 'Gorbachev's Japan Policy', *Survival* 33:2 (March/April 1991), pp. 158–172; Andrew Mack and Martin O'Hare, 'Moscow–Tokyo and the Northern Territories Dispute', *Asian Survey* 30:4 (April 1990), pp. 380–94; George Ginsburgs, 'The Territorial Question between the USSR and Japan: The Soviet Case and a Western Aperçu', *Korea and World Affairs*, Summer 1991, pp. 259–78; Tsuyoshi Hasegawa, Jonathan Haslam and Andrew C. Kuchins, eds, *Russia and Japan: An Unresolved Dilemma Between Distant Neighbours*, University of California Press, Berkeley, 1993.

[2] Peter Egyed, *Western Participation in the Development of Siberian Energy Resources: Case Studies*, East–West Commercial Relations Series, Research Report 22, Carleton University, Ottawa, December 1983.

[3] Gerald Segal, *Normalizing Soviet–Japanese Relations*, Royal Institute of International Affairs, London, 1991, p. 11; Menon, 'Gorbachev's Japan Policy' (op. cit., n. 1), page 162.

Map 2.1: The Northern Territories

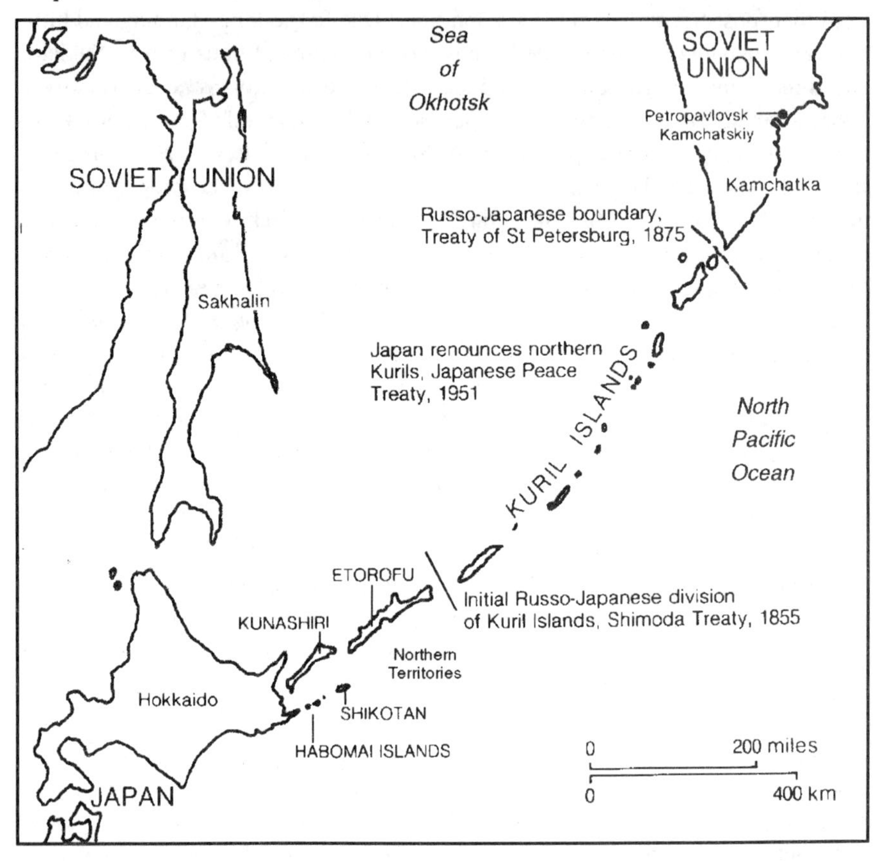

Source: Rajan Menon, 'Gorbachev's Japan Policy', *Survival*, March/April 1991, p. 160.

perestroika. In response, Japan's policy towards the Soviet Union also became more flexible. In May 1989 Foreign Minister Uno advanced a new policy of 'Balanced Expansion' (Kakudai Kinko). That is, pending the conclusion of a peace treaty which might successfully resolve the territorial dispute, Japan and the FSU would nevertheless proceed with negotiations over matters such as fishing rights, environmental protection and visits by former Japanese inhabitants of the disputed islands to their ancestors' graves.[4] This new policy, also named as a policy of

[4] The new policy of 'Balanced Expansion' lies somewhere between the entrance and exit theories. The entrance theory (Iriguchi Ron) insists on some progress on the territorial issue before Japan would commit itself to increased economic cooperation, investments,

'expanding equilibrium', was supported by Ozawa Ichiro, then Liberal Democratic Party General Secretary, who said that 'I believe we must hold talks and be willing to make mutual concessions',[5] and Kanemaru Shin, former deputy prime minister, who urged that Japan should consider a phased reversion plan as a realistic way of solving the territorial issue.[6]

A corresponding flexibility emerged in Soviet policy. In early September 1990, Shevardnadze suggested that Moscow was not yet ready to accept an unconditional return of all four islands as demanded by Japan, but this time Soviet policy appeared to be aimed at treating the territorial issue as part of a package which would involve massive Japanese aid for the development of eastern Siberia, and possibly support for demilitarizing the Northwest Pacific.[7] In October 1990 the Soviets sounded out Japan on the possibility of compromise by the return of two of the four disputed islands.[8]

Just before Gorbachev's Tokyo visit in April 1991, the Japanese government proposed $13.3 billion in assistance and emergency aid on condition that Moscow return all four islands. According to the proposal, $4 billion would be allocated for emergency financing, and $9.3 billion for a three-phase package of 20 economic projects. An oil and gas development project in the Sakhalin shelf was included in the second phase to be carried out over 10 years.[9] However, Gorbachev could not accept the offer as Soviet domestic politics did not allow him to make even a modest concession, such as acknowledging the Soviet Union's obligations under the 1956 agreement to return Shikotan and the Habomais to Japan. Anger at the new Bering Sea boundary agreement with the United States on 1 June 1990, for example, was a serious burden on the Soviet leadership at the time.[10] The only tangible

---

technology transfer, and the like. The exit theory (Deguchi Ron) posits improving relations with the FSU as a means of solving the territorial issue. See P. Berton, 'The Evolution of the Japanese–Russian Territorial Dilemma', in Allison *et al.*, *Beyond Cold War to Trilateral Co-operation in the Asia–Pacific Region* (op. cit., n. 1) Appendix F, p. 15.

[5] FBIS, Sov. 90: 70 (11 April 1990), pp. 11–12; FBIS, Sov. 90: 72 (13 April 1990), pp. 2–3.

[6] *Supar Report* 9 (July 1990), pp. 55, 58.

[7] *Far Eastern Economic Review*, 20 Sept. 1990, pp. 11–13.

[8] *The Times*, 8 Oct. 1990.

[9] The 3-phase package consists of 5 projects valued at $1.3 billion to be carried out within 5 years (1st phase); 12 projects, $3.5 billion, over 10 years (2nd phase); 3 projects, $4.5 billion, in the twenty-first century (3rd phase). A petrochemical project at Tengiz was included in the 3rd phase. See *Japan Times*, 27 March 1991. There were reports that Japan might offer $26 billion in order to get back the four islands. See *Korea Herald*, 26 March 1991; *Financial Times*, 17 April 1991.

[10] For a full text of the agreement, see *Law of the Sea Bulletin* (UN) 17 (April 1991), pp. 15–21. The hostile domestic response to the boundary agreement did not give Gorbachev any

concession to Japan was a proposal by Gorbachev to reduce military force on the four disputed islands.[11]

2.1.2 Recent developments

Soon after the failed August coup, the acting speaker of the Russian parliament Ruslan Khasbulatov visited Japan and said that in relations between Japan and Russia, an emphasis should be placed on fairness, and respect for the norms of international law. This first enunciation of 'Law and Justice' became the hallmark of Boris Yeltsin's policy towards Japan,[12] and initially the newly born Russian Federation took a positive stance. The first meeting of the peace-treaty working group after the demise of the Soviet Union was held in February 1992, and at that meeting the Russian delegation officially acknowledged the validity of the 1956 Soviet–Japanese Joint Declaration.[13] The meeting was part of the preparations for Yeltsin's visit to Japan in Autumn 1992, but his visit did not take place.[14] Its abrupt

---

breathing space for the settlement of the Kurile Islands dispute. In a contributed article entitled 'The Country's Foreign Policy Effort Came Under Suspicion', V. Guliy, USSR people's deputy and *Rossiyskaya Gazeta* staff correspondent, defended Mr Eduard Shevardnadze as a victim of a military conspiracy. Guliy argued that the main reason for the minister's resignation was Deputy Petrushenko's speech at the Fourth Congress of USSR People's Deputies, blaming Mr Shevardnadze for signing the agreement without informing the people's deputies. However, Guliy failed to answer questions such as why the agreement was prepared and signed without the knowledge of the public, the USSR Supreme Soviet and the people's deputies; why, even eight months after it was signed, the deputies had not been informed about it and why it had not been submitted to them for ratification. To make matters worse, an article by Yu. Katasonov under the rubric 'Explanations without suspicion: The Secrets of the Bering Sea' severely criticized Guliy's argument for not saying a word about oil or how the agreement would solve the main economic problem of demarcation – the distribution of rights to the potential oil regions. See FBIS, Sov. 91:29 (12 Feb. 1991), pp. 7–10; *Eastern Bloc Energy*, Feb. 1991, p. 10; *Supar Report* 12 (Jan. 1992), p. 163.

[11] FBIS, EAS 91:75 (18 April 1991), p. 7; *Japan Times*, 15 May 1991; FBIS, Sov. 91:199 (15 Oct. 1991), p. 11. In March 1992, Andrei Kozyrev, Russian Foreign Minister, announced that troops located on the southern Kuriles had been cut by 30% and that there were currently 7,000 soldiers and border guards on the islands. See FBIS, Sov. 92:55 (20 March 1992), p. 33.

[12] In his letter to the Japanese Premier Miyazawa at the end of February 1992, Yeltsin took a positive stance in stating that the two countries could conclude a peace treaty (including the delineation of the boundary) on the basis of 'law and justice'. See Berton, 'The Evolution of the Japanese–Russian Territorial Dilemma', in Allison *et al.*, *Beyond Cold War to Trilateral Cooperation in the Asia–Pacific Region* (op. cit., n. 1), Appendix F, pp. 14, 16.

[13] Berton, op. cit., p. 16.

[14] Yeltsin's decision to postpone his visit to Japan and Korea was made at a meeting of the shadowy Security Council on 9 September 1992, but the visit to Seoul was immediately rearranged. See *Financial Times*, 10 Sept. 1992; *Korea Times*, 10 and 18 Sept. 1992.

cancellation reflects the delicate situation with regard to the dispute.

It is worth noting that Yeltsin, as a president of the Russian Republic, had already suggested a five-phase solution during his visit to Japan in January 1990. According to his proposal, the first stage would be official recognition that a problem exists and the reshaping of public opinion to open the way for a settlement. This would take two or three years. The second stage would be demilitarization of the islands and might take five to seven years.

The third would be to declare the islands a free-enterprise zone open to Japan, by which Japan would be granted most-favoured-partner status. This would take three to five years. The fourth stage would be the signing of a peace treaty. This would involve a concession on Japan's part since it would have to sign a peace treaty without getting the islands back. These four stages would take 15 to 20 years. The final stage would be to let a new generation of politicians work out a solution.[15] (The fifth stage is similar to Deng Xiaoping's 'Senkaku Island Formula'.)

Vladimir B. Yakubovsky, a senior fellow at Moscow's Institute of Far Eastern Studies, said that Japan had forced Yeltsin into a corner at a time when Russian nationalists were requiring him to keep intact what's left of the crumbling Soviet empire.[16] The Russian nationalists, especially the leading figure among them, Valentin Fedorov, governor of Sakhalin Island (as of 1992), adduced three reasons against returning the islands to Japan. First of all, conceding land to Japan would set off a barrage of territorial claims against Russia by other countries, such as China and the Baltic states. Secondly, the loss of the Kurile fishing grounds would deprive Russia of around one million tonnes of fish a year, worth $1 billion. Thirdly, the islands, stretching in a long curving finger from the Kamchatka Peninsula to Japan, are strategically vital. They provide a key link in the nation's radar system, and they control the ice-free straits used by Russia's nuclear-missile submarines to reach the open Pacific in winter.[17]

By mid-September 1992 the dispute had been turned into a diplomatic nightmare for the Japanese government by the Sakhalin authorities' decision to lease a part of Shikotan Island for 50 years to a Hong Kong-based property concern, Carlson & Kaplan Co., to develop the area as a tourist resort. (In late October 1992 the company reversed the decision.[18]) Regardless of this decision, in a decree signed on

[15] FBIS, Sov. 90:26 (7 Feb. 1990), pp. 16–18; FBIS, Sov. 90:165 (24 August 1990), p. 79; Vladimir Ovsyannikov, 'Boris Yeltsin: We must free ourselves of the legacy of the past', *New Times*, June 1990, pp. 20–1.

[16] *Korea Times*, 21 Nov. 1992.

[17] *Korea Times*, 13 Sept. 1992.

[18] *Financial Times*, 12 and 13 Sept. 1992; 17 Sept. 1992; 18 Sept. 1992; *The Times*, 17 Sept. 1992; *Independent*, 17 Sept. 1992; *Korea Times*, 10 Sept. 1992; FBIS, EAS 92:205 (22 Oct. 1992), p. 5.

30 November and subject to approval by the Russian legislature, Boris Yeltsin, President of the Russian Federation, proposed that foreigners be allowed to lease land on the Kurile Islands, and the Islands be made a special economic zone with tax-free exports and imports and other tax breaks.[19] On 9 December 1992 Japan warned Russia that relations would suffer if it pursued plans to create a free-trade zone on a cluster of islands claimed by Tokyo.[20]

In August 1993 Russia's tough stance on the Kurile Islands was reconfirmed by Prime Minister Viktor Chernomyrdin's remarks that 'There is no territorial problem. We will never negotiate with anyone on this issue.'[21] Even though Yeltsin's visit to Japan was eventually made in October 1993 after twice being cancelled, and Yeltsin offered an apology on the matter of prisoners of war,[22] the trip failed to settle the territorial dispute.

At present a continuing stalemate seems more likely than resolution. A report on scenarios for new relationships among Japan, Russia and the United States, prepared for the heads of government of Japan, Russia and the USA put it this way: 'The balance of forces in the domestic politics, the governmental politics, and the bureaucratic politics of each favours continued stalemate rather than solution. In both countries, leadership is too weak, too timid, or too distracted to devise and pursue a strategy for circumventing and overcoming the very real domestic obstacles that stand in the way.'[23] If stalemate continues, it will lead to a delay in full Japanese commitment to the Russian Far East oil and gas development projects.

2.1.3 Other factors in Japanese–Soviet energy relations

The consequence of this dispute is extremely disappointing for energy relations. As already mentioned, even though Japan has explored the possibility of participating in oil and gas development in West and East Siberia and in the Far East since the 1960s, nothing has been achieved except the discovery of two oil and gas fields in offshore Sakhalin. However, the blame cannot be wholly laid on the territorial issue even though it was a decisive factor. The poor economics of field development can also be blamed, as a number of examples demonstrate.

First of all, the Soviet–Japanese consultations on the Sakhalin continental-shelf project that ended on 23 November 1990 managed to agree on some issues, like the

---

[19] *Korea Times*, 22 Sept. 1992; 4 Dec. 1992.

[20] *Korea Times*, 10 Dec. 1992.

[21] *Korea Times*, 19 Aug. 1993: 29 Aug. 1993; *Nikkei Weekly*, 13 Sept. 1993.

[22] *The Times*, 13 Oct. 1993; *Financial Times*, 13 October 1993.

[23] Allison *et al.*, *Beyond Cold War to Trilateral Cooperation in the Asia–Pacific Region* (op. cit., n. 1) pp. 38–40.

level of normal prices for the resources extracted, forms of credit and technological arrangements for the development of the deposits, but failed to agree on the approach to evaluate the likely profitability of the Sakhalin project.[24] Secondly, preliminary economic calculations submitted to SODECO (Sakhalin Oil Development Cooperation Co.) in January 1991 suggested that the Chaivo field could be developed profitably only if the Japanese party extended credits for construction of surface facilities on preferential terms, at a prime interest rate of 7.5%/year on Japanese credits and on condition that 100% of the oil and condensate were exported.[25] Thirdly, in the 13th Japan–Soviet Economic Cooperation meeting held in Tokyo in January 1991, the Sakhalin oil and gas development project made no progress because of a difference in estimates over the future price of oil and Soviet expectations of a large reduction in interest rates by the Export–Import Bank of Japan.[26]

However, poor economics was not the real reason for Japan's refusal to commit itself to Soviet projects, but an excuse. During 1973–86 when high oil prices made the economics very favourable, the Japanese found other excuses for not undertaking these projects. For example, they lent huge sums of money to countries such as Indonesia to develop LNG projects, much more than they would have needed to lend for the Soviet projects.

When Rantik Dzhavanshirovich Margulov, the first deputy chairman of the Bureau for the Fuel and Energy Complex, visited Japan to talk about the Yakutia project, MITI (Ministry of International Trade and Industry) pointed out to him all the problems involved, as follows: first, Japan's needs for this century were already taken care of; secondly, the Japanese were exploring Alaska; thirdly, there would be environmental problems with the pipeline; fourthly, Soviet policies could suddenly change; fifthly, would the Soviet Union be able to persuade North Korea?; finally, what about the current chaos in the Soviet Union?[27] These are all excuses for a project to which the Japanese government and utilities are politically opposed.

The investment environment and other factors have also caused delay in the Russian Far East's oil and gas development. During the first half of the 1990s, development of these projects has not materialized. Internal problems, like the

---

[24] FBIS, Sov. 90:230 (29 Nov. 1990), p. 19.

[25] Andrei A. Konoplyanik, S. Oganesyan and A. Retyunin, 'Sakhalin tender background detailed', *Oil and Gas Journal*, 23 March 1992, p. 129.

[26] *Supar Report* 11 (July 1991), p. 40.

[27] *Asahi Shimbun*, 13 June 1990. For details of the stance taken by Japan's policy-making ministries towards the FSU, see Tsuneo Akaha and Takashi Murakami, 'Soviet/Russian–Japanese Economic Relations', in Tsuyoshi Hasegawa, Jonathan Haslam and Andrew C. Kuchins, eds, *Russia and Japan: An Unresolved Dilemma Between Distant Neighbours*, University of California Press, Berkeley, 1993, pp. 175–80.

dispute between central and local authorities as to how to develop Sakhalin offshore projects and continuous delay in formulating petroleum law are new factors that have discouraged the Japanese from taking part in RFE oil and gas development.

2.1.4 Business interests and prospects

Despite the territorial dispute, a series of energy deals between Japan and Russia during 1991–2 shows that bilateral energy relations could be improved in the 1990s. In 1991 Tomen Corporation agreed with Soyuznefteeksport, the Soviet corporation specializing in crude-oil exports, to increase crude-oil and oil-products imports. Under the $200-million agreement, Tomen would double oil purchases to 0.5 mt in 1991 from 0.25 mt in 1990, and increase the products imports to 0.8 mt from 0.6 mt.[28] And C. Itoh & Co., a Japanese trading house, made a deal with Soyuznefteeksport and Sakhalinmorneftegaz (Sakhalin Offshore Oil and Gas Co.) to export electric appliances and other consumer goods in exchange for crude oil.[29] Reportedly, in November 1991, the Ministry of the Oil Refining Industry awarded an order to C. Itoh to double the capacity of the Komsomolsk refinery to 120,000 b/d and to equip the plant with modern equipment. The project cost was estimated at $300–400 million. Reconstruction of the Khabarovsk refinery would begin in 1991 and continue for four or five years, at a cost of $100 million.[30]

Encouraging news followed. In late September 1992, Nippon Steel Corporation and C. Itoh signed contracts with Russia's Gazcomplektimpex and state gas concern Gazprom to provide Russia with $300-million worth of export credits. A second and similar contract with Gazprom worth $400 million was to be signed. Both contracts granted Russia a five-year deferral of payments (with two years grace for repayment and an 8% interest rate) (see Chapter 6, section 1).[31]

These reports prove that Japan's business interests can outweigh the official

[28] The contract crude will be mainly Ural oil. In 1990, of the contracted volume, only 40,000 tonnes had actually been traded. See *Japan Times*, 13 Feb. 1991.

[29] The $9 million deal was the first of its kind under a new Soviet trade system giving local corporations leeway to export their products. Besides this, C. Itoh made a deal with the Soviet Union to help supply oil. The Soviets arranged for C. Itoh to take 100,000 to 200,000 tonnes of Middle East crude to India each month. In return the Soviets would supply 1 tonne of Soviet Urals crude to C. Itoh for every 1.3 tonnes of Middle East crude sent to India. See *Supar Report* 11 (July 1991), p. 45, 48.

[30] *Kommercheskii vestnik* 34 (Nov. 1991), quoted in *Supar Report* 12 (Jan. 1992), p. 111.

[31] Nippon Steel and C. Itoh represented three other Japanese steelmakers and eight other trading companies in the deal. Of $300 million credits, $200 million was for 200,000 tonnes of large-diameter pipe and 150,000 tonnes of seamless pipe for natural-gas pipelines, and $100 million for drilling equipment. See *Oil and Gas Journal*, 12 Oct. 1992, p. 26; *Russian Petroleum Investor*, Oct. 1992, p. 17; June 1993, p. 55; Sept. 1994, p. 33 (Table).

Japanese government policy of refusing to establish normal trade relations with Russia until the two nations settle their territorial dispute regarding the Kurile Islands. (It does not necessarily mean that the conservative Japanese utilities are changing their stance towards gas purchasing from Russia.) The good news is a signal that Japanese government policy is becoming more flexible. Reportedly, MITI is to provide financial aid to Sakhalin offshore gas development by revising the JNOC Law, under which JNOC (Japan National Oil Corporation) can provide financial aid to oil and gas exploration projects alone and can only guarantee liabilities related to development projects.[32]

It remains to be seen, however, whether this development will lead to a fundamental shift in Japan's policy from *Seikei Fukabun*, the inseparability of politics and economics to *Seikei Bunri*, the separation of politics from economics, without settlement of the territorial dispute. A real test will come with the Sakhalin and Yakutsk oil and gas developments.

In late 1993 SODECO decided to drop its demand that Russia repay $277 million, of which $181.5 million were in credits, $95.5 million in interest, as increased interest by major western oil companies in Sakhalin offshore oil and gas development put SODECO in danger of losing not only the $277 million, but also its claim to the Odoptu and Chaivo oil and gas fields discovered by SODECO in the late 1970s. Japan had to accept this compromise so as not to lose its vested interest, and in fact gained from it as the Arkutun-Daginskoye field was included in the deal (see Chapters 6 and 7).

In late June 1994, solid ground for the development of Sakhalin offshore oil and gas was prepared by a production-sharing agreement between Yuri Shafranik, Russia's Minister of Fuel and Energy, and officials of Sakhalin Energy Investment Co., to develop the 'Sakhalin-II' project comprising the Piltun-Astokskoye and Lunskoye oil and gas fields.[33] Even though the Japanese companies in the consortium are not the driving force of Sakhalin-II (their combined shares are 30%), they are very well positioned to influence other consortium members due to their status as main consumers. It looks likely that the start of Sakhalin-II LNG export will be tuned to Japan's gas-market situation. (The decisive factor will be when the Japanese utilities make a commitment to LNG imports from Sakhalin.)

In this situation, the unsettled territorial problem seems unlikely to act positively on the export of Sakhalin offshore gas to Japan's gas market, which probably cannot begin before early in the next decade. If the territorial problem remains

---

[32] *Japan Petroleum & Energy Trends*, 1 Oct. 1993, p. 3.

[33] Sakhalin Energy Investment Co. is the formal name of the Bermuda-based legal entity created by the MMMSM (Marathon, McDermott, Mitsui, Misubishi and Shell). See *Russian Petroleum Investor*, July/August 1994, p. 53; *Financial Times*, 24 June 1994.

unsettled until then, it can only delay Japan's active participation in Russia's East Siberian oil and gas development.

2.2 Japanese–Chinese relations

2.2.1 Strengthening of relations

The relationship between China and Japan is particularly important to the political and economic development of the Asia–Pacific region, especially Northeast Asia. China has emphasized the significance of its relation with Japan and aimed at achieving three objectives: strengthening cooperation against Soviet influence in the Asia–Pacific region, utilizing Japan's economic power, technology and financial capacity to modernize the Chinese economy, and impeding any developments that might allow Japan once more to become a military threat to China.[34]

The energy relationship with Japan was the keystone of Chinese strategy in the 1970s. China saw that an oil-centred trade partnership between itself and Japan had greater potential than one between the Soviet Union and Japan. Japan was critically influenced by its positive attitude towards China, which contrasts markedly with an historic distrust of the Soviet Union, and the prospect of large-scale oil imports from China provided a pragmatic rationale for a posture that many Japanese would have liked to adopt anyway, quite apart from economic considerations.[35] However, the Chinese had to show their cards and shrewdly used the certainties of established crude-oil reserves at Daqing and the future potential of the Bohai Gulf[36] against the Soviet Siberian and Far Eastern natural-resources development projects.

A few recent examples reflect the strong Sino–Japanese relationship that has developed during the past two decades. For instance Japan took the lead in resuming loans to China at the end of 1990, with a sum of 112.5 billion yen for 17 projects involving transportation, energy and communications.[37] According to Gu Rubai, of the Bank of China, and Yukinori Ito, of the Export–Import Bank of Japan, the total Japanese energy loans during 1979–93 reached $9.4 billion (see Chapter 6, section 1). The sheer scale of Japan's energy-development loans to China is a simple

[34] Susan L. Clark, 'Japan's Role in Gorbachev's Agenda', *Pacific Review* 1:3 (1988), p. 285.
[35] Selig S. Harrison, *China, Oil, and Asia: Conflict Ahead?*, Columbia University Press, New York, 1977, pp. 149–50.
[36] Ronald C. Keith, 'China's Resource Diplomacy and National Energy Policy', in Ronald Keith, ed., *Energy, Security and Economic Development in East Asia*, St Martin's Press, New York, 1986, pp. 20–1.
[37] *Beijing Review*, 28 Oct.–3 Nov. 1991, p. 29. In August 1991 the Japanese premier Toshiki Kaifu visited Beijing, and Japan was the first country whose leader visited China since the Tiananmen massacre of June 1989. See *Beijing Review*, 19–25 Aug. 1991, p. 4.

reflection of the strength of Sino–Japanese relations. However, it does not necessarily mean that the relationship has always been so rosy.

It could be argued that energy, and especially oil, trades have played important roles in strengthening ties between the two countries during the past two decades. Since 1973 when China began its crude-oil exports to Japan as a way of distracting Japanese interests from Soviet Far East energy development, China has kept a substantial amount of oil trade with Japan. During 1984–90, Japan's share in China's crude-oil exports hovered around 38–55% (China's total crude-oil exports were around 22–31 mt, of which 11–14 mt were allocated for Japan).

Besides this, and despite low oil prices and several years of disappointing and costly exploration, Japan has maintained its commitment to Chinese offshore development. As shown in Table 2.1, ten Japanese companies were set up for the development of Bohai Bay, Beibu Bay and Pearl River Mouth Basin fields during 1978–88. Of these, Chengbei Oil Development Corp. (CODC), Beibu Offshore Oil Development Co. (BOODC) and Japan China Oil Development Corp. (JCODC) have produced oil, and in 1990 the three companies' share in Japanese companies' overseas oil production was less than 2%. If it had not been for MITI's plan to raise the proportion of oil imports from Japanese producers from 10% to 30%, Japanese companies – having either no oil discovery or poor production records in China's offshore fields – would have withdrawn.

Another reason for continued cooperation might have been political considerations. A simplified comparison can cause misunderstanding, but it is worth mentioning. Only SODECO, whose main shareholder was JNOC (Japan National Oil Corporation), has been established, in 1974, for Far East offshore oil and gas exploration and development and the oil fields discovered during the late 1970s have not been developed so far. If the FSU and Japan had solved their territorial issue, this would not be the case.

In contrast, as mentioned above, Japan has established as many as ten companies for Chinese offshore development, and JNOC's shares were over 50% in all of them. As JNOC is a government-financed public corporation under MITI, the government's political stance towards China is clearly reflected in the decision to continue financial support for the development of unpromising fields in the Chinese offshore. Japan has been more generous to China than to the FSU, even though China has also had territorial disputes with Japan, albeit maritime ones.

2.2.2 The unresolved Senkaku issue

A three-way dispute in the southern part of the region involves claims by China, Taiwan and Japan to the Senkaku Gunto (known in Chinese as Diaoyutai), consisting of eight uninhabited islets and three rocks without vegetation, situated about

Table 2.1: Japanese companies involved in Chinese offshore development

	JCODC	BOODC	HODC	Japex Nanhai Ltd	New HODC
Established	24.4.78	26.11.82	29.9.83	29.9.83	12.12.85
Capital, initial	4.28 b yen	800 m yen	300 m yen	200 m yen	180 m yen
Capital, most recent figure	99.11 b yen (Feb. 1990)	8.88 b yen (June 1987)	6 b yen (May 1988)	4.7 b yen (May 1988)	3 b yen (May 1989)
Share composition (%)	JNOC 64.15 JAPEX 5.06 TOC 2.52 MPDC 1.66 MOECO 1.60	JNOC 49.3 IODC 17.3 INPEX 12.7 MOECO 10.1 Marubeni 5.1 Taiyo Oil 5.1	JNOC 50.0 AEDC 30.0 Nippon Oil 5.5 INPEX 2.0 MOECO 2.0 MPDC 2.0	JNOC 40.0 JAPEX 40.0 TOC 3.0 INPEX 3.0 MOECO 2.0 MPDC 2.0	JNOC 50.0 AEDC 33.7 NOOEC 5.5 INPEX 2.0 MOECO 2.0 MPDC 1.7
Area	*Bohai Bay* BZ 28–1 BZ 34–2/4	*Beibu Bay* Weizhou 10/3	*PRMB* Block 28/14 41/02 15/33 15/31	*PRMB* Block 15/33	*PRMB* Block 16/06
Remarks	A	B		C	

Note:
A Jan. 1989: Chengbei Oil Development Corp. merged.
B Aug. 1989: withdrew from WZ 10/3, prepared to close BOODC.
C Informed CNOOC not to extend block 15/33 exploration after Sept. 1989.
D Lufeng, 13-1-3, 25-1-1.
E Prepared to close JPR.
F Informed CNOOC not to extend block 13/03 exploration after 31 March 1990.
Abbreviations:
AEDC: AEC Energy Development Co. Ltd.
BOODC: Beibu Offshore Oil Development Company Ltd.
HODC: Huanan Oil Development Company Ltd.
INPEX: Indonesia Oil Exploration Co. Ltd (JNOC is the main shareholder in INPEX, with 50%).
IODC: Idemitsu Oil Development Co. Ltd.

NMC PRMODC	JAPEX New Nanhai Ltd	JPR	LBODC	JAPEX Nanhai Pearl River Ltd
12.12.85	12.12.85	26.5.86	14.1.88	26.8.88
150 m yen 1.8 b yen (June 1989) JNOC 50.0 Nippon Mining 50	180 m yen 3.08 b yen (May 1989) JNOC 50.0 JAPEX 32.22 TOC 3.02 INPEX 3.02 MOECO 2.01 MPDC 2.0	150 m yen 635 m yen (April 1988) JNOC 48.03 JAPEX 33.78 INPEX 12.99 MOECO 5.2	150 m yen 2.15 b yen (Oct. 1989) JNOC 55.81 JAPEX 15.46 AEDC 8.84 TOC 8.84 Nippon Mining 6.63 INPEX 4.42	100 m yen 500 m yen (July 1989) JNOC 50.0 JAPEX 41.0 TOC 3.0 INPEX 3.0
PRMB Block 16/06 15/33 15/31	*PRMB* Block 16/06	*PRMB* Block 27/04	*Bohai Bay* Block 13/03	*PRMB* Block 15/31
	D	E	F	

JAPEX: Japan Petroleum Exploration Co. Ltd (JNOC is the main shareholder of JAPEX, with 65.7%).
JCODC: Japan China Oil Development Corporation.
JPR: Japex Pearl River Ltd.
LBODC: Laizhou Bay Oil Development Co. Ltd.
MOECO: Mitsui Oil Exploration Co. Ltd (JNOC's MOECO share is 20.03%).
MPDC: Mitsubishi Petroleum Development Co. Ltd.
NMC PRMODC: NMC Pearl River Mouth Oil Development Co. Ltd.
NOOEC: Nippon Oil Overseas Exploration Co. Ltd.
PRMB: Pearl River Mouth Basin in the South China Sea.
TOC: Teikoku Oil Co. Ltd.

Source: Sekiyu Kogyo Renmei, Waga Kuni Sekiyu Kaihatsu no Genjo, Sekiyu Kogyo Renmei, Tokyo, 1990, pp. 72–3, 113–4, 122–5, 141–2, 153–6, 166–7, 199–200, and 253–4.

120 nautical miles Northeast of Taiwan, about 200 nautical miles west of Okinawa.[38] (It would be a two-way claim if Taiwan was to be included in China.) The East China Sea's oil potential is estimated at 10–100 billion barrels.[39] Possession of the islands would confer title over about 21,645 sq. km of the continental shelf, and at stake is an area encompassing parts of at least three possibly major oil-bearing sub-basins, with best prospects for the southwestern corner.[40] According to Mark Valencia, if China owned the Senkakus, it would possess most of the disputed area, including that with the thickest sediment, while Japan would retain thick sediments on the eastern margin of the Taiwan–Sinzi Basin and the Okinawa Trough Basin. If Japan owned the Senkakus, it would take much more of the basins, though an area which has yielded many dry holes and one Chinese oil strike would accrue to China.[41]

There would remain a potential difficulty, even if the issue of Senkaku Gunto was settled amicably in favour of China. Mark Valencia wrote:

> the equidistant line between the undisputed islands of Japan and the Chinese mainland leaves on the Japanese side of the line an area of 9,000 sq. nautical miles of the Asian continental shelf landward of the 200 metres isobath. China claims the broad adjacent continental margin, and argues that the shelf ends at the Okinawa Trough with water depths of 2,000 metres. Japan might argue that the trough is just an incidental depression in a continuous continental margin between the two countries and that the median line is the appropriate boundary.[42]

If Japan agreed to making a median-line arrangement, it might be because the arrangement would permit the area's oil development to move ahead regardless of how the question of title to the Senkaku is settled. Even if the Japanese claim were to be ignored in fixing a median line, a line drawn on the basis of the Ryukyus as 'base points' would give Japan scope for oil development in most of the areas covered in the 'provisional' concessions that it has demarcated in the East China

---

[38] Jeanette Greenfield, *China's Practice in the Law of the Sea*, Clarendon Press, Oxford, 1990, p. 127.

[39] *Far Eastern Economic Review*, 31 March 1988, p. 29.

[40] *Far Eastern Economic Review*, 28 May 1992, p. 23.

[41] Mark J. Valencia, 'Northeast Asia: Petroleum Potential, Jurisdictional Claims, and International Relations', *Ocean Development and International Law* 20 (1989), p. 48; *Far Eastern Economic Review*, 31 March 1988, p. 29. For details of the issue of delimitation of the shelf between China and Japan, see Greenfield, 'China's Practice in the Law of the Sea' (op. cit., n. 38), pp. 127–49; Choon-ho Park, *East Asia and the Law of the Sea*, Seoul National University Press, Seoul, 1983.

[42] Valencia, 'Northeast Asia' (op. cit., n. 41), p. 47.

Sea.[43] That is, regardless of the boundary issue, Japan can claim a voice in relation to oil and gas development in the East China Sea.

A main reason why Japan hesitates to make a median-line agreement with China lies in the failure so far to resolve the Taiwan issue. Even though Japan announced in March 1972 that it would deal only with China on the question of the Senkaku Gunto, it was reluctant to jeopardize its trade and investment links with Taiwan by negotiating with Beijing as the sole representative of Chinese offshore claims. It also said that it would not sanction petroleum exploration until ownership is resolved.[44] In response to the Chinese request to cooperate in joint studies on exploration and development of oil in the East China Sea, Teikoku Oil Co. was to establish a representative office in Beijing.[45]

At that time, however, China's stance towards the shelf question was ambiguous. On the one hand, China has rebuffed Japan's repeated offers to discuss the shelf question on the grounds that any solution to the boundary mark in the Yellow and East China Seas must be multilateral, involving all claimants. On the other hand, China persuaded Japan to agree to suspend its claim to sovereignty over the Senkakus as a precondition for any negotiations on cooperative oil arrangements, by suggesting that a realistic appraisal of regional economic needs and cooperation should take precedence over a narrowly 'legalistic' or 'historical' approach.[46]

Eventually China took a pragmatic stance which led to the so-called Deng Xiaoping formula in 1978, leaving the Senkaku question to future generations to resolve.[47] Since then, both countries have generally maintained an uneasy silence over the ownership of the islands in line with Deng's formula. In October 1990, however, when Taiwan made a fierce protest against Japan's preventing a group of Taiwan athletes with an Olympic torch from landing on Tiaoyutai island, using Japanese naval and air force units, Beijing stated that the islands are an 'inalienable part of China' and Japan's action was 'completely unreasonable'.[48] And in February 1992, when a new bill entitled 'The Law of the People's Republic of China on its Territorial Waters and their Contiguous Areas' and asserting control over the Senkaku Islands was passed by the Chinese parliament, Japan lost no time in making a rare public criticism of Beijing.[49] However, neither side has

---

[43] Ibid., p. 55.

[44] Ibid., p. 47.

[45] *Far Eastern Economic Review,* 31 March 1988, p. 29.

[46] Ibid.

[47] Robert E. Bedeski, *The Fragile Entente: The 1978 Japan–China Peace Treaty in a Global Context*, Westview Press, Boulder, 1983, pp. 35–7.

[48] *Free China Journal* 7: 82 (25 Oct. 1990), p. 1.

[49] *Financial Times*, 28 Feb. 1992.

wanted to be drawn into more than exchanges of protests over the islands (see Chapter 5, section 2).

2.2.3 Cooperation first, dispute next?

The implications of the new bill and the recent build up of Chinese naval forces suggest the possibility that China might resort to military force to resolve its territorial dispute. (However, it seems unlikely to resort to full-scale naval action in support of its Spratly claims in the foreseeable future as its navy is lacking a true deep-water capability for sustained action in the South China Sea.) China's desperate need for Japan's technology and equipment, and a huge investment, would argue against its opting for force to possess the Senkakus. In July 1991 CNPC signed an agreement with JNOC for the geophysical prospecting of the Tarim Basin, and this made Japan the first country to enter this forbidden and unexplored area (see Chapter 6, section 1). In April 1992, when a delegation led by Zhou Yongkang, vice-president of the CNPC, visited Japan, Mitsubishi agreed to extend CNPC loans totalling $100 million and designated for the purchase of technology and equipment for oil development in the Turpan-Hami Basin.[50]

Furthermore, in September 1992 Premier Li Peng told Japanese executives that they could explore for oil in the country's far west, and the CNPC President Wang Tao told JNOC President Kunio Komatsu in October 1992 that 'China will formally decide by the end of 1992 to open its remote inland oil fields to foreign investment'.[51] That is, China informed Japan in advance about opening the Tarim Basin to foreign investment. China had to use this card to attract Japanese interests, as the attractions of crude-oil exports diminished. In fact, in the Long-Term Trade Agreement of February 1978, China committed a total of 47.1 mt of crude-oil exports to Japan during 1978–82, but failed to meet the commitment by 7.76 mt due to its inability to increase oil production. (At that time, China's oil production target was 250 mt by 1985, 500 mt by 2000, as against the 1978 output of about 100 mt.[52]) In 1987 Japan was importing mainly crude oil, food and other commodities, but in 1992 more than half of imports from China were manufactured goods. Textiles became the biggest import item, accounting for 30% of the total.[53]

China used the opening of the Tarim Basin in the same way that it used crude-oil

---

[50] *China Daily*, 6 April 1992.

[51] *Financial Times*, 23 Sept. 1992; *Oil and Gas Journal*, 9 Nov. 1992, newsletter; *Korea Times*, 3 Nov. 1992.

[52] Chae-Jin Lee, *China and Japan: New Economic Diplomacy*, Hoover Institution Press, Stanford, 1984, pp. 103–112 (especially Table 22); Shigeru Ishikawa, 'Sino–Japanese Economic Co-operation', *The China Quarterly* 109 (March 1987), pp. 1–21.

[53] *Far Eastern Economic Review*, 22 Oct. 1992, p. 54.

Map 2.2: East China Sea contract areas

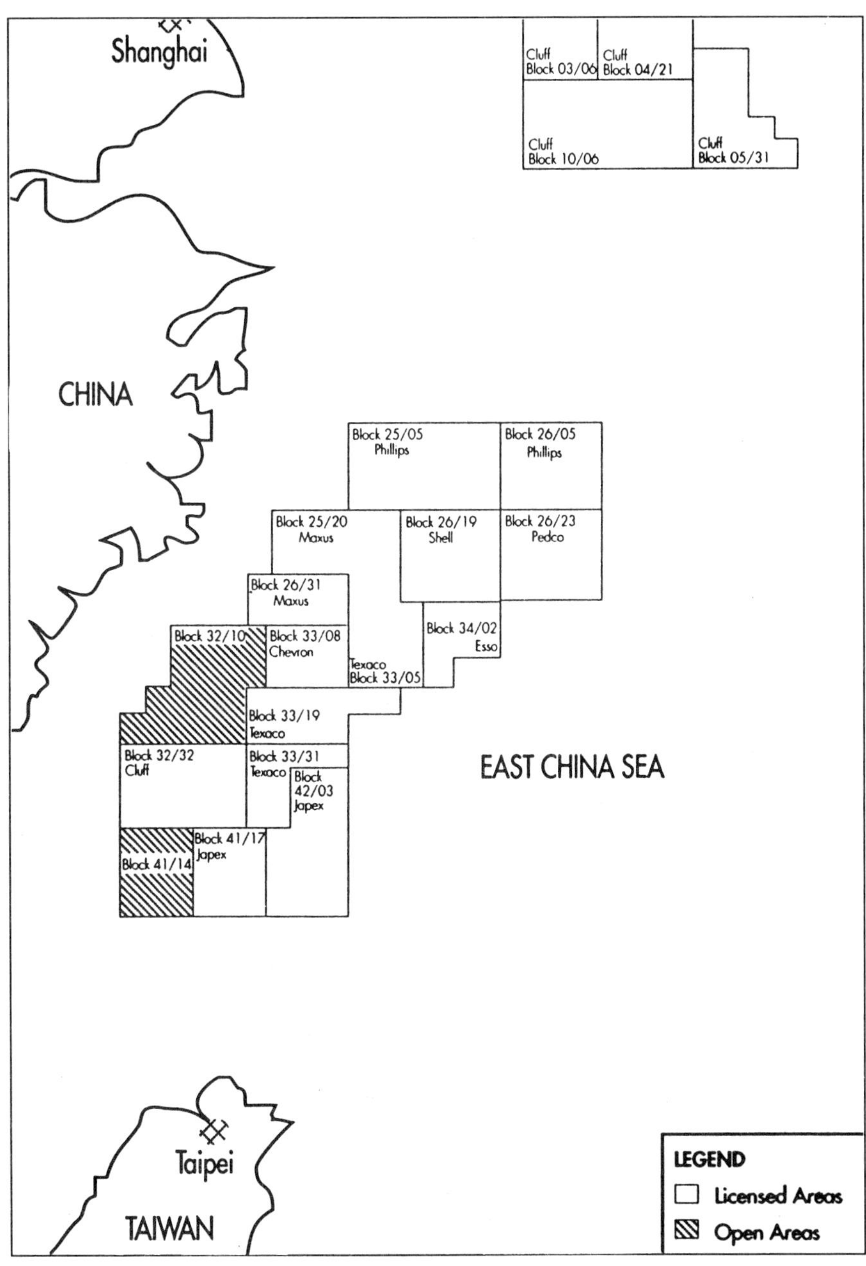

Source: China Petroleum Investment Guide, China Feature and AP Energy Business Publications, Singapore, 1994, p. 127.

exports in the early 1970s to block Japan's massive investment in Soviet Far East oil and gas development. This time crude-oil export was replaced by advance news of the opening of the Tarim Basin. As discussed in Chapter 6, section 1, during December 1993 and March 1994, eight Japanese companies took part in contracts between three consortia and CNPC for the Tarim Basin exploration: Japan did not disappoint China.

China's efforts to win Japan's favour has not been confined to the energy sector. Just before Gorbachev's Tokyo visit in April 1991, the Chinese premier Li Peng called for consultations between Japan and the FSU to resolve the Kurile issue. Unlike Li Peng's diplomatic gesture, Foreign Minister Qian Qichen made it clear that China supported Japan's attempts to retrieve four disputed islands from the FSU.[54] When a bill allowing Japanese soldiers to be deployed abroad under the UN flag was passed on 15 June 1992, China refrained from criticism.[55] In the latter case, China was confident of its leverage over Japan, that is, Japan needs China's support in its bid to become a permanent member of the UN Security Council. Both cases were examples of political strategies on the part of the Chinese aimed at winning Japan's goodwill.

By coincidence or not, China's efforts to attract Japanese interests developed satisfactorily. Soon after the cancellation of the Russian president Boris Yeltsin's Tokyo visit in September 1992, a Japanese consortium composed of Mitsubishi Corp., Marubeni Corp., Mitsui & Co., Itochu and Nissho Iwai agreed to undertake a feasibility study for a $4-billion petrochemical complex in the northern Chinese province of Liaoning.[56]

It is not certain, however, whether silence on the ownership of the islands in line with Deng's formula can be maintained once a phase of exploitation, rather than exploration, of the East China Sea oil and gas reserves begins. Unlike the Tarim contract, only one Japanese consortium composed of Japex and Teikoku has secured blocks (41/17 and 42/03) in southern acreage, by making a production-sharing contract with CNOOC in December 1993. Originally CNOOC offered 20 blocks in northern and southern acreages covering a total of 72,800 sq. km in the East China Sea, but contracts on block 32/10 and 41/14 are not yet made[57] (see Map 2.2). It cannot be said that the Senkaku issue between China and Japan has not affected the interest of Japanese companies in oil and gas development in the East China Sea.

[54] *Supar Report* 11 (July 1991), p. 59.

[55] *Far Eastern Economic Review*, 25 June 1992, p. 18.

[56] *Financial Times*, 22 Oct. 1992.

[57] *China Petroleum Investment Guide*, China Feature and AP Energy Business Publications, Singapore, 1994, p. 94 (Table 2).

So far, the agreement in 1978 between China and Japan to shelve their dispute over the sovereignty of the potentially oil-rich Senkaku Islands was a sign to their Asian neighbours, as much as to each other, of their commitment to reducing regional tension. Both countries have still to gain the confidence of their Asian neighbours and to dispel lingering suspicions of territorial ambition. This is a task which will not be assisted by allowing Sino–Japanese political differences to influence adversely the region's stability.[58] None the less there is a danger of conflict once China's 1992 decision to develop the East China Sea's oil and gas reserves results in exploitation. That is, a reconsideration of Deng's formula seems inevitable. What sort of solution can be hammered out in the 1990s remains to be seen. One thing that is very certain is that China will not allow the Senkaku issue to sour its relations with Japan.

2.3 The Korean Peninsula and prospects for unification

2.3.1 South Korea vs the Soviet Union (Russia)

One of the areas in the world most seriously affected by the end of the Cold War is the Korean peninsula. As far as South Korea is concerned, the changed environment has been favourable. It was the convergence of Gorbachev's new foreign policies directed towards Northeast Asia and South Korea's 'northern policy' that brought the establishment of diplomatic relationships between the FSU and South Korea in September 1990.[59]

In his Krasnoyarsk speech, Gorbachev said that 'In the context of a general improvement in the situation on the Korean peninsula opportunities may arise for organizing economic ties with South Korea.'[60] This was interpreted as a direct appeal to Seoul for its participation in the development of Siberia and the Soviet Far East. At the same time, it was the Soviet Union's first official indication that it intended to use South Korea as a card in Northeast Asian power politics.

In May 1989 a speech by Aleksandr N. Yakovlev, a Soviet Communist Party Politburo member, provided a clear vision of the Soviets' new policy towards South Korea. He said that 'If Japan does not take part positively in the development of the Soviet Far East, the Soviet Union will have to seek relations with China, and start

---

[58] Laura Newby, *Sino–Japanese Relations: China's Perspective*, RIIA/Routledge, London, 1988, p. 87.

[59] For details on South Korea's northern policy, see Dan C. Sanford, *South Korea and the Socialist Countries: The Politics of Trade*, Macmillan, London, 1990.

[60] The speech was made on 16 Sept. 1988 under the title 'Time for Action, Time for Practical Work'. See FBIS, Sov. 88:182 (20 Sept. 1988), pp. 29–41; *News and Views From the USSR* (Soviet Embassy, Washington), 19 Sept. 1988, pp. 1–11.

substantial relations with South Korea with which Moscow has just begun contacts.'[61] Then, in April 1990, Igor Rogachev, then Soviet deputy foreign minister, stressed the need to promote commercial and economic relations with South Korea for the purpose of integrating the Soviet Union into the international division of labour in the Far East.[62]

In the energy sector, however, the new Soviet thinking was kindled by a South Korean initiative. In January 1989 South Korea's Hyundai Business Group proposed building a pipeline grid from the Yakut ASSR to the Korean peninsula through North Korea.[63] In August 1990, Yi Won, then director of the Resources Development Bureau at the Ministry of Energy and Resources, and a leader of the Korean mission to the Soviet Union for energy-development cooperation, said that 'The Korean government has decided to promote the plan for the development of East Siberian gas fields because it would help ensure S. Korea's energy supply and also because it would help North–South Korean relations.'[64] It was the first time that the South Korean government had revealed its plan for laying pipelines through North Korea. On 19 April 1991 when Gorbachev visited Cheju Island in South Korea, both countries agreed to pursue an early joint development of natural gas in the Sakhalin region with Korean firms and with participation by third countries' business ventures.[65] (Details of South Korea's approach towards Sakhalin offshore development are in Chapter 6, section 2.)

Besides the Sakhalin project, a number of other agreements have been made in the energy sector. In January 1991 Lucky-Goldstar International Corporation made a contract with Polimerkhim to provide petrochemicals to the FSU. It was the first direct export to the country.[66] Then a joint venture (dubbed 'Lisko') by Interprom of the FSU and Lucky-Goldstar of Korea was created in the wake of Gorbachev's visit to Korea.[67] In May 1991 Hyundai Resources Development Co. (HRDC) and the

---

[61] *Korea Times*, 9 May 1989.

[62] *Supar Report* 9 (July 1990), p. 22.

[63] Hankook Ilbo, 7 Jan. 1989. In December 1988 Mr Chung Ju-Yung, founder and honorary chairman of the Hyundai Business Group, met the chairmen of the Bechtel Group and Parsons Corp. respectively to discuss a possible joint venture in Siberia. Before meeting them, he had talked with Mitsubishi and Mitsui in Japan. See *Supar Report* 6 (Jan. 1989), Chronicle, p. 20.

[64] FBIS, EAS 90:154 (9 Aug. 1990), pp. 18–19.

[65] *Korea Herald*, 21 April 1991.

[66] The $2 million contract was to provide 1,200 tonnes of acryloniprile butadiene styrene resins to the Soviet Union. See FBIS, EAS 91:26 (7 Feb. 1991), p. 23.

[67] Lisko had a starting capital of $50 million and would import Soviet coal in return for electronic goods. See *Eastern Bloc Energy*, Aug. 1991, p. 11.

Kalmyk Republic signed an agreement on joint ventures in oil drilling and refining, and in August 1991 HRDC and Mangyshlakneft, of the Republic of Kazakhstan, agreed to develop the north Buzachi oil field near the Caspian Sea.[68]

During the first half of 1992, a basis for the promotion of joint development of energy resources in Russia was created in the form of a committee named the 'Korea–Russia joint energy resources cooperation.'[69] After visiting South Korea – his first stop in Asia, not the second after his visit to Japan – the Russian president Boris Yeltsin said that 'the trip to Seoul was the first step and the right country was chosen. ...Of course, the visit was successful and necessary.'[70]

In his Seoul visit, Yeltsin confirmed the role of South Korea as an essential counterweight to Japan, which he wished to keep guessing about the prospects of economic, especially energy, cooperation. The leverage that South Korea offers Russia in relation to its frontier oil and gas development was an invisible gift to Yeltsin from Seoul. To the Russians, South Korea is too small to be politically threatening, but has enough economic muscle and technological prowess to help oil and gas development in the Russian Far East.

The South Korean response was more than Russia expected, and the agreement paved the way for the development of the Republic of Sakha's huge gas resources. In June 1994, after many twists and turns due to disagreement on the budget issue, South Korea and the Russian Federation agreed to implement a preliminary feasibility study (see Chapter 6, section 2). At present, few believe that the Korean initiative in the development of Yakutian gas will be realized before the end of the century. It could only be facilitated earlier by settlement of the unification problem currently existing between North and South Korea[71] (see box p. 50).

As for oil trade between the Soviet Union and South Korea, it officially started in March 1987, but until 1990 it had no more than a symbolic meaning.[72] In July 1991 Jindo Co. concluded a contract to buy five million barrels of Soviet oil with deliveries to begin in Autumn 1991;[73] this was the first direct and large-scale contract between the Soviet Union and South Korea. Given that West Siberia itself is heavily dependent on its own oil, however, large-scale oil exports are inconceivable. Until

---

[68] *Chosun Ilbo*, 19 May 1991 and 24 Oct. 1991.

[69] FBIS, EAS 92:102 (27 May 1992), pp. 24–25.

[70] *Korea Times*, 22 Nov. 1992.

[71] Keun Wook Paik, 'Pipeline Politics: Turkmenistan vs. Russian Far East Gas Development', *Geopolitics of Energy* (Sept. 1994), p. 6.

[72] For details, see Keun Wook Paik, 'Russian and Chinese Oil and Gas Policies in Northeast Asia: International Political Consequences and Implications', PhD thesis, University of Aberdeen, 1993, pp. 336–7.

[73] *Hankook Ilbo*, 30 July 1991; FBIS, Sov. 91: 151 (6 Aug. 1991), p. 13.

the implementation of the Far East and East Siberia oil and gas projects, the scale of the FSU's oil exports to South Korea will not be substantial.

2.3.2 North Korea vs the Soviet Union (Russia)

When the Soviets decided to establish a relationship with South Korea, they did so at the expense of North Korea. Immediately after South Korean–Soviet talks in San Francisco in June 1990, the Soviet Union withdrew its technicians from Yongbyon, where they were helping to build large-scale nuclear reactors, and stopped the transfer of all associated technology. Then, in late August 1990, the Soviet Union decided to make North Korea pay hard currency for its crude-oil delivery beginning on 1 January 1991.[74] The decision was a serious blow to North Korea.[75] The dwindling crude-oil delivery from the Soviet Union resulted in a temporary shutdown of North Korea's largest refinery.[76]

Ironically, the Soviet Union's lukewarm stance towards North Korea opened the way for inter-Korean trade.[77] In April 1991 Honam Refinery exported 29,800 barrels (worth $1.4 million) of high-sulphur diesel oil to North Korea for the first time, despite a US protest on the grounds that such an export was against COCOM (Coordinating Committee for Export to Communist Areas) regulations. The company judged the US protest groundless for two reasons: first, South Korea is not a member country of COCOM and, second, high-sulphur diesel oil is not a strategic

[74] One report claimed that the FSU allowed North Korea a moratorium on paying for 1991's 0.5 million tonnes of crude in hard currency in consideration of the latter's financial difficulties. See FBIS, EAS 91:75 (18 April 1991), p. 32. The decision was all part of the break-up of the CMEA.

[75] According to a JETRO (Japan External Trade Organization) Report, North Korea's oil imports from the FSU have declined sharply in recent years, from 0.8 mt in 1987 to 0.506 mt in 1989, and to 0.41 mt in 1990. See *Asian Wall Street Journal*, 1 Oct. 1991; FBIS, Sov. 92:38 (26 Feb. 1992), p. 32; *Chosun Ilbo*, 26 Jan. 1993. In 1991 North Korea spent $306.8 million for 2.44 mt of crude-oil imports. The breakdown is as follows: 1.1 mt from China ($145.68 million), 1 mt from Iran ($120 million), and 0.34 mt from the CIS ($40.8 million). See *Korea Times*, 24 Nov. 1992.

[76] *Supar Report* 12 (Jan. 1992), p. 65. As of 1991, the capacity of North Korea's two refineries was around 3.5 mt per year. One is Seungli Chemical Plant located in Najin, near Vladivostok; its refining capacity is 2 million tonnes. The plant has kept refining Soviet crude oil. The other is Bonghwa Chemical Plant located 13 km off Shineiju, near Dandong city, Liaoning province, in China, and its capacity is 1.5 million tonnes. Chinese crude has been refined here. See Chung Hae-Seok, 'North Korea's Oil Industry', *Korea Petroleum Association Journal*, June 1991, p. 41.

[77] In 1992, inter-Korean trade recorded $210.2 million on an approval basis, a 9.4% increase from the $192.2 million in 1991. See *Korea Times*, 16 Jan. 1993.

item, but a fuel used by fishing boats. This episode confirms the United States' diminishing influence in South Korea, and illustrates how the political environment in Northeast Asia is changing.

The latter is not necessarily favourable to Russia. Due to the worsened relationship between the Soviet Union (later Russia) and North Korea, Russian influence there has diminished substantially. In this context, some doubts can be raised as to the safety of the proposed gas pipeline passing through North Korean territory. Even though North Korea has continuously stated that it has no objections to a gas pipeline through Soviet or Russian channels,[78] no one can guarantee its safety. In other words, there is no way to stop North Korea's blocking or disruption of a gas pipeline passing through its territory. Surely, the North Korean factor is the weak link in the implementation of the East Siberian gas-pipeline project.

2.3.3 China's pragmatic stance towards the two Koreas

China has also lost influence in North Korea, but not to the extent that Russia has. It has taken a more pragmatic stance towards North Korea. Originally it intended to adopt payment in hard currencies instead of open accounts in commodity exchanges with North Korea from 1992, but decided to postpone doing so until 1993 in consideration of North Korea's poor foreign-currency holdings and its anger over the establishment of diplomatic relations between South Korea and China in August 1992.[79]

However, at the end of 1992 China decided to end its barter trade with North Korea. In the oil talks between the two countries in November 1992, China asked North Korea to settle 0.65 mt of crude-oil shipment with hard currencies, but North Korea refused to accept the proposal. Then China offered a compromise, suggesting that North Korea pay with its iron or zinc in 1993, and with hard currency from 1994. As North Korea refused this as well, China informed North Korea of its decision to suspend delivery of 0.65 mt of crude-oil on 31 December 1992.[80] To North Korea, a cash payment for its crude-oil imports was almost impossible, and China's decision to stop the barter trade seemed to strike a fatal blow to the energy situation.[81]

---

[78] FBIS, EAS 90:222 (16 Nov. 1990), p. 28. However, North Korea refused to acknowledge the agreement between the FSU and South Korea in April 1991 on joint gas development in Sakhalin. See FBIS, EAS 91:78 (23 April 1991), pp. 11–12.

[79] The bilateral trade between North Korea and China amounted to $620 million in 1991. See *Korea Times*, 24 Nov. 1992.

[80] In 1992 China supplied about 1.2 mt/year of crude oil to North Korea, of which 0.65 mt was in the form of barter trade and the remaining 0.55 mt on credit. See *Korea Times*, 24 Feb. 1993.

[81] Since 1990 North Korea has suffered from a serious crude-oil shortage and China's supply became a lifeline. During the 1980s China supplied around 1–1.5 mt of its crude oil to North Korea at a special price. For example, in 1989–90, if international oil prices had been

Paradoxically, the decision was the clearest indication that Beijing had abandoned ideological correctness in favour of economic development. The first direct deal on a long-term basis with South Korea had been made in May 1989,[82] and annual Chinese crude imports by four Korean companies during 1989–91 amounted to roughly one million tonnes.[83] The scale of the oil trade during the period was quite significant even though no diplomatic relations existed between the two countries.

The coincidence of political and economic interests seemed to spark a rapid expansion in oil trade between China and South Korea, creating an important new energy axis in Northeast Asia. Politically ambitious, South Korea has aimed to transform its expansive oil-refining sector into the hub of a crude-oil and products trade network running through northern China, Russia and North Korea. As for China, priority has been given to finding steady new sources of oil products to ensure the success of its economic reforms, as traditional suppliers, like Singapore, Hong Kong and Japan, seemed unlikely to have the needed processing capacity.[84]

The Chinese market was ideal for South Korean refiners under pressure to increase exports due to surplus capacity.[85] By 1992 the surplus capacity was 0.4 million b/d.[86] In 1991 South Korea exported a mere 0.744 million barrels of products to China due to high import tariffs and a lack of formal diplomatic ties, while around 20,000 b/d of crude oil and 2,670 b/d of products were imported.[87] Thanks to ratification of a most-

applied, North Korea would have paid $113.2 million and $137.1 million respectively. But North Korea paid only $61 million and $67.7 million. In 1992 North Korea's electricity generation and coal production declined by 9.3% and 4.1% from the previous year respectively. See *Korea Times*, 17 Feb. 1993; *Korea Times*, 31 Dec. 1992; *Chosun Ilbo*, 31 Dec. 1992; *Financial Times*, 5 Jan. 1993.

[82] A South Korean company, Sunkyung Ltd, representing its affiliate Yukong Ltd, made a contract to import 745,000 barrels/year of Chinese crude oil with a Hong Kong SINOCHEM branch office. The import prices were to be determined at least $2 lower than those of Middle East crude oil. See *Korea Times*, 17 May 1989.

[83] The four companies are Yukong Ltd., Honam Oil Refinery Co., Kyung In Energy Co. and Kukdong Oil Co. (now Hyundai Oil Co.) The Chinese crude mainly came from Shengli and Chengbei oil fields.

[84] *Petroleum Intelligence Weekly*, 16 March 1992, p. 2.

[85] In early 1991, South Korea's refining capacity was 0.974 mb/d (including a heavy-oil-cracking and desulphurizing capacity of 0.034 mb/d). By 1992, the refining capacity already reached 1.675 mb/d. According to an early 1991 estimate, the refining capacity at the end of 1993 would be 1.509 mb/d, including 0.23 mb/d of heavy-oil-cracking capacity and 0.16–0.17 mb/d of desulphurization capacity. See *Chosun Ilbo*, 10 March 1991; *Petroleum Intelligence Weekly*, 23 Sept. 1991, p. 6; a report (unpublished) prepared by the Korean Petroleum Association.

[86] *Petroleum Intelligence Weekly*, 16 March 1992, p. 2.

[87] Ibid.

favoured-nation trade agreement on 1 February 1992, Chinese import duties on South Korean oil products were slashed by more than half, to 6–8%. The establishment of formal diplomatic relations followed. This made South Korea's oil more competitive with alternative suppliers such as Singapore, Hong Kong and Japan, and other sources, like the United States. In 1992, as a result, South Korea's oil-products exports to China amounted to 6,024 million barrels (worth $115.2 million).[88]

Apart from the oil trade, until the end of 1991 only one other deal in the energy sector was reported.[89] Soon after the establishment of diplomatic relations, Samsung Engineering won a bid to build a $200-million ethylene plant in Jilin city, Jilin province, in northeastern China. It was the first important Chinese contract awarded to a South Korean company since the establishment of diplomatic relations.[90]

China's pragmatic stance towards North and South Korea indirectly contributed to inter-Korean energy cooperation. In early 1992 North Korea's Seungli (Victory) Chemical Co. asked Lucky-Goldstar Co. to supply them with around 30 million barrels of crude oil (worth $0.2 billion) annually. They suggested that payment be made in the form of refined products and non-ferrous metals, like zinc ingot.[91] North Korean companies have made more such suggestions since November 1992, including a deal on grains.[92] In short, the Chinese decision to end barter trade with North Korea at the end of 1992 and the consequent shortage in North Korea's crude-oil supply has strengthened the South's role as a middleman in supplying crude oil to the North, possibly leading to inter-Korean joint offshore development.

North Korea has undertaken offshore exploration and development since the late 1970s.[93] In 1981 a 2,000-km marine seismic survey was begun in the central portion

---

[88] A report (unpublished) prepared by the Korean Petroleum Association; *Oil and Gas Journal*, 20 July 1992, p. 26.

[89] In November 1991, Hyundai Heavy Industries Co. won a contract for $32.4 million worth of oil-drilling equipment for a project in Hainan province in southern China. The company took part in the biddings for a $55-million platform-installing project in December 1992, and a $13-million pipeline project in January 1993 respectively, and is waiting the result. See *Korea Times*, 18 Feb. 1993.

[90] *Financial Times*, 22 Sept. 1992. In November 1992, South Korea and China agreed to undertake ten joint projects including a joint research project for natural-resources development in the Yellow Sea in 1993. See *Korea Times*, 27 Nov. 1992.

[91] *Chosun Ilbo*, 19 Feb. 1992.

[92] *Korea Times*, 5 Jan. 1993.

[93] In 1977 North Korea signed a protocol with Asia Exploration Consultants (AEC) of Singapore regarding oil exploration and development, but this never went beyond the protocol stage. Seismic work was first undertaken in September 1979, and a jack-up dubbed *Enda Star* was used to drill a well near the Chinese-claimed boundary, beginning in September 1980. This activity stopped in January 1981. See Valencia, 'Northeast Asia' (op. cit., n. 41), p. 41.

of Korea Bay by Geoco technicians and equipment on a 15,000 sq. km seismic option granted in 1979 to INAP *et al.*, Yugoslavia's national company.[94]

China has also carried out a seismic survey of the western Korea Bay, including parts of the boundary. Two Western-designed jack-ups drilled close to the border in 1980. Some minor oil and gas discoveries were apparently made in the same region earlier, and the structures continue across the boundary into North Korean jurisdiction. This was why China was interested in assisting North Korea in its exploration efforts. However, both sides have left the demarcation issue unsettled,[95] and there have been no reports of Chinese participation in North Korea's offshore exploration and development since the second half of the 1980s.

Reportedly North Korea discovered 425 b/d of crude oil in Zone C in the Yellow Sea at the end of 1988 with the help of an Australian company, Meridian Oil NL,[96] which made a contract with North Korea covering the western Korea Bay on 31 July 1987. It was also reported that North Korea confirmed gas reserves in the Heungnam area.[97] Until recently the North has not yet responded to South Korea's proposal of inter-Korean joint offshore oil and gas development. If North Korea accepts the proposal, it will be a turning point in inter-Korean energy relations.

---

[94] Ibid.; G. L. Fletcher, 'Oil and Gas Developments in the Far East', *American Association of Petroleum Geologists Bulletin* 67 (1983), pp. 1888, 1895–6.

[95] If China maintains the silt-line principle, based upon the concept of the 'natural prolongation' of the continental shelf, or alternatively claims an exclusive economic zone (EEZ) extending from Haiyang Island, 69 km off Liaodong Peninsula, problems could arise. A boundary along the silt line would give almost the entire Korea Bay Basin to North Korea, whereas if the equidistant-line boundary was applied, only a small pod of possible oil-bearing sediment would lie on the North Korean side of the line. See Valencia, 'Northeast Asia' (op. cit., n. 41), pp. 40–41; *Far Eastern Economic Review*, 31 March 1988, p. 28.

[96] The area's oil potential is estimated at 200 million barrels. In 1990 Leeward Petrochemical Products Ltd took over operatorship and a 92% working interest while Meridian retained an 8% stake. See *Petromin*, Dec. 1993, pp. 37–8; *Chungang Ilbo*, 1 Jan. 1989; *Kookbang Ilbo* (Defence Daily), 11 April 1992. According to PIW, a half-dozen European and Australian companies were invited to examine prospects after North Korea's Ministry of National Resources Development drafted framework laws governing production-sharing contracts. See *Petroleum Intelligence Weekly*, 6 April 1992, p. 7, and 2 Sept. 1992, p. 7. A North Korean delegation attending the Offshore South East Asia conference in Singapore in 1986 indicated that Norwegian and Yugoslavian companies had undertaken seismic activity. See *Offshore*, Aug. 1986, p. 13; M.J. Valencia, *Offshore North–East Asia: Oil, Gas and International Relations*, Economist Intelligence Unit, London, 1988, p. 22.

[97] *Meil Kyungje* (Economic Daily), 8 Feb 1992. In February 1993, Swedish independent Taurus Petroleum secured two seismic option blocks covering 11,000 sq. km in the Yellow Sea. See *Petromin*, Dec. 1993, p. 38.

2.3.4 The dormant offshore boundary issue

In the past, China recognized North Korea as the only legitimate government in the Korean peninsula, and therefore disputed the outer boundaries of all South Korean leases.[98] It is not an exaggeration to say that the Yellow Sea has rarely been explored. As a result so far no discovery has been made despite the area's potential of around 1–10 billion barrels of oil.[99]

The boundary issue is the crucial factor. According to Mark Valencia, the silt-line boundary in the Yellow Sea would place the entire basin on the Chinese side of the line. If the boundary was the equidistant line, most of the basin would be on the Chinese side but half a pod of potentially oil-bearing sediment, including a tip of the area with the best prospectives, would be on the South Korean side.[100] Meanwhile, in the northern East China Sea an equidistant line between China, South Korea and Japan would bisect the Taiwan–Sinzi Basin so that the largest area would go to China.[101] If the silt-line was the boundary, most of the basin would go to Japan and South Korea, though China would get a tongue of the extreme northern core. In short, the silt-line boundary is advantageous for China in the Yellow Sea, but disadvantageous in Korea Bay and the East China Sea.[102]

Leaving this intractable boundary issue unsettled, both sides have explored the possibility of Yellow Sea joint development in recent years. Following a secret symposium on Yellow Sea oil and gas exploration in October 1990,[103] CNOOC officially proposed joint development of the Yellow Sea in March 1991,[104] and the

---

[98] A series of South Korean–US seismic surveys of the Yellow Sea in May and June 1971, and Gulf's drilling operations in Korea's seabed-mining Block II from February to June 1973, were suspended because of fierce reactions from China and North Korea. See Harrison, 'China, Oil, and Asia' (op. cit., n. 35), pp. 125–45; Kim Woodard, *The International Energy Relations of China*, Stanford University Press, Stanford, 1980, pp. 147–90.

[99] *Far Eastern Economic Review*, 31 March 1988, p. 28.

[100] Ibid., pp. 28–9; Richard T. S. Hsu, 'A Rational Approach to Maritime Delimitation in the Yellow Sea', and Comments by Jin-Hyun Paik, in Choon-ho Park *et al.*, *The Regime of the Yellow Sea: Issues and Policy Options for Cooperation in the Changing Environment*, Institute of East and West Studies, Seoul, 1990, pp. 133–58. For further information, see Park, 'East Asia and the Law of the Sea' (op. cit., n. 41).

[101] The Longjing I well was more than 40 m beyond a hypothetical Chinese–South Korean median line suggested by Seoul. See Valencia, 'Northeast Asia' (op. cit., n. 41) p. 52.

[102] Ibid., p. 48; *Far Eastern Economic Review*, 31 March 1988, p. 29. For more detailed information, see Greenfield, 'China's Practice in the Law of the Sea' (op. cit., n. 38), pp. 117–49.

[103] In late February 1990 the EOOC, a subsidiary of CNOOC, delivered its message to South Korea through Lucky-Goldstar International Corp., and the symposium was held in Shanghai 23–25 Oct. 1990. See Ministry of Energy and Resources' press release material.

[104] *Chosun Ilbo*, 23 April 1991.

Map 2.3 Potential boundary dispute between China and South Korea: the East China Sea

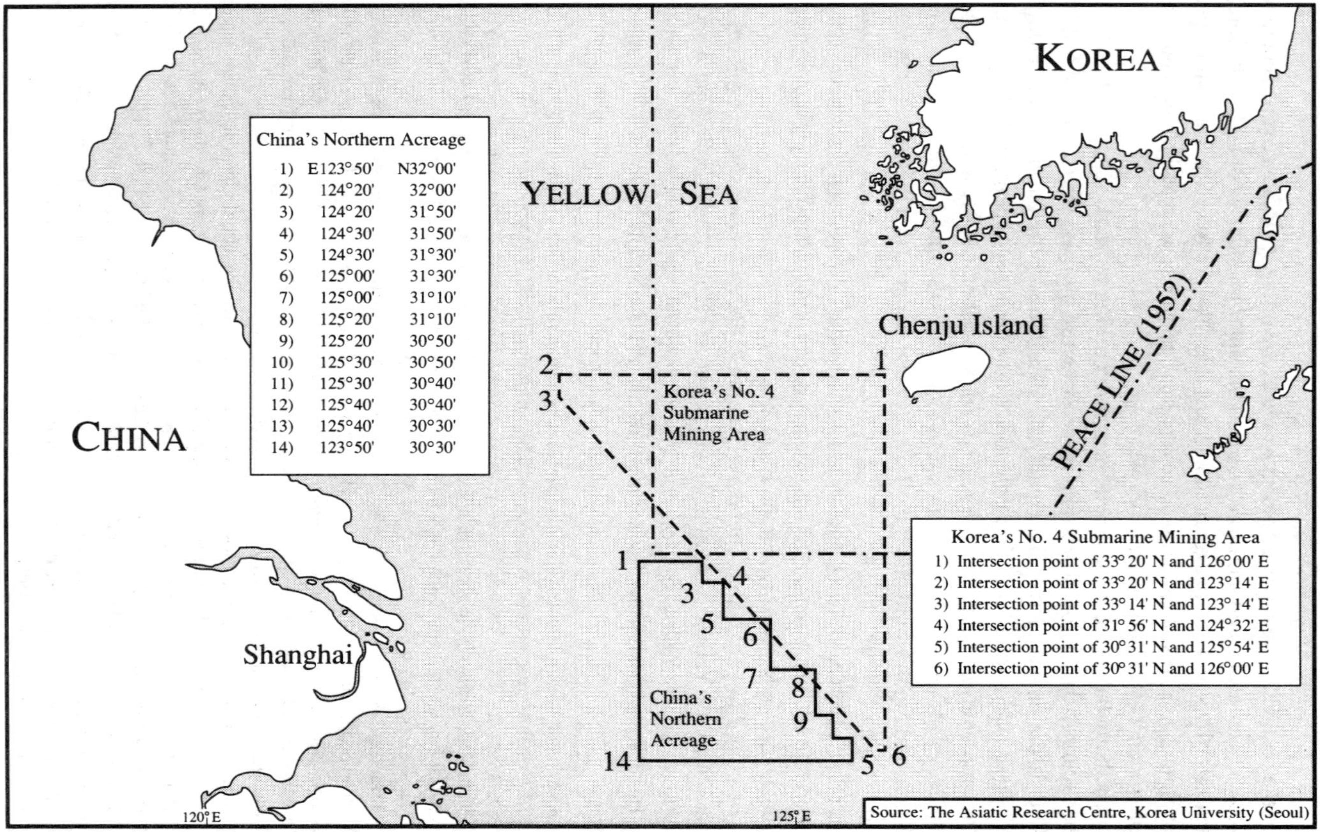

KOREA

YELLOW SEA

CHINA

Shanghai

Chenju Island

PEACE LINE (1952)

Korea's No. 4 Submarine Mining Area

China's Northern Acreage

120° E

125° E

China's Northern Acreage

	E	N
1)	E123°50'	N32°00'
2)	124°20'	32°00'
3)	124°20'	31°50'
4)	124°30'	31°50'
5)	124°30'	31°30'
6)	125°00'	31°30'
7)	125°00'	31°10'
8)	125°20'	31°10'
9)	125°20'	30°50'
10)	125°30'	30°50'
11)	125°30'	30°40'
12)	125°40'	30°40'
13)	125°40'	30°30'
14)	123°50'	30°30'

Korea's No. 4 Submarine Mining Area

1) Intersection point of 33° 20' N and 126° 00' E
2) Intersection point of 33° 20' N and 123° 14' E
3) Intersection point of 33° 14' N and 123° 14' E
4) Intersection point of 31° 56' N and 124° 32' E
5) Intersection point of 30° 31' N and 125° 54' E
6) Intersection point of 30° 31' N and 126° 00' E

Source: The Asiatic Research Centre, Korea University (Seoul)

next month a South Korean mission was dispatched to discuss the CNOOC proposal. In June 1992 CNOOC repeated its request for South Korean companies' participation in the Yellow Sea development, through a formal diplomatic channel.[105] Soon after the establishment of diplomatic relations in August 1992, the second South Korean–China international symposium on the petroleum potential of the Yellow Sea and the East China Sea was held in Seoul.[106]

In late 1992 a Korean consortium composed of eight companies decided to take part in the fourth international bidding for the East China Sea's oil and gas exploration and development, announced on 30 June 1992, and to purchase the data package.[107] Sino–South Korean oil and gas development cooperation in the Yellow Sea and East China Sea seems thereby to be strengthened. For a fully fledged development of the Yellow and East China Seas, however, a compromise on the problem of delimitation of the continental shelf has to be made (see Map 2.3).

South Korea's recently improved relations with both Russia and China could be conditioned by factors such as North Korea's nuclear problem,[108] the unsettled boundary dispute and power politics among the regional powers. In particular the death of North Korea's President Kim Il-Sung in July 1994 has brought a bundle of new uncertainties. One positive aspect of the situation arises from North Korea's virtually non-existent oil and gas industries.

2.4 Taiwanese issues

2.4.1 'One country, two systems'

China's policy towards Taiwan can be summed up by the proposition that there is only one China, thereby negating Taiwan's political existence. Officially, the concept of 'one country, two systems'[109] was put forward by Deng Xiaoping in January

---

[105] *Maeil Kyungje Shinmoon*, 7 Dec. 1992. For details of the consortium, see Chapter 6, section 2.

[106] The symposium was held on 21–26 September 1992. See *Korea Times*, 22 Sept. 1992; 27 Sept. 1992.

[107] *Maeil Kyungje Shinmoon*, 7 Dec. 1992.

[108] In October 1994, the United States reached an accord with North Korea to ease the threat of North Korea's nuclear-weapons programme. South Korea would build two light water reactors (a generating capacity of about 1,000 MW each) in the North based on its own version of technology originally licensed from ABB Combustion Engineering. In return, North Korea froze its nuclear-weapons programme. South Korea would finance more than half of the $4 billion project. The reactor contract will be handled by the Korean Peninsula Energy Development Organisation (KEDO), the US-led international consortium. See *Business Week*, 24 April 1995, p. 52; *Financial Times*, 13 and 14 June 1995.

[109] There are four modes, the Vietnam, German, Korean, and Chinese modes, of achieving unification. See *Beijing Review*, 10–16 Aug. 1992, pp. 22–5.

Prospects for Korean unification

The issue of Korean unification[1] is obviously important for the region's energy relations. The pattern of German unification looks unlikely to be followed as South Korea cannot afford to bear the financial burden involved. The most likely possibility is the adoption of federation before actual unification. The sudden collapse of the Kim Jung-Il regime could place South Korea in a very difficult situation.

The question of how unification would affect energy relations is simplified by the fact that North Korea has virtually no energy-industry base to speak of. Even if a breakthrough on its nuclear problem is made, the provision of two light-water reactors would make only a limited contribution to the North's dire energy situation. If unification is settled before the end of this decade or by early next decade, the North's oil and gas industries would have to start from scratch. A huge increase in oil and gas consumption would follow, and require a stable energy-supply source due to the peninsula's poor indigenous oil and gas resources.

As a result, South Korea has good reason to take a very positive stance towards Russian Far East oil and gas development. Geographically, North Korea is very well positioned to take a free ride on Russian Far East development. Until the unification issue is settled, however, South Korea's policy will be seriously influenced by a power struggle in the region among countries reluctant to lose any vested interests and anxious to explore new business opportunities in the Korean peninsula.

[1]Aidan Foster Carter, *Korea's Coming Reunification: Another East Asian Superpower?*, Economist Intelligence Unit, London, 1992.

1982.[110] Since then, it has became the concept underlying the Communist Party's solution to the Taiwan issue. The 'one country, two systems' formula was written into the joint declaration on the issue of Hong Kong between China and Britain on 19 December 1984. Deng admitted that the formula, originally proposed to break the deadlock in the Sino–British negotiation, was ultimately intended to solve the Taiwan question.[111] The crux of Deng's formula is that within the unified People's Republic of China, the mainland would practise socialism, while the current capitalist systems of Taiwan, Hong Kong and Macao would remain unchanged.[112]

[110] An elaborated 'nine-article statement' on reunification was announced by Ye Jianying, then chairman of the Standing Committee of the National People's Congress, on 30 Sept. 1981. See *Beijing Review*, 13–19 Aug. 1990, pp. 14–15. Deng's official proposal of 'one country, two systems' was made in Sept. 1982 when the British premier Margaret Thatcher visited Beijing. See C. L. Chiou, 'Dilemmas in China's Reunification Policy toward Taiwan', *Asian Survey* 26: 4 (April 1986), p. 469.

[111] Chiou, op. cit., p. 469–71.

[112] *Beijing Review*, 13–19 Aug. 1990, p. 15. In his interview with *China Times* in Sept. 1990, President Yang Shangkun said Taiwan would be a special administrative region under the

It was not until the late 1980s that Taipei began to signal changes in its policy towards mainland China. The first was the lifting of martial law from July 1987. (In November 1992, Taiwan announced the lifting of 36 years of martial law in the fortress islands of Quemoy and Matsu off China's coast, which were excluded from the 1987 decision because of their strategic importance.[113]) In November 1987 the ruling Kuomintang (KMT) decided to open the door to mainland visits by Taiwan residents, even though Beijing had already proposed a 'three-communications' policy of mail, travel and business links as early as 1979.[114] And official approval by the KMT's 13th national congress of indirect trade with the mainland followed in July 1988.[115] Then in May 1989 Finance Minister Shirley Kuo attended the Asian Development Bank (ADB) meeting held in Beijing, as the first senior Taipei official to visit Beijing since 1949.[116] This, however, was Taiwan's first move to back up President Lee Teng-hui's 'one nation, two governments' formula floated in April 1989 to counter Deng's 'one country, two systems', under which Taiwan would attempt to resume participation in international organizations.[117]

Its approach became clearer with the adoption by the State Reunification Commission of a three-stage programme for reunification which became a guiding principle for future mainland policy in February 1991. A key point in the programme was the demand for 'not negating the other party's status as a political entity'. China regarded this as Taiwan's attempt to join the international community as an equal 'political entity' with China and to seek diplomatic 'dual recognition', contrary to the proposition of one China.[118]

2.4.2 'One China, one Taiwan'

During 1990–1 Taiwan's efforts to find its natural place in the new power equation (based more on economic than political factors, using its status as the world's thirteenth largest trading nation) were intensified, as Taiwan took advantage of the

---

jurisdiction of one China, and its armed forces could be retained. See Parris H. Chang, 'China's Relations with Hong Kong and Taiwan', *Annals of the American Academy of Political and Social Science* 519 (Jan. 1992), p. 134.

[113] John F. Copper, *Taiwan: Nation-State or Province?*, Westview Press, Boulder, 1990, pp. 57–8; *Korea Times*, 7 Nov. 1992.

[114] *Far Eastern Economic Review*, 5 Nov. 1987, p. 21.

[115] *Far Eastern Economic Review*, 21 July 1988, p. 21.

[116] *Far Eastern Economic Review*, 18 May 1989, p. 37.

[117] *Far Eastern Economic Review*, 4 May 1989, pp. 27–8; Lee Lai To, 'Taiwan and the Reunification Question', in David S.G. Goodman and Gerald Segal, *China in the Nineties: Crisis Management and Beyond*, Clarendon Press, Oxford, 1991, pp. 183–98.

[118] *Beijing Review*, 8–14 July 1991, pp. 32–4; *Far Eastern Economic Review*, 25 July 1991, p. 21.

shift in international opinion on China in the wake of the Tiananmen massacre in June 1989. The result was encouraging. The upgrading of functional relations with West European countries has been substantial, and as of 1991 Taiwan had become a member of eleven international organizations under its official name, the Republic of China.[119]

The establishment of relations between South Korea and China in August 1992 was a fatal blow to Taiwan's foreign policy. However, it was compensated for by a dramatic change in the policy of western trading partners towards Taiwan. In November 1992, two important arms deals were made: the purchasing of 150 modified F16 a/b warplanes and other weapons (worth $5.8 billion) from the United States, and 60 Mirage 2000-5E fighter jets and 1,000 Mica air-to-air missiles ($3.8 billion) from France.[120] The US deal, coupled with the decision that US trade representative Carla Hills would attend an annual joint business conference in Taipei in early December 1992, meant a significant change in US policy towards Taiwan.[121] In September 1994 the US government revealed its plans to upgrade US–Taiwan relations.[122]

Taiwan's improved relationships with powerful western countries were not the only driving force behind the dual-recognition policy. Another influence was a domestic independence movement recently gaining momentum. The Taiwan Democratic Progressive Party (DPP), formed in September 1986, adopted a resolution calling for the establishment of a 'Republic of Taiwan' on 13 October 1991.[123] The DPP's 'one China, one Taiwan' policy, demanding that Taiwan be allowed to participate in international affairs and join such organizations as the Gatt and UN, competed with the government's 'one China' policy.[124] The result of the December

---

[119] *Far Eastern Economic Review*, 14 Nov. 1991, pp. 30–3.

[120] Other weapons from the United States are 900 Sidewinder and 600 Sparrow air-to-air missiles, 500,000 rounds of cannon shells and 40 spare engines. See *Korea Times*, 19 Nov. 1992; *Far Eastern Economic Review*, 3 Dec. 1992, pp. 8–10; *Financial Times*, 3 Sept. 1992.

[121] A ban on high-level exchanges was imposed by US president Jimmy Carter. See *Far Eastern Economic Review*, 3 Dec. 1992, p. 8. US arms sales to Taiwan are based on section 3 of the 1979 Taiwan Relations Act (TRA), stating that 'the United States will make available to Taiwan such defense articles and defensive services in such quantity as may be necessary to enable Taiwan to maintain a sufficient self-defense capability.' See Dennis Van Vranken Hickey, 'Will Inter-China Trade Change Taiwan or the Mainlands?', *Orbis*, Fall 1991, p. 527.

[122] *Beijing Review*, 19–25 Sept. 1994, p. 5.

[123] The DPP prepared the draft Constitution of Taiwan on 25 August 1991. See *Beijing Review*, 28 Oct.–3 Nov. 1991, p. 6; 8–14 June 1992, p. 20.

[124] *Far Eastern Economic Review*, 24–31 Dec. 1992, p. 25; 12 Nov. 1992, pp. 16–18; 17 Sept. 1992, p. 21; *Financial Times*, 16 Sept. 1992; *Korea Times*, 8 Nov. 1992; *Korea Times*, 18 Aug. 1992.

1992 election, in which the KMT won only a 53% majority,[125] proved its attraction.

Taiwan's success in upgrading relations with western countries, in particular with the United States, and the real victory of the opposition DPP in December 1992 election have shaken the Beijing government's expectation that reunification was only a matter of time. Beijing seems to have been too optimistic about the strengthened economic ties across the Taiwan Strait. According to the Ministry of Foreign Economic Relations and Trade (MOFERT), during 1979–90 the volume of indirect trade between opposite sides of the Taiwan Strait totalled $15.74 billion, with an average annual growth rate of 43.3%, and more than 2,000 enterprises have been built on the mainland with funds from Taiwan investors.[126]

By 1989 China had become Taiwan's fifth largest trading partner, and Taiwan ranked sixth on the mainland's list. Indirect bilateral trade between the two countries was $3.5 billion in 1989, and reached $7.3 billion in 1992.[127] In 1992 Taiwan, with a massive $84 billion of foreign reserves, was ranked as China's second biggest source of investment funds.[128] With Taiwanese banks allowed to deal directly with overseas branches of Chinese banks and Taiwanese businessmen to remit money to the island from the mainland, by a decision made in November 1992 to increase civilian and economic contacts,[129] Taiwan's investment seems set to increase unless a serious clash on reunification occurs.

2.4.3 Taiwan's energy relations with China and Russia

Unlike the strengthened economic ties between China and Taiwan, energy cooperation has been seriously constrained by political and economic considerations. In March 1990 Mr Wang Yung-Ching, chairman of Taiwan's Formosa Plastics Group (FPG), announced that Formosa would build a naphtha cracker in Haicang, Fujian province, but the implementation of the proposed $7 billion petrochemical project was blocked by political pressure from Taiwan's government.[130] Ma Ying-jeou,

---

[125] *Korea Times*, 22 Dec. 1992. The basis of the DPP lies in the 'Tangwai' (outside party) movement in the 1970s. The DPP's legal recognition was granted in May 1989. See James Cotton, 'Redefending the Taiwan Polity: "One Country, Two Governments"', *Korea and World Affairs*, Fall 1989, p. 463.

[126] *Beijing Review*, 15–21 July 1991, pp. 5–6.

[127] Hickey, 'Will Inter-China Trade Change Taiwan or the Mainland?' (op. cit., n. 122), p. 518; *Korea Times*, 29 Jan. 1993; Chi Schive, *Taiwan's Economic Role in East Asia*, Center for Strategic and International Studies, Washington, DC, 1995.

[128] *Korea Times*, 29 Jan. 1993.

[129] The decision was made in November 1992, *Korea Times*, 10 Nov. 1992; 14 Nov. 1992.

[130] In May 1990 China approved the project. However, FPG decided to delay the project following pressure by Taipei officials. See *Oil and Gas Journal*, 11 June 1990, p. 25; *Far Eastern Economic Review*, 15 Nov. 1990, pp. 76–7; *Financial Times*, 4 Nov. 1992.

vice-chairman of the Mainland Affairs Council (MAC), defended the government's opposition to the FPG project by the simple explanation that 'Wang's investment would take away one third of our industrial base'.[131] In December 1992 FPG confirmed that the project was suspended.[132]

Another casualty of the political situation was China's offer to supply crude oil to Taiwan. The crisis caused by the Iraqi invasion of Kuwait in early August 1990 led to the cut-off of Kuwait oil supplies to Taiwan, which made up about 17% of Taiwan's oil imports. Soon after the Gulf crisis, in a bid to expedite reunification, Beijing offered to sell oil to Taiwan at 'privileged prices' to help alleviate Taiwan's dependence on Middle East supplies, but the offer was immediately rejected due to Taiwan's policy of having no direct contact with Beijing.[133] In November 1990 Chiang Ping-Kun, deputy economic affairs minister, said that 'Taiwan policy seemed unlikely to permit a crude oil deal with the mainland'. He added that 'the wax levels of mainland crudes were too high to meet Taiwan requirements'.[134]

Interestingly, in the same month, Chiang said that 'preliminary analysis shows that some crudes from the FSU are suitable for Taiwan refineries, but limited supplies could be a problem'. He added that 'Sakhalin Island could only fill a 0.1 mt tanker for Taiwan every two months, and shipments from western parts of the FSU through Europe would be costly and take over 30 days to get here'.[135] In late January 1991 Chiang reconfirmed that the Taiwanese government was studying the feasibility of buying Soviet crude oil.[136] Then it was reported, in July 1991, that the Chinese Petroleum Corp. (CPC) was seeking partners to explore for oil in Siberia and also negotiating to buy crude oil from the FSU. The report added that CPC was also interested in buying crude oil from Sakhalin after Taiwan's economic ministry allowed its ten state enterprises to barter with the FSU in an effort to beef up business exchanges between the two countries.[137] Soon after the report, a barter deal including a small amount of oil was made. In September 1991 CMP Enterprise Co., a computer manufacturing and trading firm in Taiwan made an agreement in principle with the FSU to barter $200-million worth of consumer goods for Soviet raw materials, including 8,000 tonnes of aluminum ingots, 30,000 tonnes of

---

[131] *Far Eastern Economic Review*, 17 Sept. 1992, p. 23.

[132] There was disagreement on whether the produced ethylene would be exported or sold to China. While Beijing favoured exports, FPG wanted a 100% commitment to domestic sales. See *Oil and Gas Journal*, 7 Dec. 1992, p. 35.

[133] *South China Morning Post*, 6 Sept. 1990.

[134] FBIS, Sov. 90: 214 (5 Nov. 1990), pp. 57–8.

[135] FBIS, Sov. 90: 214 (5 Nov. 1990), pp. 57–8.

[136] FBIS, China 91: 17 (25 Jan. 1991), pp. 68–9.

[137] *Supar Report* 12 (Jan. 1992), p. 105.

petroleum, 20,000 tonnes of heavy duty oil, 3,000 tonnes of chemical raw materials and 90,000 tonnes of copper. The barter deal was signed by the Soviet Far East Foundation and Soyuzkoopvneshtorg, a Soviet timber import and export company.[138]

During 1991–2, reportedly, Taiwan and the Soviet Union (Russia) explored the possibility of oil-and-gas-development cooperation very seriously. In September 1991, a meeting between a Soviet delegation led by Vladislav Gribkov, deputy general director of the Yuganskneftegaz Production Association, and officials of CPC was held in Taipei to discuss a possible CPC role in the development of Salyn oil field in Tyumen.[139] In mid-June 1992 a group of officials from Lukoil (Russian State Oil Co.) led by Vitalii Shmidt, vice-chairman of Lukoil, visited CPC, and called for CPC to invest an unspecified amount of capital in exchange for exploration rights in Lukoil's Siberian concession. The CPC response was to choose the oil fields in Siberia and Sakhalin for initial cooperation.[140]

However, the Russians, like the Soviets, were determined to separate economics from politics and rule out any official and political ties with Taiwan for fear of undermining recently improved Sino–Soviet relations.[141] This sort of pragmatic stance towards the Taiwanese issue can be seen in remarks by Victor Yaroshenko, then minister of foreign economic relations of the Russian Soviet Federated Socialist Republic (RSFSR), in January 1991, when he said that 'the RSFSR regards Taiwan as an inalienable part of China and does not intend governmental relations. RSFSR companies, being private, however, can trade with whomever they desire, even countries with which the RSFSR has no diplomatic relations'.[142] In July 1993 Boris Kutovskii, a Foreign Ministry spokesman said that 'Russia does not plan to establish diplomatic relations with Taiwan either in the near or the distant future'.[143] In 1993 trade between Russia and Taiwan reached $708.8 million, up 14% from the previous year.[144] This boils down to 'politics is one thing, economics is another thing'.

The most important example of the limits to improved economic relations between China and Taiwan came from oil and gas development cooperation. China

---

[138] Ibid., p. 77.

[139] FBIS, China 91: 180 (17 Sept. 1991), p. 71; *Oil and Gas Journal*, 23 Sept. 1991, newsletter. In October 1991, CPC confirmed that it had been in contact with Yuganskneftegaz about forming a joint venture exploration company in West Siberia. See FBIS, China 91: 199 (15 Oct. 1991), p. 84.

[140] FBIS, China 92: 114 (12 June 1992), p. 53; *Oil and Gas Journal*, 29 June 1992, newsletter.

[141] For a detail of the FSU's improved relations with Taiwan, see Paik, 'Russian and Chinese Oil and Gas Policies in Northeast Asia' (op. cit., n. 72), pp. 339–42.

[142] FBIS, Sov 91: 5 (8 Jan. 1991), pp. 49–50.

[143] Tass, 23 July 1993, quoted in *RA Report* 16 (Jan. 1994), p. 54.

[144] *Izvestia*, 2 April 1994, quoted in *RA Report* 17 (July 1994), p. 74.

has been keen to initiate joint oil exploration with Taiwan because the Taiwan Strait is estimated to contain 3–4 billion tonnes of oil.[145] Academics in Taiwan have responded positively to China's appeal. At the end of 1990, the Institute of Oceanology at the National Taiwan University and China's Academia Sinica's South China Sea Institute of Oceanology in Guangzhou agreed on formal and regular exchanges of information on oil reserves and geophysical structure, ocean flows and geological features in the Taiwan Strait.[146] This move is understood to be the first step towards a future joint oil-exploration effort. In March 1991 Fan Xin-Fa, a member of the People's Political Consultative Conference, urged the Beijing government to think seriously about joint exploration and development of the East China Sea with Taiwan.[147]

2.4.4 Offshore development cooperation and reunification

CPC, in charge of oil prospecting and exploration work in the Taiwan Strait has shown no sign of wanting cooperation.[148] At the end of 1990, Chen Yao-Sheng, chairman of CPC, confirmed that CPC's involvement was a matter of Taipei's mainland policy.[149] Recently, however, signs of change in CPC policy emerged. From early January to early February 1994, a high-level delegation from CPC visited China National Offshore Oil Corp. (CNOOC) to promote cooperation and exchanges between the two sides in offshore oil exploration and development, refining, and the production and marketing of petrochemicals.[150] Taiwan has also allowed CPC to cooperate with CNOOC in offshore exploration through foreign subsidiaries, even though it barred CPC from onshore exploration and development in China.[151] More surprising news is that CPC, CNOOC and Chevron Corp. agreed to form a joint venture for oil exploration in the East China and South China Seas.[152] In late April 1995, the Taiwanese government let slip that Chinese officials were

---

[145] *Hong Kong Standard*, 4 Dec. 1990.

[146] *Hong Kong Standard*, 14 Sept. 1990; 4 Dec. 1990.

[147] *Wen Wei Po*, 27 March 1991.

[148] *Hong Kong Standard*, 3 Dec. 1990; *Hong Kong Standard*, 14 Sept. 1990.

[149] *Wen Wei Po*, 27 March 1991.

[150] *China Oil, Gas & Petrochemical* 2: 3 (1 Feb. 1994), p. 3. OGJ reported that the CPC would commission private entities to evaluate prospects onshore and in the South China and Bohai Seas. See *Oil and Gas Journal*, 24 Aug. 1992, newsletter.

[151] *Oil and Gas Journal*, 28 March 1994, newsletter. OGJ also reported that China and Taiwan agreed to conduct joint surveys of waters surrounding the Spratly Islands. See *Oil and Gas Journal*, 21 Feb. 1994, newsletter.

[152] *Far Eastern Economic Review*, 31 March 1994; *World Journal*, 25 April 1994; 12 Sept. 1994.

coming to Taipei to plan joint oil explorations in the East and South China Seas.[153]

If these reports are true, they constitute a major shift in Taiwan's policy given that Taiwan has asserted its title to virtually all of the Taiwan Strait and East China Sea, stopping short only at claims to the Yellow Sea. After the US–China rapprochement, however, oil exploration off China's coasts by US companies working for Taiwan was regarded as provocative to Beijing and was discouraged. What makes the continental-shelf controversy so critical is the fact that it embodies fundamental political and juridical issues related to the future status of Taiwan. That is why the United States has not explicitly 'de-recognized' claims to the seabed that derive from Taiwan's mainland claims, while 'de-recognizing' Taiwan as a government with jurisdiction over the mainland.[154]

In early 1981 China decided to proceed with Longjing I, located in the Texfel concession let by Taiwan (see Map 2.4).[155] However, in the same year, just a few weeks after announcing the successful development of wells, China made a nine-point proposal to Taiwan for reunification talks including joint offshore development.[156] This confirms that China could not ignore the question of Taiwan. Leaving the reunification issue unsettled, China decided to open the disputed East China Sea in late June 1992, after passing a controversial law in February (see Chapter 5, section 2) – an indication that China is determined not to recognize Taiwan's status as a separate government with de facto jurisdiction over its own territory.

In the 1970s Selig S. Harrison foresaw that China's response to any oil or gas development by Taiwan was likely to be governed primarily by whether this took place as part of the island's gradual movement towards implicit or explicit provincial status within a 'one China' framework, or rather as part of an effort to develop the independent economic strength necessary to become a sovereign republic.[157] The current approach of China–Taiwan's united front on exploration in the East and South China Seas shows the application of Harrison's prediction in the 1990s.

It remains to be seen whether China and Taiwan will take this pragmatic stance towards East China Sea oil and gas development until the unification problem is settled. If any serious confrontation rises, it would be in the exploitation stage rather than the exploration one. If the reunification issue is settled before the exploitation stage, the settlement itself will pave the way for oil and gas development cooperation between the two countries in the East China Sea, and possibly then in the Tarim Basin area.

---

[153] *The Economist*, 29 April 1995, p. 83.

[154] Valencia, 'Offshore North-East Asia' (op. cit., n. 96), pp. 18–19); Valencia, 'Northeast Asia' (op. cit., n. 41), pp. 53–4.

[155] Valencia, 'Northeast Asia', p. 53.

[156] *Far Eastern Economic Review*, 31 March 1988, p. 29.

[157] Harrison, 'China, Oil , and Asia' (op. cit., n. 35), p. 123.

Map 2.4: Petroleum concession areas: East China and Yellow Seas

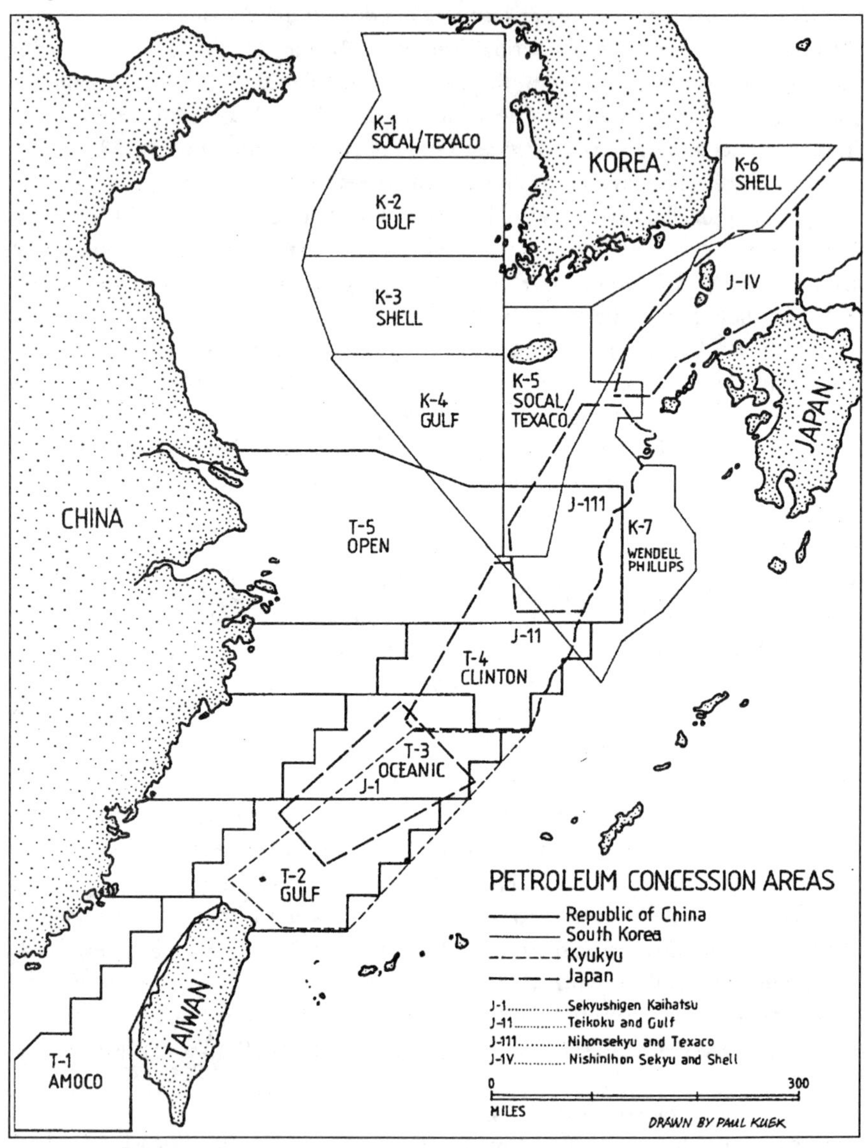

Source: US State Dept. Map No. 261 7-71 (State RGE), quoted in Jeanette Greenfield, *China's Practice in the Law of the Sea*, Clarendon Press, Oxford, 1992, p. 126

Reportedly, in November 1992 Deng Xiaoping ordered a study of the possibility of federation. He added that for peaceful unification between the mainland and Taiwan, it would not be possible to concede any policy revision.[158] But a major shift in both China's and Taiwan's policies then followed. In late April 1993, their first formal meeting, in Singapore, marked the initial, tentative steps towards resolution of one of the world's most intractable conflicts. However, the talks centred on Taiwan's insistence that China offer some legal framework for the protection of its investments on the Chinese mainland, for political matters were originally excluded from the exchange.[159] The significance of this meeting was that it allowed both sides to begin to gain confidence.

However, no breakthrough has been made in political relations, even though common ground on 'functional issues', like the repatriation of hijackers, fishing disputes and the return of mainland Chinese working illegally in Taiwan, had been achieved by the sixth round of talks since the ground-breaking sessions in April 1993.[160] If current efforts are continued, both sides could hammer out an ideal solution for unification. It remains to be seen whether a peaceful settlement will be made before the end of this decade. Clearly, real cooperation in offshore and onshore oil and gas development depends on the outcome.

2.5 The changing environment and the influence of superpower relations

2.5.1 The changing environment

During the past four decades, Northeast Asia has been an arena of East–West confrontation. In the wake of the Cold War, however, new links have been established in the region between countries formerly operating in economic isolation. New developments in the past few years include the Sino–Soviet rapprochement, establishment of diplomatic relations between the FSU and South Korea, and China and South Korea, and admission to the United Nations of both Korean states. (But, although many relationships have changed in the period, that of Japan and Russia has not.) These advances present the countries of Northeast Asia with new possibilities for reshaping international relationships in the region to meet the challenges of the post-Cold War world. That is, geopolitical realignments are taking place, and geo-economic patterns are assuming a much greater importance than in the Cold War period.

In fact, the framework of geopolitical alignments in Northeast Asia has also

---

[158] *Jingbao*, 5 Nov. 1992, quoted in *Kookmin Ilbo*, 6 Nov. 1992.

[159] *Financial Times*, 28–30 April 1993.

[160] *Financial Times*, 9 Aug. 1994.

changed: there is greater recognition of the region's multipolarity, and a more explicit departure from the previously bipolar East–West policy framework by which policy attitudes were largely set or circumscribed. This is associated with the changed, and for the most part diminished, role and influence of the superpowers. The result is a realignment of the balance of power among the four major powers, namely the United States, Russia, Japan and China. China and Japan figure as the major regional powers in the area, with the decline of superpower influence since the end of the Cold War.[161]

The emergence of major regional powers in Northeast Asia seems likely to promote a more complex pattern of international relations which would permit the exploitation of differences between adversaries, and between the United States and its allies. In parallel with this new alignment of power relations, the idea of multilateral security cooperation in Northeast Asia is being seriously considered. In July 1994, Asia–Pacific countries launched the Asean Regional Forum (ARF), a multilateral security group composed of 18 countries, including Russia, China, the United States, the six ASEAN members (Brunei, Indonesia, Malaysia, the Philippines, Singapore and Thailand), Japan, Australia, New Zealand, Canada, South Korea, Vietnam, Laos, Papua New Guinea and the European Union.[162] Reportedly, the organization, the first of its kind in Asia, would discuss North Korea's nuclear programme, the Cambodian civil war, and territorial disputes over the islands and oil fields of the South China Sea.[163]

This sort of development was inconceivable until recently. The United States, especially, has been strongly against a new regional security process, as it had an overriding interest in opposing the establishment of any forum that could lead to the erosion of its strong political and military position in the area. Since US–Soviet rivalry ceased to be the dominant factor in the region, however, US policy has switched from tackling the direct threat from Moscow to maintaining a balance of power, and preventing the appearance of any new problems presented by the power vacuum that emerged following the decline of Soviet power.

Another fact that should be emphasized is that the Asia–Pacific region's emergence as America's largest trading partner has driven the United States to rethink its policy towards the region. In fact, America's trans-Pacific commerce now totals more than $300 billion in annual two-way trade, nearly one-third larger than that

---

[161] Stuart Harris, 'The End of the Cold War in Northeast Asia: The Global Implications', in Stuart Harris and James Cotton, eds, *The End of the Cold War in Northeast Asia*, Lynne Rienner Publishers, Boulder, 1991, pp. 258–74.

[162] *Financial Times*, 29 July 1994.

[163] Ibid.

across the Atlantic.[164] And US firms have invested more than $61 billion in the region, with over $95 billion of Asian investments in the United States. In particular, North America has been the most important market for Northeast Asian exports, with its share up from 28% in 1965 to nearly 40% in 1987. North America's share in Northeast Asian imports fell from 28% to 21%. Consequently, the Northeast Asian economies, accounting for about 20% of world output and about 18% of world exports as of the early 1990s, emerged as a net capital export source.[165]

The scale of the Northeast Asian economies is such that any development that is unfavourable to them also affects the US economy adversely. The most vulnerable point is oil-supply security. Northeast Asia's heavy dependence on imported Middle East oil means that any disruption in supply could be fatal to regional economies. (If China becomes a massive oil importer at the end of this decade, it would add an even greater burden to the supply problem.) If the worst case occurs, the impact to the US economy would be considerable. As of 1992, the United States imports 42% of its oil from potentially unreliable suppliers half a world away.[166]

The US National Energy Strategy (NES)[167] is not necessarily focused on the Middle East, but the United States regards Persian Gulf oil as a vital interest. In other words, the Northeast Asian region's heavy dependency on Persian Gulf oil could impose a burden on the United States, and the region needs to explore ways of reducing its dependence. A reduction could be achieved by acceleration of regional oil and gas development.

2.5.2 The US stance towards Russia's and China's frontier oil and gas development

US interest in oil and gas development in the Soviet Far East and China dates back to the early 1970s. The Yakutsk gas development project was promoted by a consortium composed of Occidental Petroleum, the El Paso Gas Company, the Bechtel Corporation of the United States, and several Japanese firms since the early 1970s, but was suspended in the wake of the Soviet invasion of Afghanistan in

[164] James A. Baker III, 'America in Asia: Emerging Architecture for a Pacific Community', *Foreign Affairs*, Winter 1991/2, pp. 4–5. For the global significance of the Pacific economy and its trade pattern, see Peter A. Petri, 'One Bloc, Two Blocs, or None?: Political-Economic Factors in Pacific Trade Policy', in Kaoru Okuizumi, Kent E. Calder and Gerrit W. Gong, eds, *The US–Japan Economic Relationship in East and Southeast Asia*, Center for Strategic and International Studies, Washington, DC, pp. 39–70.

[165] Christopher Findlay, 'Northeast Asia and the World Economy' in Harris and Cotton, eds, *The End of the Cold War in Northeast Asia* (op. cit., n. 162), pp. 28–49.

[166] *Oil and Gas Journal*, 31 Aug. 1992, p. 29.

[167] Arlen I. Erdhal, 'US Energy Policy in the Post-War Era', paper presented at the International Conference on 'Oil and Money: Asia and the Pacific', Singapore, 14 May 1991.

December 1979.[168] Thus, the project became a casualty of power politics between the United States and the FSU, and US oil companies' interests were diverted from the Soviet Far East to China's offshore.

During 1982–92 US companies played an important role in Chinese offshore exploration and development. A total of 70 contracts were made with 50 foreign companies, of which 37 were with 15 US companies. US companies discovered 19 oil-bearing payzones after drilling 97 wells and spending $1.04 billion, while a total of 67 oil-bearing payzones were found by all the foreign companies after drilling 286 wells and spending a total of $3.1 billion.[169] As for onshore development, Chinese domestic politics prevented the timely opening of promising onshore areas and lost large-scale investment by US companies. It was not until the first half of 1992 that Amoco Orient Petroleum Co. became the first major western oil company to make an onshore exploration contract in China.[170] In short, Chinese offshore and onshore oil and gas exploration and development have benefited from US investment which might have been placed in East Siberian gas development had power politics between the United States and the FSU not blocked US participation in the project.

American companies did not resume their study of Soviet Far East oil and gas projects until the late 1980s. In December 1988 McDermott of the United States moved into the Sakhalin offshore area by signing a protocol with the FSU's Ministry of Oil and Gas Industry,[171] and in early 1989 Far East Energy Inc. began to explore the possibility of resurrecting the project (for US interests on Russian Far East oil and gas projects, see Annex 2.1 to this chapter).

Paradoxically, US companies' active participation in Russian Far East gas development projects could lead to a further delay in Alaskan gas export to the Northeast Asian market. In 1993 US LNG exports to Japan recorded 1 million tonnes,[172] but

---

[168] Bruce W. Jentleson, *Pipeline Politics: The Complex Political Economy of East–West Energy Trade*, Cornell University Press, Ithaca, 1986, pp. 132–71.

[169] *Oil and Gas Journal*, 28 Sept. 1992, p. 23.

[170] The contract between Amoco and the China National Oil Development Corp. covers 1.27 million acres in the Fuyang basin of Anhui Province, 600 km northwest of Shanghai. See *Oil and Gas Journal*, 25 May 1992, p. 29.

[171] The Soviets asked for US cooperation for the development of Piltun-Astokhskoye and Lunskoye oil and gas fields in May 1987 when the US–Soviet summit meeting was held. See Institute for Soviet and East European Economic Studies, Japan Association for Trade with the Soviet Union and Socialist Countries of Europe, *The Soviet Union's Presence in International Oil Market* [Kokusai Sekiyu Sizyou ni Okeru Soren no Purezesu], SEEES, Tokyo, 1991, p. 91.

[172] *BP Statistical Review of World Energy*, June 1994, p. 24. Alaska was the first supplier to ship LNG to Japan in 1969 from fields located in the Cook Inlet area. See John Choon Kim, 'Alaska Energy Resource Potential: Opportunities and Constraints', *Resources Economics Study* (Seoul) 1: 2 (Summer 1989), p. 109.

the scale of LNG exports would be increased enormously if either the proposed Trans-Alaska Gas Pipeline System (TAGS) project is implemented or North Slope equity producers decide to develop the project by themselves (see Chapter 6, section 1). This is a dilemma which US government policy towards Russian Far East oil and gas development has to cope with.

Another factor that could cause some hesitation in US policy towards Russian Far East oil and gas is strategic. The US government is reluctant to see Russian military forces expand in the area, but it is also reluctant to see the upsurge of regional powers, leading to a diminished US influence in Northeast Asia. In this context, as long as Russian Far East oil and gas development makes a minimum contribution to reducing the vulnerability of oil supplies to the Russian Far East military forces, and provides a new opportunity for US oil companies, US policy towards Northeast Asia's oil and gas development seems likely to be positive.

The positive change in US policy towards Northeast Asia has to do with the rapidly changing environment in the region. In recent years Northeast Asian countries have explored possibilities for multilateral economic cooperation very seriously. Tendencies towards the formation of exclusive economic groupings in Europe and North America, threatening not just Japan but also other dynamic but highly trade-dependent East Asian economies, which experienced dynamic economic growth in the 1980s, seem to have driven Northeast Asian countries to think of forming a smaller economic circle in the region, as an initial step to creating an Asia–Pacific circle. Consequently, a soft regionalism, lacking organizational structure as yet, and based on economic interaction across ideological-political boundaries, is emerging in the area.[173]

2.5.3 Soft regionalism

Strictly speaking, the base of this soft regionalism in Northeast Asia has been laid down by a Chinese initiative. In the mid-1980s the Chinese began to explore the possibility of multilateral economic cooperation, mainly focused on a Soviet–Chinese–Japanese trilateral economic network in Northeast Asia. That is, what has occupied the Chinese is an international division of labour among northeast China,

[173] Robert A. Scalapino, 'Northeast Asia – Prospects for Cooperation', *Pacific Review* 5: 2 (1992), p. 102; Mark J. Valencia, 'Economic Cooperation in Northeast Asia: The Proposed Tumen River Scheme', *Pacific Review* 4: 3 (1991), p. 263; Shi Min, 'Northeast Asia's Economic Development and the Trend Toward Regionalism', *Proceedings of the Conference on Economic Development in the Coastal Area of Northeast Asia*, held in Changchun, 29–31 Aug. 1991, compiled by Won Bae Kim and Burnham O. Campbell, East–West Center, Honolulu; Cen Cai *et al.*, 'Regional Cooperation in Northeast Asia and the Exploitation of the Triangle Area of Lower Tumen River', paper presented at the 1991 Changchun Conference.

the Mongolian People's Republic, the Soviet Far East, Japan and the Korean peninsula, with the Chinese northeast at its hub.[174] Some steps have been taken to achieve multilateral economic cooperation. In September 1988 a Northeast Asia Research Centre in Changchun city, Jilin province, with nearly 200 specialists and experts was founded, and in January 1989 a conference on the Northeast Asian Economic Circle was held in Beijing.[175]

In July 1990, when a mission from Japan, representing China's Northeast Development Council, led by Tabuchi Setsuya, head of the Nomura Securities Co., visited Harbin, Shao Chihui, governor of Heilongjiang province, proposed concrete cooperation among Japan, China and the FSU for the development of the Japan Sea rim. The governor's proposal includes a timber-processing combine, a home electric-appliance-manufacturing enterprise, and an oil and natural gas combine, all to be built in the Soviet Far East, using Japanese capital, equipment and technology, Chinese labour and Soviet raw materials.[176] The proposal reflected China's earnestness about multilateral economic cooperation.

Formation of the Northeastern Economic Region covering three provinces of Heilongjiang, Jilin and Liaoning, three leagues of Hulun Buir, Hinggan and Jirem, and Chifeng city in the eastern part of Inner Mongolia, could be further evidence of Chinese enthusiasm. The Beijing leadership has given special attention to the northeastern frontier area, as one of three economic development zones in China's overall development strategy for the 1990s, mapped out in the Seventh Plenary Session of the 13th Central Committee in December 1990.[177] In short, the Chinese have set out to build a 'new economic order' in Northeast Asia, integrating the FSU, as stated by Deng Xiaoping in response to Gorbachev's call at Krasnoyarsk in 1988 for international economic cooperation in the Far East.[178]

The Soviets, like the Chinese, were also very positive about multilateral economic cooperation in Northeast Asia, as its implementation would lead to the Soviet Far East's integration into the dynamics of regional cooperation. After the

---

[174] In 1986 the idea of Soviet–Chinese–Japanese trade and investment was further articulated. See Gaye Christofferson, 'Economic Reforms in Northeast China: Domestic Determinants', *Asian Survey* 28: 12 (Dec. 1988), pp. 1255–6.

[175] According to Chen Longshan, the deputy secretary-general of the centre has sponsored a journal named *Northeast Asia Studies*. See FBIS, China 91: 128 (3 July 1991), p. 5; *Supar Report* 7 (July 1989), p. 30.

[176] *Supar Report* 10 (Jan. 1991), p. 40.

[177] Yufan Hao, 'The Development of the Soviet Far East: A Chinese Perspective', *Korea and World Affairs* 15:2, Summer 1991, pp. 245–6.

[178] Steven M. Goldstein, 'Diplomacy amid Protest: The Sino–Soviet Summit', *Problems of Communism*, Sept.–Oct. 1989, p. 56.

Krasnoyarsk speech, having confirmed the FSU's interest in the idea of developing tripartite Chinese–Japanese–Soviet economic activity, the necessity for the establishment of a Free Economic Zone (FEZ) in Sakhalin (1990) and Nakhodka (1991)[179] were recognized as a means of adjusting the Soviet Far East to the trend towards regional economic cooperation. In April 1991 Gorbachev repeated a proposal, similar to the 1988 Krasnoyarsk proposal but somewhat extended, for creating a zone of prosperity around the Donghae Sea (Sea of Japan), combining Japanese and South Korean cash, Chinese and North Korean manpower, and Soviet natural resources. The Japanese gave a cautious welcome to the idea.[180]

To the Japanese, this sort of proposal was nothing new. In September 1985 when China's State Science and Technology Commission proposed the idea of a trilateral Soviet–Chinese–Japanese regional economic network at a meeting of the Sino–Japanese Economic Technology Exchange Conference, the Japanese reacted with both scepticism and enthusiasm.[181] Since then the concept has been studied seriously by the Japanese. In May 1989, when the first intergovernmental Sino–Soviet meeting in 30 years was held, it was reported that Japan was planning to dispatch a large-scale trade mission to northeast China and the Soviet Far East in July 1989. It was a signal that Japan had begun to explore the possibility of an economic community established around the Sea of Japan.[182] In November 1990, an international conference entitled 'For the Development of Cooperation in the Sea of Japan Area' was held in Niigata on the initiative of the Japan Socialist Party and with the active support of Niigata prefecture authorities.[183] Then in July 1992, the Japanese government was reportedly examining the possibility of a new economic zone around the Sea of Japan that would act as a bridge between the Pacific rim economies and the EC.[184]

At the moment, the most likely project based on multilateral economic cooperation in Northeast Asia is the Tumen River Economic Development Area (TREDA)

---

[179] On 14 July 1990 the RSFSR (Russian Soviet Federal Socialist Republic) Supreme Soviet declared Sakhalin Oblast a free economic zone (FEZ). See *Supar Report* 10 (Jan. 1991), pp. 15–17. After the coup in August 1991, Nakhodka went ahead and unilaterally implemented the necessary regulations for its free economic zones. See *Supar Report* 12 (Jan. 1992), p. 94.

[180] *Supar Report* 11 (July 1991), p. 28.

[181] Christofferson, 'Economic Reforms in Northeast China' (op. cit., n. 175), p. 1255.

[182] The mission was composed of about 130 of Japan's most high-powered executives from the securities, life insurance, banking, trading and manufacturing industries. See Akihiro Tamiya, 'Trade Mission targets Manchuria, Soviet Asia: Thaw attracts Trade Mission', *Japan Economic Journal*, 20 May 1989, pp. 2–3.

[183] FBIS, Sov. 90: 217 (8 Nov. 1990), p. 9.

[184] *Nikkei Weekly*, 18 July 1992, p. 3, quoted in *RA Report* 14 (Jan. 1993), p. 24.

project, encompassing Hunchun in China, Chongjin in North Korea and Russia's Vostochnyy port.[185]

2.5.4 Multilateral energy cooperation

The concept of multilateral energy cooperation in Northeast Asia is also gaining ground. Energy relations have undergone their own peculiar brand of perestroika following the collapse of communism. The process has turned the area, one of the most heavily armed on earth, into a region with commercial opportunities. In fact, as shown in Figures 2.1(a) and (b), during the past few years bilateral energy relations in Northeast Asia have been transformed compared with the previous two decades. In the 1990s and early next century, implementation of oil and gas development projects in Sakhalin offshore, the East Siberian (Republic of Sakha) area of the Russian Federation and the East China Sea and Tarim Basin would give rise to fundamental changes in regional energy relations (see Figure 2.1(c)) towards a multilateral pattern. To this end, the establishment of a regional energy regime is badly required.

At the moment two mechanisms handle regional economic cooperation in the Pacific rim: the Pacific Economic Cooperation Conference (PECC)[186] and Asia Pacific Economic Cooperation (APEC).[187] The PECC's Minerals and Energy

[185] The UN-sponsored Tumen River Area Development Programme (TRADP) closed its New York office on 31 Oct. 1994. Its role has been given to the TREDA project. See *Far Eastern Economic Review*, 10 Nov. 1994, p. 47; *Financial Times*, 31 May 1995. For details of TRADP, see Paik, 'Russian and Chinese Oil and Gas Policies in Northeast Asia' (op. cit., n. 72), p. 384, reference no. 28.

[186] Together with the scholarly Pacific Trade and Development Conference (PAFT-AD), and the business-oriented Pacific Basin Economic Council (PBEC), the multi-party PECC, one of three international non-governmental organizations in the Asia-Pacific region, was founded in Sept. 1980. For details, see Lawrence T. Woods, 'Non-governmental Organizations and Pacific Cooperation: Back to the Future?', *Pacific Review* 4: 4 (1991), pp. 312–21.

[187] In January 1989, the Australian premier Bob Hawke proposed a start to ministerial-level consultations, and in November 1989 the first high-level meeting of APEC was held in Canberra. Original members were six members of ASEAN, S. Korea, Japan, Australia, New Zealand, the United States and Canada. See Andrew Elek, 'The Challenge of Asian-Pacific Economic Cooperation', *Pacific Review* 4: 4 (1991), pp. 322–32; Richard L. Grant *et al.*, *Asia Pacific Economic Cooperation: The Challenge Ahead*, Center for Strategic and International Studies, Washington, DC, 1990; Okuizumi *et al.*, 'The US–Japan Economic Relationship in East and Southeast Asia' (op. cit., n. 165). In 1991, at APEC's third annual meeting in Seoul, the three Chinas (China, Hong Kong, Taiwan) became full members, and in 1992 the fourth meeting decided to create an APEC secretariat in Singapore. See *Financial Times*, 12, 13 and 23 Sept. 1992.

Forum (MEF)[188] has facilitated discussion and consultation on key issues relating to the minerals and energy sectors in the Asia–Pacific region since 1986. Professor Gaye Christoffersen has argued that the MEF is emerging as an international resource regime for the Asia–Pacific region, appropriate for dealing with problems requiring collective action, but whose findings and recommendations are non-official and non-binding.[189] The latter is a weak aspect of the MEF, and if any sort of coordinated official initiative is taken on energy policy in the area, it will come from the Energy Group of the APEC conference as the only government-level organization in the Asia–Pacific area.

Even if Russia was to be accepted as a member of APEC in the foreseeable future, it is questionable whether APEC members can agree to give priority to the energy development of Northeast Asia, especially the Russian Far East, in the near future. In the current situation, an active role for APEC in the region's oil and gas development is doubtful. Until APEC pays attention to the region, establishment of the 'Northeast Asian Energy Regime' (NAER), whose aim is not to make a self-reliant energy system, but to lay down guidelines for multilateral energy cooperation in Northeast Asia, is strongly needed as an intermediate step or as APEC's sub-regional mechanism.[190]

The concept of the NAER is surely a by-product of the changing environment in Northeast Asia, and its establishment would be ideal not only to accelerate realization of multilateral energy cooperation but also to satisfy the need for a new Northeast Asian policy framework arising from the extensive interdependence of political and strategic as well as economic aims. However, tacit power struggles, and competition for foreign investment, could make the establishment of a regional energy regime very difficult.

As is discussed in Chapter 6, if the Energy Silk Route project to connect the rich gas-prone fields of Central Asia with end-users in Northeast Asia, for example, is implemented during the second half of this decade, Russia's East Siberian gas-

---

[188] The general purpose of the Forum on Minerals and Energy is to promote discussion and consultation among officials, industry leaders and independent researchers on minerals and energy issues of regional interest. The inaugural meeting of the Forum was held in Jakarta, Indonesia, 6–8 July 1986.

[189] Gaye Christoffersen, 'Socialist Integration and Energy Regimes', *Pacific Review* 3: 1 (1990), p. 24. For the concept of an international regime, which provides the theoretical background for that of a resource regime, see Oran R. Young, *International Cooperation: Building Regimes for Natural Resources and the Environment*, Cornell University Press, Ithaca, 1989, pp. 11–30.

[190] Keun Wook Paik, 'Towards a Northeast Asian energy charter', *Energy Policy*, May 1992, pp. 433–443.

Figure 2.1: A simplified pattern of bilateral energy relations in Northeast Asia

(a) until the mid-1980s

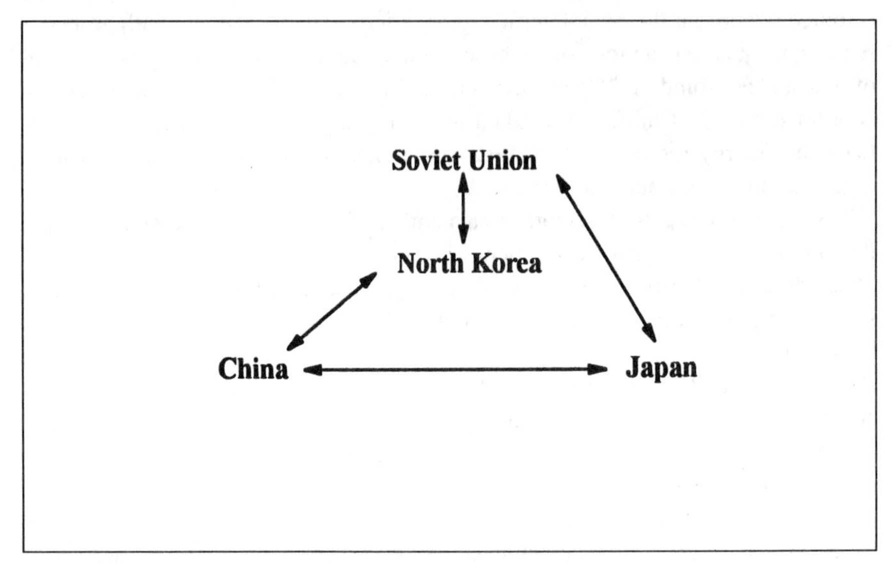

(b) from the late 1980s to the present

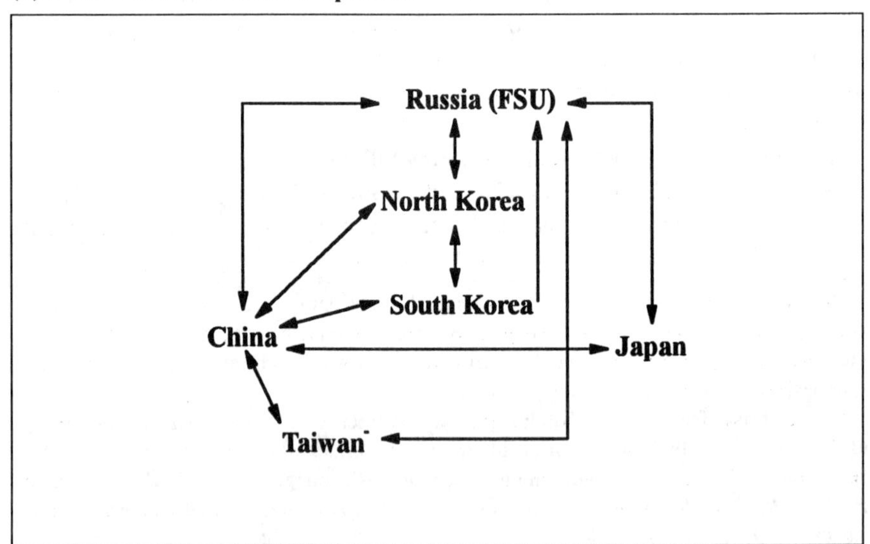

Source: Keun-Wook Paik, 'Towards a Northeast Asia energy charter', *Energy Policy*, May 1992, p. 428.

Figure 2.1 (c): Anticipated multilateral energy relations with bilateral ones in Northeast Asia: mid 1990s to 2010

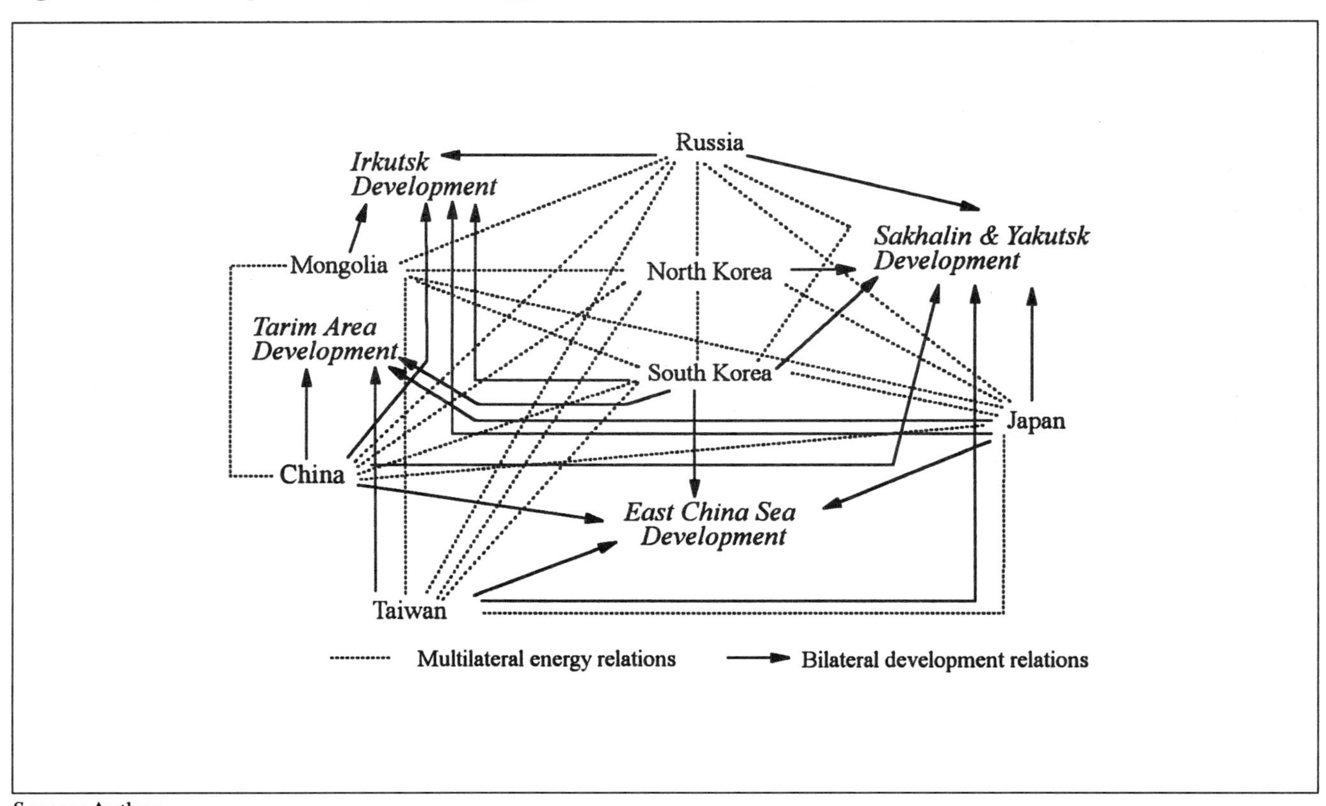

Source: Author

development project will be a casualty. This will repeat the situation that occurred in the early 1970s. At that time China succeeded in blocking Japan's massive investment in Soviet Far East oil and gas development by arranging Daqing crude-oil exports to Japan, thereby distracting Japanese interest from the Soviet Far East. In this instance, China and Japan will use Turkmenistan gas to block Russia's entry into the Northeast Asian gas market. This case provides an excellent example of the dynamics of the energy politics that could emerge in Northeast Asia in the 1990s.[191]

Energy relations in Northeast Asia could be a casualty of the region's power politics. On the other hand, its frontier oil and gas development projects could open a new chapter in multilateral cooperation, but only with the full support of all powers in the region. The second half of the 1990s will witness how deeply energy relations are influenced by power politics in the region.

2.6 Conclusion

This chapter examined how political relationships have interacted with the region's energy developments. Many politically delicate issues remain unresolved. In summary, first of all, the northern-territory dispute between Japan and Russia remains a stumbling block in both countries' energy relations, and looks unlikely to be settled very soon. It would act unfavourably on Russian Far East, except Sakhalin offshore, oil and gas development. Secondly, the establishment by South Korea of relationships with both Russia and China opened the way for Korean companies' active participation in both countries' frontier oil and gas development; and North Korea's poor oil and gas industries will be a full beneficiary of the Russian Far East gas development once unification is settled.

Thirdly, a peaceful settlement of the Taiwan–China reunification issue after Hong Kong's return to China in 1997 is required for development of oil and gas in the East China Sea. Fourthly, the energy relationship between Japan and China could be constrained due to the unresolved Senkaku issue, but any serious confrontation between the two countries due to the territorial dispute seems very unlikely. Finally, the unresolved offshore boundary issue between the Korean peninsula and China remains a stumbling block to accelerating Yellow Sea oil and gas exploration and development. Of these issues, surely some will be resolved during the second half of the 1990s.

If the territorial dispute between Japan and Russia is settled in the coming years, it would fundamentally affect not only the region's frontier oil and gas development but also its energy-supply balance. It remains to be seen, however, whether settlement will occur in this decade or be considerably delayed. If the latter is the

[191] Paik, 'Pipeline Politics' (op. cit, n. 71), pp. 1–8.

case, then it would be regrettable not only for Japan and Russia but also for the Northeast Asian region as a whole. A golden opportunity for multilateral energy-development cooperation, making all the regional countries participants as well as beneficiaries, could slip away.

The following chapters 3 and 4 will examine the realities of both Russia and China's oil and gas production, focusing on potential and constraints. The study will be useful for an understanding of the goals of Russian and Chinese oil and gas policy in Northeast Asia.

Annex 2.1: US interests in Russian Far East oil and gas projects

1 In December 1990 Atlantic Richfield Co. (ARCO) signed preliminary agreements for the exploration and production of oil and gas in the northeast shelf, and a subsidiary named ARCO Alaska Russian Exploration Co. was set up in February 1991.[192]

In March 1992, the government of Chukotka and Alaska Russian Exploration Co. signed a protocol of intent to undertake negotiations that will grant to the American company exclusive rights to carry out surveys, and develop and produce hydrocarbons both on land and on the Chukotka shelf.[193]

Then, in July 1992, Northeast Petroleum Operating Agency (NEPO), formed in November 1991 by the administrations of Magadan Oblast and the Chukotka Autonomous Okrug, Rosgeolkom, and a series of financial and commercial organizations, revealed its plan to hold a series of international tenders for the development of Russia's northeastern shelf largely divided into eight large parcels. According to NEPO, a series of tenders for the parcels will be held: in 1992–3 two of them, Primagadan in the Okhotsk Sea, and Vostochno-Khatyrskii (Eastern Khatyrsk) in the Bering Sea, and in 1994–5 the remaining six parcels on the shelf of the Sea of Okhotsk, the East Siberian and Chukotka Seas.[194]

2 In March 1991 a venture of the US Halliburton Geophysical Services and the Soviet Oil and Gas Ministry's Dalmorneftegeofizika Trust, dubbed Polar Pacific Co. of Geophysics, was reported to have planned a 1991 programme covering the Okhotsk and Kamchatka Seas, Anadyrskii Gulf, Chukchi Sea, East Siberia Sea and Laptev Sea.[195]

---

[192] *Supar Report* 10 (Jan. 1991), p. 181; 11 (July 1991), pp. 108–9; *RA Report* 14 (Jan. 1993), pp. 103–4.

[193] Vostok Rossii 13 (March 1992), p. 7, quoted in *Supar Report* 13 (July 1992), p. 108.

[194] *Vostochnyi Ekspress* 32 (1992), p. 4, *Commersant*, 6 Oct. 1992, p. 9, both quoted in *RA Report* 14 (Jan. 1993), pp. 103–4; *Oil and Gas Journal*, 29 June 1992, newsletter.

[195] *Oil and Gas Journal*, 4 March 1991, newsletter.

3 In January 1992, the Salt Lake City-based Equity Oil Co. and Houston-based Coastline Exploration Inc. formed Symskaya Exploration Inc. for exploration and development in Krasnoyarsk Krai. Symskaya has signed a protocol with Eniseygeofizika and Eniseyneftegazgeologiya (ENI). After purchase of a geological and geophysical data package, Symskaya will have the right to select 10% of about 45,000 sq. km in the Symskaya area of Krasnoyarsk Krai.[196]

4 In January 1992, Dallas-based Maxus Energy Corp. and Yakutskgeofizika signed a technical evaluation agreement covering a 148-million-acre area covering the Lena-Anabar trough, Verkhoyansk fold belt and foredeep, and Predpatom trough. Martin Schuepbach, Maxus senior vice-president of exploration, cited at least five major discoveries, each with estimated reserves of as much as 6 tcf of gas and 500 million barrels of oil, adjacent to Maxus's technical evaluation areas.[197]

5 In February 1992 it was reported that an American firm, Grynberg Production Corp. was undertaking a survey of the Khabarovsk shelf for oil and gas.[198]

6 In March 1992 it was reported that Smith-Everidge of the United States and Sameko of Sakhalin formed a joint venture named 'Petrosakh' in 1991, and Petrosakh has begun work to develop the Okruzhnoe oil deposit whose reserves are estimated at producing 0.3–0.4 mt/year for 20 years.[199]

7 As discussed in chapter 7, many US companies like Marathon, McDermott, Exxon, Texaco and Mobil are involved in Sakhalin offshore oil and gas projects.

---

[196] Equity owned 80% of the stock of Symskaya, and Coastline the rest. See *Oil and Gas Journal*, 20 Jan. 1992, p. 28.

[197] Maxus will conduct an eight-month initial evaluation of its area, then select one or more technical evaluation areas, ranging in size to as much as 50,000 sq. km. A 12- to 24-month evaluation will follow. Ibid., pp. 28–9.

[198] Sovetskii Sakhalin, 6 Feb. 1992, quoted in *Supar Report* 13 (July 1992), p. 80. In August 1992 it was reported that Russian geologists found promising oil/gas deposits in the republic's far-eastern Khabarovsk Territory. See *Oil and Gas Journal*, 10 Aug. 1992, newsletter.

[199] *TVD Delin* 9 (March 1992), p. 3, quoted in *Supar Report* 13 (July 1992), p. 105.

Chapter 3

Russian oil and gas: resources, production and industries

The importance of the energy industry in the Russian economy has never been questioned. In 1994 the energy sector represented over 15% of GDP, 17% of gross industrial output (including electrical energy) and 42% of exports by value. In the same year, the combined oil and gas sectors accounted for 12% of GDP, 85% of primary energy supply expressed in tonnes of oil equivalent and 98% of fuel exports by value.[1]

After the breakup of the Soviet Union, Russia became the main inheritor of its energy industry, in which the oil and gas sectors were dominant in terms of production, consumption and exports, as shown in Figure 3.1. Russia also inherited problems in these industries.

During the past few years Russia's oil production has fallen unprecedentedly and gas production also began to show signs of strain. Important questions can be asked as to what caused the current crisis in the oil industry and brought stagnation to the gas industry, and what the implications are for Russian Far East oil and gas development in the coming years. This chapter will study the great potential of Russia's oil and gas reserves, the predicaments it faces in oil and gas development, the unreasonable economics of the industry caused by unbalanced investment and controlled prices, and energy resources that might serve as alternatives to oil given the crises in the industry.

3.1 The potential of oil and gas reserves

3.1.1 The Soviet Union and the Russian Federation

Oil: Oil and gas resources are widely scattered throughout Russia, but are poorly located with respect to areas of demand. Thanks to severe environmental conditions, inadequate economic infrastructure and high development costs, a number of major potential hydrocarbon-bearing regions, like East Siberia, offshore basins in the Barents and Kara Seas, and Sakhalin Island in Russia, remain virtually unexplored.

[1] 'The Russian Federation; Taxation of the Oil and Gas Sectors', paper prepared by Emil M. Sunley, Christopher E. Lane and David C. L. Nellor, International Monetary Fund, Dec. 1994, p. 3.

Figure 3.1: Soviet energy balance, selected years: 1960–89

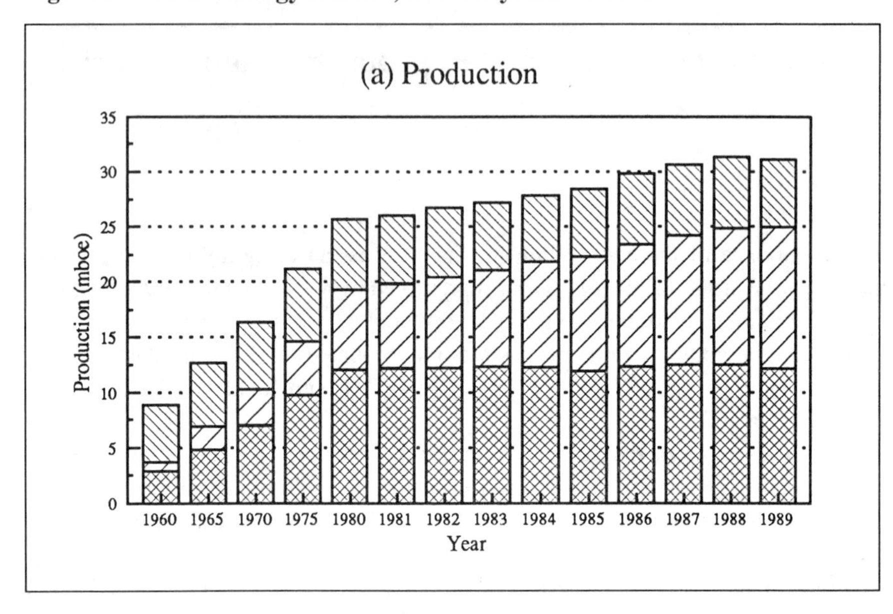

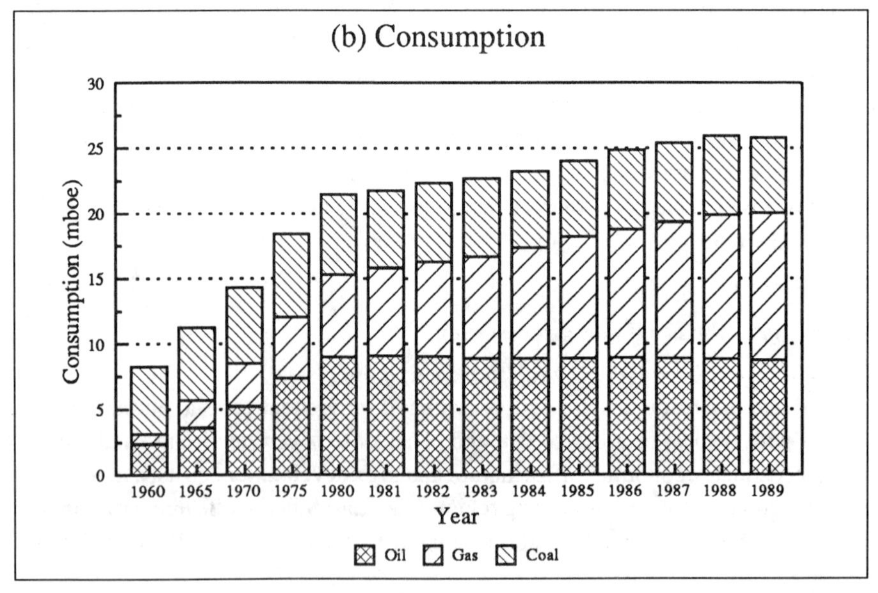

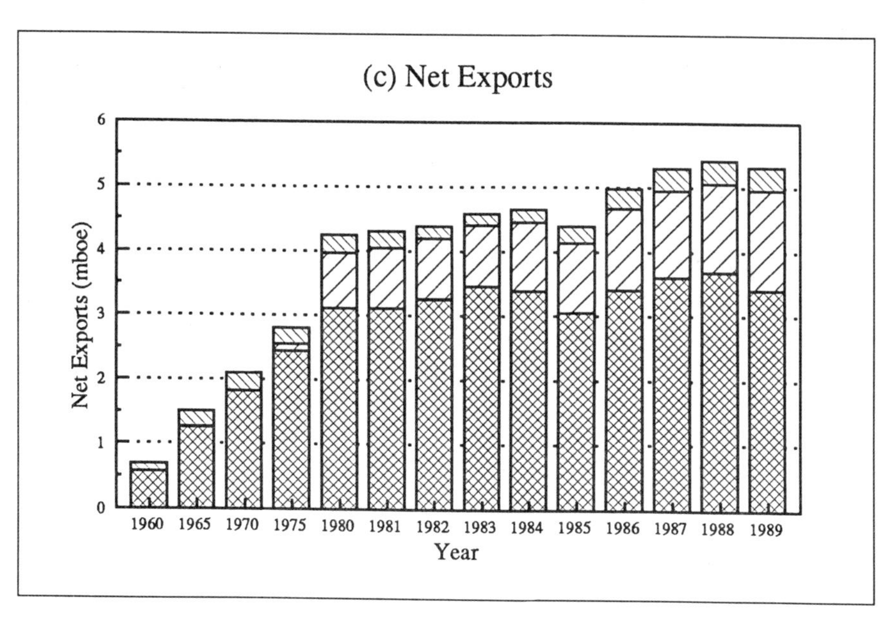

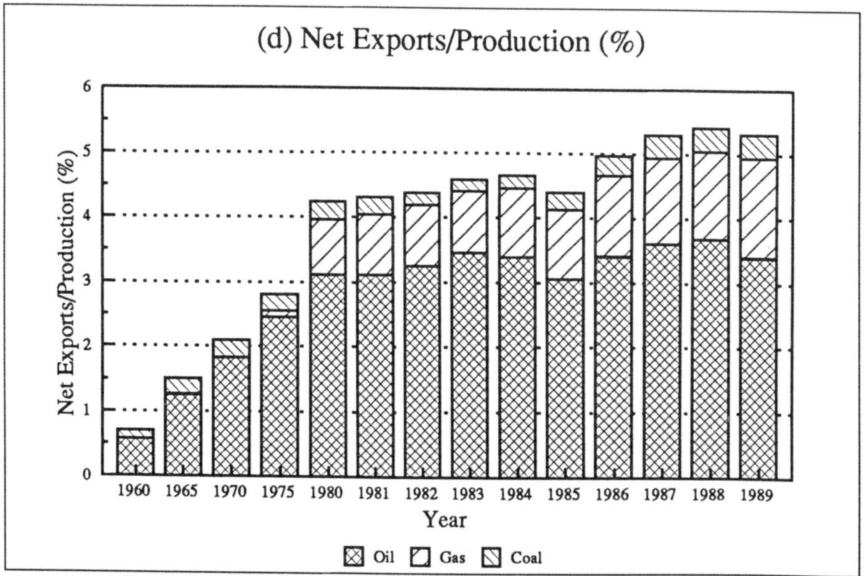

Sources: 1960–75: 'Energy, Economics and Foreign Policy in the Soviet Union', ed. A. Hewett, The Brookings Institute, Washington DC, 1984, pp. 150–1; 1980–9: Plan Econ report 5:4 (7 March 1990).

Official data on the oil reserves of the Soviet Union were a state secret from 1947, but in July 1991 the first ever public statement of Soviet oil reserves was released. It confirmed 23.5 billion tonnes (172.3 billion barrels) of 'industrial reserves' (referring to proved + probable + possible reserves, or A + B + C1 + C2 in Soviet terminology) as of 1 January 1991 (see Table 3.1).[2] More detailed but slightly different figures for oil reserves are provided by Valery Neverov, a researcher for the commodity-trading firm Hermes. Neverov put the figure as high as 36.6 bt (268.3 billion bbl).

According to Neverov, by the beginning of 1991 the CIS (Commonwealth of Independent States; the Soviet Union was bigger than the CIS as it included the Baltic states) had already produced 15 bt (110 billion bbl) of the country's oil demand. Consequently 21.6 bt (158.3 billion bbl) remained to be produced. West Siberia's total reserves are 20.9 bt, and 15.3 bt remained to be produced as 5.6 bt had already been produced up to 1 January 1991.[3] Including C3-category reserves, reserves remaining to be produced in the CIS become 23.1 bt.[4] Neverov's figure of 13.8 bt in the Tyumen area was confirmed by V. Isayev, a director of the Russian Federation Academy of Sciences' Institute for Oriental Studies.[5]

There has been a steady growth in oil reserves since the early 1980s, according to Valentin Bykov from VNIIOENG. Out of a total of 2,800 discovered fields, 182 giant fields account for 68% of the country's initial explored reserves, and the ratio of initial reserves to ultimate potential resources in the FSU is estimated to be as low as 40%. Most reserves are concentrated within a small number of larger fields – 3.4% of fields (with initial recoverable commercial oil reserves of categories A, B and C, over 100 million tonnes, and with proved and probable reserves in excess of 750 million bbls each) provide 72% of production.[6]

Western experts regard the Soviet figures as somewhat inflated, and put Soviet

---

[2] It was revealed by Lev Churilov, then Minister of Oil and Gas, that the share of industrial reserves to be found in the largest high-yield fields has gradually declined during the past 30 years from 90% to 51%, and 60% of these fields are now exhausted. See *Eastern Bloc Energy*, Nov. 1991, p. 11, Feb. 1992, p. 2.

[3] *Eastern Bloc Energy*, Feb. 1992, p. 2.

[4] The breakdown is as follows: Russia, 19.6 bt, of which West Siberia 15.2 bt (Tyumen 13.8 bt, Tomsk 1.4 bt), Kazakhstan 2.1 bt, Azerbaijan 0.53 bt, Turkmenistan 0.46 bt and other states 0.4 bt. See *Eastern Bloc Energy*, March 1992, p. 12.

[5] Isayev's figure is in the explored category (including A, B, and C1 classifications). See *Oil and Gas Journal*, 5 Oct. 1992, p. 102.

[6] In West Siberia, the ratio of initial reserves to ultimate potential resources increased from 20% to 40% in the 20-year period of 1965–85. See Valentin F. Bykov, 'Development Prospects of the Resource Base of the Soviet Oil Industry', paper presented at the Oil and Gas USSR Conference, London, 11 Dec. 1991.

Table 3.1: Different estimates of Soviet/Russian/CIS oil (and gas) reserves (bt/tcm)

Reserve Classification	Country	Reserves Oil	Reserves Gas	Source and date of estimate
A+B+C1 (proven)	Soviet Union	102.2		Lev Churilov (then minister of oil and gas): Jan 1991
		83.3		US Geological Survey: Jan 1990
		50–100		Western experts: during the 1970s
			49.2	Gazprom Kontsern: start of 1988
			50–5	J.P. Stern: 1990
	Russia		46.9	A.T. Shatalov (first deputy minister of energy and fuels): start of 1991
	CIS	57		*Int. Petroleum Encyclopedia*: Jan. 1992
			73.3	A.T. Shatalov: start of 1991
C1 (probable)				
C2 (possible)	Soviet Union	172.3		Lev Churilov: Jan. 1991
			105	Gazprom Kontsern: start of 1988
	CIS	268.3		Valery Neverov, Hermes' researcher: start of 1991 (Trading Firm, Hermes' Researcher)
C2 + D1 (hypothetical)				
D2 (speculative)				
Others:				
In place	Soviet Union		330	Gazprom Kontsern: start of 1988
Recoverable	CIS	158.3		V. Neverov: start of 1991
	Soviet Union	54.4–227		US Geological Survey: Jan. 1990
			20.9–81	US Geological Survey: Jan. 1990

Source: Keun Wook Paik, 'Russian and Chinese Oil and Gas Policies in Northeast Asia: International Political Consequences and Implications', PhD dissertation, University of Aberdeen, 1993, p. 151.

proved oil reserves in the range of 50–100 billion barrels, and the ratio of reserves to production at around 13:20.[7] However, Meyerhoff estimates that Soviet onshore

[7] Keun Wook Paik, 'Russian and Chinese Oil and Gas Policies in Northeast Asia: International Political Consequences and Implications', PhD dissertation, University of Aberdeen, 1993, p. 116 (reference nos 5–6).

Soviet reserve classification[1]

The Soviet explored category (A, B, C1) was not only more inclusive than the US/Canadian/Saudi proved category but also broader than the French, German and Dutch proved-reserves category. Soviet reserve categories – A, B, C1, C2, D1 and D2 – are based primarily on the degree of exploration and delineation drilling that has been carried out and cannot be directly equated to the Western categories of proved, probable, and possible reserves, which are based on prevailing economic and technological factors (see Table 1.4).

[1] *Oil and Gas Journal*, 5 Oct. 1992, pp. 102–3; Leslie Dienes, 'The Soviet Oil Industry in the Twelfth Five-Year Plan', *Soviet Geography* 38 (Nov. 1987), pp. 625–7; Arthur A. Meyerhoff, 'Soviet Petroleum: History, Technology, Geology, Reserves, Potential and Policy', in Robert G. Jensen, Theodore Shabad and Arthur W. Wright, eds, *Soviet Natural Resources in the World Economy*, University of Chicago Press, Chicago, 1983, pp. 327–30.

and offshore reserves of proved, probable and predicted total 60 bt (441 billion bbl).[8] The US Geological Survey put the identified reserves at 11.3 bt (83.3 billion bbl) as of January 1990 and estimates undiscovered (recoverable) oil resources to be between 54.4 billion and 227 billion barrels, with 12.5 bt (92 billion bbl) the most likely amount.[9] US experts are in the habit of downgrading the figures on the grounds that even Soviet A and B reserves do not fully correspond to the rigorous requirements of the American Petroleum Institute's 'demonstrated' (proved) reserve category.

Whatever the debate on the scale of the FSU's oil reserves, great potential exists in Russia and can be confirmed by the claim of Lev Churilov, then chairman of Rosneftegaz, that 4.9 bt (35.9 billion bbl) of untapped reserves can be brought on stream before the end of this decade.[10] (This claim is now doubtful, but demonstrates Russia's potential.)

[8] Marshall I. Goldman, *The Enigma of Soviet Petroleum: Half-Full or Half-Empty?*, George Allen & Unwin, London, 1980, p. 118.

[9] Charles D. Masters, David H. Root and Emil D. Attanasi, 'World Resources of Crude Oil and Natural Gas', in the *Thirteenth World Petroleum Congress Proceedings*, Vol. 4: *Reserves, Management, Finance and General*, John Wiley & Sons, Chichester, UK, 1992, pp. 51–64, Table 1.

[10] According to Churilov, there are 14 bt (102 billion bbl) of oil reserves in Tyumen Oblast, of which 11 bt (80 billion bbl) are accumulated in fields that are currently in production. The remaining 3 bt (22 billion bbl) are in fields awaiting development. Hence, Tyumen Oblast alone would contain about 60% of the officially announced 23.5 bt of oil reserves in the territory of the FSU. See *CIS* (formerly *Review of Soviet Oil*) 27: 2 (Feb. 1992), p. 113. For the development plan for Russian oil reserves, 1992–2000, see *Petroleum Intelligence Weekly*, 24 Aug. 1992, p. 4.

Table 3.2: CIS: natural-gas reserves, 1990–2030 (tcm)

	1990	2000	2010	2020	2030
Proved & probable	223	230	235	225	225
Possible	52	70	85	100	105
Total	275	300	320	325	330
Cumulative Output	10	20	32	45	58

Note: The figures are from a new long-term plan for gas, drawn up by the Gazprom Kontsern.
Source: *Eastern Bloc Energy*, Aug. 1991, p. 2.

Table 3.3: Soviet Union: natural-gas reserves, as of 1 Jan. 1988 (tcm)

	Proved & probable	Possible	Total	Cumulative Output
W. Siberia	35.3	77.4	112.7	2.8
E. Siberia & Far East	0.6	31.3	31.9	0.06
C. Asia & Kazakhstan	6	21.3	27.3	0.9
European USSR	5.7	19.8	25.5	3.1
Shelf	0.7	57.4	58.1	0.2
Others (Urals, etc)	0.9	11.9	12.8	1.14
Total	49.2	219.1	268.3	8.2

Source: *Eastern Bloc Energy*, Aug. 1991, p. 2.

Gas: As far as natural-gas reserves are concerned, no one disagrees that the FSU not only has immense proven gas reserves, but that additional sizeable discoveries are possible in the future. According to a new long-term plan for gas drawn up by the Gazprom Kontsern, as shown in Table 3.2, ultimate reserves of 330 trillion cubic metres (including proved and probable reserves of 105 trillion cubic metres) are forecast.[11] Table 3.3 shows detailed data on the FSU's gas reserves published for the first time since 1977. As of 1 January 1988, the proved and probable reserves are 49.2 tcm, of which West Siberia's share is about 70%.[12]

[11] *Eastern Bloc Energy*, Aug. 1991, p. 2. Here 1 tcm equals 35.3 tcf.
[12] As of 1992, Gazprom revised that figure to more than 54 tcm with total potential reserves assessed at 260 tcm. See *Eastern Bloc Energy*, April 1992, p. 10.

Here special attention should be paid to East Siberia, the Far East and the offshore shelf where possible reserves are estimated at 88.7 tcm, but proved and probable reserves are put at merely 1.3 tcm. Even though this figure was inflated three times by Anatoly T. Shatalov, then first deputy minister of energy and fuels, Russian Federation,[13] it confirms that these regions are almost untapped and have great potential given that only 5% of natural-gas-resource potential has been explored in the fields of Yakutia and Sakhalin.[14]

Shatalov said that Russia's share in the CIS is around 64% (which indicates that CIS gas reserves are approximately 73.3 tcm). His figures on gas reserves are as follows: West Siberia (37.8 tcm), European region (5.2 tcm), East Siberia and the Far East (1.9 tcm) and the offshore shelf (2.0 tcm). Consequently, the Russian total is 46.9 tcm, of which more than 14 tcm has not yet been explored.[15] (In 1993, the Russian total became 49.5 tcm.[16])

According to Western estimates, the FSU possess 49–57 tcm of gas, or around 40% of world proven reserves.[17] The ratio of reserves to production is estimated at 72.[18] One expert, Jonathan P. Stern, put the proven reserves at 40–45 tcm, but added that the figure would be around 50–55 tcm if huge offshore reserves discovered in the late 1980s are included.[19] The US Geological Survey put the identified reserves of gas at 43.9 tcm as of January 1990 and estimates undiscovered (recoverable) gas

---

[13] Anatoly T. Shatalov, 'Production and Consumption of Gas: The Outlook in Russia', paper presented at an International Conference 'Opening Up the Post-Soviet Gas Industry', London, 14–15, April 1992.

[14] Eugene M. Khartukov, 'Russian Far East: Energy Review and Outlook to 2000', *Petroleum Advisory* 105, East–West Center, Honolulu, 15 Sept. 1992, p. 1.

[15] In Russia, 699 gas concentrate and oil–gas fields have been opened up, and the reserves there are about 25 tcm, i.e. 53% of all Russian reserves. Some 56 fields with about 14 tcm are ready for industry. About 200 more fields are being opened up, which accounts for more than 8 tcm. Approximately 143 fields are being kept in reserve, and these are fairly small. The average reserves are approximately 1.5 to 2 mcm each. See Shatalov, *Production and Consumption of Gas* (op. cit., n. 14).

[16] This rise could hide the emergence of a trend which may pose serious problems in the future since not enough new possible gas is being found. In 1993 only 500 bcm was discovered, less than 23% of the 2,200 bcm found in 1988 and less than the 1993 output of 617 bcm. See *Eastern Bloc Energy*, May 1994, p. 3.

[17] *BP Statistical Review of World Energy*, June 1994; *Petroleum Economist*, Aug. 1991, p. 10; *FT International Gas Report*, 26 July 1991, p. 16.

[18] *BP Statistical Review of World Energy*, June 1994.

[19] Jonathan P. Stern, *European Gas Markets: Challenge and Opportunity in the 1990s*, Dartmouth, Aldershot, 1990, p. 52. In his recent publication, Stern put the figure at 48–9 tcm. See Jonathan P. Stern, *The Russian Natural Gas 'Bubble': Consequences for European Gas Markets*, Royal Institute of International Affairs, London, 1995, p. 3.

Table 3.4: Oil fields in East Siberia and the RFE at the beginning of 1992

Region	No of fields	Large			Average			Small			
		DE	UD	UE	DE	UD	UE	DE	UD	UE	CL
East Siberia	16		2	4		1	4		3	2	
Krasnoyarsk	10		1	4			2		1	2	
Irkutsk	6		1			1	2		2		
Far East	58		2	3		2	1	24	3	14	9
Sakha Rep.	11		1	1		1	1		1	6	
Magadan	3									3	
Sakhalin incl. offshore	44		1	2		1		24	2	5	9

Key: DE = developed; UD = undeveloped; UE = under exploration; CL = closed.
Note: Classification of oil fields is based on size and development stage: large (30–300 mt); average (10–30 mt); small (less than 10 mt). There are no giant fields (more than 300 mt).
Source:'Interim, Summary Report on Study of Energy Resources in East Siberia and 'Russia's Far East', prepared by Northern Regions Centre (Tokyo), Feb. 1993 (unpublished)

resources to range between 20.9 and 81 tcm, with 34.8 tcm the most likely amount.[20] A paper prepared for the World Bank estimates that approximately 22 tcm of gas, one-third of the world's reserves, are contained in the West Siberian basin, and in addition 10.3 tcm of gas can be classified as probable to inferred.[21]

3.1.2 Oil and gas potential in East Siberia and the RFE

Oil: At the beginning of 1992, 74 oil fields were known in East Siberia and the RFE: 16 in East Siberia, 58 in the RFE (11 in the Sakha Republic, 3 in the Magadan region and 44 in the Sakhalin region – see Table 3.4). As stated in Chapter 1, total oil reserves, including unproven ones, of both East Siberia and the RFE are equally 8.9 bt. The proven oil reserves in East Siberia and the RFE are around 640 mt, split almost equally between East Siberia and the RFE.

[20] Masters, Root and Attanasi, *World Resources of Crude Oil and Natural Gas* (op. cit., n. 9), pp. 54–5.

[21] George Pavloff and Richard Spears, 'Russian Federation Petroleum Development and Production: Background Information', paper prepared for the World Bank, March 1992. According to a paper by Dr J. D. Grace, roughly 33 tcm of remaining recoverable gas is concentrated in 16 fields that constitute Russia's key gas resources. *Oil and Gas Journal*, 6 Feb. 1995, p. 71.

Table 3.5: Oil reserves in East Siberia and the RFE (100 mt)

Region	Discovered reserves	Undiscovered reserves	Total reserves
East Siberia	7.64	80.73	88.37
Krasnoyarsk	5.02	63.52	68.54
Irkutsk	2.62	17.21	19.82
Far East	7.06	82.16	89.22
Onshore	4.43	30.54	34.96
Sakha Rep.	2.63	26.45	29.08
Magadan	0.1	0.97	1.07
Kamchatka	–	0.16	0.16
Sakhalin	1.7	1.16	2.87
Amur	–	0.03	0.03
Khabarovsk	–	0.31	0.31
Primorskii	–	0.01	0.01
Offshore	2.63	51.63	54.26

Note: Reserves are classified according to Russian standards. Discovered: A + B, C1, C2, cumulative production. Undiscovered: C3, D1, D2. Total: A + B, C1, C2, D1, D2, cumulative production.
Source: 'Interim, Summary Report on Study of Energy Resources in East Siberia and Russia's Far East', prepared by Northern Regions Centre (Tokyo), Feb. 1993 (unpublished).

Initial potential oil reserves in the RFE are estimated at 8.9 bt (see Table 3.5), of which 0.33 bt is proven reserves (A + B + C1), 0.28 bt is inferred reserves (C2), 79.3 mt is the estimated prospective reserves (C3) and 95 mt is cumulative production. As shown in Table 3.6, the balance of oil in place and reserves (A + B + C1 + C2) in the RFE are estimated at 2.8 bt, of which 1.1 bt are in the Sakha Republic and 1.6 bt in the Sakhalin region. The total recoverable balance of oil reserves (A + B + C1) is estimated at 328 mt, of which 294 mt is represented by the C1 category (including 131 mt in the Sakha Republic).

Gas: As for natural gas, 105 gas fields were known in East Siberia and the RFE: 33 in East Siberia, 92 in the RFE (30 in the Sakha Republic and 55 in the Sakhalin region – see Table 3.7). As mentioned in Chapter 1, total gas reserves including unproven ones are estimated at 56 tcm, of which East Siberia has 57%, the RFE 43%. Proven gas reserves in East Siberia and the RFE are around 2.5 tcm, with two-thirds of this in the RFE.

Initial potential gas reserves in the RFE are estimated at 24.2 tcm (see Table 3.8),

Table 3.6: Explored reserves of crude oil in the RFE, as of Jan. 1992 (mt)

Area	No of fields	Reserves category				
		A	B	C1	A + B + C1	C2
Sakha Rep.	11	–	–	438.3 131.4	438.3 131.4	667.4 131.5
Magadan Region	3	–	–	13.7 3.4	13.7 3.4	26.8 6.2
Sakhalin Region	45	85.4 12.3	110.8 21.7	677 159	873.2 193	753.3 146
Total	59	85.4 12.3	110.8 21.7	1129 293.8	1325.2 327.8	1447.5 283.7

Note: a numerator tells oil-in-place reserves, a denominator tells recoverable balance reserves.
Source: Oil and Gas in the Russian Far East, prepared by FACTS (Honolulu), Feb. 1994, p. 39 (Table 3).

of which 45 bcm is cumulative gas production and losses, 1.6 tcm is proven reserves (A + B + C1), 614 bcm is inferred reserves, and the estimated prospective reserves are 255 bcm. As shown in Table 3.9, gas-in-place reserves in the RFE are estimated at 2.2 tcm, of which 1.3 tcm is in the Sakha Republic and 0.84 tcm in the Sakhalin region. The total recoverable balance of gas reserves (A + B + C1) is 1.6 tcm, of which 0.96 tcm is located in the Sakha Republic.

Despite this great potential in oil and gas reserves, the RFE region has contributed almost nothing to cumulative oil output and negligibly to gas output. (Details on oil and gas output in Sakhalin and the Sakha Republic will be discussed briefly below.) For the time being, what matters for Russian oil and gas production are the provinces west of the Yenisey River, as RFE potential will be important only regionally. Even though oil output from the RFE will have a very minor effect on oil prospects in Russia, and a negligible impact on the world oil market, gas output from the RFE will have a very strong impact on the region's gas market.

The Russian Federation has great potential in oil and gas reserves, but development will be very difficult without the active participation of foreign companies, given that undeveloped reserves are located in remote and environmentally harsh areas. This is particularly the case for oil and gas development in the RFE.

Table 3.7: Natural-gas fields in East Siberia and the RFE

Region	No of fields	Large			Average				Small			
		DE	UD	UE	DE	UD	UE	CL	DE	UD	UE	CL
East Siberia	33	1	5	6	1	4	5	1			4	6
Krasnoyarsk	23	1	3	5	1	1	3	1			3	5
Irkutsk	10		2	1		3	2				1	1
Far East	92	1	8	6	2	5			10	19	20	21
Sakha Rep.	30	1	5	4	1	4			1	1	7	6
Magadan	2										2	
Kamchatka	4					1				1	2	
Khabarovsk	1										1	
Sakhalin incl. offshore	55		3	2	1				9	17	8	15

Key: DE = developed; UD = undeveloped; UE = under exploration, CL = closed.
Note: Classification of natural-gas fields is based on size and development stage: large (30-500 bcm); average (10-30 bcm); small (less than 10 bcm). There are no giant fields (more than 500 bcm).
Source: 'Interim, Summary Report on Study of Energy Resources in East Siberia and Russia's Far East', prepared by Northern Regions Centre (Tokyo), Feb. 1993 (unpublished).

3.2 Russian oil and gas production

3.2.1 Oil

During the past few years, the Russian oil industry has been in a state of chaos because of structural reorganization from separate state-owned enterprises operating in different segments of the industry to a few large, vertically integrated (and privatized) oil companies.[22] The most serious problem facing the Russian oil industry is a sharp decline in production.

As shown in Tables 3.10 and 3.11, and Map 3.1, in 1990 West Siberia's share in the FSU's total oil and gas production was 66% and 70% respectively. It is at the centre of the current production crisis. Table 3.12 shows that oil production in the FSU slumped to 352 mt in 1994 from 571 mt in 1990, and that Russia recorded 309 mt in 1994, from 516 mt in 1990.

[22] A key aspect of this new structure is the creation of a new state oil-managing body, Roseneft, to take over the management of government shares in the new integrated companies, like Yukos, Surgutneftegaz and Lukoil. For details of this reorganization, see Matthew J. Sagers, 'The Energy Industry of the Former USSR: A Mid-Year Survey', *Post-Soviet Geography*, June 1993, pp. 351–5.

Table 3.8: Natural-gas reserves in East Siberia and the RFE (bcm)

Region	Discovered reserves	Undiscovered reserves	Total reserves
East Siberia	1.85	10.34	31.91
Krasnoyarsk	1.28	8.54	24.94
Irkutsk	0.57	1.8	6.97
Far East	2.26	8.39	24.21
Onshore	1.51	3.02	12.18
Sakha Rep.	1.35	2.63	10.43
Magadan	0.01	0.09	0.38
Kamchatka	0.02	0.17	0.85
Amur	-	-	0.06
Khabarovsk	-	0.03	0.18
Primorskii	-	-	0.01
Sakhalin	0.12	0.09	0.3
Offshore	0.75	5.37	12.03
Sakhalin	0.55	0.5	1.25

Note: Reserves are classified according to Russian standards. Discovered: A + B, C1, C2, cumulative production. Undiscovered: C3, D1, D2. Total: A + B, C1, C2, C3, D1, D2, cumulative production.
Source: 'Interim, Summary Report on Study of Energy Resources in East Siberia and Russia's Far East', prepared by Northern Regions Centre (Tokyo), Feb. 1993 (unpublished).

In particular, crude-oil production in West Siberia fell by 53 mt in 1992, from 329 mt to 276 mt. The absolute decline in West Siberia alone represents over 80% of the overall decline in Russian crude-oil production in 1992. The region's output has declined by 139 mt from a peak of 415 mt in 1988, when the region accounted for 67% of the Soviet total. As shown in Table 3.13, over 90% of the output decline of 139 mt during 1988–92 came from just 5 of Tyumen province's 12 oil producers, notably the largest, Nizhnevartovsk field, which was alone responsible for over half the decline during the period.

3.2.2 Gas

Already in the mid-1980s the Soviets were warning against repeating the same mistakes as those made in the oil industry.[23] Gas production, as shown in Table 3.12, for

[23] Jonathan P. Stern, *Soviet Oil and Gas Exports to the West*, Gower, Aldershot, 1989, p. 8; Thane Gustafson, *Crisis amid Plenty: The Politics of Soviet Energy under Brezhnev and Gorbachev*, Princeton University Press, Princeton, 1989, p. 141.

Table 3.9: Balance of reserves of natural gas in the RFE, as of Jan. 1992 (bcm)

Region and field status	No of fields	Cumulative production	Current reserves A + B + C1	C2
Sakha Rep., all fields	30	18.5	959	375
of which UP	4	16.95	197.3	28.2
PCD	6	1.43	502.4	50.6
UE/A	15	0.11	241.5	282.8
UC	5	0.04	17.7	13.4
Magadan region, all fields	2	–	6.9	7.8
of which UE/A	2	–	6.9	7.8
Kamchatka region, all fields	4	–	16	6.6
of which PCD	2	–	13.7	0.8
UE/A	2	–	2.3	5.8
Sakhalin region, all fields	55	26.4	615.2	223.2
of which UP	22	24.8	45.6	11.1
PCD	7	0.07	480.7	145.4
UE/A	10	0.44	85.7	66.5
UC	16	1.06	3.3	0.1
Khabarovsk Territory, all fields	1	–	0.4	1.6
of which UE	1	–	0.4	1.6
Total Russian Far East	92	44.9	1597.6	614.2

Key: UP = under production; PCD = prepared for commercial development; UE/A = under exploration/appraisal; UC =under conservation.
Source: *Oil and Gas in the Russian Far East*, prepared by FACTS (Honolulu), Feb. 1994, p. 48 (Table 9).

the first time ever in Soviet history, declined in 1991, down from 814.8 bcm in 1990 to 810.4 bcm, despite the fact that gas production in Russia increased by 0.4%, from 540.2 bcm in 1990 to 643 bcm in 1991, an increase that was offset by decline in the republics. Russia's gas production also then recorded a 4% decline, by falling from 643 bcm in 1991 to 617.6 bcm in 1993.[24] Here it is worth noting the comparatively

[24] According to N. Shamrayev, Deputy Minister of Economy, Russian Federation, gas production in 1994 was expected to be 607 bcm. See *Proceedings of the Third International Conference on 'Natural Gas: Trade and Investment Opportunities in Russia and the CIS'*, London, 13–14 Oct. 1994, p. 39.

Table 3.10: Regional output of crude oil in the Soviet Union (million bbl/day)

Region	1955	1960	1965	1970	1975	1980	1985	1990
W. Siberia	0	0	0.02	0.63	2.96	6.29	7.58	7.51
Tyumen	0	0	–	0.56	2.86	6.07	7.33	7.33
Other areas	0	0	–	0.07	0.1	0.22	0.25	0.18
North Caucasus	0.13	0.24	0.42	0.7	0.48	0.42	0.24	0.12
Azerbaijan	0.31	0.36	0.43	0.4	0.34	0.39	0.28	0.24
Volga-Urals	0.83	2.09	3.45	4.17	4.53	3.86	2.64	2.35
Tatar	0.29	0.93	1.54	2.04	2.07	1.66	0.92	
Bashkir	0.29	0.51	0.88	0.78	0.78	0.76	0.7	
Other areas	0.25	0.65	1.03	1.35	1.68	0.44	1.02	
Other USSR	0.15	0.27	0.56	1.16	1.51	1.1	1.22	
Total USSR	1.42	2.96	4.88	7.06	9.82	12.06	11.96	11.44

Sources: E.A. Hewett, *Energy, Economics and Foreign Policy in the Soviet Union*, The Brookings Institution, Washington DC, 1984, p. 50; D. Wilson, *Soviet Energy to 2000*, The Economist Intelligence Unit, London, 1986, pp. 16–17; R.W. Campbell, *The Economics of the Soviet Oil and Gas Industry*, John Hopkins University Press, Baltimore, 1968, p. 124; *Soviet Geography*, April 1991, p. 253.

large net addition of 12.8 bcm in 1993, reinforcing the Gazprom assertion that production is being shut in because of lack of markets, both domestic and export.[25]

The gas industry's relatively strong performance is partly because it has not experienced the same kind of breakdown in organizational structure as has the oil industry, and financial pressures too are not nearly as great.[26] (However, the possibility of structural change in the gas industry cannot be totally ruled out.) The problem for gas production and transmission lies not with the resource itself, but with rising investment costs for fields located in the arctic, far from centres of consumption, and the need to protect the environment.[27]

[25] In 1994 the net addition was estimated at 9–10 bcm. See Stern, *The Russian Natural Gas 'Bubble'* (op. cit., n. 19), pp. 30–31.

[26] Sagers, *The Energy Industry of the Former USSR* (op. cit., n. 22), p. 379; Jonathan P. Stern, *Oil and Gas in the Former Soviet Union: The Changing Foreign Investment Agenda*, Royal Institute of International Affairs, London, 1993, pp. 19–21.

[27] Stern, *European Gas Markets* (op. cit., n. 20), pp. 52–3; *Eastern Bloc Energy*, April 1989, p. 6; David Wilson, 'USSR Environmentalists threaten the Energy Industry', *Petroleum Review*, April 1990, pp. 191–4; Michael Kaser, 'Soviet Energy Production', *Energy Policy*, May 1991, p. 327.

Table 3.11: Regional distribution of gas production in the Soviet Union (bcm)

Region	1960	1965	1970	1975	1980	1985	1990
European USSR and Urals	44.5	109.7	138.9	154	n.a.	n.a.	n.a.
Ukraine	14.3	39.4	60.9	68.7	56	42.9	29
Azerbaijan	5.8	6.2	5.5	9.9	11.6	14.1	9
North Caucasus	13.7	40	47	23	21	7.5	5.4
Orenburg	0.5	0.6	1.3	20.1	48	n.a.	n.a.
Komi	1	0.8	6.9	18.5	19	17.9	13
Others	9.2	22.7	4.8	13.8	n.a.	n.a.	n.a.
East of Urals	0.8	18.3	59	135	n.a.	n.a.	n.a.
W. Siberia	0	0	9.3	35.7	156	375.8	567
Kazakhstan	0	0	2.1	5.2	3	5.5	7.1
Uzbekistan	0	16.5	32.1	37.2	36	34.6	40.8
Turkmenistan	0	1.2	13.1	51.8	70.5	83.2	87.8
Others	0	0.6	2.4	5.1	n.a.	n.a.	n.a.
Total USSR	45.3	128	197.9	289	435.2	642.9	814.7

Sources: L. Dienes and T. Shabad, *The Soviet Energy System: Resource Use and Policies*, V.H. Winston & Sons, Washington, DC, 1979, pp. 70–1; J.P. Stern, *Soviet Natural Gas Development to 1990*, Lexington Books, Lexington, 1980, p. 28; D. Wilson, *Soviet Energy to 2000*, The Economist Intelligence Unit, London, 1986, p. 60; *Soviet Geography*, April 1991, p. 266.

3.2.3 Offshore

As far as offshore production is concerned, Russia is producing a negligible amount of oil and gas, as the Soviet offshore production centre, the Azerbaijan Republic, is no longer within Russia's boundary. (However, Russia is still an influence in the republic.) During the Soviet era, the share of offshore oil and gas production in the total had never been over 5%. As shown in Table 3.12, the figure was less than 2% of the total during 1977–87. Russia can find solace in a string of major offshore discoveries, like Odoptu, Chaivo, Lunskoye and Piltun-Astokskoye oil and gas fields in Sakhalin offshore, Shtockmanovskoye gas field in the Barents Sea, Prierazlomnoye oil field in the Pechora Sea, and Rusanovskoye gas field in the Kara Sea.[28] The scale of offshore oil and gas production will be substantial, once these fields are fully developed. Production will start with Sakhalin offshore.

[28] Paik, *Russian and Chinese Oil and Gas Policies in Northeast Asia* (op. cit., n. 7), pp. 183–5, 239–44.

Map 3.1: Main oil and gas production base in the CIS

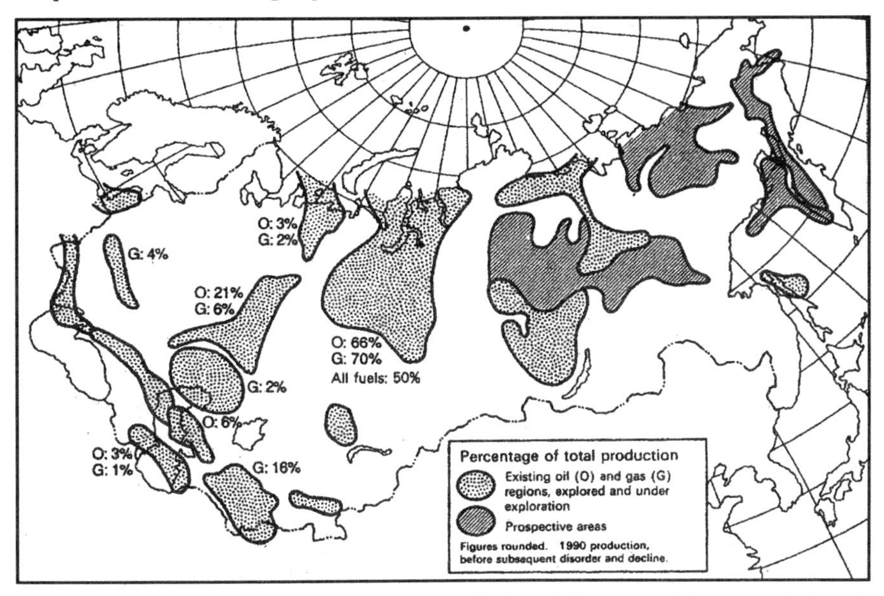

Source: Leslie Dienes, Istvan Dobozi and Marian Radetzki, *Energy and Economic Reform in the Former Soviet Union*, Macmillan, London, 1994, p. 37.

3.2.4 The RFE

Oil: In the RFE, only the Sakhalin region has produced a small amount of oil. In 1992 crude-oil production totalled 1.67 mt (Sakhalin 1.61 mt, the Sakha Republic 0.06 mt), declining from 2.6 mt in 1985. The region's oil production is expected to reach 4.5–7 mt in 2000,[29] but this amount will have virtually no impact on oil prospects in Russia.

As stated in Chapter 1, the RFE's annual oil demand is roughly 20 mt, of which around 9 mt is for crude oil for the region's two oil refineries. A substantial part of the RFE's crude-oil demand should be covered by imports in the future. In fact, the feedstock of the RFE's two refineries, Khabarovsky NPZ in Khabarovsk and Komsomolsky NPZ in Komsomolsk-on-Amur, is supplied from Sakhalin and West Siberia, and the latter represents over three-quarters of total refinery intake.[30]

[29] *Oil and Gas in the Russian Far East*, a study report prepared by FACTS (Fesharaki Associates Consulting and Technical Services, Inc.), Honolulu, Feb. 1994, pp. 55, 61 (Tables 13, 16).

[30] Ibid., p. 65.

Table 3.12: Soviet Union (Russia): oil and gas production (mt/bcm)

	Oil				Gas			
Year	FSU	RF	West Siberia	Off-shore	FSU	RF	West Siberia	Off-shore
1950	37.9				5.8			
1955	70.8				9			
1960	147.9			7.1	45.3			
1965	242.9		1	11.4	127.7		0.03	2.2
1970	353		31.4	12.8	198		9.3	3.3
1975	490.8		148	11.4	289.3		35.7	8
1980	603.2		312.6	9.8	435	254	156	12.7
1981	608.8		334	9.8	465		176.1	13.8
1982	612.6		352.9	9	501		230.5	14.2
1983	616.3		369	8.7	536	363.3	270.0*	14.8
1984	612.7		380	9	587	412.1	320.0*	15.2
1985	595.8		368	9.5	642.9	462	375.8	14.8
1986	610.8		389.6	10	686.1	503	419.1	14.8
1987	624.2	569.5	409.5	10.6	727.4	544.2	464.8	15
1988	624.3	568.8	415.1	11	770	589.6	510.8	15.2
1989	607.3	554.9	405.1	11	796.1	615.8	539.6	
1990	570.8	516.2	375.2	12.1	814.8	640.2	568.9	
1991	515	461.1	328.8		810.4	643	574	
1992	449.5	395.8	275.7		781.2	640.4	574.6	
1993	393.4	354.6			757.7	617.6		
1994	351.5	309.4			727	607.3		

Key: * = planned figure.
Sources: 1986: Gerald E. Dixon, ed., *Soviet Petroleum Outlook*, Vol. 1, International Energy Services, London, 1989, pp. 20–1; oil (1987-92): Matthew J. Sagers, 'The Energy Industries of the Former USSR: A Mid-Year Survey', *Post-Soviet Geography* 34: 6, pp. 344 (Table 1) and 378 (Table 5); oil (1993): *BP Statistical Review of World Energy*, June 1994; RF gas (1983–93): from proceedings of Conference on 'Natural Gas: Trade and Investment Opportunities in Russia and the CIS', convened by the RIIA, London, 13–14 Oct. 1994 (Fig. 11.3); Stephen Lewarne, *Soviet Oil: The Move Offshore*, Westview Press, Boulder, 1988, p. 62; *Offshore*, 20 June 1982, p. 145; *Soviet Geography*, April 1989, p. 316; *Petroleum Review*, Oct. 1989, p. 521; *Petroleum Economist*, Sept. 1990, p. 26; *World Oil*, Aug. 1991, p. 84.

In 1994, reportedly, Komsomolsky NPZ cut production as a result of high transport costs from West Siberia. The refinery bought Siberian oil for 70,000 roubles/tonne, but paid 100,000 roubles/tonne in delivery costs. In other words, it could not make ends meet as its oil became 35% more expensive than oil from the Angarsk

Table 3.13: Oil and gas production in the RF and West Siberia (mt)

		1970	1980	1985	1988	1990	1991	1992
Russian Federation	Oil				568.8	516.2	461.1	395.8
	Gas		254	462	489.8	640.6	642.9	640.4
W. Siberia	Oil	31.4	312.7	368.1	415.1	375.2	328.8	275.7
	Gas		156.4	375.8	510.8	569.3	574	574.6
Tyumen oblast	Oil	28.5	307.9	361.1	405.7	365	319	267.5
	Gas		156.2	375.4	505.3	568.9	573.7	574.3
Tomsk oblast	Oil	2.9	4.8	7	9.4	10.2	9.8	8.2
	Gas		0.2	0.4	0.2	0.4	0.3	0.3
Sakhalin	Oil		2.5	2.6	2.2	2.2	1.8	1.7
	Gas		0.8	0.8	1.6	1.8	1.9	1.7
Sakha Rep.	Gas		0.8	1	1.3	1.4	1.4	1.5

Source: *Soviet Geography*, April 1991, p. 257; *Post-Soviet Geography* 34: 6 (1993), pp. 344 (Table 1) and 378 (Table 5).

refinery in central Siberia. Fuel oil cost 20% more. If this situation continues, it will drive Komsomolsky NPZ to buy oil abroad.[31]

Crude-oil delivery to the refineries from Sakhalin is by way of a 624-km twin pipeline connecting Okha on Sakhalin Island with Komsomolsk-on-Amur. At present only one pipeline with a 529-mm diameter, commissioned in 1970, is in operation. Crude-oil delivery from West Siberia is mainly by rail over a distance of more than 2,400 km, from Irkutsk to Khabarovsk. From West Siberia to Irkutsk, delivery is made by pipeline.[32]

In 1992 the two refineries produced 10.5 mt of oil products: 5.7 mt at Khabarovsky NPZ and 4.8 mt at Komsomolsky NPZ.[33] The same year, oil-products

[31] *Russian Petroleum Investor*, July/Aug. 1994, p. 40.

[32] Another pipeline with a 325-mm diameter, commissioned in 1962, is no longer in operation. See *Oil and Gas in the Russian Far East* (op. cit., n. 29), p. 90.

[33] The breakdown of products in Khabarovsky NPZ is as follows: Gasoline 0.75 mt, jet fuel 0.47 mt, diesel/gasoil 1.06 mt, fuel oil 1.51 mt, bitumen/tar 0.18 mt and liquefied refinery gas 0.04 mt. In Komsomolsky NPZ: aviation gasoline 0.075 mt, gasoline 0.81 mt, jet fuel 0.29 mt, diesel/gasoil 1.89 mt, fuel oil 1.77 mt and petroleum coke 0.03 mt. Ibid., p. 67 (Table 19).

consumption in the RFE doubled, to 21 mt, roughly a 17% jump since 1985.[34] The deficit was covered by oil products imported mainly from East Siberia. In 1992 product deliveries from East Siberia to the RFE were around 13 mt, of which 55% was delivered to the Maritime Territory, 20% to Yakutia and 16% to the Amur region.

Gas: As for the RFE's gas production, as shown in Table 3.13, the combined output of the Sakha Republic and Sakhalin was merely 3.2–3.3 bcm during 1990–2, accounting for roughly 0.5% of Russia's total gas production. The two regions' production in 2000 is expected to be 15–20 bcm. If 20 bcm is achieved,[35] the RFE's share in Russia's total gas production will be 2.6%, assuming that total production in 2000 is 755 bcm.[36]

During 1985–92 the RFE's gas consumption rose from 1.8 bcm to 3.3 bcm, but gas use is limited to Yakutia, Sakhalin and the Khabarovsk Territory due to underdevelopment of the gas distribution system. During the same period, gas consumption in Yakutia rose from 1 bcm to 1.5 bcm, while that of Sakhalin dropped to 0.75 bcm. The Khabarovsk Krai began to use gas after the gas trunkline (length 445 km, diameter 720 mm) between Sakhalin and Komsomolsk-on-Amur was commissioned in 1987. Gas consumption in the Khabarovsk Krai totalled 1–1.1 bcm.[37]

In the Sakha Republic, whose hydrocarbons industry ceased to be under the control of Moscow in 1992, two gas pipelines are in operation. One is in the centre of the Republic, connecting Tas-Tumus with Yakutsk (278 km), and was commissioned in 1968; later a 370-km pipeline connecting Mastakh with Yakutsk was added because of the depletion of gas reserves at the Ust-Vilyuiskoye field. The other (172 km) in the west, delivers gas from the Sredne-Botuobinskoye field to Mirnyy.[38] (For further discussion, see Chapter 7.)

Long delays in development have restricted the RFE's oil and gas industries. But with the realization of the Sakhalin offshore development in the coming years, and the possibility that the Sakha Republic and Irkutsk region will be seriously explored, a totally different picture is likely to emerge in the next decade. What is urgently needed is massive foreign investment.

---

[34] 21 mt is broken down as follows: liquefied petroleum gas 0.12 mt, gasoline 2.5 mt, jet fuel 2.1 mt, diesel/gasoil 9.2 mt, fuel oil 6.5 mt, lube oils 0.3 mt, and bitumen/tar 0.3 mt. Ibid., pp. 75–86 (Table 25–31).

[35] Ibid., p. 61 (Table 16).

[36] *Eastern Bloc Energy*, Jan. 1994, p. 3.

[37] *Oil and Gas in the Russian Far East* (op. cit., n. 29), pp. 76 and 78, Table 24.

[38] Ibid., p. 101.

3.3 Problems of onshore production and offshore development

3.3.1 Onshore production

The main reasons for the current crisis in the oil industry are the over-rapid depletion of reservoirs, decline of productivity and drilling activity, shortage of equipment or delays in putting equipment into service, lack of advanced technology, reduced investment and unreasonably low oil prices. Of these, depletion of reservoirs and decline of productivity are basically long-term problems dating back to well before Russia's current economic crisis. Eugene Khartukov, head of the World Energy Analysis and Forecasting Group, Moscow Institute of International Relations, summarized the main factors as follows: depletion of the resource base, a very poor technological base and poor oil economics caused by the drive for production at all costs.[39]

Depletion of oil reserves: The depletion of oil reserves in major fields has reached alarming levels: 50% in the largest fields in West Siberia. The exhaustion rate of the giant Samotlor field is almost 60%, and that of the similarly vast Romashkino field in the Tatar Republic is 83%. Given that half the country's current proven oil reserves are accumulated in 46 fields, 30 of which are in Tyumen oblast, the depletion of large fields is a serious problem.

On top of this, the proportion of marginal reserves in the total balance of recoverable reserves discovered between 1977 and 1988 grew by half to 30%.[40] Consequently the proportion of reserves exploited with well-production rates of less than 20 tonnes/day exceeded 50% of the national additions to reserves.[41] The significance of the discovery of smaller oil fields is demonstrated by the following statistics: in the mid-1970s Russia was finding 50 new oil fields a year and in 1975 each new Siberian field had reserves averaging 53 mt of recoverable reserves. By 1985 the average new field had 15 mt and in 1992–3 some 11–12 mt. With the development of smaller fields, average well yields dropped sharply, from 21 t/d in 1975 to 15.2 t/d in 1985 and 8 t/d in 1993.[42] To offset declines at older, larger fields, production is increasingly shifting to widely scattered smaller fields, leading to problems in providing needed infrastructure and access as well as to lower rates of flow.

---

[39] *Financial Times*, 26 Oct. 1990.

[40] Here marginal reserves seem to mean the reserves found in small and medium-sized fields. See Bykov, *Development Prospects of the Resource Base of the Soviet Oil Industry* (op. cit., n. 6).

[41] Ibid. In January 1986 total Soviet recoverable oil reserves in fields that were not in production amounted to 6.9 bt (50.4 billion bbl), but in January 1990 the figure declined to 5.4 bt (39.3 billion bbl). See *CIS*, Feb. 1992, p. 42.

[42] *Eastern Bloc Energy*, May 1994, p. 2.

Non-producing wells: Losses in oil production due to non-producing wells are immense. For example, in 1990, Soviet oil production (without condensate) reached 551 mt, and wells with a production capacity of 124 mt were shut in or depleted.[43] The same year, Russia had 123,100 operating oil wells, with about half of these in West Siberia.[44] The number of shut-in wells, mainly the result of lack of equipment and technical resources, increased by 2,100 in 1989, 6,700 in 1990 and 5,900 in 1991.

Most shut-ins are in West Siberia. As of 1 March 1992, a quarter of its wells were shut in.[45] Producing enterprises estimated their average lost oil production at 8 tonnes per day per well. The average loss of oil production throughout Russia because of well shut-ins is about 30 million tonnes (219 million bbl)/year with an estimated export value of $3.6 billion.[46]

Restoration of idle oil wells is the first step in the Russian approach to rejuvenation of its oil-producing sector. It is an urgent task. At the end of 1993, the number of inoperative oil wells in Russia was placed at 33,341, or more than 1 in 5 production wells, up from some 27,600 wells standing idle at the beginning of the year. Of these 33,341 wells, roughly 7,800 were considered 'surplus', exceeding the norm of 25,500 set by the government for wells out of production.[47] Once the more than 20,000 perfectly good but currently non-producing wells are restored,[48] a substantial reduction will be made in the scale of oil-production decline.

Declining productivity: Declining productivity poses another problem for the Soviet oil industry. In 1990 the industry had to replace 19.4% of its total production potential by completing new wells, while in 1980 the figure was 13.1%. That is, the yearly oil-production-replacement rate was increasing continuously during the period. In 1990, 166 wells had to be completed to replace one million tonnes of oil production, 2.3

---

[43] *CIS*, Feb. 1992, p. 42.

[44] Leslie Dienes, 'Prospects for Russian Oil in the 1990s: Reserves and Costs', *Post-Soviet Geography*, Feb. 1993, p. 92.

[45] West Siberia's shut-in wells numbered 17,900. See *Oil and Gas Journal*, 10 Aug. 1992, p. 19.

[46] Ibid., pp. 19–20.

[47] Of 7,800, some 2,109 were shut for lack of materials and replacement equipment, such as well tubing, pumps, christmas trees and the like, representing a production loss slightly in excess of 187,000 b/d. See Robert E. Ebel, *Energy Choices in Russia*, Center for Strategic and International Studies, Washington, DC, 1994, p. 28. In 1991 the number of non-producing Russian wells was 23,472, but at the end of 1992 the figure reached 30,457, and in 1993 increased by 1,400 to 31,860. See *Eastern Bloc Energy*, March 1994, p. 8.

[48] *Financial Times*, 23 Sept. 1992. For a comprehensive report on non-operating wells, see *Eastern Bloc Energy*, Nov. 1991, pp. 2–5.

times more than in 1980. It is anticipated that 240–50 new wells will have to be drilled in 1995 to replace one million tonnes of lost oil-production capacity.[49]

Declining productivity is directly connected with the increase in well numbers. In January 1986 there were 856 oil-producing fields in the Soviet Union, but in 1990 the number increased to 1,099. Production from four-fifths of these fields is declining.[50] In fact, average nationwide oil-well yield has been continuously declining, from 103 b/d of oil 1986 to 74.5 b/d in 1990.[51] The average flow of new wells in the Soviet Union was 285 b/d of oil in 1980 but only 128.5 b/d in 1990, and in West Siberia the figure recorded was only 103 b/d in 1990, down from 1173 b/d in 1975.[52] (The *Moscow News* reported that in 1990 the average yield of Tyumen's more than 57,000 wells was 125.6 b/d, sharply decreasing from 196 b/d in 1985 and 284 b/d in 1980.[53])

According to a mid-1992 assessment for Roseneftegaz, the wells installed before 1991 and still operating in West Siberia will experience a fourfold decrease in productivity until 2000. The Roseneftegaz report projected a 17.6% annual average decline for the rest of the 1990s, the yearly rate slowing down from 24.6% in 1992 to 14.5% by 2000 as the reservoirs deplete. This means that wells that produced 11–12 t/d in 1991 will pump only about 3.2 t/d in 2000.[54]

Poor drilling performance: It is estimated that production wells totalling 64 million metres (Mm)/y must be drilled to reach an annual production level of 510 Mm/y in 1995.[55] However, this target is unlikely to be achieved given that Soviet rigs are very heavy and drilling performance is poor due to the low quality of drillbits.[56]

---

[49] *CIS*, Feb. 1992, p. 42; *Oil and Gas Journal*, 27 Jan. 1992, p. 40.

[50] *CIS*, Feb. 1992, p. 42

[51] Ibid., p. 38.

[52] It was expected that the average yield of new wells will decline to 80–88 b/d by 1995. Ibid., p. 40; Leslie Dienes, 'Siberia: Perestroyka and Economic Development', *Soviet Geography*, Sept. 1991, p. 451. In West Siberia, in 1985 the flow rate of new oil wells was 285.9 b/d, and in the whole USSR it was 190.6 b/d. See Ibrahim A. H. Isamil, 'The Oil Production Decline in the Former Soviet Union and its Impact on OPEC', *OPEC Bulletin*, Feb. 1992, p. 17 (Table 1).

[53] *Oil and Gas Journal*, 3 Feb. 1992, p. 21.

[54] Dienes, *Prospects for Russian Oil in the 1990s* (op. cit., n. 44), p. 90.

[55] Bykov, *Development Prospects of the Resource Base of the Soviet Oil Industry* (op. cit., n. 6).

[56] Russian drillbits drill three to four times less footage than equivalent Western bits. As of 1 January 1991, 4,699 land and platform rigs and 24 mobile offshore rigs either idle or active were stationed in the CIS. Among them, 1,306 rigs were in West Siberia and 1,058 in the Volga-Ural province. See Joseph P. Riva, Jr, *Petroleum Exploration Opportunities in the Former Soviet Union*, Pennwell Books, Tulsa, 1994, p. 50; *Oil and Gas Journal*, 27 April 1992, p. 24; *Eastern Bloc Energy*, March 1991, pp. 2–4.

The Soviet Union's drilling activity peaked in 1988 with 49.1 Mm, but then declined to 37.1 Mm in 1991 and 30.9 Mm in 1993. The 1993 figure was far below that for 1985, some 35.7 Mm.[57] During 1988–93, exploratory/appraisal drilling went down by 63%, from 8.4 Mm in 1988 to 3.1 Mm in 1993. And development drilling in the same period decreased by 32%, from 40.7 Mm in 1988 to 27.8 Mm in 1993.[58]

In Russia, the total drilling footage was 44.1 Mm in 1988, but dropped by 38%, to 27.4 Mm in 1993. During 1988–93, exploratory drilling went down by 68%, from 6.1 Mm in 1988 to 1.9 Mm in 1993, and development drilling decreased by 33%, from 38 Mm in 1988 to 25.4 Mm in 1993. In West Siberia, during 1990–3, drilling by oil companies decreased by 24%, from 25.2 Mm in 1990 to 19 Mm in 1993.[59]

Complaints by Russian oilmen that exploration focuses too much effort on the appraisal of existing fields and not enough on the discovery of new ones are understandable. The results are quite clear. Initial recoverable reserves at fields not yet being exploited have declined from 6.9 billion tonnes (50.37 billion bbl) in January 1986 to 5.4 billion tonnes (39.42 billion bbl) in January 1990, and no new large fields have been found in recent years.[60] According to Lev Churilov, then chairman of Rosneftegaz, drilling of new wells had fallen sharply, with 10.2 Mm drilled instead of the planned 13 Mm in the first half of 1992. If the trend continues, he said, average daily oil production would fall by 10,000 tonnes/day.[61]

Other factors: Exploration and development conditions have deteriorated. (Strictly speaking, these are partly indicators of a maturing oil sector.) The average development-well depth has increased from 2,003 metres in 1980 to 2,340 metres in 1990, and the ratio of average watercut has increased from 57.4% in 1980 to 77.5% in 1990.[62] During 1985–88 the annual increase of watercut in West Siberia recorded 4%, and that of old oil fields was 1%. The average water content of produced oil in Tyumen province has started to increase seriously in recent years, from 5% in 1970

---

[57] *Eastern Bloc Energy*, March 1994, p. 7 (Table). In 1985 exploration drilling was 6.9 Mm, and development drilling was 28.8 Mm. See Alexander A. Arbatov *et al.*, *Soviet Energy: An Insider's Account*, Centre for Global Energy Studies, London, 1991, Annex, Table 8.

[58] *Eastern Bloc Energy*, March 1994, p. 7 (Table). From 1989 to 1991 exploratory drilling dropped more than 20%, resulting in 27% smaller growth in explored oil reserves; and development drilling decreased by 7.01 million metres, with about 3,000 fewer wells completed each year. See *Oil and Gas Journal*, 27 Jan. 1992, p. 38.

[59] *Eastern Bloc Energy*, March 1994, p. 8.

[60] *Oil and Gas Journal*, 27 Jan. 1992, p. 38.

[61] *Financial Times*, 21 July 1992.

[62] *CIS*, Feb. 1992., p. 43.

to 56.3% in 1985 and 74.5% in 1990. The figures for the FSU are 44.2 % in 1970, 69.6% in 1985 and 77.4% in 1990.[63] In early 1990 it was reported that 75% of Tyumen gas wells had experienced water encroachment and that by 1995 the figure would exceed 90%.[64]

Problems of oil production were further compounded by the economic and political fragmentation of the FSU, causing severe disruption in materials and equipment supply to the Russian oil industry. For example, in 1990 just before the break-up of the FSU, shortage of casing pipe cut Tyumen oil output by 5 mt, and lack of wellhead valves left over 300 newly drilled wells uncompleted.[65] It was reported that deliveries of equipment and materials amounted to only 80% of the planned volumes for the year.[66] However, in 1991, when the FSU dissolved, total deliveries of equipment and materials to the Nizhnevartovsk association were only 40–60% of requirements for the year. As the main equipment suppliers, like Azerbaijan, Georgia and Ukraine (the principal supplier of pipelines and tubing), are now demanding close to world prices for their goods (key equipment prices have risen between 4 and 22 times), some producing associations have been supplied with less than half the equipment they need.[67]

Massive quantities of associated liquids have been wasted each year owing to frequent pipeline accidents and lack of transport capacity, although many petrochemical plants are running well below capacity.[68] Losses of oil in transport and storage were estimated at between 12 and 15 mt/year.[69] As for wastage of gas, the volume of gas flaring in the CIS is even bigger than annual Chinese gas production (during 1986–8, over 15 bcm/y of gas was flared, a figure never surpassed by the annual Chinese gas production). Since 1970 some 270 bcm of casing head gas plus about 50 mt of valuable gas liquids have been lost by flaring.[70]

The above examples confirm that Russia is experiencing the same sort of crisis in its oil industry as the Soviet Union. The problem of idle wells is clearly a short-

---

[63] Isamil, 'The Oil Production Decline in the Former Soviet Union and its Impact on OPEC' (op. cit., n. 52), p. 17 (Table 2).

[64] Kaser, 'Soviet Energy Production' (op. cit., n. 27), p. 328.

[65] The record was made during Jan.–Aug. 1990. See *Eastern Bloc Energy*, Aug. 1990, p. 5.

[66] *Eastern Bloc Energy*, Dec. 1990, pp. 2–3.

[67] *Financial Times*, 24 July 1992. Equipment deliveries from Azerbaijan to West Siberian oil associations have practically stopped, while shipments of Grozny-made equipment have been sharply reduced. See *Oil and Gas Journal*, 3 Feb. 1992, p. 21.

[68] The explosion of the pipeline carrying 3 mt/year of unstable gasoline near Ufa in June 1989 was a typical accident. See *Eastern Bloc Energy*, June 1989, pp. 1–3.

[69] Kaser, *Soviet Energy Production* (op. cit., n. 27), p. 327.

[70] *Eastern Bloc Energy*, Sept. 1989, p. 2.

term, systematic difficulty following on from the breakup of the Soviet Union, but depletion of reservoirs, decline of productivity and drilling activity, reduced investment, etc., are relatively long-term ones.

It is important here to distinguish Soviet experience from post-1991 Russian policy, especially when trying to separate technical and resource problems – mostly historically determined – from the organizational and political crisis of the post-1991 period. Since the breakup of the Soviet Union, a great deal of oil-production decline is specifically due to organizational chaos, although some of it would have happened anyway.

Unlike the trouble-ridden oil industry, Russia's gas industry put in a fairly impressive performance given the severe economic crisis in the country. It does not necessarily follow that the gas industry is problem-free, as it has also faced financial difficulties, mainly because of low prices and non-payment by delinquent customers, and demand challenges such as pressures on internal consumption, declining consumption in the other former Soviet republics and stagnating exports abroad.

The recent gas explosion near Ukhta region in the Komi republic is a fresh reminder of the problems the gas industry faces. Reportedly, much of the Russian gas-export system was built using imported German steel pipe, but few of the pipelines were properly coated with PVC; until recently they were coated to a depth of 1 mm, woefully inadequate by the European or US standard of 3 mm.[71] The industry's long-distance pipeline grid urgently needs investment. It is doubtful whether the plan to extend the gas-supply network, that is, construction of 300,000 km of gas-distribution grid by 2005 (30,000 km/year), can be implemented as planned.[72]

In short, while Russia's oil industry is itself in crisis, the gas industry is in difficulty only to the extent that it is affected by the crisis in the economy as a whole. The latter is the much larger problem inherent in the creation of a new economic and political system which the oil and gas industries can then adapt to. Some of the difficulties they face seem to be manageable once the controlled prices that deprive enterprises of any initiative to invest are freed to the level of world-market prices, and conditions for foreign participation are improved.

3.3.2 Offshore development

The Soviet Union and now Russia has faced a chain of problems in offshore development during the past four decades. These are, technical, environmental and

---

[71] *The Times*, 28 April 1995.

[72] Currently, construction of only 13,000–17,000 km/y is being made. See I. Dudin, 'Sales through the Distribution Network', *Proceedings of the International Conference on Natural Gas: Trade and Investment Opportunities in Russia and the CIS*, convened by the Royal Institute of International Affairs, London, 13–14 Oct. 1994.

financial constraints, ecological and social problems, an unfavourable foreign-investment environment, fluctuation of world oil prices, maldistribution of gas resources and unresolved territorial disputes.

First, though the Soviet Union made some progress in deep-water development, until the end of the 1980s there was no technology for offshore development at a water-depth range of 200-350 metres because the Soviets focused on developing the Caspian offshore up to a depth of around 100 metres.[73] Since the breakup of the Soviet Union the Caspian Sea is offshore for four sovereign nations: Russia, Azerbajan, Kazakhstan and Turkmenistan. Development here will be given priority, in parallel with that of Sakhalin offshore, where all the major oil and gas fields are located at water depths far below 100 m. Deep-water technology will be necessary for Russia if it is to pursue a self-reliant policy for the development of the Barents Sea. For example, Shtokmanovskoye gas field in the Barents Sea is located at 280–380 m.

Besides this deep-water problem, another serious constraint on the technical side comes from harsh environmental conditions, notably ice in the Sea of Okhotsk and Soviet Arctic seas. In the Sea of Okhotsk, ice floes are usually about 2 m thick, and move at a speed of 1 m/sec (2.2 mph), and the ice sometimes scours the bottom of the shelf as it ploughs into the seabed.[74] In northeastern Sakhalin offshore, normal operations are possible only 107 days a year, from 1 July through 15 October, because of this ice problem. Ice 1–1.2 m thick extends 1 km from the coast in March. In southwestern Sakhalin offshore, above a latitude of 47°30' N, work can proceed for 261 days a year, from 15 March to 30 November, but all personnel and equipment must be removed by 15 December. Below this line 291 days are available for operations, from 15 March to 31 December, and personnel and machinery must be out by 15 January.[75]

The Soviet Arctic seas have a minimum of 6–8 months of ice cover, and pack ice (so-called dangerous ice, 2–6 m thick) generally moves at an average speed of 3 cm/sec from the Siberian shelf to the Fram Strait, where the speed accelerates to 10–15 cm/sec.[76]

---

[73] Paik, *Russian and Chinese Oil and Gas Policies in Northeast Asia* (op. cit., n. 7), pp. 171–5.

[74] The pressure on offshore platforms is estimated to be 800 tonnes per sq. mile. See *Oil and Gas Journal*, 18 March 1991, p. 35; 10 June 1974, p. 95.

[75] Allen S. Whiting, *Siberian Development and East Asia: Threat or Promise?*, Stanford University Press, Stanford, 1981, p. 146. Soviet officials pointed out that rough water and ice in the Sea of Okhotsk made it 2.5 times more difficult to drill there than in the Caspian Sea. See *Oil and Gas Journal*, 10 June 1974, pp. 94–6.

[76] Helge Ole Bergesen, Arild Moe and Willy Ostreng, *Soviet Oil and Security Interests in the Barents Sea*, Frances Pinter, London, 1987, pp. 58–61; Tore Gjelsvik, 'Basic Features of the Arctic', in Louis Rey, ed., *Arctic Energy Resources*, Elsevier, Amsterdam, 1983, p. 30.

For the exploration and development of the Barents Sea, Igor B. Dubin argued, innovative and costly technical facilities and technologies, like fixed ice-resistant platforms (capable of withstanding high ice loads up to 15,000 tonnes) and technical facilities for underwater oil and gas production, are necessary.[77] This is something that Russian Arctic offshore development has to deal with. On top of the ice problem, the extreme cold makes matters even worse; in January the average temperature of Yamburg and Yamal regions is minus 20–27° Celsius.[78]

These technical and environmental constraints mean an increase in Russia's Arctic Sea development costs. According to A. Arbatov, costs of net prospecting and reconnaissance drilling in the Barents Sea are seven times higher than those in West Siberia, and exploration and production costs amount to over $40 per barrel, which means that Arctic oil would not be competitive on the world market without a substantial price rise.[79] On the other hand, according to the more positive view expressed by A. Konoplyanik, exploration costs in terms of capital investment per unit of accretions to reserves will decline in the Arctic and will prove substantially less than costs in the Caspian Sea because of the large size of the fields awaiting discovery. But, Konoplyanik added, the costs will be increased for development of oil fields in Far Eastern seas.[80]

---

[77] Igor B. Dubin, 'Offshore Production Area: The Barents and Kara Seas, the Sea of Okhotsk', paper presented at the International Conference on 'Opening up the Post-Soviet Gas Industry', London, 14–15 April 1992, p. 5; Svein Fjeld, 'Structures in Ice Covered Waters', in L. Rey, ed., *Arctic Energy Resources*, pp. 201–216; *Petroleum Review*, Oct. 1989, pp. 524–6.

[78] A. S. Astakhov, A. D. Khaitun and G. E. Subbotin, 'Socioeconomic Aspects of Oil and Gas Development in West Siberia', *Annual Review of Energy* 14 (1989), pp. 118–19. If the temperature is minus 30–35° Celsius, sailors in Arctic conditions stop outside work, and if minus 50, all cranes stop work. See A. A. Meyerhoff, 'The USSR Northern and Far Eastern Coasts: Petroleum Geology and Technology, Mining Activities, and Environmental Factors', working draft prepared for Department of Indian and Northern Affairs, Ottawa, Canada, pp. 208–9; Erik Solem, 'Arctic Resources and their Development', paper presented at the 4th Annual North Sea Conference held by BIEE, London, 5–6 June 1989, p. 8.

[79] According to Arbatov, the cost of one well in the Beaufort Sea is 10–15 times more than in the Gulf of Mexico, and in the Chukotsky Sea it is 25–30 times more. See *Petroleum Review*, Oct. 1989, p. 520. However, it is said that Arbatov's estimates are exaggerated to support his view that oil and gas exploration should be scaled down with greater emphasis placed on energy saving. See *Eastern Bloc Energy*, Nov. 1989, p. 2.

[80] According to Konoplyanik, during 1996–2000 unit oil and gas exploration costs will be respectively 87.5% and 44% of those of 1991–5, and in 2001–2005 will have fallen to 81.2% and 44%. Furthermore, the costs of Arctic exploration in 1991–5 will be only 76% of those of the Caspian Sea for oil and 56% for gas, even though Caspian costs should rise substantially as work proceeds into waters over 200 m deep while most Arctic work will take place in less than 75 m of water. See *Petroleum Review*, Oct. 1989, pp. 521–3, especially Tables 2 and 3; *Eastern Bloc Energy*, Nov. 1989, p. 2.

Secondly, ecological and social problems hindered Soviet offshore development, and Russia could face the same situation. In late 1986 work at D-6 field in the Baltic Sea was suspended because of environmental considerations, and was not resumed for two years, and in March 1989 the Soviet Union decided to suspend further development of the Yamal Peninsula in consideration of environmental damage.[81] These examples reflect the burgeoning of the Green movement within the country. Since ecological accidents, like oil leakage, can happen at any time in Russian offshore exploration and transportation, the ecological factor will be a potential threat to further offshore development.[82] This problem, however, can to some extent be handled by the introduction of clean technology from the West.

During the late 1980s ethnic unrest in Azerbaijan and Armenia confirmed that disruption of essential oil- and gas-equipment production or delay in equipment delivery could compound the difficulties already being experienced by the Soviet energy industry. In 1989 the country's production of oil equipment fell by 15%,[83] since the Baku area was still manufacturing as much as 60% of the country's oil- and gas-field equipment.[84] However, *Russian* offshore development will not be directly affected by this region's ethnic problem.

Third, the unfavourable foreign-investment environment, caused mainly by bureaucratic irresponsibility and sluggishness, restrictions on currency convertibility and an inadequate legal framework, as well as high taxes and lack of proper investment protection, was another obstacle to Soviet offshore development, as it is to Russian development. The country is lagging behind China in dealing with the problem.

Unlike the above constraints, which could be manageable in the long run, the following factors are independent of Russia's intention to accelerate its offshore development. First, low world oil prices will surely be unfavourable to Russian offshore development. In June 1986 the FSU and Japan agreed to reassess their plans to develop the Sakhalin offshore fields, because the oil-price collapse of 1986 had led both sides to lose interest in the project.[85] By contrast, rising world oil prices

---

[81] *Financial Times*, 31 Aug. 1990; *Petroleum Review*, April 1990, p. 194.

[82] According to A. Cherny, director general of Sakhalin Oil and Gas, environmental factors will play a major role because the Sea of Okhotsk is a substantial salmon-fishing area and provides large-scale employment. See *Oil and Gas Journal*, 18 March 1991, p. 33. If oil leakage occurs in Arctic Seas, it is 20–50 times hard to decompose it than in southern latitudes and the ice sheet makes it much more difficult to eliminate. See *Petroleum Review*, Oct. 1989, pp. 521 and 524–6; H. R. Hume *et al.*, 'Arctic Marine Oil Spill Research', in L. Rey, ed., *Arctic Energy Resources* (op. cit., n. 77), pp. 313–341.

[83] *Oil and Gas Journal*, 19 Feb. 1990, p. 26.

[84] Ibid.; *Lloyds List*, 18 Jan. and 23 Jan. 1990; *Financial Times*, 8 March 1990.

[85] *Petroleum Economist*, June 1986, p. 225; *Eastern Bloc Energy*, Aug. 1989, p. 7.

in 1990 rekindled Soviet as well as Japanese interest.[86] Given that Arctic oil cannot be competitive on current world oil markets (during the first half of the 1990s prices hovered far below $20 per barrel) with exploration and production costs alone amounting to over $40 per barrel, current low prices will cause Russia's offshore development to be suspended or delayed.

Secondly, maldistribution of natural gas in the Russian Arctic seas places another burden on Russian planners wanting to promote Arctic offshore development. At present, Russia is more serious about developing giant oil and gas deposits in the north of West Siberia than in its Arctic seas. Why, after all, should priority be given to the development of Russian Arctic offshore gas deposits – suspending meanwhile onshore gas development – in the absence of any supergiant oil-field discoveries there. If the Shtockmanovskoye and Rusanovskoye fields in the Barents and Kara Seas had been supergiants, the timetable for Arctic-seas development would be far more advanced.

Finally, unresolved territorial disputes in offshore areas have been an intractable obstacle to development. Besides the Caspian Sea, where territorial disputes among the four claimants are hampering development, two major territorial problems exist in the Barents Sea (with Norway) and the Sea of Okhotsk (with Japan), and two minor ones in the Bering Sea (with the United States) and the Baltic Sea (with Sweden).[87] Declining crude production and failure to find oil reserves in undisputed areas of the seas will give Russia the pretext it needs to overcome military objections and move into the disputed territories.

3.4 Investment

During the past two decades, capital investment in the energy industry increased 4.8 times and spending on the production of oil and gas grew 5.8 times, while the national income increased 2.2 times.[88] The oil industry absorbed 17% of all industrial investment in the 11th five-year plan (1981–5). In other words, while total investment in the country's industry increased by less than 20%, investment in fuel production grew by 53% to reach 80 billion roubles (in 1984 prices). Of this amount, 50 billion roubles were invested in the oil industry. This amount exceeded the overall increase in investment in oil production for the preceding ten years. Approximately 1 out of every 6 roubles invested in the country's industry in the

[86] *Review of Soviet Oil*, Oct. 1990, p. 84.

[87] For details on these territorial disputes, see Paik, *Russian and Chinese Oil and Gas Policies in Northeast Asia* (op. cit., n. 7), pp. 190–2.

[88] Arbatov *et al.*, *Soviet Energy* (op. cit., n. 57) p. 14, especially Annex Tables 38–43.

1981–5 period went to the national fuel sector (1 out of 10 roubles during 1971–5, and 1 out of 8 roubles in 1976–80).[89]

By 1988 the oil industry absorbed almost 20% of all industrial investment.[90] As shown in Table 3.14, in 1988 it accounted for 49% of investment in the energy industry, while oil constituted only 36.5% of total energy output.[91] This demonstrates that the huge capital investment in the oil industry has been employed inefficiently, a fact confirmed by returns on investment. During 1980–8 capital returns for industry overall have progressively decreased from 1.29 roubles per rouble of investment to 1.06. In the fuel industry the figure has sharply declined from 0.9 to 0.54.[92] This trend cannot be allowed to continue.

Capital investment in the oil and gas industries in 1989–90 remained at the 1988 level of 14 billion roubles. Then, in 1992, it collapsed to 7 billion roubles (in 1988 prices).[93] This suspension of capital investment was inevitable, as the Soviet Union had no capital to invest, and could be interpreted as an actual investment decline in the oil and gas-extraction industry in consideration of rising production costs.

During 1975–89, the average production costs of natural gas increased by one-third and those of coal rose, on the whole, by a half. As for oil, the costs increased more than threefold.[94] (A well-known study by Tretyakova and Heinemier estimated that average production costs increased almost four times during 1970–86.[95]

---

[89] Alexander A. Arbatov, 'Prospects of Creating Joint Ventures dealing with Fuels and Raw Materials in the Context of Economic Restructuring in the USSR', paper presented at the Joint BIEE/SAEE 2-Day Seminar 'Soviet Energy in the New Europe: Joint Ventures and Prospects for Co-operation', London, Sept. 1990; A.A. Arbatov, 'How will the USSR cope with falling output?', *Petroleum Intelligence Weekly*, 1 Jan. 1990, p. 6.

[90] Arild Moe, 'The Future of Soviet Oil Supplies to the West', *Soviet Geography*, March 1991, p. 147. During the same period, total energy investment absorbed 90% of the total growth in Russia's industrial investment, but produced a mere 13% increase in energy output. See *The Economist*, 25 Nov. 1989, p. 116.

[91] Kaser, 'Soviet Energy Production (op. cit., n. 27), p. 326, Table 1.

[92] Arbatov *et al.*, *Soviet Energy* (op. cit., n. 5), Annex, Table 46.

[93] Ilya Leshchinets, 'Capital Requirements – Domestic and Foreign Dimensions', paper presented at the 2nd Annual Russian Oil Conference entitled 'The Russian Oil Industry: Foreign Investment Opportunities', London, 11–12 Feb. 1992.

[94] Eugene M. Khartukov, 'Soviet Energy Price Reform: Its Domestic and International Implications', paper presented at the Joint BIEE/SAEE 2-Day Seminar on Soviet Energy in the New Europe: Joint Ventures and Prospects for Co-operation, London, Sept. 1990.

[95] The average production costs were estimated at 4.56 roubles in 1970, but rose to 17.7 roubles in 1986. See *Soviet Geography*, March 1991, pp. 145–6; Albina Tretyakova and Meredith Heinemier, 'Cost Estimates for the Soviet Oil Industry: 1970 to 1990', CIR Staff Paper 20, Center for International Research, US Bureau of the Census, Washington, DC, June 1986.

Table 3.14: The Soviet Union's capital investment in oil and gas production (billion roubles)

Year	Energy Total	Oil & Gas Total	Oil	Gas
1982	17.7	12.3	9.6	2.7
1983	18.7	13.1	10	3.1
1984	22.2	13.9	10.3	3.6
1985	25.3	15.7	11.5	4.2
1986	27.4	17.6	12.9	4.7
1987	30.1	19.7	14.6	5.1
1988	31.8	20.8	15.3	5.5
1989	36.3	20.9	15.5	5.4
1990		20.7	15.5	5.2

Sources: *Eastern Bloc Energy*, April 1990, p. 2; Thane Gustafson, *Crisis amid Plenty: The Politics of Soviet Energy under Brezhnev and Gorbachev,* Princeton University Press, Princeton, 1989, p. 25; A.A. Arbatov *et al., Soviet Energy: An Insider's Account*, Centre for Global Energy Studies, London, 1991, Annex Table 38.

According to Liefert's study, which pointed out that differential rent and depletion costs are excluded in Tretyakova and Heinemier's study as they base their estimates on average costs, the full cost of producing a unit of oil in the Soviet Union increased sixfold, while that of gas rose only 40%.[96])

For example, the production costs for 1 tonne of oil rose from 13.68 roubles in 1985 to 17.12 roubles in 1988. The total amount of exploitation expenditure increased accordingly from 7.7 billion roubles to 10.3 billion roubles.[97] During the same period capital investment in the oil industry increased from 12.9 billion roubles to 15.3 billion roubles. However, as discussed earlier, capital investment in both the oil and the gas industries in 1989–90 was halted. The actual investment decline in the oil industry despite soaring production costs has been the most

[96] William Mark Liefert, 'The Full Cost of Soviet Oil and Natural Gas Production', *Comparative Economic Studies*, Summer 1988, pp. 1–20.

[97] The proportion of expenditures for MFP (maintaining of formation pressure) and water production makes up about 30% of total expenditure. See L.P. Gujnovcki, 'Some Economical Problems of the USSR Oil Industry', paper presented at the Joint BIEE/SAEE 2-Day Seminar 'Soviet Energy in the New Europe: Joint Ventures and Prospects for Co-operation', London, Sept. 1990.

immediate cause of the current oil-production crisis.[98]

According to the then oil minister Lopukhin, as of March 1992 oil-production costs were 1,650 roubles/tonne, but oil was sold at the state-set price of 650 roubles/tonne.[99] The difference of 1000 roubles/tonne was subsidized by government.[100] This situation deprived enterprises of any incentive to invest in new wells or repair ailing equipment.

Unlike the sagging oil industry, capital investment in the gas industry has paid off. Despite an estimated tripling of gas-transportation costs during the past two decades, extremely low production costs have helped to keep the industry in the black. It was reported that the 1990 profits target was as high as 6.68 billion roubles, with production costs of 2.9 roubles per thousand cubic metres.[101]

However, if the trend of capital-investment decline experienced in 1988–90 continues during the 1990s,[102] the gas industry will face harsh times. In 1991 the industry already became a casualty of falling investment. In fact, investment from the centre was cut by 60% for 1991, and Gazprom and the production associations were unable to make good the deficit from higher rouble prices on the internal Soviet gas market.[103]

A real burden for the industry is that a huge amount of investment is being requested during the 1990s. Gazprom estimates that to finance the planned programme of pipeline construction, 220 billion roubles (at 1991 prices) in investment is needed between 1992 and 2010 plus $13–15 billion of imports of western piping during 1992–2000.[104] The CIS gas-supply network stretching over a distance of

---

[98] In 1989 the oil and gas industries received 12.9 billion roubles, but the figure dropped to 8.6 billion roubles in 1991. See *Financial Times*, 24 July 1992. This is the reason why the Soviet government has agreed on emergency measures to channel 25 billion roubles of extra investment into its ailing oil industry in 1991 to prevent a further collapse of production. See *Financial Times*, 29 Jan. 1991, and 21 Feb. 1991.

[99] *Financial Times*, 19 March 1992.

[100] As of October 1991, the industry is currently subsidized to the tune of 19 billion roubles, and only $16 million of foreign capital investment so far had been forthcoming. See *Financial Times*, 9 Oct. 1991.

[101] Stern, *European Gas Markets* (op. cit., n. 19), pp. 53–4; *Eastern Bloc Energy*, March 1990, p. 2.

[102] Investment was cut back from 10.5 billion roubles in 1988 to 4.9 billion roubles in 1990. See *Eastern Bloc Energy*, May 1992, p. 2.

[103] *Petroleum Economist*, Aug. 1991, p. 12.

[104] *Eastern Bloc Energy*, May 1992, p. 3; *Petroleum Economist*, June 1992, p. 5. For example, the new NGL transportation system, which will replace the NGL line and was explored near Ufa in 1989, is estimated to cost $2 billion and 8 billion roubles. See Paul Davies *et al.*, 'The Challenge of New Pipeline Systems in Russia and the Republics', paper presented at the

some 215,000 km was laid during the past two decades, but pipelines are failing to survive anywhere near as long as their target 25-year lifespan.[105] The single most important reason for this widespread decay is that the Soviets laid pipelines without corrosion protection. Welds and joints, hastily put together as construction teams raced to meet demanding targets, are also key points of weakness.[106]

During the Soviet period the state bore the burden of capital investment in the oil and gas industries. The policy that Russia has pursued so far suggests that capital investment will become the responsibility of the industry.

3.5 Financing, pricing and prospects

According to Professor Gueorgi Matyukhin, chairman of the Central Bank of the RSFSR, the power sector, including oil, gas and coal production facilities, needs a capital investment in 1991–95 of 193 billion roubles.[107] Such funding is out of the question. Amidst a rocketing deficit and hyperinflation, resulting in capital investment in 1992 being cut by 46%,[108] the government cannot afford to increase investment in the energy industry.

In the current situation, one way to revitalize the country's crisis-ridden oil industry would seem to be oil-price liberalization, but the steps already taken by the government show that this will be achieved only gradually. According to Eugene

---

International Conference on the 'New Realities in Pipeline Design, Construction and Operation', London, 28–29 Jan. 1992. Besides this, it seems that the cost of pipeline reconstruction will be enormous during the 1990s with some 3.5 billion roubles expected to be invested in upgrading the system in the first half of the 1990s. See *Petroleum Review*, Dec. 1990, p. 617.

[105] According to A. Baiko, department chief of gas transportation, Gazprom, as of 1993, 37% of the pipelines are up to 10 years old, 58% are 10 to 20 years old and 25% are over 20 years old. Plans have been made to replace 40% of those that are worn out and damaged by corrosion. Work is to be carried out at an annual rate of 1,500 km, and so far the objective has been met. See *Proceedings of the 2nd International Conference on 'Opportunities for Trade and Investment in the Russian and CIS Gas Industry'*, London, 11–12 Oct. 1993, p. 45.

[106] *Petroleum Economist*, June 1992, p. 5; P. Davies *et al.*, *The Challenge of New Pipeline Systems in Russia and the Republics* (op. cit., n. 104).

[107] By this investment in the oil-production sector more than 100 low-production deposits located in northern parts of West Siberia would be put into operation, and drilling 184 million oil wells and putting 70,000 on stream could be implemented. See Gueorgi Matyukhin, paper (with no title) presented at the International Conference on 'Eastern and Central Europe: The New Energy Picture', Budapest, 4 March 1991.

[108] As of September 1992, the budget deficit stands around 7% of GNP, or at 800 billion roubles, and hyperinflation is running at 4.4% a week, or more than 20% a month. See *Financial Times*,15 and 23 Sept. 1992.

Table 3.15: Russia: changes in oil price (roubles/tonne)

Year		Average oil prices	Average production costs
1986		24.89	14.88
1990		25.70	21.92
1991		70	
1992	Jan.–May	350	
	June–Sept.	1,800 –2,200	
	Sept.–Jan. 93	4,000 –5,000	
1993	Feb.	9,000	

Note: According to a paper entitled 'Investment in the Oil and Gas Industry of the Former USSR: Possibilities, Conditions, and Problems', prepared by Institute for Economic Strategies (anonymous), average oil production costs in 1985 were 13.7 roubles/tonne, and 23–5 roubles/tonne in 1991 (but later it changed).
Sources: 1986 and 1990: CIS (formerly *Review of Soviet Oil*), Feb. 1992, p. 44; 1991–2: *Financial Times*; 1993: *Post-Soviet Geography*, June 1993, p. 350.

Khartukov, until the end of the 1980s, Soviet domestic prices for fuel and energy were revised twice, during the price reforms of 1965–7 and 1980–2. The latter raised average enterprise prices for crude oil by 135%, from 10.6 up to 24.8 roubles/tonne, and for oil products by an average of 60%.[109]

However, during 1975–89 average oil-production costs increased more than threefold. Consequently the actual profitability of the Soviet oil-producing industry dropped by the end of the 1980s to 3.6% (in relation to fixed assets) as against the normative rate of 36.5%. The after-tax ROR (rate of return) of the gas industry, which carries a burden of turnover tax, went down to 2.4% in 1989 as against 18.8%, established as the industry's norm at the beginning of 1982. In short, declining profitability lowered further by rising production costs and frozen domestic prices of the main fossil fuels made a new energy-price reform inevitable.

As shown in Table 3.15, as a result of four successive price reforms, average oil prices jumped from 25.7 roubles/tonne in 1990 to 4,000 roubles ($20)/tonne in September 1992 (less than $3/barrel). Then, in February 1993, the crude-oil price was raised to 9,000 roubles/tonne. Just prior to this price change, the average selling price for crude oil in January 1993 was 13,500 roubles/tonne ($1 = 550 roubles) – around $3.4 per barrel, or under 20% of the world market price. At some reasonable

[109] Similar wholesale prices for natural (free and associated) gas went up, on average, by 33% (to 6–35 roubles/1000 cm, depending on production costs). See Eugene M. Khartukov, 'Soviet energy price reform' (op. cit., n. 94).

estimate of the purchasing-power parity rate of the rouble, this translates into a price of around $9–10 per barrel, or some 55–75% of world market prices.[110]

As for gas, the prices were adjusted twice in 1992. A five-fold increase was made on 1 January, and then a six-fold increase to 1,600–1,800 roubles per thousand cubic metres was made on 18 May. During the year, there was a fourteen-fold increase in the price for gas, while Russia's retail price index increased about 17.5 times.[111] In early 1993 the base price for gas rose to 3,600 roubles, from 1,100 roubles per thousand cubic metres (established in May 1992). However, the price of gas sold to the population remained highly subsidized, even though it more than doubled from 260 to 600 roubles per thousand cubic metres. As of 1993, the domestic price of gas (for industrial consumers) is only 10% of the world market price. At a more reasonable estimate of the purchasing-power parity rate, it could be put at 25% of the world market price.[112]

Oil and gas prices are still far below world market prices. A dilemma that the Russian government has to solve is how simultaneously to minimize the impact of oil- and gas-price increases on its collapsing economy and to revitalize its energy industry. The burden of investment in the energy industry will not to be alleviated until energy prices are brought to world levels.

At present, one option is to utilize foreign investment. According to a study by Jonathan P. Stern, by May 1993 out of 93 oil and gas joint ventures in Russia and the other CIS states, in various stages of development from study to full production, slightly more than one-third had progressed beyond the study and negotiation phases to an actual agreement. Of these, only five have seen actual investment expenditures exceeding $100 million – a reasonable benchmark for projects that will yield significant volumes of oil and gas in the future.[113]

Another study by the US International Trade Commission revealed that over 40 joint-venture oil and gas projects operating in Russia have generated $200–300 million in foreign investment as of spring 1993.[114] But this figure is relatively small

[110] Sagers, 'The Energy Industries of the Former USSR' (op. cit., n. 22), p. 350. According to an IEA study, by the end of 1993 oil and gas had reached 30% and 20% of world market prices respectively. See International Energy Agency, *Russian Energy Prices, Taxes and Costs 1993*, IEA, Paris, 1994, p. 14.

[111] By the end of 1992, half of the gas-producing enterprises in Russia were running at a considerable loss. See Sagers, 'The Energy Industries of the Former USSR' (op. cit., n. 22), p. 379.

[112] Ibid., pp. 379–380.

[113] Stern, *Oil and Gas in the Former Soviet Union* (op. cit., n. 26), pp. 29–39.

[114] US International Trade Commission, *Trade and Investment Patterns in the Crude Petroleum and Natural Gas Sectors of the Energy Producing States of the Former Soviet Union*, Publication 2656, June 1993.

given the vast amounts of capital needed to revitalize industry. Risks such as lack of a legal and regulatory framework, an uncertain taxation regime, oil- and gas-price controls, uncertain property rights, unclear jurisdiction, oil-export controls, currency restrictions, differences in business practices and political uncertainty are stumbling blocks to foreign investment.[115] Unless and until macro-economic problems are addressed satisfactorily, it will be very difficult for the Russian energy industry to become efficient.

3.6 Alternative energy resources

If there is any alternative to oil it has to be gas. The Long-Term Energy Programme, announced in 1984 and covering the period 1980–2000, saw natural gas acting as an 'energy bridge' between the present era of large-scale liquid-fuel use and a future energy balance in which open-cast coal and nuclear power would dominate.[116]

Isabel Gorst has pointed out that the role of gas within the Programme has been completely altered for a number of reasons rooted in the events of 1986, such as Gorbachev's economic reconstruction plans under the banner of perestroika, the accident at Chernobyl nuclear reactor 4 on 26 April in that year and the collapse of oil prices. She saw that the energy bridge provided by natural gas would be extended much further into the twenty-first century than originally envisaged, and added that only a few steps have so far been taken across it.[117]

According to a new long-term plan drawn up by the Gazprom Kontsern in 1991, gas production will reach 1.12 tcm in 2000, 1.26 tcm in 2010, 1.3 tcm in 2020 and 1.36 tcm in 2030. If implemented as planned, gas could meet as much as 55–60% of the country's energy need, compared to the current 40%.[118] At the end of 1993, when Russia's Ministry of Fuel and Energy announced a preliminary draft of its new long-term energy plan, the figures became 680–95 bcm in 1995 and 820–60 bcm in 2010.[119]

The readjustment was necessary. Given that the size of the 'gas bubble' – defined as production that remains shut in because of lack of markets – was increasing

---

[115] Ibid., Chapter 3.

[116] Stern, *European Gas Markets* (op. cit., n. 19), p. 51. For the Long-Term Energy Programme, see David Wilson, *Soviet Energy to 2000*, Economist Intelligence Unit, special report 231, 1986, pp. 6–13.

[117] *Petroleum Review*, Dec. 1990, pp. 616–18; *Petroleum Economist*, July 1991, pp. 18–19.

[118] *Eastern Bloc Energy*, Aug. 1991, pp. 2–4. However, the figures were readjusted downwards in the new 'conception of energy policy' prepared by the Russian government to 850 bcm in 1995 and 1.05 tcm in 2010. See *Eastern Bloc Energy*, Aug. 1992, p. 2.

[119] *Eastern Bloc Energy*, Dec. 1993, pp. 2–5 and Jan. 1994, pp. 2–6.

rapidly in 1993–4,[120] the decline in gas production in the same period was determined by domestic and international demand rather than by production failures. Russia's gas industry has enough strength to overcome the current crisis and could lead the way for other sectors in the future.

The prospects for Russia's oil industry look much less promising, as suggested above. Robert E. Ebel has predicted that oil-production levels in Russia will not return to the heights of 1987–8 before the end of the century.[121] Oil seems unlikely to maintain its attraction as an earner of hard currency, and natural gas is likely to assume the dominant role. Few have challenged this prediction. It does not necessarily follow, however, that oil's role as a hard-currency earner will disappear.

Turning to the coal industry, the verdict here is even more depressing than for the oil industry. The Russian minister of fuels and energy has described the situation as, 'worse than in any other energy sector',[122] and warned that those mines considered uneconomic must close if the industry is to rationalize itself.[123] In 1993, for example, the cost of coal production at certain enterprises began to exceed revenues.[124] Is Russia's coal industry worth financing? The answer is not positive.

The nuclear industry may have a slightly different story. The April 1986 Chernobyl accident and the December 1988 earthquake in Armenia leading to the closure of the Metsamor nuclear power plant in early 1989 were major setbacks for the Soviet nuclear-power industry. None the less Russia has explored the possibility of expansion. A bold but achievable vision for the industry was provided by Russia's premier Chernomyrdin in December 1992. But the Russian government is still delaying taking a firm line on the industry.[125]

If it decides to undertake ambitious plans for nuclear-power expansion despite the problem of funding and local protests against the siting of plants (coupled with a strong environmental movement), it may be because of concern about its export earnings. The explanation by Robert E. Ebel is as follows:

> Given the continuing difficulties with oil and coal supply, if nuclear is not a viable option, much of the country's new power generating capacity will be based on burning natural gas, thus cutting into exportable surpluses. Rejuvenation of the nuclear power industry assumes more importance to ensure that a surplus of gas is available for export.[126]

---

[120] Stern, *The Russian Gas 'Bubble'* (op. cit., n. 19).
[121] Ebel, *Energy Choices in Russia* (op. cit., n. 47), p. 126.
[122] Stern, *Oil and Gas in the Former Soviet Union* (op. cit., n. 26), p. 22.
[123] Ebel, *Energy Choices in Russia* (op. cit., n. 47), p. 93.
[124] Ibid., p. 88.
[125] Ibid., pp. 65–85.
[126] Ibid., pp. 128–9.

Russia has vast energy resources, including renewable ones. As the country has insufficient capital for the development of its four main energy sources, and domestic energy demand is currently quite depressed and seems unlikely to grow substantially in the coming years, there is no strong incentive to support a rapid development of renewable energy resources. For the time being therefore Russia will concentrate on its main energy industries. At the present time gas is Russia's only energy hope, but if much greater emphasis is placed on conservation and improved efficiency during the 1990s, the burdens carried by the energy industry could be substantially alleviated.

3.7 Conclusion

The authors of Russia's new energy plan itemized the causes of Russia's energy-industry crisis as follows: lack of an economic mechanism for ensuring the rational use of energy, with the result that consumption per unit of national income is twice as great as in the leading West European countries; and the chronic shortage of capital investment and unrealistic prices, accompanied by the steady growth of fuel exports and overconsumption of artificially cheap fuel on the internal market.[127]

In the current political and economic situation, Russia cannot afford to pay serious attention to oil and gas development in the Far East, except the Sakhalin region. Development of the RFE's oil and gas has been discussed for over two decades, but no significant development has yet taken place (this will be discussed later, in Chapter 7). Consequently, the RFE has become an oil importer rather than an exporter despite its huge oil and gas potential. Until the collapse of the Soviet empire, most of the RFE's oil imports came from West Siberia. Thereafter, even the delivery of West Siberian oil has declined significantly as the RFE could not pay for it. Further delays in oil and gas development in the RFE will simply prolong its status as an oil importer.

The implications of the current crisis for oil and gas development in the coming years are twofold: first Russia cannot look eastwards. Energy planners have always given top priority to European Russia where the core of its oil and gas industries and massive consumption are located. This trend seems likely to continue.

Secondly Russia's lack of investment capacity offers two choices for Russia in its policy towards oil and gas development in the RFE: acceleration of development in cooperation with foreign partners or delay in development until the next century. The former would be Russia's preference, but many stumbling blocks would have to be overcome. In Chapters 5 and 7, this study will discuss Russian policy towards the RFE's oil and gas development and the megaprojects that will change its supply and demand structure.

---

[127] *Eastern Bloc Energy*, Dec. 1993, p. 3.

Chapter 4

Chinese oil and gas: resources, production and industries

As economic development progresses in China, a more diversified energy mix becomes necessary. Coal is the principal energy source, representing 71–4% of energy production and 72–6% of energy consumption in the past decade, as shown in Figures 4.1 (a) and (b). The dominance of coal in China's energy balance seems unlikely to be challenged in the foreseeable future. None the less, the roles of oil and gas as important energy sources as economic development speeds up are now recognized.

It is inconceivable, however, that oil and gas can make a major contribution to China's energy sector in the foreseeable future, despite the country's vaunted oil and gas reserves. Without a substantial improvement in its stagnating oil production and poor gas production, economic development could be seriously restricted by oil and gas shortages. This chapter will study China's potential oil and gas reserves, problems in oil and gas development, the burden imposed by unbalanced investment and controlled prices, and the energy alternatives to oil.

4.1 Potential reserves of oil and gas

According to the Ministry of Energy, China has a total of 246 sedimentary basins covering 5.5 million sq. km, of which 4.2 million sq. km are onshore and 1.3 million sq. km are offshore. Total oil and gas reserves are estimated at 78.75 bt, of which 62.6 bt are onshore and 16.7 bt are offshore, and 33.3 trillion cubic metres (1,176.6 tcf) respectively.[1] These figures seem to refer to a total of A + B + C1 + C2 + Prognosticated (D1 + D2). In Chinese terms, as shown in Table 1.4, they combine class I (Tanming Chuliang), class II (Kongzhi Chuliang), class III (Yuce Chuliang), class IV Qianzai (Ziyuanliang) and class V Tuice (Ziyuanliang). Here the prognosticated onshore oil reserves are estimated at 62.7 bt (460 billion bbl).[2]

[1] Ministry of Energy, People's Republic of China, *Energy in China*, Ministry of China, Beijing, 1990, p. 19; Zhou Xiaoqian, '40 Years of Energy Industry of China', *Zhongguo Nengyuan* (Energy of China) 2 (1991), pp. 26–7. The Ministry of Geology and Mineral Resources put these figures at 81.4 bt and 51 tcm respectively. See *China Oil, Gas & Petrochemical (China OGP)* 1: 5 (1 Aug. 1993), p. 3.

[2] *China Petroleum Investment Guide*, China OGP and AP Energy Business Publications, Singapore, 1994, p. 75 (hereafter, *China Petroleum Investment Guide*).

Figure 4.1: China's energy production and consumption balances, selected years

(a) Energy production

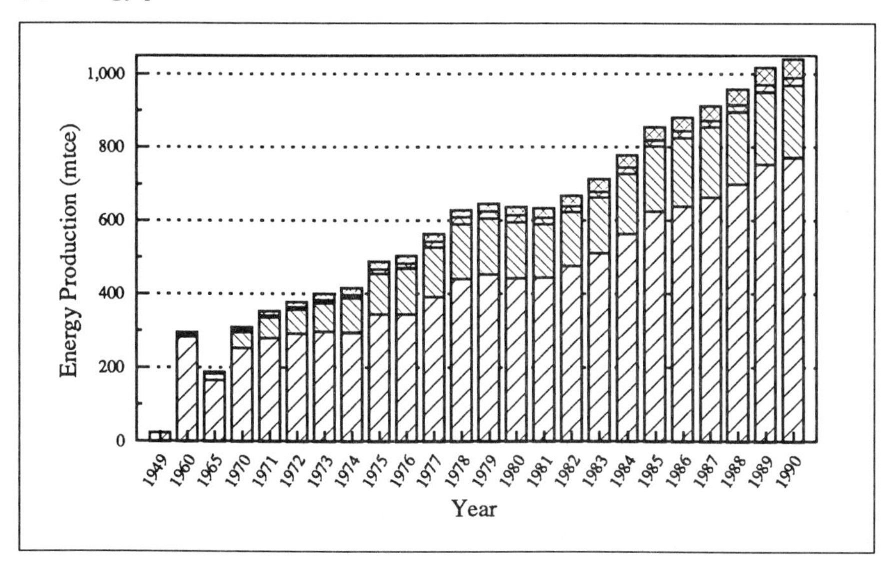

(b) Energy consumption

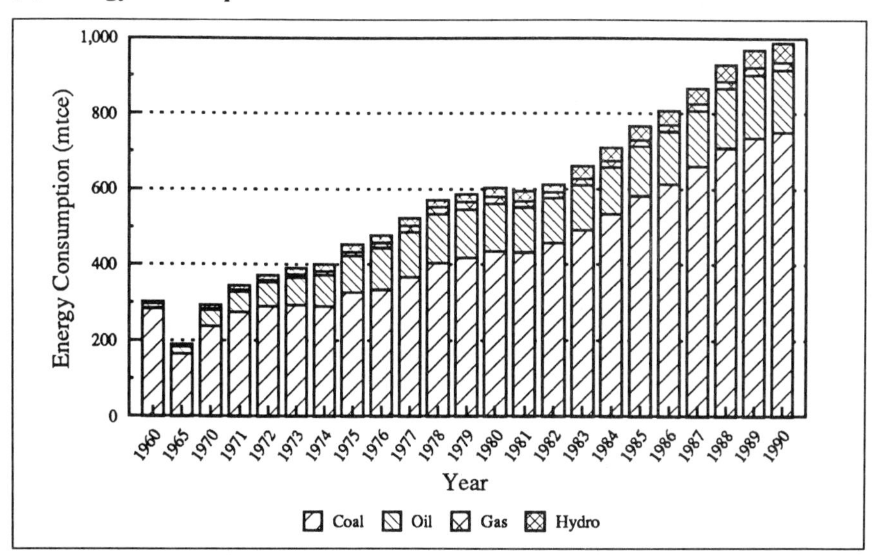

Source: Zhongguo Nengyuan Tongji Nianjian 1991, p. 135

Somewhat different figures are also suggested. According to Zhou Feng-Qi of the Energy Research Institute, State Planning Commission, oil resources range from 60 to 80 bt and there are dozens of trillions of cubic metres of gas.[3] Liu Guangding suggests that hydrocarbon reserves in place in China are roughly estimated as 30–60 bt.[4]

Two articles published in the monthly Chinese energy journal *Zhongguo Nungyuan* (Energy of China) confirm that the figures for class I (Tanming Chuliang) are not high. One put proven oil and gas reserves at 3.27 bt and 10.23 tcm respectively as of 1989,[5] and the other estimated oil reserves at 2.199 bt as of 1990 (the ratio of reserves to production is currently around 16, a decline from 18.6 in 1985).[6] The difficulty of establishing exact figures for Chinese oil and gas reserves is expressed by *China Daily*'s comment that 'exact figures on oil and gas reserves verified in 1991 remained secret'.[7]

The Chinese are not, however, reluctant to release figures on Xinjiang province, especially the Tarim Basin's oil and gas reserves. In an interview with *World Oil* in late 1989, Dr Wang Tao, president of CNPC (China National Petroleum Corp.), suggested that a third of all potential oil resources and half of total gas resources in China lie in the far west.[8] (Here 'potential' seems to mean class III.) In the early 1990s Chinese geologists estimated that geological reserves in the Tarim Basin, discovered on 22 September 1984, comprise as much as 74 billion bbl of oil and 283 tcf of natural gas, equal to about one-sixth and one-quarter of national totals.[9] Recently, *China OGP* reported that the Tarim Basin, similar in size to France, has estimated crude resources of 19.76 bt and natural-gas resources of 8.39 tcm.[10]

According to CNPC, by the year 2000, Xinjiang's recoverable oil reserves will total 14 billion bbl (including heavy oil), compared to current total reserves of

---

[3] Zhou Feng Qi, 'The Status and Prospects of Energy in China to 2005', *Energy Exploration & Exploitation* 7: 5 (1989), p. 307.

[4] Liu Guangding, 'An Overview of Geophysical Activities in China', *Geophysics: The Leading Edge of Exploration*, March 1988, p. 23.

[5] Zhou Dadi, 'Potential Crisis of China's Energy', *Energy of China* 3 (1992), p. 8.

[6] Planning Division of Ministry of Energy, 'Main Problems in the Developmental Process of 7th FYP of Energy Industry of China and the Later 10 Years Prospect of this Century', *Energy of China* 3 (1991), p. 7.

[7] This report said that the oil reserves verified in 1991 had exceeded the government plan by 10%, and gas, by 2.7 times. See *China Daily*, 15 Jan. 1992.

[8] *World Oil*, Jan. 1990, p. 28.

[9] *World Oil*, April 1992, p. 75; *Petroleum News*, July/Aug. 1989, p. 33; *Petroleum Economist*, June 1991, p. 17.

[10] *China OGP* 3: 1 (1 Jan. 1995), p. 3.

22–5 billion bbl.[11] Apart from the figures provided by the above-mentioned Chinese organizations, more inflated ones put the Basin's identified oil reserves in a range of 18–18.45 bt.[12] It remains to be seen how large the Tarim Basin's oil potential is. Seismic surveys and recent wildcat successes suggest that one structure, Tazhong, is more than 2.5 times the size of the largest structure at Daqing, China's largest oil field to date (for further details, see Chapter 7).[13]

As for offshore oil and gas reserves, recently the China National Offshore Oil Corp. (CNOOC) revealed that China offshore reserves are 1.2 bt and gas reserves, 180 bcm.[14] In the early 1990s CNOOC suggested figures for oil and gas reserves of 870 mt and 133 bcm respectively (these seem to be recoverable resources).[15] Chinese newspapers have reported some details about the reserves in offshore subregions. By the end of 1989, a total of 6.4 bt had been estimated in Bohai Sea,[16] and in 1990, East China Sea's oil reserves were estimated at 4 bt.[17] One report said that an initial geological survey had found that China's offshore deposits of oil and gas account for one-third of its total reserves.[18] Whether that is so remains to be seen.

Often quoted estimates by Western scholars for total continental petroleum resources are 63.8 bt (469 billion bbl) of oil and 30 tcm (1,059 tcf) of gas.[19] These suggest that Chinese figures are somewhat overestimated. At the end of the 1970s A.A. Meyerhoff and J.O. Willums put the onshore petroleum potential at 42 billion bbl. The breakdown is as follows: 4.3 billion bbl (produced) 15 billion bbl (proved), 5 billion bbl (probable) and 18 billion bbl (potential). They estimated 'reasonable' offshore reserves at 30 billion bbl (here 'reasonable' seems to mean class III).[20]

As regards gas reserves, Meyerhoff and Willums assign 200 tcf of ultimate recoverable gas to onshore and 100 tcf to offshore, but added that the figures may be conservative. As shown in Table 4.1, Hills put the estimated remaining reserves at 1.8 bt. According to a World Bank report, China's recoverable reserves of onshore

---

[11] *China Business Review*, March–April, 1990, p. 14.

[12] *Japan Petroleum and Energy Trends*, 12 July 1991, pp. 8–9; *Hong Kong Standard*, 1 Dec. 1990.

[13] *Energy Compass* (weekend review), 26 Oct. 1990.

[14] *China OGP* 3: 1 (1 Jan. 1995), p. 4.

[15] *China Daily*, 21 Oct. 1991; *South China Morning Post*, 11 Nov. 1991.

[16] *China Daily*, 29 Oct. 1990.

[17] *Ta Kung Pao*, 3 Sept. 1990.

[18] *China Daily*, 19 July 1990.

[19] Geological surveys of over 300 sedimentary basins onshore, covering 4.5 million sq. km have identified 170 potentially oil-bearing structures. See *China Business Review*, March–April, 1990, p. 6.

[20] *Offshore*, Jan. 1979, pp. 54–6.

Table 4.1: Estimates of oil and gas reserves in China (bt/bcm)

Region	Oil			Gas		
	Original recoverable reserves	Cumulative production	Remaining recoverable reserves	Associated gas reserves	Non-associated gas	Total reserves
Northeast[1]	1.32	0.59	0.73	25	–	25
North[2]	0.46	0.08	0.38	5	–	5
East[3]	0.41	0.161	0.249	10	3.5	13.5
Central-south	0.09	0.01	0.08	2.5	–	2.5
Northwest	0.4	0.04	0.36	15	–	15
Southwest[4]	0.013	0.001	0.012	0.5	70	70.5
Total	2.693	0.882	1.811	58	73.5	131.5

Notes:
1 Includes Daqing and Liaohe fields.
2 Includes Renqiu and Dagang fields.
3 Includes Shengli field.
4 Includes Sichuan gas field.
5 Original recoverable oil reserves seem to be Class I.
Source: Peter Hills, *The Development of the Petroleum Industry in the People's Republic of China*, International Labor Office, Washington, DC, 1987, p. 23.

oil have been estimated at 5.5 bt (40 billion bbl) by international experts, and much higher, at 8–15 bt, by Chinese experts. CNOOC estimates offshore at 2.7–10 bt.[21]

The US Geological Survey estimated identified reserves of oil at 31.4 billion bbl as of 1990 and put undiscovered (recoverable) oil reserves at between 18.4 and 87.2 billion bbl, with the most likely amount being 32 billion bbl. In the case of gas, the Survey estimated identified reserves at 5.25 tcm and put undiscovered reserves at between 16.52 tcm and 69.03 tcm, with 27.96 tcm as the most likely.[22] BP statistics put proved Chinese oil reserves at 3.2 bt (2.4% of the world total), with the ratio of reserves to produced at around 23:1. As for gas reserves, they were estimated at 1 tcm, only 0.8% of the world total, and the ratio of reserves to produced at 67.3:1.[23]

[21] World Bank, 'The Energy Sector', Annex 3 to 'China Long-Term Development Issues and Options', World Bank, Washington, DC, 1985, p. 111.
[22] Charles D. Masters, David H. Root and Emil D. Attanasi, 'World Resources of Crude Oil and Gas', *Thirteenth World Petroleum Congress Proceedings 4: Reserves, Management, Finance, and General*, John Wiley & Sons, Chichester, 1992, pp. 52–5.
[23] *BP Statistical Review of World Energy*, 1992.

Petro Asian Business Report put China's onshore remaining recoverable reserves as of 1993 at 24 billion bbl of oil and condensate and 29.5 tcf of gas (in 1983 the figures were 32 billion bbl and 34 tcf). Original total reserves, or ultimate recovery, defined as cumulative production plus estimated reserves of existing discoveries, are estimated at 43 billion bbl of liquids and 53 tcf of gas (1983 figures: 41 billion bbl and 44 tcf).[24]

The scale of Chinese oil and gas reserves cannot be compared with that of the Russian Federation. For example, as of 1991, Tyumen province alone had 10 gas fields with reserves of over 1 tcm,[25] while in 1994 the whole of China had 8 basins with prospective gas reserves exceeding 1 tcm.[26] Even though China has bragged about its oil and gas reserve potential in untapped or undeveloped areas, like the Tarim Basin and the East China Sea, it remains to be seen whether China's last frontier-area reserves prove to be another Persian Gulf, as the country has hoped.

4.2 China's oil and gas production

A Chinese energy expert, David Fridley, pointed to declining real prices, rising taxes and production costs, spiralling losses, a high debt burden, insufficient investment, low productivity and low efficiency as the major problems facing China's energy industries.[27] When it comes to upstream oil and gas, stagnation of oil production and the relatively small scale of gas production account for the major problems.

4.2.1 Oil production

According to the China Oil and Natural Gas Corp.'s development plan for the eighth five-year plan (1991–5), published in February 1991, output of crude oil in 1995 will be 145 mt, a substantial scale-down from the original target of 175 mt.[28] It

[24] *China Petroleum Investment Guide 1994*, pp. 75, 79 (Fig. 15) and 83 (Fig. 19).

[25] *Oil and Gas Journal*, 6 Jan. 1992, p. 30.

[26] Tarim Basin's and Sichuan Basin's prospective gas reserves are over 5 tcm; and six sedimentary basins, East China Sea, Yinggehai, Bohai Bay, Southeast Qiong, Junggar and Zhujiangkou, have over 1 tcm of prospective gas reserves. See Shi Xunzhi, 'Present Situation and Forecast of Natural Gas Exploitation and Utilization in China', paper presented at the International Conference on Northeast Asian Natural Gas Pipeline, convened by National Pipeline Research Society of Japan, 3 March 1995, Tokyo, p. 4.

[27] David Fridley, *China's Energy Outlook*, East–West Center, Honolulu, March 1991, p. 38.

[28] Si Bo, 'Strategic Plan for China's Oil Industry (1991–95)', *China Market* 5 (1991), p. 26; Xin Dingguo, 'China Energy Security in the 1990s', paper presented at Specialist Group Meeting on Energy Security Issues in the Pacific Region, Minerals and Energy Forum, Pacific Economic Cooperation Forum, Seoul, 23–5 July 1991.

Table 4.2: Crude production in China's main fields (mt)

Area	1980	1985	1988	1990	1991	1992	1993
Daqing	51.501	55.289	55.703	55.622	55.62	55.66	55.9
Shengli	18.318	27.031	33.303	33.506	33.55	33.46	32.7
Liaohe	5.091	9.002	12.584	13.602	13.7	13.58	14.2
Xinjiang[1]	3.906	4.994	6.15	6.801	7.02	7.3	7.6
Zhongyuan		5.501	7.221	6.3	6.1	5.81	5.5
Huabei	18.935	10.311	6.12	5.35	5	4.8	4.6
Dagang	2.909	3.651	4.22	3.83	3.8	3.9	4.05
Jilin	1.764	2.13	3.151	3.55	3.41	3.42	3.34
Henan	2.309	2.432	2.57	2.52	2.38	2.13	2.13
Changqing	1.369	1.456	1.417	1.465	1.35	1.64	1.8
Jiangsu	0.309	0.514	0.72	0.855	0.86	0.87	0.86
Qinghai	0.151	0.199	0.64	0.808	0.86	1.05	1.08
Yumen	0.583	0.058	0.528	0.546	0.69	1.05	0.44
Jianghan	1.041	1.024	1.017	0.83	0.73	0.76	0.81
Sichuan	0.098	0.117	0.119	0.131	0.13	0.14	0.15
Total (incl. offshore)	105.8	124.9	137	138.3	139.8	142	144

Note: [1]Includes all producing fields in this autonomous region, except Tarim and Turfan–Hami.
Sources: *Zhongguo Nengyuan Tongji Nianjian 1989*, p. 127; and *1991*, p. 113; *China Petroleum Investment Guide 1994*, p. 84; *BP Statistical Review of World Energy 1990* and *1994*.

was based on an assumption that the production targets of 15.7 mt from Xinjiang region (5 mt from Tarim, 2 mt from Turpan-Hami and 8.7 mt from the Jungar Basin) and 8 mt from offshore by 1995 would be achieved, and output decline in old fields would be compensated.[29] The ambitious target of 200 mt by 2000 has also been scrapped, replaced by a more modest 175 mt/year.[30]

Production stagnation is the main reason why China has revised its original production target. Oil production reached over 100 mt in 1978 and 131 mt in 1986. It then took five years to achieve 140 mt. In 1988–91, as shown in Table 4.2, only

[29] *Asian Oil and Gas*, Feb. 1991, p. 7; *China Daily*, 22 Sept. 1991. In the case of Turpan–Hami Basin, CNPC was asked to double the target. See *China Daily*, 27 Nov. 1991.
[30] Si Bo, 'Strategic Plan for China's Oil Industry (1991–95)' (op. cit. n. 28), p. 26; *OPEC Bulletin*, June 1992, p. 69.

3 mt of production increase was achieved. In 1994 oil production reached 145.8 mt, of which onshore production amounted to 95.6% (139.4 mt).[31]

As a result the goal of 145 mt of crude-oil production in 1995 was achieved one year earlier than planned: surely good news for China, though it does not necessarily mean that the problem of stagnation in oil production has been resolved. Crude-oil output has declined year by year since 1986, from more than 10 mt in the record year of 1985. In 1989 and 1990 respectively, annual increases of only 0.59 and 0.67 mt were recorded. During 1991–4, the annual production increase was slightly improved, by 2 mt (but the increase rate was merely 1.4–1.5%).

The economy grew by 13% in 1993 and 12% in 1994, and is projected to grow by 9–10% in 1995,[32] and so an earlier projection that oil production must increase by 5 mt/year in order to keep up with demand[33] was too conservative. And in the current situation, even this figure looks difficult to achieve. Even if it's met, it would be far short of China's fast increasing oil consumption. Oil consumption reached 143.3 mt in 1993; the estimated figure for 1994 is 160 mt; and 183 mt is projected for 1995.[34]

Even if projected production of 151 mt in 1995 is realized,[35] there would be a shortage of 22 mt. If the Chinese government continues to exercise its controls on imports, introduced by the price and distribution reform enforced on 1 May 1994,[36] the projected figures will have to be changed. (After the reform was introduced, crude-oil imports were scaled down to 10.5 mt, from the projected 20 mt in 1994.[37]) As currently China's oil production cannot satisfy demand, however, most of the supply and demand gap will have to be covered by imports eventually. For example, projected oil consumption of 173 mt in 1995 is close to China's revised oil-production target of 175 mt in 2000. Given the lack of hard currency, the creeping oil-production increase alongside galloping demand threatens to burden China's economic development.

4.2.2 Gas production

Natural gas has been largely neglected in China. Production represents around 2–3% of total energy consumption, compared with Asia's average of 8–9%. Although

[31] *China OGP* 3: 1 (1 Jan. 1995), p. 2.

[32] *China OGP* 2: 24 (15 Dec. 1994), p. 1; *China OGP* 3: 1 (1 Jan. 1995), p. 2; *BP Statistical Review of World Energy*, June 1994, p. 7.

[33] To achieve it, net additions to reserves of at least 44–51 million bbl/year are needed to offset natural declines in mature fields. See *Oil and Gas Journal*, 28 Sept. 1992, p. 23.

[34] *China OGP* 3: 1 (1 Jan 1995), p. 2.

[35] *China OGP* 2: 24 (15 Dec. 1994), p. 1.

[36] For details on the May 1994 reform and its impact, see *China OGP* 2: 10 (15 May 1994), pp. 1–2; *China OGP* 2: 11 (1 June 1994), pp. 1–2.

[37] *China OGP* 3: 2 (15 Jan. 1995), p. 2.

Table 4.3: China: gas production by field (bcm)

Area	1980	1985	1988	1990	1991	1992	1993
Sichuan	6.278	5.542	5.938	6.427	6.49	6.5	6.79
Daqing	3.395	2.5	2.226	2.247	2.27	2.287	2.23
Shengli	1.421	1.142	1.419	1.439	1.44	1.443	1.37
Liaohe	1.794	1.497	1.637	1.748	1.76	1.772	1.76
Zhongyuan		0.574	1.288	1.351	1.27	1.22	1.15
Huabei		0.207	0.209	0.248	0.304	0.284	0.27
Xinjiang[1]	0.353	0.546	0.461	0.502	0.55	0.675	0.84
Dagang	0.8	0.57	0.391	0.354	0.36	0.371	0.35
Henan	0.026	0.044	0.041	0.038	0.036	0.04	0.04
Jilin	0.091	0.076	0.097	0.098	0.13	0.168	0.2
Changqing	0.012	0.023	0.022	0.027	0.048	0.051	0.05
Jianghan	0.02	0.026	0.06	0.076	0.073	0.082	0.08
Yumen	0.015	0.016	0.013	0.013	0.06	0.03	0.01
Jiangsu	0.032	0.041	0.04	0.038	0.036	0.03	0.03
Qinghai	0.008	0.005	0.033	0.051	0.07	0.052	0.05
Total	12.2	11.5	12.6	13.2	13.4	13.6	14.6

Note: [1]Includes all producing fields in this autonomous region, except Tarim and Turfan–Hami.

Source: *Zhongguo Nengyuan Tongji Nianjian 1989*, p. 127; and *1991*, p. 113; *China Petroleum Investment Guide 1994*, p. 84; *BP Statistical Review of World Energy 1990* and *1994*.

crude-oil production rose by 30% in the 1980s, gas production fell sharply, and at the end of the 1980s it had recovered only to the peak achieved a decade earlier.

In 1994 gas production amounted to 16.6 bcm, but China aims at producing 20–2 bcm in 1997, and 25–30 bcm by 2000.[38] As shown in Table 4.3, as of 1993 there were two groups of gas fields producing over 2 bcm, and five major gas fields accounted for over four-fifths of China's total production. The largest Sichuan gas-field group alone accounted for over 43% of total production in 1993, with annual production running at around 6.5 bcm. Sichuan's importance is heightened by the fact that it has the highest ratio (90%) of commercial sales to production and accounts for more than 60% of national sales. Nationally an average of 700–1,060

[38] Shi Xunzhi, 'Present Situation and Forecast of Natural Gas Exploitation and Utilization in China' (op. cit. n. 26), p. 1.

cubic feet of gas is burned per tonne of oil transported, and low heater efficiency and lack of transport facilities lead to high use and waste by fields.[39]

Gas-production costs are high because of complex geology and high sulphur content (averaging 0.27% by weight).[40] In Sichuan province, exploration cost per metre rose 2,285 yuan in 1991 to 4,200 yuan in 1993 (the planned cost was 2,941 yuan), while the number of exploration wells decreased from 40 in 1991 to 21 in 1993 (planned number: 29).[41] In the case of Weiyuan gas field, located in central Sichuan province, more than 50% of wells have been shut in and production has been cut due to water incursion.[42] As gas provides fuel or feedstock to one-third of industrial operations and many residential customers in Sichuan province, the field's production is unable to satisfy the region's heavy demand. (By 1995 provincial production is estimated at 726 mmcf/d, but demand is estimated at 822 mmcf/d.)[43]

CNPC aims to step up gas exploration and development in the Shaanxi-Gansu-Ningxia Basin, where more than 100 bcm of proven gas reserves are confirmed.[44] Besides this, CNPC wants to accelerate the exploration of coal-bed gas. According to Shi Xunzhi, assistant president of CNPC, coal-bed gas represents more than one-third of China's proven gas reserves, and significant progress has been achieved in the exploration of coal-bed gas related to Jurassic coal in the northwest part of China, for example, the Tarim Basin, Junggar Basin and Tu-Ha Basin.[45] The CNPC approach reflects China's determination to increase the role of gas as an important energy source.

---

[39] Alexander Li and David Fridley, 'China's Natural Gas: A Disappointing Decade', a report of the China Energy Study, Energy Programme, East–West Center, Honolulu, Aug. 1990, p. 4. By 1992, a total of 15,698 km of oil pipeline and 7,116 km of gas pipeline were established. See *China Petroleum Investment Guide 1994*, p. 180.

[40] The drilling depth is more than 13,000 ft. Drilling costs average 6,560 yuan ($1,263)/ft, and the drilling success ratio is only 50%. See *Oil and Gas Journal*, 21 Jan. 1991, p. 17; *China Petroleum Investment Guide 1994*, p. 142.

[41] Investment in exploration increased from 409 million yuan in 1991 to 500 million yuan in 1993. See *China Petroleum Investment Guide 1994*, p. 142 (Table 3).

[42] *Oil and Gas Journal*, 21 Jan. 1991, p. 17.

[43] Ibid.

[44] *China OGP* 2: 24 (15 Dec. 1994), p. 4.

[45] West of Sichuan Basin and East of Songliao Basin also show high potential in exploration of coal-beds related to Jurassic coal measures. Coal-bed gas related to coal measures between Carboniferous and Permian prospect well in Junggar Basin, Bohai Bay Basin and Qinshui Basin. And coal-bed gas related to Tertiary coal measures also shows potential in the southeast Qiong Basin, Yinggehai Basin and East China Sea Basin. See Shi Xunzhi, 'Present Situation and Forecast of Natural Gas Exploitation and Utilization in China' (op. cit., n. 26).

4.2.3 Offshore production

The foundations of China's offshore development were laid between 1957 and 1979, when de facto development began.[46] Until the end of 1993, CNOOC had drilled a total of 327 exploratory wells, of which 223 were wildcats and 104 were appraisal wells. As a result, a total of 78 oil- and gas-bearing structures have been found, and half of these are deemed recoverable.[47] In 1994 China's offshore production totalled 6.4 mt, 4.3% of total oil production, jumping from a mere 2.4 mt (1.7% of total output) in 1991.

As shown in Tables 4.4 and 4.5, the Pearl River Mouth Basin (Nanhai East) is China's main offshore production area. In 1994 the Basin produced 3.7 mt. Four fields (Huizhou 21-1 and 26-1, Lufeng 13-1 and Xijiang 24-3 fields) are currently producing, and during 1995–6 five more fields (Xijiang 30-2, Liuhua 11-1, Huizhou 32-2 and 32-3 and Lufeng 22-1 fields) are expected to be on stream. The remaining 2.7 mt were produced by the Bohai Sea (1.6 mt) and Beibu Gulf Basin (1.1 mt). In the Bohai Sea Basin, there are currently six producing fields: Chengbei, Xi-428, Bozhong 28-1 and 34-2/4, Jinzhou 20-2 and Suizhong 36-1 fields. In addition, Jinzhou 9-3 is expected to be on stream in 1995. In the Beibu Gulf Basin (Nanhai West), there are two producing fields, Weizhou 10-3 and 11-4.[48]

Given that in the period 1982–94 four international bidding rounds for China's offshore development were invited, and a total foreign investment of $4.3 billion was forthcoming,[49] the result is not very impressive. The biggest oil-field discovery so far is Amoco Orient Petroleum's Liuhua 11-1 field which will be on stream in 1996 with a peak production of 65,000 b/d. Some solace was offered by the discovery of Yacheng 13-1 gas field, located in the Yinggehai Basin, 100 km off Hainan Island. This, China's largest offshore gas field, will be on stream in January 1996 with a production of 3.4 bcm, of which 2.9 bcm will be allocated to Hong Kong through a pipeline 800 km long (with a 28 inch diameter) completed in November 1994, and 0.5 bcm to Sanya, the southern tip of Hainan Island, through a 94-km (14-inch diameter) pipeline.[50]

---

[46] Keun Wook Paik, 'Russian and Chinese Oil and Gas Policies in Northeast Asia: International Political Consequences and Implications', PhD dissertation, University of Aberdeen, 1993, pp. 192–4.

[47] *China Petroleum Investment Guide 1994*, p. 96.

[48] For details on these fields, see Paik, 'Russian and Chinese Oil and Gas Policies in Northeast Asia' (op. cit. n. 44), pp. 197–203; *China Petroleum Investment Guide 1994*, pp. 104–38; *Petroleum Review*, Feb. 1995, pp. 67–8.

[49] *China OGP* 3: 1 (1 Jan. 1995), p. 4.

[50] *China OGP* 2: 23 (1 Dec. 1994), p. 6; *China Petroleum Investment Guide 1994*, p. 135 (Table 21).

Table 4.4: China: offshore oil production (mt/y)

	On stream	Average prod./y	1989	1990	1991	1992	1993	1994
Bohai Sea			0.625	0.865	0.944	n.a.	1.123	1.6
Chengbei	1972	0.3						
Xi-428		0.03						
Bozhong 28-1	Sept. 1989	0.09						
Bozhong 34-2/4	July 1990	0.31						
Jinzhou 20-2	1992	0.11						
Suizhong 36-1	Aug. 1993	1.17						
Jinzhou 9-3	1995	0.9						
Pearl River Mouth Basin			0.128	0.305	1.162	n.a.	2.942	3.7
Huizhou 21-1	Sept. 1990	0.59						
Huizhou 26-1	Dec. 1991	1.02						
Lufeng 13-1	Sept. 1993							
Xijiang 24-3	Nov. 1994	2.5*						
Xijiang 30-2	1995							
Liuhua 11-1	1996	3						
Huizhou 32-2	1996	1.5*						
Huizhou 32-3	1995							
Lufeng 22-1	1995							
Beibu Gulf Basin			0.201	0.262	0.304	n.a.	0.568	1.1
Weizhou 10-3	1986	0.095						
Weizhou 11-4	Oct. 1993	0.5						
Total			0.907	1.39	2.4	3.82	4.63	6.47

Note:* = a combination of Xijiang 24-3 and 30-2, and Huizhou 32-2 and 32-3.
Source: *China Petroleum Investment Guide 1994*, pp. 91–140; *China OGP* 2: 23 (1 Dec. 1994), pp. 5–6; *China OGP* 3: 2 (15 Jan. 1995), p. 4; *Petroleum Review*, Feb. 1995, p. 67.

CNOOC aims at verifying 100–150 mt of oil reserves and producing 1–2 mt of crude oil by 2000 in the East China Sea, where, in 1993, some 26 exploration wells were drilled: 5 have resulted in industrial oil and gas flows and 9 have had high-yield flows.[51] As shown in Map 4.1, Pinghu 4 gas field, whose development has

[51] *China Petroleum Investment Guide 1994*, p. 128 (Table 15).

Table 4.5: China's offshore oil and gas fields: discoveries and development

Field	Discovery	Contract area	Operator	Production start	Estimated peak
Chengbei	1972	Bohai Sea	JCODC (1987 to BOC)	Zone B:1985/ Zone A: 1987	0.4 mt
Bozhong 28-1	Dec. 1982	Bohai Sea	JCODC	May 1989	0.34 mt
Bozhong 34-2/4E	1982/4	Bohai Sea	JCODC	June 1990	0.4–5 mt
Suizhong 36-1	May 1986	Liaodong Bay	BOC	1992	1–1.8 mt
Zinzhou 20-2	Oct. 1984	Liaodong Bay	BOC	1992	550 mcm
Pinghu 4	Dec. 1988	East China Sea	SHOC	1997	440 mcm
Huizhou 21-1	July 1985	PRMB 16/08	ACT	Sept. 1990	1.15 mt
Huizhou 26-1	April 1988	PRMB 16/04	ACT	Nov. 1991	2 mt
Liuhua 11-1	March 1987	PRMB 29/04	AMOCO	1995–6	2.5 mt
Lufeng 13-1	Jan. 1987	PRMB 16/06	JHN	Aug. 1993	1 mt
Lufeng 22-1		PRMB 17/16	Occidental	Feb. 1991	0.5 mt
Xijiang 24-3	April 1985	PRMB 15/11	Phillips	1994	1.6 mt
Yacheng 13-1	Aug. 1983	Yinggehai Basin	ARCO	1996	5 bcm
Weizhou 10-3	Nov. 1982	Beibu Gulf	Total (1988 to NHWOC)	Aug. 1986	0.4 mt
Weizhou 11-4	1978	Beibu Gulf	NHWOC	1993	0.5 mt

Key: PRMB = Pearl River Mouth Basin; JCODC = Japan Chengbei Oil Development Corp.; ACT = Joint Group of AGIP, Chevron, and Texaco; JHN = Japex Huanan Oil Operating Co.
Sources: Keun Wook Paik, 'Russian and Chinese Oil and Gas Policies in Northeast Asia: International Political Consequences and Implications', PhD Dissertation, University of Aberdeen, 1993, p. 248; *China Petroleum Investment Guide 1994*, p. 128.

Map 4.1 Oil and gas fields in the East China Sea

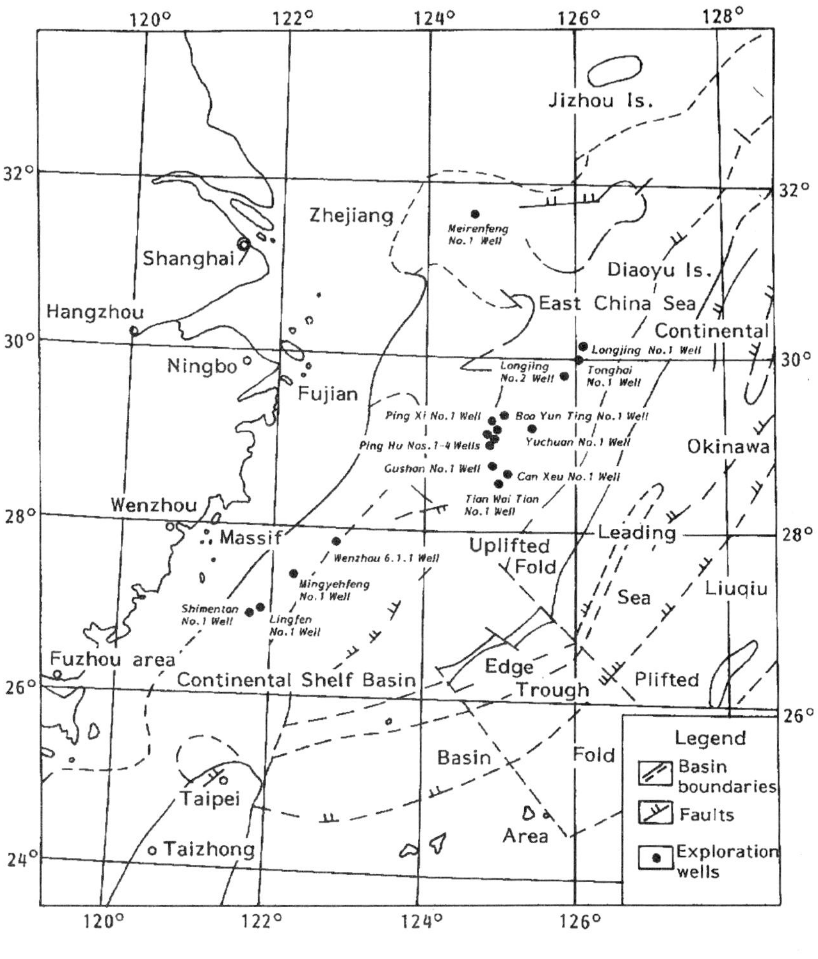

Source: China Oil (1989), p. 17.

been promoted since the early 1990s, is expected to be on stream and supply gas to Shanghai in 1997. If development is realized, 0.44 bcm/year will be delivered by a 260-km pipeline. (It is uncertain whether the development will take place as planned because Texaco terminated its joint-venture agreement with the Shanghai Offshore Petroleum Corp. in February 1994.)[52]

[52] Ibid.; Paik, 'Russian and Chinese Oil and Gas Policies in Northeast Asia' (op. cit., n. 45), pp. 202–3.

The results of offshore oil and gas development fell short of CNOOC's and foreign investors' expectations. Hopes of discovering a giant field comparable to onshore's Daqing were not realized. Consequently, offshore oil makes only a limited contribution to total production. According to CNOOC, it will total 12 mt by 1997 and thereafter an output of 8–10 mt will be maintained for 10 years.[53] When production reaches 12 mt, offshore will be the fourth largest oil-production base in China. As for gas, CNOOC aims at producing 4 bcm/year by 1997, a realistic target. Once this amount is achieved, offshore will be the second largest gas-production base in China,[54] unless a big gas discovery is made in the Tarim Basin. (Even if these plans are actually implemented, however, China will still be a relatively small gas producer in a region full of much larger producers.)

4.3 Problems of onshore and offshore production

4.3.1 Onshore problems

The downward readjustment of the oil-production goal from 200 mt to 175 mt by 2000 was painful, but China had no choice but to take the decision because of major problems with onshore fields. As shown in Table 4.2 and Map 4.2, among 15 major onshore fields, only Shengli and Liaohe showed substantial production increases. During 1980–93, a 14.4-mt rise at Shengli and a 9.1-mt rise at Liaohe were undermined by a decrease of 14.3 mt in output at Huabei. Another problem is output decline in smaller fields (15 fields, excluding Daqing, Shengli and Liaohe). During 1988–90 output averaged 33–4 mt.

One of the greatest difficulties facing the Chinese energy industry is the uneven distribution of oil and gas resources. As shown in Table 4.6, over 80% of oil and gas reserves are located in north, east and northeast China, and at present more than 90% of crude oil is produced at the maturing fields of the northeast corridor of which Daqing alone accounts for 40% of total production. Since regional production is important because of the country's poor transport system, and there is little likelihood that major contributions to oil and gas production this decade will come from the offshore and northwest frontiers, uneven distribution of resources is a real problem for the economy, one that is unlikely to be alleviated this century.

Furthermore, more than half of workable reserves have been extracted from most of the fields and output is stagnating or declining, although the Daqing field has been able to keep its annual output above 50 mt for 19 years since 1976.[55] The

---

[53] *China Petroleum Investment Guide 1994*, p. 96.

[54] Ibid., p. 115.

[55] *China Daily*, 12 March 1992.

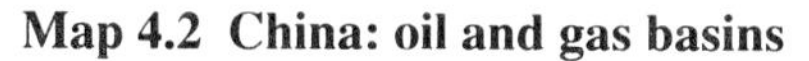

Map 4.2 China: oil and gas basins

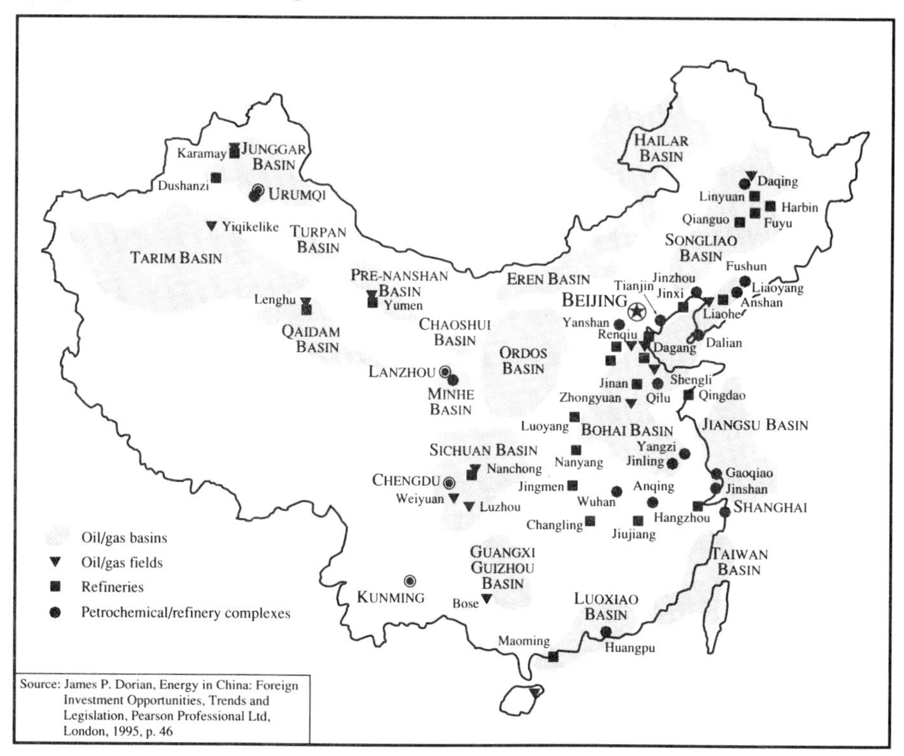

production of 55 mt at Daqing is expected to continue until 1997, and during 1998–2005 a level of 50 mt is expected to be maintained.[56] According to one Chinese newspaper, this is possible because of the discovery of the 'Tertiary Oil Extraction Technology' (Sance Chaiyu Jisu), which can extract 150–250 tonnes of oil using 1 tonne of chemical materials.[57]

According to Daqing officials, a polymer flood can increase Daqing production by as much as 400,000 b/d above its natural decline during the next 30 years. Without it, Daqing production is expected to drop by 13 mt to about 42 mt by 2000.[58] Here is a possibility that should not be overlooked. Application of intensive infill

---

[56] *China OGP* 3: 1 (1 Jan 1995), p. 2.

[57] The report said that production of 55 mt could be maintained until the end of this century. See *Wen Wei Po*, 28 Nov. 1991. Reportedly, Daqing field can increase its output by between 1.9 and 3.2 mt when 1 tonne of chemical reagent is used. See *China Daily*, 31 Dec. 1992.

[58] It is estimated that implementation of a polymer flood can boost Daqing recovery by 2.2 billion bbl. See *Oil and Gas Journal*, 28 Sept. 1992, p. 24.

Table 4.6: China: regional distribution of energy resources (%)

Region	Energy Total	Coal	Oil and Gas	Hydropower
North China	43.9	64.0	14.4	1.8
Northeast China	3.8	3.1	48.3	1.8
East China	6.0	6.5	18.2	4.4
Central-south China	5.6	3.7	2.5	9.5
Southwest China	28.6	10.7	2.5	7.0
Northwest China	12.1	12.0	14.0	12.5

Source: Ministry of Energy, *Energy in China: 1990*, Ministry of Energy, Beijing, 1990, p. 70.

drilling and water-injection techniques to maintain Daqing's production record of over 50 mt, has required installation of hundreds of imported electric submersible pumps together with other equipment, and consequently much of the $2 billion in foreign imports was for Daqing's enhanced oil recovery.[59]

Thus, maintaining Daqing's current record means an increase in production costs, ultimately leading to burdensome investments. Throughout China, artificial lift grew substantially in the 1980s.[60] In 1980, artificial lift produced 20.8% of all fluid and 26.2% of all oil in the country. In 1989 the figures were 95.3% and 90.9% respectively. In the same period, the number of rod-pump installations increased five times. In 1989 electrical submersible pumps, not introduced until 1980, were operating in some 3,000 wells. During 1979–89, oil-field equipment imports from 13 countries cost $3.4 billion.[61]

China's second largest field, Shengli, also has a high water content, as much as 85%.[62] This rate is too high given that fields developed by water flooding are experiencing a high water cut, ranging from 60–80% in 1990.[63] Shengli has also been plagued by drilling problems, like abnormal pressures, salt and gypsum intervals that can cause casing damage, and H_2S (in the far northeastern fields).[64]

As important oil fields in east China enter a high water-content stage their oil-exploiting index drops considerably. Water consumption for the exploitation of 1

[59] *China Business Review*, March–April 1990, p. 16.
[60] *World Oil*, Dec. 1990, pp. 60–2.
[61] *China Business Review*, March–April, 1990, p. 16.
[62] *China Daily*, 31 Dec. 1991.
[63] Water cut is increasing at a rate of 2% water per 1% of the original oil in place produced in China's oil fields. See *World Oil*, Dec. 1990, p. 60.
[64] *World Oil*, March 1990, pp. 69–75; *China Business Review*, March–April 1990, p. 16.

tonne of oil increased by 1.8 cubic metres, from 3 cm in the sixth FYP (1981–5) to 4.8 cm in the seventh; it seems to have reached 6.93 cm in the eighth FYP.[65] On the whole, output stabilization has been accomplished at the expense of ever-increasing water injection with (currently) over five million bbl per day of water being injected into Chinese oil fields and the rate increasing by about 3% per year.[66]

In the case of Liaohe, the third largest oil field, where heavy oil and condensate account for 60%, or 4.4 billion bbl of the field's total liquids reserves, a somewhat different problem has emerged. Drilling at Liaohe is a challenge for Chinese technology. Heavy oil here lies at an average depth of 1,600 m, compared with a typical depth of about 500 m for heavy-oil deposits elsewhere in the world. In addition, the crude has a combined wax and asphalt content of 40–60 wt%, and a pour point of 67°C, among the world's highest for condensate.[67]

China's onshore production is heavily dependent on three major oil fields, Daqing, Shengli and Liaohe. In 1993 production at these three fields totalled 103 mt, about 70% of total onshore production. The same year, Daqing and Shengli bureaux alone accounted for around 27% of the exploratory and 44% of the development wells drilled.[68] The gradual decline of Shengli since 1991, when production reached a peak of 33.55 mt, places further strain on the other large existing fields which must maintain production levels.

During the 1980s China placed too much emphasis on field development, and not enough on exploration, to increase onshore production. In 1981–8, the number of wells drilled for exploration increased 1.7 times, while that of wells drilled for oil-field development increased 3.5 times.[69] The effects of China's failure to emphasize exploration work is illustrated by the following example: during the seventh FYP (1986–90), oil-prospecting work fulfilled two-thirds of the plan's targets (that is, only two-thirds of reserves were verified) owing to shortage of funds. Consequently, output has gradually overtaken new exploitable reserves in recent years.[70] To make matters worse, the number of oil wells in production has more than doubled, from 20,993 in 1981 to 44,059 in 1988, but average output has dropped from 96 b/d to 62 b/d in the same period.

Flowing wells accounted for 10% of the total in 1988 (compared with 39% in 1981). This decline was partly caused by the increased use of infill drilling to

---

[65] *China Market* 5 (1991), p. 26.
[66] *China–Britain Trade Review*, July 1988, p. 1.
[67] *Oil and Gas Journal*, 28 Sept. 1992, p. 24.
[68] *China Petroleum Investment Guide 1994*, p. 60.
[69] *World Oil*, Jan. 1990, p. 28 (Table).
[70] *China Market* 5 (1991), p. 26.

maximize total output from field complexes like Daqing.[71] This productivity decline was directly connected to the rising unit cost of capital investment in the oil industry. In 1985 average costs for development of one barrel per day of production capacity had fallen to 6,520 yuan (at 1980 prices) and in 1989 the cost soared in real terms to 33,570 yuan per b/d, or almost 85,000 yuan per b/d (at 1991 prices). With a 40% fall in the average output per well from 1980 to 1988, higher investment was inevitable to maintain output.[72]

Crude consumption in the oil and gas extraction industries rose to 10.7 mt, or 9.1% of total crude consumption in 1990, from 7.5 mt, or 7.9% of total consumption in 1985.[73] During the 1980s crude-oil losses in fields amounted to around 2.3–2.6 mt,[74] and during the 1990s production losses and oil-field self-use seem to be increasing with further development of marginal fields, where more crude is consumed in fuelling enhanced recovery processes.

As shown in Table 4.7, one problem presented by the nature of Chinese crude is significant. Even though the crude has a very low sulphur content, it is mostly extremely waxy, requiring adaptation of transportation and processing systems to handle it. On top of this, Chinese crudes yield a high proportion of heavy products, contrary to domestic and overseas demand patterns which show an increasing proportion of light products.[75]

Wang Naiju, director of the development department, CNPC, summarized China's onshore production problems as follows:[76] first of all, it is necessary to produce 10 mt of oil by stimulation and another 10 mt of oil by drilling new wells to maintain the main oilfields' production levels, given that the decline in the natural production of old wells in the main oil fields is up to 14–15%. Secondly, increased recoverable reserves in old and new oil-bearing regions fail to compensate for the production decline. To keep the annual increment of production stable, the production load of old oil fields must be a heavy one, resulting in a rising recovery rate of residual recoverable reserves year by year.

Thirdly, daily oil production of development wells in new oil fields and the adjustment welsl in old oil fields, as wells as the oil increment by down-hole servicing,

---

[71] *World Oil*, Jan. 1990, p. 28, especially the figure entitled 'Drilling and Production in China, 1979–1988'; David Fridley, 'China's Oil Industry: A Decade in Review and Challenges Ahead', a report of the China Energy Study, East–West Center, August 1990, p. 8.

[72] Fridley, *China's Energy Outlook* (op. cit., n. 27), p. 38.

[73] *Zhongguo Nengyuan Tongji Nianjian 1991*, p. 149.

[74] Ibid., pp. 221–2.

[75] *Opec Bulletin*, March 1986, p. 42.

[76] Wang Naiju, 'Current Situation and Future Development of Onland Oil Production in China', *China Oil and Gas* 1: 1 (1994), p. 23.

Table 4.7: Selected onshore crude-oil specifications

Attribute	Daqing	Shengli	Dagang	Liaohe	Jianghan	Zhong-yuan	Xinjiang
API	33.1	25.4	30.4	28.7	29.7	35.9	33.4
Density (20°C)	855.4	898	869.7	879.3	87.4	841	853.8
Viscosity (50°C)	20.19	74.2	10.83	17.44	21.9	10.1	18.8
Freezing point (°C)	30	27	23	21	26	32	12
Asphaltene (%)	0	0.4	0	0	1.11	0	0
Gum (%)	8.9	18.6	9.7	11.9	22	8	10.6
Wax content (%)	26.2	14.6	11.6	16.8	10.7	21.4	7.2
Residues:							
Carbon (%)	2.9	6.3	2.9	3.9	4.33	3.6	2.6
Sulphur (%)	0.1	0.73	0.13	0.18	1.83	0.45	0.05
Nitrogen (%)	0.16	0.44	0.24	0.32	0.3	0.15	0.13
Nickel (%)	3.1	30	7	29	12	2.5	5.6
Vanadium (%)	0.4	1.8	0.1	0.7	0.4	1.1	0.1
Crude type[1]	A	D	B	B	C	A	B

Note: [1]A = low sulphur, paraffin base; B = low sulphur, intermediate; C = sulphur, paraffin base; D = sulphur, intermediate.
Source: Selected from *China Petroleum Investment Guide 1994*, p. 89 (Table 9).

decrease continuously because of the newly developed reserves of low grade, and the complicated sub-surface conditions of old oil fields. In fact, the average daily production of new wells decreased from 9.2 tonnes per well in 1990 to 8 tonnes in 1993, and the yearly increment of oil production per well/stimulation also decreased from 510 tonnes in 1990 to 450 tonnes in 1993. Naiju's countermeasure for the production problems of the main oil fields was that China should leave no stone unturned to prolong the stable production period or reduce the production decline of oil fields in eastern China, focusing on increasing recoverable reserves and enhancing the oil-recovery factor.

China needs a breakthrough in the far west. The government has already announced a strategy of stabilizing the east and developing the west, and allocated 100 billion yuan for oil exploration during the eighth FYP (1991–5).[77] Experts predict the west will replace the east as China's major energy source. However, oil reserves in the west are deep, usually more than 5,000 m under ground, and it takes about six months to sink a test well.

The development of the west would be costly not only because of the harsh environment but also because of the absence of infrastructure and a transportation system. Since 1989, when large-scale prospecting started in the region, China has poured more than 3 billion yuan ($550 million at the current exchange rate) into it.[78] But this is a small beginning. Desert drilling in the Tarim Basin costs about $825 per foot, or $16 million for a 20,000-ft well, almost as much as an offshore well in the South China Sea.

Furthermore, the Tarim Basin's location far away from the main energy-consuming areas requires construction of a long-distance pipeline grid costing many billions of dollars. Despite this cost, China has to do something to ease the transportation constraints. For example, Tarim's crude-oil production in 1994 reached 1.95 mt, but due to a poor transportation system, a number of producing wells had to be shut down, leading to a production cut of 0.4 mt.[79] This is the reason why the government has completed plans to construct a major 4,500-km trunk oil pipeline from the Tarim Basin eastwards. The initial pipeline route leading to Lianyungang via Louyang Henan province was redrawn because of the location of domestic demand and the new route passes Mainyan in Sichuan province.[80] As of 1990 China has built 15,900 km of oil and gas pipeline, of which 8,700 km is for oil transportation (with 225 pipelines) and 7,200 km for gas (with 223 pipelines).[81] However, there is as yet no pipeline grid to connect eastern coastal areas with the west.

This pipeline grid matters greatly to the gas industry. Most of China's gas-transmission pipelines are located in Sichuan province, with south and north trunks, while those in East China and elsewhere are short in length and small in size. To

---

[77] *Ta Kung Pao*, 26 Oct. 1990.

[78] *China Daily*, 17 March 1992.

[79] *China OGP* 3: 1 (1 Jan. 1995), p. 2; *China OGP* 3: 3 (1 Feb. 1995), p. 3.

[80] The construction cost is estimated at 7–8 billion yuan ($805–920 million). See *China Petroleum Investment Guide 1994*, pp. 90, 182.

[81] *China Statistical Yearbook 1991*, State Statistical Bureau, Beijing, 1991, pp. 483–4. From 1980 to 1988, total pipeline mileage grew at 6.4% per year, compared to 27% per year between 1970 and 1978. See Li and Fridley, *China's Natural Gas* (op. cit. n. 39), p. 6.

increase the share of gas in China's energy mix, the construction of a nationwide gas-pipeline grid in parallel with increased gas production is urgently needed. This is why CNPC is promoting a rapid expansion of the gas-transmission system. But, though CNPC aims at accelerating gas development in the coming years, for the time being the role of gas is limited due to the remote location of gas fields and lack of transportation and infrastructure facilities.

4.3.2 Offshore problems

The problems facing China in offshore development during the 1980s can be divided into two categories. One comprises dependent variables for oil and gas policies, like importing technology and foreign capital, and complaints about contract terms. The other comprises independent variables, such as the fluctuation of world oil prices and absence of supergiant oil and gas fields. The former has been dealt with reasonably well, but the latter still burdens offshore development.

First, so far as introducing foreign technology and capital are concerned, the results were better than China had expected. Initially China had to depend heavily upon imports of highly advanced equipment, but with the establishment of CNOOC and promulgation of petroleum regulation, China found a way of introducing technology along with considerable amounts of foreign capital. These imports enhanced China's exploration and drilling operations substantially.

For example, an early 1980s licensing deal for Baker Hughes Inc. drillbit technology has made China virtually self-sufficient. Then, 3-D seismic technology for improving drilling efficiency and output without increasing the number of oil rigs, logging and coring technology for enhancing deep-drilling operations, and horizontal drilling technology for China's deep offshore wells were also imported. During 1984–6, the United States alone exported $653.6-million worth of drilling and oil field equipment to China.[82]

According to a 1987 US–China Business Council study, the Bohai Development Corp. hoped to purchase 67% of $290 million in imports for its Suizhong 36-1 field from the United States.[83] However, in 1987 China's drilling and oil field equipment imports from the United States were worth only $71.9 million. Two factors seem to have dampened China's buying spree. The first was the collapse of oil prices in 1986. The second was a side effect of China's frenetic import programme. Some equipment turned out to be ill-suited to local conditions. For example, a number of foreign drilling rigs proved too heavy for China's marsh, beach and shallow-water areas.[84]

[82] *China Business Review*, March–April 1990, p. 16 (Table 5).

[83] Ibid.

[84] Ibid.

As for attracting foreign investment, by the end of 1989, total foreign investment recorded was $2.65 billion, of which $2.22 billion constituted exploration investment and $0.43 billion development investment.[85] (As mentioned above, by 1994 total foreign investment amounted to $4.3 billion.) Through cooperation with foreign companies, CNOOC has improved its self-reliance capacity remarkably. Oil and gas discoveries like Suizhong 36-1, Jinzhou 20-2, Weizhou 11-4 and Pinghu 4 oil and gas fields confirm this. That is, the cost of technology is no longer a burden on Chinese offshore development, but CNOOC will persist in a policy of 'walking on two legs', as it needs a considerable investment to conduct its own exploration. For example, to drill 10–15 wells and complete 20,000 km of seismic lines annually, a fund of 0.3 billion yuan is needed.[86]

Secondly, China took full advantage of high oil prices to create a fiscal and regulatory regime that was not very favourable to foreign oil companies and service companies wanting to be part of its offshore scene. The contractual terms laid down in the 1983 model contract became a target of investors' complaints,[87] but it worked well until 1986, by which time the euphoria surrounding the original Chinese offshore contract awards in 1983 had evaporated. However, complaints by foreign companies led China to take a relatively more flexible stance in the second round of bidding,[88] and real and innovative contract terms were applied to the bilateral negotiation between BP and CNOOC in 1987. The new terms were formally stipulated in the third round of bidding in 1989.[89]

In 1993, after the announcement of fourth-round offshore bidding in June 1992 and the first round of onshore bidding in March 1993, China relaxed its production-sharing terms.[90] The renewal of contracts signifies a more realistic appraisal by the Chinese government of the prospects for developing its offshore, and is a reflection of its determination to attract more foreign investment.

---

[85] *China Oil* 23 (1990), p. 7.

[86] *China Oil* 14 (1987), p. 10.

[87] *China Business Review*, March–April 1990, p. 24.

[88] What China has stipulated is that oil fields with an annual oil output of less than 1 mt would be exempted from paying the 12.5% concession royalties. See *China Oil* 6 (1985), p. 23.

[89] For a comparison of the conditions between 1983 and 1989, see *China Business Review*, March–April 1990, pp. 24–5; *China Oil* 20 (1989), pp. 39–45; Wu Kang, *China's Offshore Oil Prospects*, a report of the China Energy Study, Resource Systems Institute, Honolulu, March 1988, pp. 34–6; *Petroleum News*, July/Aug. 1988, p. 25; *Petroleum Advisory* (Honolulu), 1 May 1991, pp. 6–7: *China Oil* 18–19 (1988), pp. 4–5.

[90] Wang Shali, 'China's Model Contracts: Onshore and Offshore Comparisons', paper presented at PSC '93 (Oil and Gas Production Sharing Contracts, Concessions and New Petroleum Ventures in the Asia Pacific Region), convened by the Institute for International Research, Singapore, 15–17 Sept. 1993; *Petromin*, Dec. 1993, pp. 64–9.

Thirdly, and contrary to the above problems, the fluctuation of world oil prices seriously affected the pace of Chinese offshore exploration and development. Especially after the nosedive taken by world oil prices in 1986, most of the contracts and development projects made before 1986, which assumed oil prices closer to $25 per barrel (not to mention current projects), came under pressure from falling oil prices. Simply as participants in projects, in which China played the role of host, foreign companies were greatly affected by the fall in prices.

Once foreign companies estimate that exploration and operation costs are too high (for example, it was estimated that the exploration costs for wildcats and appraisal wells were as high as $10 million per well in 1989, and full operation and capital costs for each barrel of oil produced offshore might be around $15 dollars), they are reluctant to take part in projects. In such cases, the Chinese government cannot simply soften its stance towards foreign companies. If current low oil prices, hovering below $20, continue in the coming years, they will act unfavourably on China's offshore development, as the development of medium or small oil and gas fields in an era of low oil prices will not be attractive to foreign companies.

Finally and most seriously, the failure of supergiant oil discoveries, equal to Daqing, in offshore China during the 1980s was a disappointing and embarrassing result of development efforts. Naturally enough most western companies moved into China at a time of record high oil prices expecting a bonanza of discoveries; they left after spending a lot of money and finding virtually nothing. Even though the Chinese believe that their offshore basins have just been slow to reveal their secrets (indeed, only around one-third of its 1.3-million-sq.-km continental shelf has been opened up), the absence of supergiant discoveries was a fatal blow to its ambitious offshore plans.

Taking the characteristics of Chinese offshore geology into consideration (for example, the northern continental shelf in the South China Sea is a complex and flawed oil and gas area with multifault blocks), a big discovery may not be made easily, but cannot be ruled out. The final verdict on the existence of giant oil and gas fields in China's offshore will be possible only after exploration work is completed in the East China and South China Seas, where boundary disputes remain to be settled.

4.4 Controlled prices and the burden of investment

4.4.1 Unreasonable oil prices

If the outlook for Chinese self-reliance in oil is gloomy, factors such as demand outpacing supply, inadequate reserves, irrational domestic oil prices, rising production costs and excessive oil exports must bear the blame.[91] Interestingly enough, China has already experienced, in the early 1980s, what Russia is currently experiencing in relation to production decline and price reform.

The adoption of a new pricing system, the so-called 'two-tier pricing system' was inevitable following the production decline in 1980–2. In 1983 a second tier of higher crude prices was established, pegged to 1982 international prices and applied to crude produced above the state quota.[92] The aim of the reform was to promote marginal production by allowing producers to sell the above-quota amounts directly to end-users without guidance from state plans.

This new system was quite effective during the rapid expansion of onshore oil production in the early 1980s and in creating a favourable environment for the development of offshore deposits. But it was weakened when rising production costs and falling profits wiped out the gains the system had brought. In fact, a situation in which the oil industry was highly controlled while most other industries enjoyed price deregulation, compounded by frequent devaluations of the yuan before 1986, forced production costs up above the higher costs associated with enhanced recovery efforts and declining productivity at many fields.[93]

In 1989 crude production costs reached 100 yuan/tonne, from 44 yuan/tonne in 1980. As a result, the 11 billion yuan ($7.3 billion) upstream profit in 1980 had been transformed into a 780-million-yuan ($210 million) deficit by 1988, and a 2.9-billion-yuan deficit by 1990.[94] By the end of 1989, the total debts of the oil industry reached nearly 20 billion yuan ($5.4 billion), half of which was in the form of foreign loans, mostly denominated in Japanese yen.[95]

It was in the early 1990s that China began to take the problem of its unreasonable oil-price system seriously. In early 1992 subsidized oil was increased to 200 yuan/tonne ($5/bbl, based on the 1992 exchange rate), while in the years 1972–88 subsidized oil was distributed at 100 yuan/tonne ($6.6/bbl at the exchange rate prevailing for most of the period). In short, the price of China's oil in real terms has been dropping for more than two decades.[96] This is why, on 1 September 1992, China announced its decision to remove price ceilings on key raw materials, such as crude, refined products, steel, iron, copper and aluminum, once state quotas for

[91] Robert E. Ebel, 'Rethinking China's Oil Industry', *Geopolitics of Energy*, Nov. 1990, pp. 5–9.

[92] David Fridley, 'China's Oil Industry' (op. cit., n. 71), p. 7.

[93] Ibid.

[94] Ibid.; *Zhongguo Nengyuan Tongji Nianjian 1991*, p. 309.

[95] David Fridley, 'China's Oil Industry' (op. cit., n. 71), p. 8.

[96] *Far Eastern Economic Review*, 12 Nov. 1992, p. 52.

these goods were fulfilled.[97] The key aim of the reform was to channel money to China's cash-starved oil producers. During 1985–90 CNPC lost 6 billion yuan/year, though the loss had declined to 4 billion yuan/year in 1991.[98]

The 1992 decision was regarded as part of the government's efforts to gradually dismantle the two-tier price structure, and ultimately to free up prices for domestic oil. However, no serious move towards liberalization of oil prices was taken in the price reform enforced in May 1994, aimed at the state control of wholesale and retail prices for both crude and products, and cutting down on tiers of sales channels, as well as establishing a risk fund for oil importers.[99] China's price reforms will have only a limited success unless production quotas and supply allocations for state companies are removed.

4.4.2 The burden of investment

Like price reform, investment policy is still off the track. Despite production-cost increases and productivity decline, spending on exploration has fallen considerably during the past decade. For example, the costs entailed in uncovering new oil reserves rose by an average of 24.8%. It cost 560 million yuan to discover 100 mt in 1986, but the corresponding figure for 1898 was 1,360 million yuan.[100] However, exploration spending represented 35.6% of total investment in the oil industry during the period 1980–5, and the figure fell to 27.3% in 1985–90.[101] The consequence was stagnating oil production in the late 1980s.

The government increased investment in onshore development to $5 billion in 1990 from $3 billion in 1986, and has earmarked 1.5 billion yuan ($319 million) for exploration and development in the Tarim Basin during 1992–3.[102] However, when oil subsidies rose to an estimated $0.7 billion in 1991 from $0.26 billion in 1989, the government expressed its unwillingness to increase these subsidies.[103]

---

[97] *Petroleum Intelligence Weekly*, 14 Sept. 1992, p. 3.

[98] *Far Eastern Economic Review*, 12 Nov. 1992, p. 53.

[99] *China OGP* 2: 10 (15 May 1994), pp. 1–2; and 2: 11 (1 June 1994), pp. 1–2. Just before the May 1994 reform, the average crude-oil price was $7.8/bbl. After the reform, the crude price for priority consumers and ordinary consumers became $11/bbl and $19.7/bbl respectively. See *China OGP* 2: 18 (15 Sept. 1994), p. 1.

[100] Tatsu Kambara, 'The Energy Situation in China', *China Quarterly* 131 (Sept. 1992), p. 627.

[101] *China Petroleum Investment Guide 1994*, p. 84. Another source records that until 1985 exploration accounted for 45% of total Chinese investment in its oil sector. See *China Daily*, 6 Nov. 1990.

[102] *Oil and Gas Journal*, 29 July 1991, p. 25; *Oil and Gas Journal*, 15 Oct. 1990, p. 27.

[103] *Petroleum Intelligence Weekly*, 4 Feb. 1992, p. 4.

The move away from state allocation of investment capital at no interest to a combination of financing channels during the 1980s suggests the government's investment policy in the energy sectors. In 1981 capital-construction investment from the state in the coal, oil and power industries accounted for 66.5%, 79.6% and 54.6% respectively, but by 1988 it had dropped to 59.5%, 30.3% and 16.7%.[104]

That is, the coal industry's heavy reliance on state investment has continued during the period, while the oil and power industries have obtained financing from other sources. In 1988 domestic loans and self-financing investments in the power industry represented over 50% of the total, while over half of capital-construction investment in the oil industry was covered by foreign loans. The shift from central funding to a dependence on foreign loans has worsened the financial position of the oil industry.

During the seventh FYP (1986–90) oil and gas exploration dwindled relatively due to a shortage of funds, and this was reflected in the increase of proved reserves. Figures for investment during the period increased 1.78 times compared with those of the sixth FYP (1981–5), but the actual investment increase was trifling owing to price rises, production costs and exploration difficulties.

As a result, basic exploration work during the seventh FYP equalled that of the sixth. However, only 51% of planned exploration development was achieved, and 74.2% of planned proved reserves secured. (In onshore areas, the total was 79.6% of that in the sixth FYP.) During the seventh FYP, as the investment needed for securing 100 mt of proved oil reserves doubled compared with the sixth FYP, investment deficiency was calculated at around 12–16 billion yuan short of what was needed to achieve the original goal.[105] In this situation, a considerable decline in the number of exploration wells, from 1,323 in 1988 to 951 in 1993, is hardly surprising.[106]

Fixed-asset investment in the oil and gas industries during the 1980s demonstrates the situation more clearly. As shown in Table 4.8, in the years 1981–8, investment in the energy industry amounted to around 14–15% of investment in total fixed assets, but this was increased to 19% in 1990. Considering that total fixed-asset investment in 1989–90 was lower than in 1988, fixed-asset investment in the energy industry has substantially increased in the same period.

Among the different energy sectors, however, more investment has gone to electric power than to oil and gas, which were not a priority in the 1980s. A similar

---

[104] The figures are calculated from *Zhongguo Nengyuan Tongji Nianjian 1989*, p. 29.

[105] Chen Juan, 'Prospect and Exploitation of Oil and Natural Gas Resources of China', *Energy of China* 2 (1992), p. 7.

[106] *World Oil*, Jan. 1990, p. 28 (Table); *China Petroleum Investment Guide 1994*, p. 88 (Table 8).

Table 4.8: China: fixed-asset investment (billion yuan)

Year	Total investment	Energy investment	(%)	Coal	Oil/gas	Electric power	Refining	Coking and Town Gas
1981	96.1	14.12	(14.7)	3.61	4.69	4.76	0.72	0.36
1982	123.04	17.34	(14.1)	4.82	6.12	5.52	0.69	0.11
1983	143.01	21.24	(14.9)	6.14	7.42	6.89	0.64	0.15
1984	183.29	27.77	(15.2)	8.11	9.46	8.84	0.98	0.37
1985	254.32	36.64	(14.4)	8.72	13.03	12.62	1.2	1.07
1986	301.96	44.40	(14.7)	9.25	13.78	18.14	1.62	1.6
1987	364.09	54.30	(14.9)	9.87	16.62	23.55	2.62	1.64
1988	449.65	64.50	(14.3)	10.67	19.69	28.14	4.1	1.91
1989	413.77	70.56	(17.1)	12.23	23.29	29.57	3.47	1.99
1990	444.93	84.67	(19.0)	16.45	23.11	37.22	4.55	3.34

Note: Figures in brackets indicate energy as % of total.
Source: State Statistical Bureau, *China Energy Statistical Yearbook 1991*, Statistical Bureau Press, Beijing, 1992, p. 23.

story is found in capital-construction investment. Table 4.9 shows that investment in the oil and gas extraction industry was less than one-fifth of the energy industry total.

In these circumstances, self-reliance in the oil and gas sector during the 1990s cannot be achieved. The estimate by the China Oil and Natural Gas Exploration and Development Corp., that 0.8–1 bt annually would have to be proved during the period to maintain a rational proportion between oil reserves and production,[107] was a sort of warning. As if recognizing the seriousness of the estimate, the government announced that during the eighth FYP (1991–5), more than 100 billion yuan ($20 billion) would be spent on oil and gas exploration and development.[108]

According to Xin Dingguo, of the State Planning Commission, during the eighth FYP (1991–5) 32 billion yuan annually should be allocated to the coal and power industries, and to oil and gas recovery. Of this, 8–9 billion yuan seems to have been allocated to coal, 11 billion yuan to power and 3.5 billion yuan to oil and gas recovery (excluding exploration in new oil-field areas).[109]

During 1995–9, if China's economic growth is to be maintained at 9–10%, as shown in Table 4.10, it is projected that a $45-billion investment will be needed for

[107] *Oil and Gas Journal*, 14 Jan. 1991, p. 17.
[108] *People's Daily*, 29 Oct. 1990.
[109] Xin Dingguo, 'China Energy Security in the 1990s' (op. cit., n. 28).

Table 4.9: China: investment in the oil and gas industries (billion yuan)

	1985	1986	1987	1988	1989	1990
A	36.641	44.396	54.301	64.502	70.564	84.674
B	13.029	13.782	16.621	19.689	23.294	23.113
C	20.529	26.709	34.006	41.157	44.638	55.827
D	2.707	2.975	4.222	6.108	7.198	7.556
E	2.208	2.818	4.065	5.947	7.018	
F	0.498	0.157	0.157	0.162	0.18	
G	5.592	6.906	7.934	11.347	11.556	12.511
H	0.915	1.032	1.184	2.764	2.595	1.973

Key: A = fixed-assets investment in energy industry.
B = fixed-assets investment in oil and gas extraction industry.
C = capital-construction investment in energy industry.
D = capital-construction investment in oil and gas extraction industry.
E = capital-construction investment in oil extraction industry.
F = capital-construction investment in gas extraction industry.
G = technical-updating and transformation investment in energy industry.
H = technical-updating and transformation investment in oil and gas extraction industry.
Source: *Zhongguo Nengyuan Tongji Nianjian 1989*, p. 30 and *1991*, pp. 6, 23, 25, and 30.

the oil and gas sectors; $15.3 billion for oil development and $5.5 billion for gas. On the same assumption, during 2000–2004, the projected investment is $40.5 billion, of which $16 billion is for oil and $6 billion for gas.

To have a more effective energy structure by 2000, Chinese energy planners assume that the share of coal in primary energy consumption will have to decrease by 3.64%. In the cases of oil and gas, consumption will have to rise by 17.78 mt and 10.5 bcm respectively. Hydropower and nuclear power must increase by 34.7 billion kWh and 22.4 billion kWh. This requires an estimated investment of 37.2 billion yuan at 1990 prices, or an annual average increase of 7.4 billion yuan.[110]

The question is whether the Chinese government can allocate a large capital sum to the energy industry in the 1990s. The country's large fiscal deficit seems likely to prohibit such a huge investment, and has driven the government to take a more

[110] Ibid.

Table 4.10: Projected investment in the oil industry, 1995–2004 ($ b)

	1995–9	2000–2004
Exploration	8.5	9
Development		
Oil	13.3	16
Gas	5.5	6
Refining expansion	1.2	
Petrochemical complexes	10.5	5
Infrastructure	4	4.5
Total	45	40.5

Source: *China Petroleum Investment Guide 1994*, p. 7.

flexible stance to foreign investment. The external environment too is forcing China to be more aggressive in attracting foreign investment. It remains to be seen whether its oil and gas potential, and investment climate, will be attractive enough to distract potential investors from Russia and other CIS countries.

4.5 Alternative energy resources for oil

China's long-term energy outlook is causing concern as currently oil meets only 20% of internal requirements – an insufficient proportion for a modern economy. According to Professor Lu Yingashong of the Institute of Technoeconomics and Energy Systems Analysis, well before 2030 the minimum reserves required to sustain China's economy will exceed current maximum estimates of total recoverable reserves. Professor Lu proposed oil as the only option for the economic development of the Chinese coastal zone, even though internal resources are inadequate. Therefore, China could become a major oil importer by the turn of the century.[111]

In an article contributed to a Chinese quarterly *Guoji Shiyou Jingji* (International Petroleum Economy), Song Wu-Cheng forecast China's crude-oil shortage in 2000 as 51.9 mt, assuming production in 2000 of 170 mt, a GNP growth rate of 10% and an average annual oil-consumption growth rate of 7% (if an oil-consumption

[111] *OPEC Bulletin*, Sept. 1988, p. 49. However, Chow argued that China has the capability to maintain the present level of oil exports for the foreseeable future. See Larry Chuen-ho Chow, 'The Changing Role of Oil in Chinese Exports, 1974–89', *China Quarterly*, Sept. 1992, pp. 750–65.

growth rate of 8% is applied, the crude-oil shortage in 2000 will be 71.6 mt).[112] Song's forecast suggests that the scale of China's oil imports could be substantial by the end of this decade.

As for gas, it meets merely 2% of domestic requirements as of 1990. China plans an expanded role for gas in domestic industrial, residential and power-generation uses in order to allow oil to be exported. To that end, it aims to double gas production to about 2.9 bcf/d by 2000 and to substitute gas as a feedstock for its rising petrochemical industry, currently fed by oil.[113] However, the ratio of oil to gas produced in China on an energy-equivalent basis is merely 1 to 0.1.[114] Even though the Chinese are estimating their natural gas reserves at 1.165 quadrillion cubic feet (33 trillion cubic metres),[115] replacement of oil by gas seems impossible in view of proved reserves.

Compared to this dearth of oil and gas, China's coal resources are abundant. The aggregated coal resources within a depth of 1,500 m amount to 4,000 bt. As of January 1990, 901.5 bt have been verified, and around 300 bt are proved, of which anthracite accounts for 70% (coking coal makes up 30%), bituminous coal 16% and lignite 14%.[116] In 1990 coal production was recorded at 1.08 bt, but only 17.3 mt were exported.[117]

In the same year coal exports represented only 1.1% of the country's total export receipts, amounting to $667.3 million.[118] The main constraints on the development of coal exports seem to have been competition from foreign coal and the lack of a proper transportation and distribution infrastructure. Professor Lu suggested that one alternative to running an energy deficit could be nuclear power, as the construction of the infrastructure necessary to transport coal from northern China to the

---

[112] During 1981–90, China's GNP growth rate was 9% and its annual oil-consumption growth rate was 5.94%. Assuming that a GNP growth rate of 9% is maintained until 2000, Song estimated that, the demand for four major oil products (gasoline, kerosene, diesel, heavy oil) will be 70–9 mt in 1995, and 95–106 mt in 2000. He also estimated that China's oil-products shortage in 1995 and 2000 would be 40 mt and 60 mt respectively, and as for crude oil, the demand in 1995 and 2000 would be 160 mt and 220 mt respectively. See Song Wu-Cheng, '2000 Nian Zhongguo Shiyou Xuqiuliang Yuce' (Forecast on China's oil consumption scale in 2000), *Guoji Shiyou Jingji* (International Petroleum Economy) 1: 4 (1993), pp. 3–6.

[113] *Oil and Gas Journal*, 28 Sept. 1992, p. 23.

[114] The world ratio is 1 to 0.7. In the United States and the FSU, it is about 1 to 1 and gas is even ahead. See *World Oil*, Jan. 1990, p. 28.

[115] Ibid.

[116] Xin Dingguo, 'China Energy Security in the 1990s' (op. cit., n. 28).

[117] *Zhongguo Nengyuan Tongji Nianjian 1991*, p. 208.

[118] *Almanac of China's Foreign Economic Relations and Trade*, China Resources Advertising Co. Ltd., Hong Kong, 1991, p. 413.

southern and eastern provinces would be difficult and extremely costly.[119] However, this option would also be expensive.

China has a great potential of hydroelectricity (380 GW), but the country had developed only 9% (35 GW) by the early 1990s. Even with the new 20 GW of capacity under construction, China will have developed only 15% of its potential, leaving 85% untapped. At the beginning of 1992 the National People's Congress gave permission for a massive 18-GW project at the Sanxia (Three Gorge) Dam.[120] The major factors impeding hydro exploitation are the high costs of projects, the great distances between major resources and local centres, decentralization of the power industry and limits on the rates of return to investors.[121]

Currently, the share of nuclear power in China's energy mix is virtually nil. China is running two nuclear plants: one is a 300-MW plant in Zhejiang province, owned by the Chinese government, the other is the 1,800-MW Daya Bay plant near Hong Kong, a joint venture with the Hong Kong utility. (In April 1995 the latter was shut down after one of the two reactors failed a safety test.) China aims at increasing its nuclear capacity to 3.5 GW in 2000 and 22.3 GW in 2010. If the target is achieved, nuclear power's share in China's energy balance will be 4.7% in 2010.[122] However, neither nuclear power nor hydroelectricity can substitute for oil.

Even though coal is and will remain the main energy source for Chinese economic development, it too is no substitute for oil. Consequently, more emphasis seems to be being placed on oil as the only option for the economic development of the Chinese coastal zone. But transport and heat-up fuels in South China are expensive, and so competition between oil and coal is inevitable. The question follows as to whether enough oil can be supplied to maintain current high economic-growth rates. The answer is that China's domestic oil demand during the 1990s seems unlikely to be satisfied if oil production fails to increase substantially. In this context, debate over China's future oil export and import policy is of special interest.

The prospect of massive Chinese oil imports is not remotely realistic. An article contributed to *Energy of China* by staff of the State Planning Committee argues that crude-oil imports of 30–50 mt are manageable, and more economical than maintaining exports at a level of 20 mt. Ammunition for the committee's argument came from the finding that $4.6 billion was paid for the import of petrochemical feedstocks in 1988 while only $2.6 billion was earned from the export of around 20

---

[119] *OPEC Bulletin*, Sept. 1988, p. 49.

[120] Kambara, 'The Energy Situation in China' (op. cit., n. 100), pp. 623–4.

[121] Fereidun Fesharaki, Allen L. Clark and Duangjai Intarapravich, eds, *Pacific Energy Outlook: Strategies and Policy Imperatives to 2010*, East–West Centre, Occasional Papers, Energy and Mineral Series, no. 1 (March 1995), p. 93.

[122] Ibid., pp. 86–7, 98; *Financial Times*, 4 April 1995.

mt of crude oil.[123] This suggests that the role of oil in China's energy balance can be maintained with massive oil imports.

4.6 Conclusion

Balancing energy supply and demand in China is essential if the pace of economic development is to be maintained. As pointed out by Tatsu Kambara, the balance can be maintained, but China will still suffer a chronic shortfall in energy supplies.[124] The country has reason to worry about oil and gas production, even though the target of oil production in 1995 was achieved one year earlier than planned, and crude-oil imports in 1994 were far less than projected.[125] Onshore oil production in recent years has made virtually no contribution to China's total. Even offshore production will make only a limited contribution to the total production increase from the late 1990s onwards. As for gas, even if production doubled by 2000, its contribution to China's energy-production structure would not be significant.

Until the end of the 1990s, massive oil imports look inevitable as the western frontier region's infrastructure and energy-delivery system will not otherwise be fully supplied. This region cannot contribute to easing the energy shortage until at least early next century. And this prediction is based upon an assumption that a string of major discoveries will be made in Xinjiang province, especially in the Tarim Basin.

Investment availability will be the problem. China's large fiscal deficit seems likely to prevent a huge investment in the oil and gas industries. This internal situation drove China to take a more flexible stance towards attracting foreign investment. The external environment is having the same effect, as neighbouring countries, like Russia and the Central Asian republics, are competing for foreign capital. Consequently, invisible competition to invite the investment will be intensified especially between China and Russia.

The condition of China's oil and gas industries can be summarized as follows: potential but not proven resources which anyway will be high-cost (even in a low-price environment); rapidly increasing demand; low finance availability; and messy internal prices. All this could certainly be construed as a crisis, albeit of an

[123] Yang Xingxian and He Xiwu, 'Ponder upon the Strategy of Long-term Supply of Energy in China after the Gulf War', *Energy of China* 3 (1992), pp. 25–28.

[124] Kambara, 'The Energy Situation in China' (op. cit., n. 100), p. 635.

[125] China imported 10.5 mt of crude oil, slightly over half of the projected 20 mt. If not for the May 1994 reform, the projected 20 mt would have been correct. See *China OGP* 3: 2 (15 Jan. 1995), p. 2.

entirely different kind from the one that Russia currently faces. In Chapters 5 and 7, this study will suggest what sort of policy China is pursuing for its frontier oil and gas development and explores the reality of the Tarim Basin's oil and gas development.

Chapter 5

The goals of Russian and Chinese oil- and gas-development policy in Northeast Asia

This chapter examines the key elements of policies towards oil and gas development in the two main resource countries of Northeast Asia: Russia and China. It traces the relevant domestic political and economic context in these countries, and the development of policies towards oil and gas development, including the involvement of foreign companies, over the past two decades. This provides a basis for understanding both Russia's and China's oil and gas development policies in Northeast Asia.

5.1 Russia

5.1.1 Political goals

Russia in the Asian region: Even though the former Soviet Union has always been a presence in East Asia, with more than 31% of its land surface lying east of Lake Baikal, it has not yet been integrated into the East Asian region. Gerald Segal put it this way: 'The Soviet Union is a power in Asia but is not an Asian power yet.'[1] This symbolic expression of Soviet frustration gives a hint as to the political goals of the FSU's oil and gas policy in Northeast Asia during the last two decades.

In the 1970s the Soviet Union aimed to use oil and gas development to contain China and to weaken the US alliance system in East Asia. It failed in both aims. The Soviet defence buildup in the region and expansion by military means have brought a loose anti-Soviet coalition of virtually all the non-communist countries in East Asia plus China.[2] The United States, Japan and China were very suspicious of the Soviet Union's ambitious approach towards Far East oil and gas development which, as a result, was adversely affected by its political goals.

It was Gorbachev's historic Vladivostok speech in 1986 that heralded a new Soviet policy towards Asia. Gorbachev made it clear that the Soviet Union wanted

[1] Hiroshi Kimura, 'Soviet Focus on the Pacific', *Problems of Communism*, May–June 1987, p. 3.

[2] Donald S. Zagoria, 'The Strategic Environment in East Asia', in Donald S. Zagoria, ed., *Soviet Policy in East Asia*, Yale University Press, New Haven, 1982, p. 13; Osamu Miyoshi, 'Soviet Strategy in Asia: A Japanese View', *Comparative Strategy* 6: 1 (1987), pp. 1–27.

to take part in and benefit from the much vaunted economic dynamism and potential of the Asian-Pacific basin.

This was an admission that the Soviet Union had been a sideline player in the region. A Soviet historian, E. Bazhanov, pointed out that Soviet policy there had been fundamentally misguided for decades and was leading to deadlock; perestroika, however, introduced radical changes in the old policy.[3] A similar appraisal was made by Yuri D. Fadeev, of the Ministry of Foreign Affairs, at a seminar held in Seoul in June 1991. Fadeev said that

> New thinking was especially noticeable in the Soviet foreign policy in Asia and the Pacific. It might be due to the fact that this is a relatively new sphere of our policy as we have only recently turned our eyes towards the region. This was done belatedly; we failed to recognize in time the appearance of a dynamically developing centre of the world economy; benefits forgone are impossible to estimate. However, as the [Russian] proverb says, 'better late than never'.[4]

These remarks suggest that integration into the Asia-Pacific region in the 1990s is a priority, and that Soviet oil and gas policy in Northeast Asia will be seen as a means to achieving the political goal.

Regionalism in the Russian Far East: At the end of 1991 the Russian Federation (RF) emerged in the wake of the disintegration of the Soviet Union. The political goal of Soviet oil and gas policy in Northeast Asia seems unlikely to change as the RF inherited the whole of the Soviet Union's Far Eastern region. A serious problem is presented, however, by the voices of nationalism and regionalism in the area following the dissolution of an empire.[5] In fact, demands from Siberia and the Far East for economic, state-political and cultural autonomy, to reduce their dependence on a

---

[3] In an article contributed to *Pravda*, Bazhanov argued that 'the Soviet policy in the Asia-Pacific region is increasingly determined by three principal motives: to ensure the Soviet Union's security, to solve internal economic problems, and to acquire the status of a respected participant in political and social life in Asia and in the Pacific area.' See *Tass*, 16 Jan. 1990, quoted in *Supar Report* 9 (July 1990), p. 21.

[4] Yuri D. Fadeev, 'New USSR Foreign Policy: A Product of Soviet Perestroika', in Institute of Foreign Affairs and National Security (IFANS), *ROK–USSR Cooperation in a New International Environment*, IFANS, Seoul, 1991, p. 45.

[5] Mette Skak, 'Post-Soviet Foreign Policy: The Emerging Relationship between Russia and Northeast Asia', *Journal of East Asian Affairs* 7: 1 (Winter/Spring 1993), pp. 155–6; Vera Tolz, 'Regionalism in Russia: The Case of Siberia', *RFE/RL Research Report* 2: 9 (26 Feb. 1993), pp. 1–9; Sergei Manezhev, 'The Russian Far East, Post-Soviet Business Forum', Royal Institute of International Affairs, London, 1993, pp. 9–16.

super-centralized administration, are gaining ground. In July 1993 the parliament of the Maritime Territory in Vladivostok decided to grant itself the status of republic.[6]

The appearance of an Association of Far East Soviets of People's Deputies (FEA)[7] and the possibility of a Far Eastern Republic (FER)[8] are reflections of the area's dissatisfaction with its flagging economic development despite huge energy resources, and expressions of its willingness to separate itself from the Europe-oriented centre, if proper steps for the area's economic development are not immediately taken. In short, the area is reluctant to continue to provide resources for the national economy at the expense of its own development.[9] What it wants is access to the Pacific to finance a new role as a comprehensively developed economic region.[10] Essentially the FEA is asking for the power to develop independent financial and trade arrangements, and by implication political relationships, with Pacific powers.

---

[6] *The Times*, 9 July 1993; *Daily Telegraph*, 9 July 1993.

[7] On 11 August 1990 the FEA was formed at a meeting in Khabarovsk to promote economic and social cooperation. In October 1991 it practically issued an ultimatum by saying that if the necessary means for normal life were not injected into the Far East then it would have the right to absolute autonomy. For details, see Keun Wook Paik, 'Russian and Chinese Oil and Gas Policies in Northeast Asia: International Political Consequences and Implications', PhD dissertation, University of Aberdeen, 1993, pp. 251–3.

[8] The idea of the FER, which existed in 1920–2, was resurrected at the FEA meeting in August 1990. The name of the new movement is 'Vozrozhdenie' (Rebirth). Ibid.

[9] The Russian president Boris Yeltsin ceded a large amount of authority to the region to achieve economic independence in a decree of 11 November 1991, giving the right of control and use of both land and continental natural resources to the region, but the Republic of Sakha did not believe the Russian government would live up to the decree. See *Supar Report* 13 (July 1992), p. 74. The Yakut ASSR proclaimed the sovereignty of the Yakut-Sakha SSR within the Russian Federation in September 1990. Later its name was changed to Republic of Sakha. Sakha is the name of the principal ethnic group. See *Supar Report* 10 (Jan. 1990), p. 203; 11 (July 1991), p. 122.

[10] Here it is worth noting a proposal by Vladimir Balakhonov to form three or four Russian-speaking states out of those parts of the RSFSR (Russian Soviet Federated Socialist Republic) where the Russians predominate. Balakhonov thought that the creation of independent states in Siberia and the Far East would enable the Russian nation to participate in, and benefit from, the development of the 'Pacific Community' in the twenty-first century. Balakhonov divided the democratic and sovereign states as follows: i) Russia proper, embracing Moscow and historic Russian lands to the west of the Urals; ii) West Siberia; iii) East Siberia (Balakhonov did not rule out the possibility of a single Siberian state); iv) the Russian Far East. See Vladimir Balakhonov, 'Preservation of the Empire or Self-Preservation by Way of National Sovereignty – the Main National Problem of the Russian People', *Russkaya Mysl'*, 23 June 1989, p. 6, quoted in Roman Szpoluk, 'Dilemmas of Russian Nationalism', *Problems of Communism*, July–Aug. 1989, p. 26.

An interesting development is the recent campaign of the Primorskii Krai governor, Yevgeny Nazdratenko, to overturn the 1991 border treaty in which Russia agreed to return a 5.5-sq.-mile area (including the disputed Damansky Island) in its Far East territory to China.[11] This campaign will not seriously affect Russia's policy towards China, but confirms the dilemma the Russian Far East is facing. On the one hand, it expects its early integration into the Asia-Pacific economy. On the other, it fears Chinese economic expansion and their massive migration into the region.

As far as Chinese peaceful expansion is concerned, Moscow has responded by removing 20 Russian border checkpoints from the control of local governments and putting them under Moscow's control.[12] At present, separation of the Russian Far East from the Russian Federation is no more than a vaguely articulated wish, and no organized political movement seems to be behind it. None the less a genuine separatist movement in the Far East in the foreseeable future cannot be ruled out.

It remains to be seen whether regionalism will lead to the appearance of an FER or remain a means to obtaining more authority from the central government. Moscow's response towards the movement for separatism in the Far East seems to be greatly conditioned by the achievement level of its political goal, especially improvement in its uneasy relations with Japan. As Russia recognizes the importance of having a politically friendly environment for the promotion of its long-delayed oil and gas development, the political goal of its oil and gas policy in Northeast Asia in the 1990s seems to be to secure its status as a regional power by improving its relations with the other major countries of the region.

5.1.2 Strategic goals

During past decades Soviet military buildup in the Far East seems to have been driven by superpower competition and strategic considerations that now embrace three of the world's largest oceans and reach well beyond the immediate East Asian theatre. Instigating factors were the Sino-Soviet conflict and border clashes in the Far East, the greater independence and economic resurrection of Japan, and US influence and involvement in the region. As a result, the strategic importance of the

---

[11] *Financial Times*, 1 March 1995; *The Times*, 9 June 1995.

[12] This step was taken in January 1994. Besides this, Moscow terminated the liberal visa system and restricted visa insurance to Chinese businessmen. See Tsuneo Akaha, 'Russia in Asia in 1994: An Emerging East Asian Power', *Asian Survey* 35: 1 (Jan. 1995), p. 103. In Spring 1994 estimates presented to the State Duma varied from 0.3 million to 2 million people. If the trend continues, the Chinese could form the majority of the population in the regions bordering China within 20 years. It is now being called 'Chinese peaceful expansion'. See Zhores A. Medvedev, 'Sino-Russian borders', *Times Higher Educational Supplement*, 13 Jan. 1995.

Map 5.1: The Baikal–Amur main line, 1981

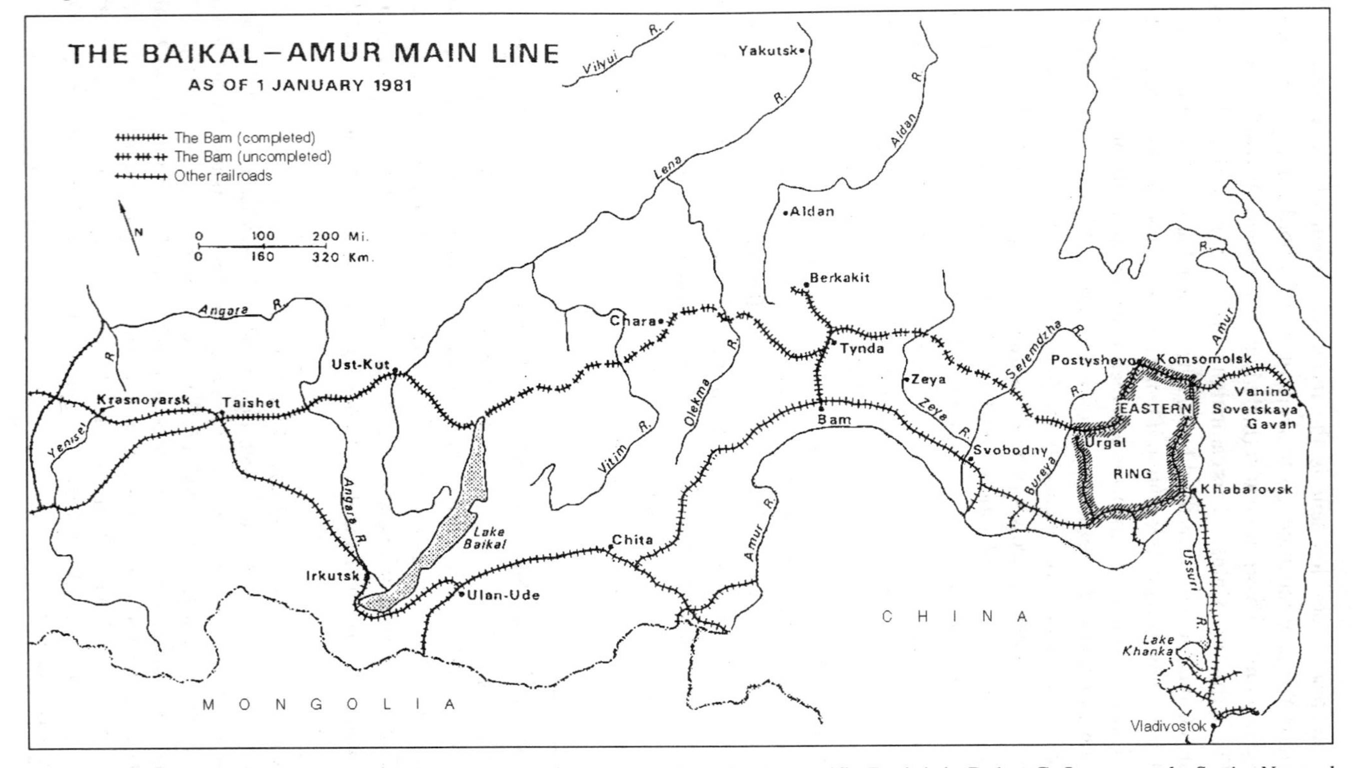

Source: Victor Mote, 'The Baikal–Amur Main line and its Implications for the Pacific Basin', in Rober G. Jensen et al., *Soviet Natural Resources in the World Economy*, University of Chicago Press, Chicago, 1983, p. 134.

Soviet Union as a gateway to the Pacific received greater attention in Moscow, with a substantial increase in the Soviet military presence in the Far East.[13]

Following the border clashes of 1969, Soviet appreciation of its Far Eastern vulnerabilities was heightened; the 1979 confrontation between China and Vietnam intensified this sense of insecurity. The Soviets responded with a military buildup in the region. The idea of building the Baikal–Amur Main line (BAM), which first arose in 1932 after the Japanese seizure of Manchuria, was resurrected.[14] Construction of the 3,145-km line, from Ust-Kut to the Amur at Komsomolsk, began in 1974 and suggested the growing strategic importance of the region (see Map 5.1). In 1975 the Trans-Siberian Railway (TSR) could supply only four-fifths of the estimated annual logistical demand of Soviet armed forces in the Far East.[15] The BAM construction was aimed at easing the overloading of the TSR and was expected to satisfy the logistical demands of the region's military forces.

The BAM project led China, Japan and the United States to keep a watchful eye on the effect of Siberian development on Moscow's maritime presence in the Pacific, as it would augment the logistical flow to the military in the Far East. In 1978 the Soviet Union set up the headquarters of a Theatre of Military Operations (TVD)[16] in the Far East, and in 1979 located its largest out-of-area air and naval base in the Pacific at Cam Rahn Bay in Vietnam. By the end of the 1980s the Soviet Union had formed a formidable military force in its Far East composed of two groups (one to counter US forces in Japan, Alaska and along the Pacific coast, and the other to cover the land force).[17]

---

[13] Gary Hausladen, 'Perestroyka and Siberia: Frontier Resource Development', in Michael J. Bradshaw, ed., *The Soviet Union: A New Regional Geography?*, Belhaven Press, London, 1991, p. 110; Harry Gelman, 'The Siberian Military Buildup and the Sino–Soviet–US Triangle', in Rodger Swearingen, ed., *Siberia and the Soviet Far East: Strategic Dimensions in Multinational Perspective*, Hoover Institution Press, Stanford, 1987, pp. 179–225.

[14] Theodore Shabad and Victor L. Mote, *Gateway to Siberian Resources (The BAM)*, John Wiley & Sons, New York, 1977, p. 71; Victor L. Mote, 'The Baikal–Amur Mainline and its Implications for the Pacific Basin', in Robert G. Jensen, Theodore Shabad and Arthur W. White, eds, *Soviet Natural Resources in the World Economy*, University of Chicago Press, Chicago, 1983, pp. 133–87.

[15] Victor L. Mote, 'The Communications Infrastructure', in Rodger Swearingen, ed., *Siberia and the Soviet Far East* (op. cit., n. 13), p. 52.

[16] The TVD was set up six years before similar headquarters were established in Europe and the Caucasus. See Malcolm Mackintosh, 'Soviet Military Strategy and Operational Capacities in the 1990s', in Ross Babbage, *The Soviets in the Pacific in the 1990s*, Pergamon Press, Oxford, 1989, pp. 34–5.

[17] The number of Soviet forces deployed in the region totalled almost 0.6 million. The first group, with 0.326 million men (excluding combined units and units in the region of the

The worst failure of Soviet policy in Northeast Asia was the incapacity to turn a massive military buildup in the area to political advantage. That is the main reason why, during his visit to Beijing in May 1989, Gorbachev for the first time provided details of pending unilateral force reductions in Asia and the Pacific.[18] Reportedly, the new Russian military command, created at the beginning of 1992, plans to slash the three-million-strong military to around two million by 1995, and to 1.5 million by the end of the decade.[19]

Another reason why the Soviets came to take a defensive military posture in Asia might have been the burden of defence spending and the energy situation. In 1985–7 fewer Soviet naval vessels (including submarines) were detected in the South China Sea, and Malcolm Mackintosh has argued that this was partly due to Gorbachev's interest in cutting defence spending, presumably in order to restrict energy flow to a navy whose main priority was preparing for a basically defensive war in the North Pacific.[20]

The tardy completion of the BAM should be blamed to some extent for the low level of its energy shipment to the Far East.[21] The BAM railway was laid by late 1984, but it was not until November 1989 that it was in commission. Reportedly, facilities allowing only 9 mt of freight, just 25% of estimated capacity, have been

---

Chinese border) deployed in the Far East Military District, had 870 combat aircraft, including 470 strike aircraft; about 4,500 tanks, 4,100 infantry combat vehicles and armoured personnel carriers; about 7,000 aircraft; 55 major surface ships; and 48 nuclear-powered submarines (submarines carrying strategic ballistic missiles are not included in this number). The second group, with 0.271 million men deployed in the Far East and Transbaikal military districts and in Mongolia, had 820 combat aircraft, 8,100 tanks, 10,200 infantry combat vehicles and armoured personnel carriers, and 9,400 artillery systems. See *FBIS*, Sov. 89: 102 (30 May 1989), pp. 9–10.

[18] Gorbachev pledged cuts of 12 divisions (including three in Mongolia), 11 air-force regiments and 16 warships from the Pacific fleet. See *Far Eastern Economic Review*, 1 June 1989, p. 22.

[19] Russian analysts estimate that forces stationed in the Far East will make up 25% of this total, compared with 14% as of 1992. Furthermore, they are also contending that Russian military strategy in the region is swinging from a reliance on quantity to quality. See *Far Eastern Economic Review*, 26 Nov. 1992, pp. 27–8.

[20] Malcolm Mackintosh, 'Soviet Military Strategy and Operational Capacities in the 1990s' (op. cit., n. 16), p. 38.

[21] The original 1975 freight-flow analysis of the BAM forecast a possible total of 35 mt of shipments in 1985, including 25 mt of West Siberian oil, and some 5 mt of south Yakutian coking coal. See Victor Mote, 'The Communications Infrastructure', in Rodger Swearingen, ed., *Siberia and the Soviet Far East* (op. cit., n. 13), p. 53.

equipped.[22] In short, the BAM's future role remains in question until its full operation is implemented.

Important lessons can be learnt from the Soviet Union's military buildup in the northeast Pacific. It not only failed to achieve a favourable regional balance of power, but it also generated fear of its intentions in the region and undermined its broader economic and political objectives. In the 1990s Russia seems unlikely to repeat the mistake of a policy that would only cause another delay in oil and gas development in the Russian Far East. Instead, it will probably take a roundabout route to achieve its strategic goal.

That is, it will explore the possibility of making RFE military forces a beneficiary of the region's oil and gas development. Russian Far East oil and gas, once developed would give the military a free ride. In the 1990s the strategic goal of Russia's oil and gas policy in Northeast Asia will be served by achievement of political and economic goals.

5.1.3 Economic goals

The failure of regional economic development: The economic goals of Soviet oil and gas policy in Northeast Asia aimed at easing the chronic regional energy shortages and subsequently helping comprehensive economic development and the region's integration into the Asia-Pacific economies. The Far East was rarely integrated into the mainstream of the Soviet economy, as remoteness and the harsh environment prevented the generation of major export flows to pay for the high cost of development and the expense of naval and military installations so prevalent through its territory. Professor Leslie Dienes described the Far East's weak integration in the Soviet Union as a 'parasitic' relationship.[23]

Had the Soviets implemented Far East oil and gas development the story would have been quite different. The delay in development caused a serious energy shortage in the area. As shown in Table 5.1, Sakhalin crude-oil production in 1991 was less than 2 mt. Since the RFE's two refineries, located in Khabarovsk and Komsomolsk, require around 9 mt of crude oil, and the RFE's total oil demand is around 20 mt/year, a substantial amount of oil had to be imported. In 1991 around

---

[22] The reason why the capacity availability of the BAM was so low is not known. See *Supar Report* 8 (Jan 1990), pp. 72–3; Matthew J. Sagers, 'News Notes', *Soviet Geography*, Dec. 1989, p. 772. In 1987 the main east–west axis of BAM carried only 1 mt, even though the BAM railway jurisdiction generated 16 mt of coal (from South Yakutia) and 9 mt of other freight. See Victor Mote, 'New Soviet Economic Strategy in Asia and the Pacific', *Acta Slavica Iaponica* 8 (1990), p. 97.

[23] Leslie Dienes, *Soviet Asia: Economic Development and National Policy Choices*, Westview Press, Boulder, 1987, p. 89.

Table 5.1: The RFE oil and gas situation (mt/bcm)

	1985	1990	1991
1 Khabarovsk and Komsomolsk refinery's capacity:			
Khabarovsk Refinery	4.12	4.246	4.471
Crude oil from Sakhalin Island	0.1	—	—
Crude oil from W. Siberia	4.02	4.246	4.471
Komsomolsk Refinery	5.2773	5.5684	5.6456
Crude oil from Sakhalin Island	2.4804	1.6207	1.632
Crude oil from W. Siberia	2.7969	3.9477	4.0136
2 Sakhalin crude-oil production and distribution:			
Crude production	2.588	1.8882	1.8323
Allocation for			
Sakhalin Island	0.058	0.068	0.06*
Khabarovsk	2.477	1.765	1.6353*
export to Japan	—	0.062	0.137
3 Natural-gas production and consumption:			
Gas production	1.826	3.2343	3.4162
from Yakutia	1.017	1.402	1.528
from Sakhalin	0.809	1.8323	1.8882
Yakutian gas consumption	1.024	1.528	1.402
in Yakutia	1.024	1.528	1.402
Sakhalin gas consumption	0.926	1.847	1.8883
in Sakhalin	0.926	0.882	0.874
in Khabarovsk	—	0.965	1.0143

Note: * = estimates.
Source: The figures are provided by the Economic Research Institute Russian AS in Khabarovsk.

8.5 mt of West Siberian crude oil was delivered to the RFE, compared with 6.8 mt in 1985. In 1993 the RFE's crude-oil and oil-products imports amounted to 6.2 mt and 11mt (including 3.1 mt of fuel oil) respectively.[24] As for natural gas, in 1991 (insufficient) indigenous production totalled 3.4 bcm, up from 1.8 bcm in 1985, which

[24] In 1992 the RFE imported 7 mt of crude oil, 3 mt of fuel oil and 8 mt of other oil products. See Yevgeni Khartukov and Fereidun Fesharaki, 'Russian Far East: Energy Review and Outlook to 2000', *Energy Advisory* 105 (15 Sept. 1992), p. 3; *Eastern Bloc Energy*, Oct. 1992, p. 2; Yevgeni Khartukov, 'Oil and Gas in the Russian Far East: Its Impact on the Asia-Pacific Region', *Petromin*, Oct. 1994, p. 68 (Tables 4 and 5).

was consumed within regional boundaries.[25]

The dire oil and gas situation in the Soviet Far East was part of the overall failure in the region's economic development. Groundwork for the development programme was carried out in the late 1970s. In 1978 work began on drawing up 'The Comprehensive Programme of Development of Productive Forces of the Soviet Far East' (SFE),[26] of which oil and gas development formed a part. In October 1980 a conference at Vladivostok agreed to set up a single Comprehensive Programme for the development of oil and gas reserves in the Primorskii Krai, Sakhalin Island, and Kamchatskaya and Magadanskaya oblasts. Then, at the beginning of 1982, another programme was announced to organize the extensive exploration of East Siberia.[27] Despite these efforts, no comprehensive programme materialized until 1985, when fuel and energy shortages in the Soviet Far East equalled 4–5 mt, rising from 1 mt in 1980.[28]

Finally a comprehensive programme did appear, in August 1987. This was the 'Long Term State Programme for the Complex Development of the Productive Forces of the Far Eastern Economic Region, the Buryat ASSR, and Chita Oblast to the year 2000'.[29] It was a very ambitious plan, but not realistic. Professor Dienes pointed out that to invest the proposed sum of 198 billion roubles by the year 2000 would require an annual growth of over 9%. This seemed unlikely considering that

[25] As of 1991, the share of Far East oil and gas production in total Russian oil and gas output was merely 0.4% and 0.5% respectively. See Khartukov and Fesharaki, 'Russian Far East' (op. cit., n. 24), p. 4 (Table 2).

[26] The programme was later identified as the 'Dalnii Vostok' programme. Priority within Dalnii Vostok was given to the structural transformation of the economy, solving social problems, and the development and rational use of the natural resources of the region. See Elisa B. Miller, 'Economic Policy in the Soviet Far East, 1965–80: One Aspect of Soviet Economic Relations in the Asia Pacific Region', PhD dissertation, University of Washington, 1986, pp. 142–74.

[27] David Wilson, 'Exploration for Oil and Gas in Eastern Siberia', in Alan Wood and R. A. French, eds, *The Development of Siberia: People and Resources*, Macmillan, London, 1989, pp. 228–60.

[28] Yu Skorokhodov, 'The Soviet Far East: Problems and Prospects', *Far Eastern Affairs* 3 (1988), p. 7.

[29] The programme was approved by the Politburo on 24 July 1987. It called for a 2.4–2.5-times increase in industrial output: oil extraction to rise 3.1–3.8 times (6–8 million tonnes), gas production 7.2–9.3 times, electricity generation 2.6 times and coal extraction to reach 82–5 mt. To achieve that goal, however, it proposed a sum of 198 billion roubles of investment in the Far East and 34 billion roubles for the two Transbaikalian provinces of Chita oblast and the Buryat ASSR. (The official exchange rate for the rouble used here equals US$1.33.) See Leslie Dienes, 'A Comment on the New Development Program for the Far East Economic Region', *Soviet Geography*, April 1988, pp. 420–2.

during 1985–7 annual investment growth in the national economy as a whole averaged no more than 5.3%, and the 1988 plan called for only a 3.6% rise.[30] (The Programme was carried out between 1987 and the first half of 1989.[31]) Reportedly an energy shortage began to reappear in Khabarovsk Krai in 1989.[32]

New proposals and requirements for energy: At the end of the 1980s the Soviet Union began to prepare a comprehensive survey of the Far East's mineral and energy resources with special emphasis on its natural-gas export potential,[33] and in the spring of 1991 a report entitled 'Concept of Developing Yakutian and Sakhalin Gas and Mineral Resources of Eastern Siberia and the USSR Far East', commonly known as the 'Vostok (East) Plan', was produced.[34] Even though the 'Vostok Plan' has not been implemented (at least in its original form), the Plan itself was a reflection of the Soviets' keenness to accelerate Soviet Far East oil and gas development.

Like the Soviet Union, Russia gives priority to the economic development of its Far East. According to Dr Alexandre G. Granberg, a new government programme named 'The Far East' will be oriented towards cooperation in the Pacific region and will envisage the active participation of foreign capital. The Asia-Pacific countries, he said, could profitably participate in mining and processing of mineral, coal, gas, timber and oil resources.[35]

---

[30] Ibid., p. 421. Professor Pavel A. Minakir confirmed that the Programme was unrealistic by saying that 'The planned goals for energy production have not yet yielded good results. By 1990 only 50% of projected energy production will be put into operation'. See Pavel A. Minakir, 'Economy of the Soviet Far East: Prospects for Development and Cooperation in the Asian-Pacific Region', paper presented at the Third PECC Minerals and Energy Forum, Manila, 27–28 July 1989.

[31] FBIS, Sov. 91: 74 (17 April 1991), p. 7.

[32] In the Krai, the energy crisis began in 1975 and lasted about 10 years. By 1985 the problem had been overcome. See FBIS, Sov. 90: 137 (17 July 1990), p. 56.

[33] Fereidun Fesharaki and Eugene Khartukov, 'Oil and Gas of the Soviet Far East: How Big a Play?', *Petroleum Advisory* 76 (3 Sept. 1991), p. 4. In 1990 an interesting conclusion was drawn by an authoritative USSR Academy of Science commission, led by academicians M. Styrikovich and Yu. Rudenko, which prepared a feasibility study on developing the extraction and use of natural gas from the continental shelf in the Far East. The commission concluded that 'The implementation of the plans will make it possible to meet the Far East economic region's needs for power industry fuel and raw materials ... The implementation of the plans could be a major part of the USSR's foreign policy contribution to the development of the Pacific countries.' See FBIS, Sov. 90: 137 (17 July 1990), p. 56.

[34] W.C. Krueger, 'Ambitious exploration, pipeline project may tap eastern CIS', *Oil and Gas Journal*, 23 March 1992, p. 121.

[35] Dr A.G. Granberg added that 'the effectiveness of state programmes and the activity of the institutionalized Russian and foreign investors will largely depend upon the evolution of the

However, whilst the economic goals are clear, the means are far more problematic. The region simply does not have the financial, technical or labour resources to undertake the massive developments implied (see Chapter 7); and it is hard to see how the rest of Russia can provide such resources. Consequently, plans cannot be realized without very extensive foreign investment, and an influx of foreign labour. And that in turn will depend upon Russian relationships with its Pacific neighbours, including resolution of disputes such as that with Japan over the Kurile Islands (see Chapter 2).

5.2 China

5.2.1 Political goals

'Containment': China's oil policy in the 1970s and early 1980s was conditioned by the fear of Soviet oil-and-gas hegemony, which threatened to affect adversely East Asian geopolitical relations. China's main concern was whether the accelerated development of Soviet Siberian oil and gas, coupled with the projected development of supporting communications and transportation infrastructure, might result in a greatly improved Soviet logistical capacity to wage war in the Far East.[36] China used anti-Sovietism as a political weapon to obtain US and Japanese technical and economic assistance, for Sino-American and Sino-Japanese relations were rooted in a common obsession with the growth of Soviet power.

China's foreign policy has always been anti-imperialist, and its rapprochement with the United States in the 1970s seemed to break the traditional rules. In fact nothing changed, except that the Soviet Union replaced the United States as China's foremost imperialist enemy.[37] And while the United States emphasized China's role as a potential political partner, China's primary concern was to gain access to the

---

mechanism of cooperation. Such a concrete mechanism could be provided by the project, which was initiated in April 1992 by the Associations of economic cooperation of Siberia and the Far East. The project was code-named "Integrator-XXI". Its intention is to link various business interests of Russia's Eastern territories with those of the Asian Pacific Region countries'. See the statement by Dr A.G. Granberg, as a representative of the RNCPEC (Russian National Committee for Pacific Economic Cooperation), presented at the IXth General Meeting of the PECC, San Francisco, Sept. 1992. (It has not been possible to confirm whether this programme was actually prepared.)

[36] Ronald C. Keith, 'China's Resource Diplomacy and National Energy Policy', in Ronald C. Keith, ed., *Energy, Security and Economic Development in East Asia*, St. Martin's Press, New York, 1986, p. 26.

[37] A. James Gregor, *The China Connection: US Policy and the People's Republic of China*, Hoover Institution Press, Stanford, 1986, pp. 79–85

scientific and technical knowledge and equipment necessary for its development.[38]

In its relationship with Japan, China aimed at achieving three objectives: strengthening cooperation against Soviet influence in the Asia-Pacific region; utilizing Japan's economic power, technology and financial capacity to modernize the Chinese economy; and impeding any developments that might once more allow Japan to become a military threat to China.[39] The energy relationship with Japan was the keystone of Chinese strategy, which used the certainties of established crude-oil reserves at Daqing and the future potential of the Bohai Gulf against Soviet Siberian and Far East natural-resources-development projects.

The strategy worked, but China realized that the oil-export card would not be as effective in the 1980s as in the 1970s.[40] The Yakutian gas project was suspended not because of Chinese oil but because of the Soviet invasion of Afghanistan in December 1979. The promise of Chinese oil was not powerful enough to generate much political leverage.

China's pragmatic policy: In the early 1980s the task of domestic development and a fading Soviet threat brought a rethinking of Chinese foreign policy towards greater independence.[41] This signalled an end to Deng Xiaoping's earlier strategy of forging an anti-Soviet united front with the countries of the US alliance system.[42] China's main purpose now was to provide a stable international environment for internal

[38] China's petroleum exploration and production-equipment imports from Western countries during 1973–78 totalled about $577–600 million, including $169–74 million from the United States and $199 million from Japan. The figures are calculated from Table 22.1 in Kim Woodard, *The International Energy Relations of China*, Stanford University Press, Stanford, 1980, pp. 546–9. See also Randall W. Hardy, *China's Oil Future: A Case of Modest Expectations*, Westview Press, Boulder, 1978, pp. 102–3, Appendix S.

[39] Susan L. Clark, 'Japan's Role in Gorbachev's Agenda', *Pacific Review* 1: 3 (1988), p. 285.

[40] In the Long-Term Trade Agreement of February 1978, China committed a total of 47.1 mt of its crude-oil exports to Japan during 1978–82, but failed to meet the commitment by 7.76 mt due to its inability to increase oil production. At that time the production target for oil was 250 mt by 1985 and 500 mt by 2000, as against the 1978 output of about 100 mt. See Chae-Jin Lee, *China and Japan: New Economic Diplomacy*, Hoover Institution Press, Stanford, 1984, pp. 103–12 (especially Table 22); Shigeru Ishikawa, 'Sino-Japanese Economic Co-operation', *China Quarterly* 109 (March 1987), pp. 1–21.

[41] Chi Su, 'Sino-Soviet Relations of the 1980s: From Confrontation to Conciliation', in Samuel S. Kim, ed., *China and the World: New Directions in Chinese Foreign Relations*, 2nd edn, Westview Press, Boulder, 1989, p. 117; Kerry B. Dumbaugh, 'Peking's Foreign Policy Since 1987: Implications for the United States', in King-Yuh Chang, ed., *Mainland China after the Thirteenth Party Congress*, Westview Press, Boulder, 1990, pp. 197–201.

[42] Steven I. Levine, 'Sino-American Relations: Renormalization and Beyond', in Samuel S. Kim, ed., *China and the World* (op. cit., n. 41), p. 92.

economic reform and to enhance its value for its trading partners in the West.[43]

China's pragmatism in the 1980s paid special attention to the availability of Western technology, particularly from the United States.[44] During 1979–88 China spent $3.4 billion on oil-field-equipment imports from 13 countries, including about $1.4 billion for equipment from the United States.[45] China even explored the possibility of utilizing improved Sino-Soviet relations. In 1985 it explored the possibility of multilateral cooperation in Northeast Asia including the Soviet Far East.[46] Given the political, strategic and economic challenges of Siberian development and China's desperate efforts to block development during the 1970s, the Chinese initiative was something of a surprise.

The Chinese conceived of a triangular compensation-and-barter trade and investment relationship. Professor Gaye Christoffersen gives the following example: the Soviet Union supplies crude oil to China, China processes it in the Liaoning refinery, then the oil products are shipped to Japan. In return, Japan supplies capital and technology to both the Soviet Union and China.[47] The implementation of a triangular energy trade makes northeastern China a beneficiary of Soviet Far East energy development, and at the same time alleviates the burden of hard-currency payment for advanced-technology imports.

---

[43] China saw that improved Sino-Soviet relations, as a means of maximizing bargaining power with the United States, would serve the purpose of enhancing its status, and bringing pressure to bear upon western governments to facilitate technology transfers, to increase the flow of investment and to expand trade. See Leszek Buszynski, 'International Linkages and Regional Interests in Soviet Asia-Pacific Policy', *Pacific Affairs* 61: 2 (Summer 1988), p. 224.

[44] During 1981–5, two-thirds of all China's technology-import contracts were signed with the United States, Japan and Germany. In the same period China signed 319 contracts with US companies with a total value of $1,225 billion: 22.8% of the total number, and 24.7% of the total value of contracts. See Ai Wei, 'The Technology Trade Between the United States and Mainland China in Recent Years', in King-Yuh Chang, ed., *Mainland China After the Thirteenth Party Congress* (op. cit., n. 41), pp. 159–95.

[45] *China Business Review*, March–April 1990, p. 16 (Table 5).

[46] Gaye Christoffersen, 'Economic Reforms in Northeast China: Domestic Determinants', *Asian Survey* 28: 12 (Dec. 1988), pp. 1254–6.

[47] Gaye Christoffersen, 'Socialist Integration and Energy Regimes', *Pacific Review* 3: 1 (1990), pp. 26–7; *Far Eastern Economic Review*, 1 Jan. 1987, p. 47. Considering that at that time China was thinking of relying on cheaper foreign technology from the Soviet Union requiring no hard currency, due to its heavy dependence on Japanese technology and a $6-billion trade deficit with Japan in 1985 alone, this was an ideal way of killing two birds with one stone. See Walter Arnold, 'Political and Economic Influences in Japan's Relations with China since 1978', in Kathleen Newland, ed., *The International Relations of Japan*, Macmillan, London, 1990, p. 127 (especially Table 7-1).

In short, what China tried to achieve was an environment favourable to its socialist modernization drive following the Third Plenary Session of the Eleventh Central Committee in December 1978.[48] The policy boils down to avoiding any hint of an alliance with the United States and asserting that its improved relations with the Soviet Union would not constitute an alliance. It was a manifestation of the Chinese desire to ensure that international conflict would not get in the way of its economic development.[49] At the same time, it was a confession of its ambition to act as a balance in superpower relations and to expand Sino-Soviet trade.

Accelerated Sino-Russian trade based on their strengthened political relations is given priority in China's post-Soviet agenda. In 1993 the scale of Sino-Russian trade reached $7.7 billion, up from $4.3 billion in 1990. A sharp decline in 1994 due to the replacement of barter trade with trade based on cash settlement seems to be short-lived, and in 1996 the trade scale is expected to return to the 1993 level.[50] The mutual benefits of rapprochement are far beyond expectations, and politically strengthened Sino-Russian relations are bound to play a pivotal role in China's policy towards Northeast Asia in the coming years.

China took the changing international environment seriously and was determined not to allow it to upset its economic development. The political goal of Chinese oil policy in the 1990s seems to be to seek a favourable international environment for China's oil and gas development in remote or disputed areas, and consequently to initiate reform, accessibility and modernization.

5.2.2 Strategic goals

Superpower relations: The security aspect of the Sino–Soviet confrontation seriously affected various aspects of China's international energy policies in the 1970s. Kim Woodard pointed out that China had been concerned about the security implications of the location of its principal energy industries in regions vulnerable to Soviet attack, of the proposed Soviet–Japanese cooperation in energy development and transportation projects in Siberia, and of the increased Soviet naval capability in the Yellow Sea, East China Sea and the South China Sea.[51]

---

[48] For the communique of the Third Plenary Session, see *Peking Review*, 29 Dec. 1978, pp. 6–16.

[49] David M. Lampton, 'The United States, China, and the Soviet Union: Managing a Complex Triangular Relationship', in James A. Dorn and Wang Xi, eds, *Economic Reform in China: Problems and Prospects*, University of Chicago Press, Chicago, 1990, pp. 299–307.

[50] Han Baocheng, 'New Focus on Sino-Russian Economic and Trade Relations', *Beijing Review*, 8–14 May 1995, p. 18.

[51] Woodard, *The International Energy Relations of China* (op. cit., n. 38), pp. 54–5.

Chinese energy industries are concentrated in the Northeast, near the border region, which happens to be the region with the greatest strategic vulnerability.[52] Daqing oil field especially was vulnerable to attack by the Soviet Union because it is adjacent to a sharply contested area on the Sino-Soviet border.

This strategic vulnerability was heightened by the Tyumen oil-pipeline proposal.[53] The pipeline, running close to China's nothern border, was to have provided fuel for Siberian industrialization, thus adding to Soviet military potential, and it was to have transported oil to the Far East for use by the Soviet Pacific fleet.[54] Thus it was obviously seen as a security threat.

A similar strategic vulnerability existed in China's offshore areas. In the late 1970s China became concerned about Soviet naval expansion along its coastline.[55] After the Soviet invasion of Afghanistan in 1979 the Chinese stressed that the Soviet 'southward strategy' was essentially designed to outflank Western Europe in the Middle East and that it was linked to a secondary strategic thrust in the Pacific, which they dubbed the 'dumb-bell strategy'.[56]

Japan and the China Seas: By the mid-1980s, as Sino-Soviet tensions and the immediate threat from Moscow subsided, China became less interested in the strategic benefits to be gained from increased cooperation with the United States

---

[52] The strategic vulnerability of the region to Soviet attack made further development of the northeast region, China's Ruhr, hazardous in terms of security. Ibid., p. 57.

[53] The Soviet proposal envisaged Japanese credits of $2 billion for the construction of a pipeline from the Tyumen oil field in West Siberia to the Soviet Pacific port of Nakhodka, with an estimated flow of 40 mt/year of crude oil for shipment to Japan. See Peter Egyed, *Western Participation in the Development of Siberian Energy Resources: Case Studies*, East-West Commercial Relations Series 22, Institute of Soviet and East European Studies, Carleton University, Dec. 1993.

[54] Arthur Jay Klinghoffer, *The Soviet Union and International Oil Politics*, Columbia University Press, New York, p. 261.

[55] The Pacific Fleet, along with the upgrading of military facilities in the Kurile Islands in 1978 and in the Sino-Vietnam war in 1979, became the largest of the four Soviet fleets in the mid-1980s. See Woodard, *The International Energy Relations of China* (op. cit., n. 38), p. 65; Rodger Swearingen, 'The Soviet Far East, East Asia, and the Pacific-Strategic Dimensions', in Swearingen, ed., *Siberia and the Soviet Far East* (op. cit., n. 13), pp. 240–5.

[56] This dumb-bell strategy highlighted the strategic significance of Siberian resource development for Soviet expansionism in the Far East, and it placed the Strait of Malacca at the middle point of a bar that strategically joined Soviet naval activities in the Indian and Pacific Oceans. See Ronald C. Keith, 'China's "Resource Diplomacy" and National Energy Policy', in Keith, ed., *Energy, Security and Economic Development in East Asia* (op. cit., n. 36), pp. 31–32.

Map 5.2: Unilateral claims in the South China Sea

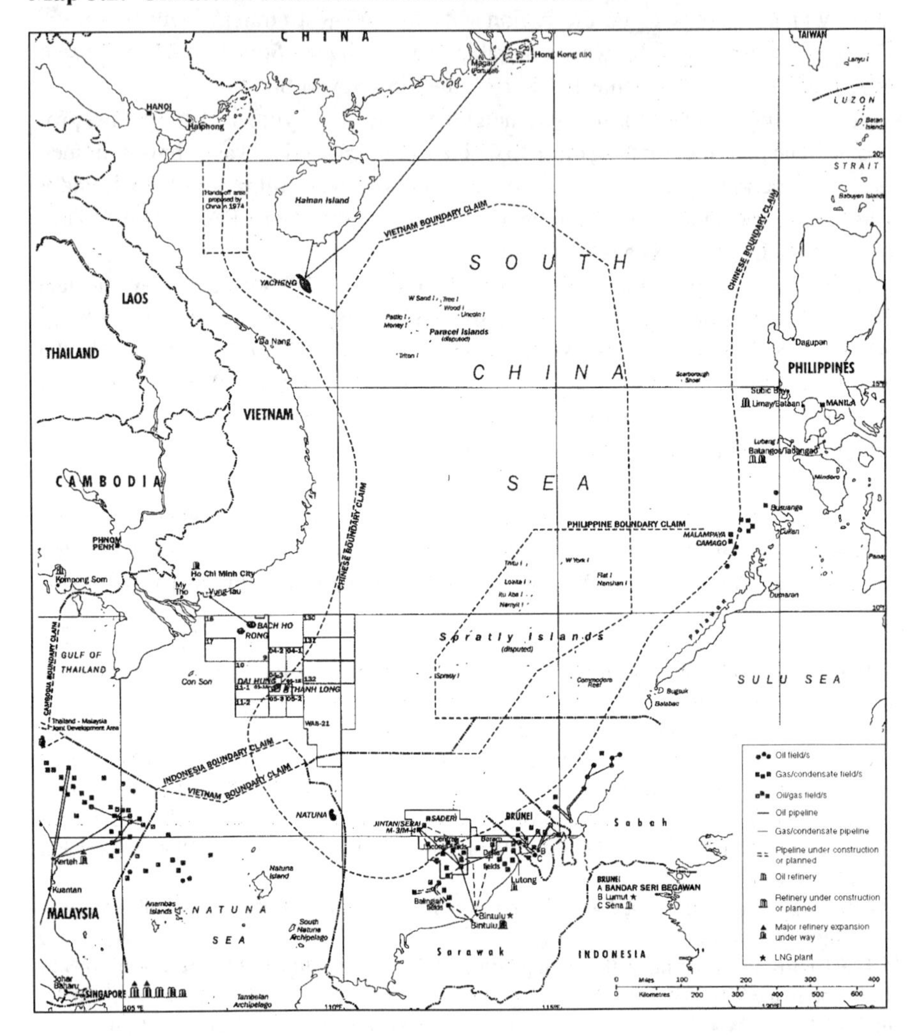

Source: Petroleum Economist, July 1995, p. 18

NOTE: The information within this map is based upon or drawn from various authoritative sources and whilst all reasonable care has been taken in the preparation of this map no warranties can be given as to its accuracy and/or no reliance can be placed upon the same without further detailed inspection and survey. The publishers cannot therefore accept any liability or responsibility for any loss or damage and indeed would be grateful to receive notification of any errors or inconsistencies. No reproduction whatsoever of this map or any part thereof is permitted without the prior consent of the copyright owners. The international and other boundaries in this map are taken from authoritative sources and believed to be accurate as at the date of publication of this map. The representation in this map of any pipelines is no evidence of the existence of rights of passage or use of the same.

and Japan.[57] At the end of the 1980s, the prospects of military disengagement by the United States in East Asia and the Pacific in the post-Cold War era presented the possibility that an unbridled Japan might seek to transform its enormous economic power into military strength and assert itself as a regional power.[58] China's concern is understandable given that the chance of a low-intensity conflict over territory or economic interests has increased and could increase further, and is closely related to offshore oil interests.

China has twice already experienced military clashes in the South China Sea. Its offshore oil interest is believed to have been one of the triggers to clashes over the Parcel and Spratly islands (see Map 5.2).[59] In February 1992 a law listing the Spratlys as sovereign Chinese territory and reserving the right to use force to expel intruders strongly hinted at the strategic goal of China's oil and gas policy in North-east Asia in the 1990s.[60] The law's significance lay in Chinese claims to the South China Sea and much of the East China Sea.[61]

In April 1992 General Zhang Xusan, in a public statement of a shift in maritime strategy, outlined that it was 'high time' for China to readjust its naval strategy and make greater efforts to recover South China Sea oil and gas resources.[62] Military

---

[57] Kenneth Lieberthal and Michel Oksenberg, *Policy Making in China: Leaders, Structures, and Process*, Princeton University Press, Princeton, p. 267.

[58] *Far Eastern Economic Review*, 13 Dec. 1990, pp. 28–9.

[59] Chi-Kin Lo, *China's Policy towards Territorial Disputes: The Case of the South China Sea Islands*, Routledge, London, 1989; Mark J. Valencia, 'International Conflict over Marine Resources in South-East Asia: Trends in Politicization and Militarization', in Lim Teck Ghee and Mark J. Valencia, *Conflict over Natural Resources in South-East Asia and the Pacific*, Oxford University Press, Oxford, 1990, pp. 103–6; Jeanette Greenfield, *China's Practice in the Law of the Sea*, Clarendon Press, Oxford, 1992, pp. 150–67; *Far Eastern Economic Review*, 13 Aug. 1992, p. 14–20; Zhiguo Gao, 'The South China Sea: From Conflict to Cooperation?', *Ocean Development and International Law* 25: 3 (July–Sept. 1994), pp. 345–59.

[60] According to *China Youth News*, a decision to increase military exercises in the Spratlys – or Nansha islands – was taken at a meeting of the command of a submarine unit in the South China Sea fleet. See *Straits Times*, 18 May 1991.

[61] The bill was entitled 'The Law of the People's Republic of China on its Territorial Waters and Their Contiguous Areas'. According to Article 2, 'The PRC's territorial waters refer to the island waters contiguous to its territorial land. The PRC's territorial land includes the mainland and its offshore islands, Taiwan and the various affiliated islands, including Diaoyutai Islands (Senkaku Islands), the Penghu Islands (the Pescadores), the Dongsha Islands (Pratas islands), Xisha Islands (Paracel islands), Nansha Islands (Spratly Islands) and the other islands that belong to the PRC'. See Harvey Stockwin, 'China's Alarming Ripple Effect: Territory Demarcation Signals Expansion Plan', *Sunday Morning Post*, 8 May 1992.

[62] General Zhang, the Navy deputy commander-in-chief, added that his forces were ready to 'offer assistance to the economic development' of the area, including the disputed Spratly islands. See *Straits Times*, 7 April 1992; *Far Eastern Economic Review*, 13 Aug. 1992, p. 20.

Map 5.3: The Crestone deal: Wannan Bei-21 area

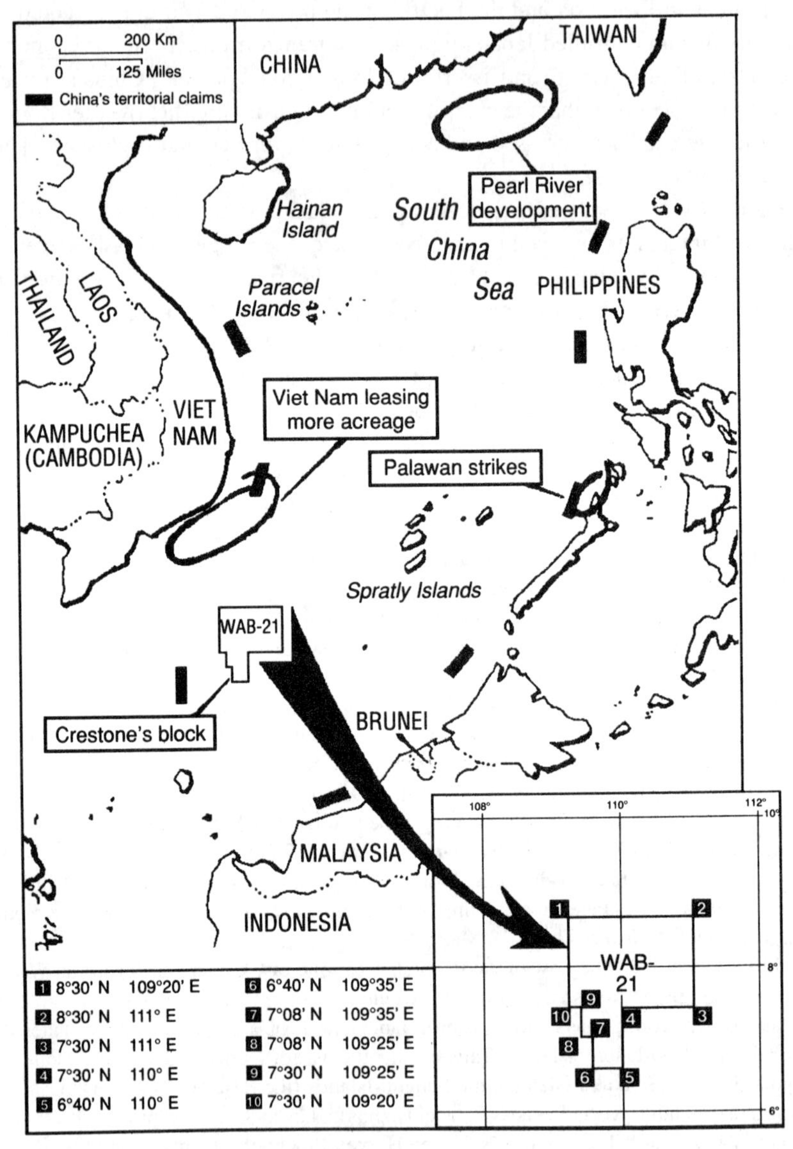

Source: Oil and Gas Journal, 13 July 1992, p. 20.

interest in pursuing a forward policy in the South China Sea seems to be supported by China's increased defence spending.[63] President Yang Shangkun revealed China's ambition to have its own aircraft carrier within ten years to increase its hold on the Spratly Islands and secure its role as a military power in Asia.[64] In short, its territorial claims to the South China Sea islands are backed up by a buildup in naval forces.

An internal document provides a vivid picture of what spurs China to pursue a forward policy in the South China Sea (and though it has been disavowed by Chinese officials it is still worth noting). According to the document, 'In terms of resources, the South China Sea holds reserves worth $1 trillion. Once Xinjiang has been developed this will be the sole area for replacement of resources, and it is a main fallback position for "lebensraum" (survival space) for the Chinese people in the coming century.'[65] In connection with its contract in May 1992 with Crestone Energy Co. for oil and gas exploration at Wanan Bei-21 area, China vowed to defend US crews with its 'full naval might' (see Map 5.3).[66]

What are the implications of China's policy towards the Spratlys for the East China and Yellow Seas? The disputed claim to the Senkaku Islands (Diaoyutai Islands) between China and Japan[67] remains unsettled, as does the Yellow Sea demarcation problem with South Korea. As China views strengthened relations

---

[63] The Chinese defence budget rose 15% in 1991 and 12% in 1992 to $6.7 billion. And a large portion of the increased military spending was already being funnelled to the Chinese navy, which was reported to be building a Chinese naval base in Myanmar to add to its three South China bases. In early 1993 China decided to increase defence spending by 12.4% to $7.5 billion, despite the budget deficit expected to reach 84.4 billion yuan ($14.7 billion) for 1993. It marks the fourth consecutive annual increase. See *Korea Times*, 30 Jan. 1992, p. 15; 17 March 1993; *Financial Times*, 17 March 1993.

[64] The speech was made at the military commanders' meeting on 27 Sept. 1992. See *South China Morning Post*, 14 Dec. 1992.

[65] The document was prepared by the theoretical department of *Zhongguo Qingnian Bao* (*China Youth News*). See *Far Eastern Economic Review*, 13 Aug. 1992, p. 16. This may seem somewhat exaggerated, but a similar view can be found elsewhere. Mu Lin wrote that 'the development of the South China Sea's oil resources is essential for the Chinese economic development'. See *Xin Bao*, 1 July 1992.

[66] The contract area's oil reserves are estimated in excess of 1 billion bbl. See *China Daily*, 12 June 1992; *Oil and Gas Journal*, 13 July 1992, pp. 20–1; Miriam Hughesman, 'China moves in...', *Energy Economist*, July 1992, pp. 2–4; Shigeo Hiramatsu, 'China's Naval Advance: Objectives and Capabilities', *Japan Review of International Affairs* 8: 2 (Spring 1994), pp. 118–32.

[67] Robert E. Bodeski, *The Fragile Entente: The 1978 Japan–China Peace Treaty in a Global Context*, Westview Press, Boulder, 1983, pp. 35–7; *Far Eastern Economic Review*, 30 Aug. 1990, p. 11.

with Japan during the 1990s as an essential step towards exerting a new influence not only on the Asia-Pacific region but on the whole world,[68] and needs Japan economically for its domestic development, the Senkaku issue lies dormant for the time being. If a huge oil field is discovered in the East China Sea and its development is implemented, however, the situation could change drastically. Nothing can guarantee that China's new Spratlys policy will not be applied in the East China Sea,[69] and the Yellow Sea too would be unlikely to remain an exception.

Besides these offshore areas, China's far western Xinjiang Uygur Autonomous Region, bordering CIS republics as well as Mongolia, Pakistan, India and Afghanistan, will also have strategic importance as a hub of oil and gas production in the next century. China has already faced unrest among ethnic minorities in the area,[70] and seems likely to keep vigil against an expansion of Islamic fundamentalism. It seems to emphasize protecting its frontier oil and gas areas, and this will complement the economic elements in its oil and gas policy.

5.2.3 Economic goals

Oil development before the 1990s: In the 1970s the economic aspects of Chinese oil policy were overshadowed by the political and strategic ones. China's decision in the early 1970s to export crude oil to Japan was originally driven by political considerations. Without the Soviet factor, a large proportion of Chinese oil exports to Japan would not have been possible.[71]

The economic effects of its oil exports were considerable.[72] Despite the decline of oil production during 1979–81, oil exports continued to rise until 1985 due to the importance attached to increasing hard-currency earnings at that stage of China's development.[73] However, the collapse of the oil price in 1986 drove China to

---

[68] *Beijing Review*, 12–18 Oct. 1992, pp. 19–21.

[69] Japan rejected the February 1992 law and made a rare public criticism of Beijing. See *Financial Times*, 28 Feb. 1992; *Straits Times*, 11 March 1992.

[70] The bordering CIS republics are Kazakhstan, Tajikistan and Kirghizia. See Terry Cannon, 'National Minorities and Internal Frontier', in David S.G. Goodman, ed., *China's Regional Development*, Routledge, London, 1989, pp. 164–79.

[71] In economic terms, the poor quality of Daqing crude oil (such as its waxiness, its high yield of heavy oil distillate – 70.5% as against Arabian crude's 44%, its high pour point) – except for its low sulphur content – made it unattractive to Japanese importers. See Selig S. Harrison, *China, Oil, and Asia*, Columbia University Press, New York, 1977, pp. 157–7; Chae-Jin Lee, *China and Japan: New Economic Diplomacy* (op. cit., n. 40), pp. 110–11.

[72] Oil and coal export earnings balanced energy plant and equipment import costs, approximately $4 billion during 1973–8. See Kim Woodard, 'China and Offshore Energy', *Problems of Communism* 30 (Nov–Dec. 1981), p. 35.

[73] Especially during 1982–5 almost all the increase in annual oil production was exported.

rethink the economics of its oil exports.[74] As a result, oil imports increased substantially, from 0.9 mt in 1985, to 3.5 mt in 1986 and 10.7 mt in 1989.[75] This confirms that Chinese oil policy in the 1980s had come to be conditioned as much by economic factors as by political ones.

In the 1990s China continues to give top priority to its modernization drive. An important question arises as to whether China can keep up its oil exports for hard currency to import technology and equipment needed for modernization, and at the same time satisfy its galloping domestic demand. The answer depends on achievements in oil and gas development.

China opened its offshore territories and part of its onshore regions to international exploration and production in the 1980s. It began offshore,[76] but despite the rosy forecasts, the result of the decade's efforts was disappointing. As discussed in Chapter 4, total offshore oil production in 1993 recorded a mere 4.6 mt,[77] or 3.2% of China's total output of 144 mt. Even if the target of 12 mt in 1997 is achieved, it would amount to little more than a drop in the ocean so far as China's growing oil requirements are concerned.

Another gloomy forecast suggested that China would be a massive oil importer by the end of this decade, a serious warning that the economic goals of its oil and gas policy in the 1990s will not be achieved unless urgent measures are taken. A major shift in China's oil and gas policy seems inevitable.

The rise and rise of foreign involvement: The decisions in 1992–3 to open China's frontier areas at the expense of the self-reliance policy were a reflection of its

See Larry Chuen-ho Chow, 'The Changing Role of Oil in Chinese Exports, 1974–89', *China Quarterly* 131 (Sept. 1992), pp. 759–60.

[74] In 1983 China exported 2 tonnes of crude oil to cover the imports of energy-intensive products with an energy content of 1 tonne of oil equivalent, but after the oil price crisis the ratio deteriorated and consequently oil exports became even more uneconomical. Ibid., pp. 761–2.

[75] *Zhongguo Nengyuan Tongji Nianjian 1991*, p. 212.

[76] Earlier results of the offshore exploration programme begun in 1974, were unsatisfactory. Presumably, the conclusion of the ECAFE (Economic Commission for Asia and the Far East) report in 1969, that 'A high probability exists that the continental shelf between Taiwan and Japan may be one of the most prolific oil reservoirs in the world', offered great hope to the Chinese, as did another report in 1969 that the continental shelf of China from the southern tip of Taiwan to Hainan Island may be one of the most promising areas. See K. O. Emery *et al.*, 'Geological Structure and Some Water Characteristics of the East China Sea and the Yellow Sea,' *UN ECAFE/CCOP Technical Bulletin* 2 (1969), pp. 3–43.

[77] *China Petroleum Investment Guide*, *China OGP* and AP Energy Business Publications, Singapore, 1994, p. 115.

determination to develop all available oil and gas resources. On 30 June 1992 a long-delayed decision to open the East China Sea was made with the announcement of the fourth round of bidding.[78] The opening of onshore frontier areas followed. The Chinese were worried that it would become more and more difficult to stabilize output in three key fields (Daqing, Shengli and Liaohe) because more than half of the workable reserves had been extracted from most of the fields and output was dropping. Hence the strategy of 'stabilizing the east and developing the west' was defined.[79]

The hurried decision to open the frontier areas after years of procrastination was a huge policy change and could be a turning point in Chinese oil and gas exploration and development. It began with a relinquishment of the 1989 decision. At the beginning of 1989 China's State Council called a meeting of senior petroleum officials, and the conference endorsed the principle of self-reliance and barred foreigners from the western basins. An article by Julia Leung pointed to four reasons for the Chinese insistence on self-reliance.

First, they worried that western capitalistic influences might contaminate the hinterland, especially Xinjiang, which was already troubled by minority unrest. Secondly, they have had bad experiences working with foreigners offshore and were frustrated at being unable to persuade foreign partners to develop offshore oil fields they have discovered. It was not until 1990, when oil prices recovered to between $18 and $20 a barrel, that a few oil companies pushed ahead with offshore production plans. Concern that they would not be able to control production of Tarim oil contributed to the decision to bar foreigners.

Thirdly, the CNPC was reluctant to give jobs to foreign companies because the state oil concern had nearly 1.4 million workers on its payroll, and with money short and mature fields drying up it would be in the country's interest to deploy the workers in frontier areas, like the Tarim Basin. Finally, the Daqing factor: many top-ranking CNPC officials who rose to their positions largely because of being associated with

[78] Exploration work in the East China Sea began In 1980, and as of 1990, of 17 exploratory wells, 8 have resulted in commercial oil and gas flows, and 6 have had good oil and gas showing. See Yang, Qi-Lun, 'A Review of Hydrocarbon Exploration in the East China Sea by the Shanghai Marine Geological Investigation Bureau, with a Discussion of Geological Aspects', in Cleavy, L. McKnight and Edmund Chang, eds, *Proceedings of the International Symposium on Tectonic Evolution and Petroleum Potential of the East China Sea*, School of Earth Sciences, Stanford University, 15–16 March 1990, p. 50; *China Daily*, 18 Sept. 1989; *China Daily*, 2 July 1990.

[79] China has earmarked 100 billion yuan ($20 billion) for oil exploration in the Tarim Basin during the eighth five-year plan period (1991–5). See *South China Morning Post*, 18 Feb. 1991; *Ta Kung Pao*, 26 Oct. 1990; *Wen Wei Po*, 6 Feb. 1991; *China Daily*, 17 March 1992.

discoveries at Daqing were confident of repeating the same feat at Tarim. And junior officials hoped Tarim would do for their career paths what Daqing had done for their seniors'. They wanted to claim sole credit for any discoveries.[80]

Three main factors have contributed to a reversal of the policy against foreign exploration in western China. First of all, dire shortages of capital have produced a big fiscal deficit,[81] and China has drastically cut back the budget for exploration,[82] to the extent that the conservative CNPC has been forced to come up with funds itself.[83]

Secondly, the Chinese were worried about flagging oil production. In the mid-1980s it was predicted that energy output by the end of this century would be doubled, not quadrupled, as planned. At that time the Chinese anticipated the difficulty of achieving a quadrupling of industrial and agricultural production with only a doubling of energy production.[84] The prediction was confirmed.[85]

Thirdly, the Chinese had to consider the impact of Russian Far East oil and gas development. They realized that once RFE development got under way it would be extremely difficult to divert the massive capital flow away from Russia towards China's sagging oil and gas industries.[86]

---

[80] Julia Leung, 'China takes Risk in Policy on Oil Basins', *Asian Wall Street Journal*, 27 May 1991.

[81] The capital shortage lead to fulfilment of only two-thirds of the oil prospecting work plan during the seventh FYP (1986–90). See Si Bo, 'Strategic Plan for China's Oil Industry (1991–95)', *China Market* 5 (1991), p. 26.

[82] The exploration budget for Tarim has been slashed to $0.3 billion for 1991–2, down from $0.6 billion allocated in 1989–90. See Qi Daqing and David Fridley, 'Tarim Basin: Hopes and Challenges for China Oil Industry', Resources Program, East-West Center, Honolulu, Jan. 1992.

[83] This is why Wang Tao, then general manager of the China National Petroleum and Natural Gas Corp. (CNPNGC), toured Japan, Canada and the United States in April 1991, and the following April another delegation led by Zhou Yongkang, deputy president of the CNPC, was dispatched to the United States and Japan for the same purpose. See *Asian Wall Street Journal*, 27 May 1991; *China Daily*, 19 May 1991; 6 April 1992.

[84] Sun Shangqing, 'China's Policies for Energy and Technology, and Economic Relations with Japan', in Andrew J. L. Armour, ed., *Asia and Japan: The Search for Modernization and Identity*, Keio University, Tokyo, 1985, p. 101.

[85] According to the Ministry of Energy Resources (MER), energy production in 1992 recorded 1,056 mt of standard coal, merely 13 million more than 1991. The electricity-generating capacity increased by 10.85% in 1992, but GNP grew by 12% and industry increased by 18%. In short, the growth of energy production failed to keep pace with the rapid economic advances. See *Beijing Review*, 4–10 Jan. 1993, pp. 5–6.

[86] Keun-Wook Paik, 'Tarim Opening: Geopolitics of Chinese Oil', *Geopolitics of Energy*, 1 April 1994, pp. 9–10.

In short, China had to consider the possibility that it might not be able to find oil in time to head off a serious energy crisis later in the decade and keep the country's economic powerhouse going into the twenty-first century unless the door was thrown open to foreign capital and technology. It is not impossible even that China will become a beneficiary of Russian Far East oil and gas development.[87] Its goal for the 1990s is to accelerate economic development,[88] and oil and gas policy will aim to prevent any delay in that development caused by energy, especially oil and gas, shortages.

5.3 Conclusion

The goals of Russian and Chinese oil and gas policies in Northeast Asia in the 1990s have common characteristics: establishing a politically friendly environment for the promotion of their frontier oil and gas development; and preventing any delay in economic development by energy, especially oil and gas, shortages. Both are giving top priority to economic factors.

However, Russia's oil and gas policy seems to be greatly conditioned by the achievement of political goals, especially the improvement of its uneasy relations with Japan. China, on the other hand, seems unlikely to be affected by political considerations, unless its new Spratlys policy is applied to the East China and Yellow Seas.

Finally, fierce competition between Russia and China for foreign investment in frontier oil and gas development cannot be ruled out. Neither, however, would want such competition to undermine their recently improved relations.

[87] For a detailed discussion on Sino-Russian oil and gas cooperation, including China's oil and gas imports from the Russian Far East, see Keun-Wook Paik, 'Energy Cooperation in Sino-Russian Relations: Focus on Oil and Gas Development', *Pacific Review* (forthcoming 1995/6).

[88] This was confirmed at the 14th National Congress of the Party in October 1992. The Party also emphasized establishing a socialist market economy. See *Beijing Review*, 26 Oct.–1 Nov. 1992, pp. 33–7.

Chapter 6

The interests and policies of importers, mainly Japan and South Korea

This chapter examines the interests of importers of oil and gas and their policies towards frontier development in both Russia and China. It focuses on Japan and South Korea as the main beneficiaries of Russian and Chinese development because of their geographical proximity, and explains where and why differences in their policies towards development occur. The discussion centres on the two countries' policies towards Russian Far East gas development as their participation here on a complementary or competitive basis will fundamentally affect the Northeast Asian gas market's supply and demand structure in the next decade.

This chapter does not see Taiwan as a main player in Russian and Chinese frontier oil and gas development as Taiwan's tense relations with China considerably limit its manoeuvrability in this respect.

6.1 Japan

6.1.1 Japan's exploration and production policy

Japan's energy-supply position is one of the most vulnerable of any country in the world. More than 50% of its energy needs are met by imports, and oil accounts for 58.3% of energy consumption. Virtually all its oil is imported, with over 70% coming from the Middle East. Given the scale of Japan's energy consumption, the fourth highest in the world, it is bound to have a strong impact on international energy markets, and energy developments in turn exert a strong influence on Japan.

Since the early 1970s Japan has pursued energy policies designed to increase energy efficiency, to create a balanced mix of energy supplies, and to secure more reliable supplies of imported and domestic energy. Japan now has one of the world's most energy-efficient economies with one of the lowest ratios of total primary energy demand per unit of GDP (0.25). A strategy of diversification of energy sources, especially through the introduction of natural gas and a determined programme to expand nuclear power, has decreased Japan's oil dependence from 78% in 1973 to 57% in 1991. The latest Japanese energy projections indicate the government's determination to pay special attention to the issue of energy security. Japan hopes to reduce oil dependence to 53% by 2000 and 48% by 2010.

Initially, the target set by MITI (Ministry of International Trade and Industry) in the late 1960s was to supply 30% of Japanese crude-oil imports in 1985 from-Japanese-developed projects. This target was re-established in 1983, when JNOC (Japan National Oil Corp.) was charged with the task of raising the share of self-developed oil to 30% of imports by 1995. During the period 1967–88 oil produced by Japanese exploration and production companies engaged in foreign upstream activities amounted to 10.6% of total Japanese crude-oil imports. In the years 1989–93 the figure ranged from 11% to 13.7%, which was the closest Japan has come to the target of 30%.[1]

Although Japanese-developed oil has ranged from 8% to 13% of total requirements over the past two decades or more, it is difficult to determine whether this has been achieved economically. To some extent, this point can be established by the role of the government-owned JNOC in Japan's overseas exploration and production activities. From its creation in 1967 until 1993, JNOC has provided equity capital and loans amounting to 1,593 billion Japanese yen and loan guarantees amounting to 1,018 billion yen to Japanese companies active in overseas oil and gas exploration and development.[2]

By the end of 1993 JNOC had provided financial assistance to 1,084 exploration wildcat wells and 788 delineation wells worldwide.[3] Almost half of the exploration and production project companies assisted by JNOC were located in the Asian region. JNOC has placed a high priority on exploration in southeast Asia and the surrounding areas, fairly close to its home market, in order to stimulate oil and gas production in a relatively poorly energy-endowed area of the world. However, most of the Japanese-produced crude oil still flows from the Middle East.

JNOC's plans for the 1990s are likely to be as ambitious as they have been in the past, even though the target of 30% for Japanese-produced crude looks unlikely to be achieved in this decade. Given that Japanese exploration companies have a very high profile in a number of petroleum provinces, like the Russian Far East, China and Vietnam, where potential oil and gas reserves are enormous, Japan's efforts to increase the level of Japanese-produced crude will presumably pay off during the next decade.

6.1.2 Financial support to China as against Russia

Japan has given special emphasis to China's and the FSU's (Russia's) oil and gas development during the past two decades. Japanese policy can be characterized as

---

[1] JNOC (Japan National Oil Corp.), *Annual Report 1994*, p. 19.

[2] Ibid., pp. 18 and 20.

[3] As of the end of June 1994, some 40 project companies assisted by JNOC were producing or about to produce crude oil and gas in 26 countries. Besides this, 79 were conducting oil exploration and development. Ibid., pp. 4–5.

Table 6.1: Japan's energy loan to China

1st loan: May 1979 Memorandum exchange	Total: $2 bn ($1 = 210 yen)	of which $1.006 bn to the petroleum industry covering the development of 11 projects, e.g. the onshore Huabei and Shengli oil fields, the offshore Chengbei oil field and the Sino-Japanese Cooperative Development Zone in south west Bohai Sea. (* Japan's EXIMBank suggests $0.73 bn, not $1.006 bn.)
2nd loan: Dec. 1984 Memorandum exchange	Total: $2.4 bn ($1 = 242 yen)	of which $1.4 bn to the petroleum industry financing the development of onshore (Liaohe, Dagang and Daqing) fields and Chinese shareholders' investment in the Sino-Japanese Cooperative Development Zone in southwest Bohai Sea. (*Japan's EXIMBank suggests $1.7 bn, not $1.4 bn.)
3rd loan: June 1992 Memorandum exchange	Total: $5 bn ($1 = 140 yen)	of which $3.5 bn to the petroleum industry financing the development of 14 onshore oil fields ($3 bn) and 4 offshore oil fields ($0.5 bn).

Source: Gu Rubai, 'Bank of China's Role in Financing Energy Sector', and Yukinori Ito, 'Financing China's Petroleum Sector', papers presented at China Petroleum Investment Conference, Beijing, 17–18 March 1994.

follows: first, Japan has rarely been slow to secure a bridgehead to both countries' oil and gas areas because of their huge potential and geographical proximity. Secondly, Japan's commitment to both China's and the FSU's (Russia's) oil and gas development has been fundamentally influenced by power relations rather than development economics.

Japan's financial aid to both the FSU and China clearly show the level of its commitment to both countries' oil and gas development. Until the end of 1993 China was the largest client of the EXIMBank (Export-Import Bank of Japan), receiving a total of $12 billion in cumulative direct loans, accounting for 13% of the Bank's total. Including cumulative indirect loans, Japan has provided China with a total of $17.8 billion, of which $11.1 billion was the united loan (also called the energy loan). As shown in Table 6.1, total Japanese energy loans during 1979–93 reached $9.4 billion, of which $5.9 billion was for oil development, accounting for around 26% of China's total investment in oil development during the same period.[4]

[4] Yukinori Ito, 'Financing China's Petroleum Sector', paper presented at China Petroleum Investment Conference, Beijing, 17–18 March 1994.

Table 6.2: SODECO's share composition

Establishment:	I Jan. 1974			
Capital:	Initial 40 million yen			
Share composition:	as of March 1990:			
	JPDC[1]	19.5%	JNOC	42.8%
	OPC[2]	19.5%	JAPEX[4]	10.4%
	C. Itoh	15.5%	OPC	10.3%
	Marubeni	15.5%	C. Itoh	7.6%
			Fuyo	5.2%
			Cosmo	2.9%
			Marubeni	2.3%
	Gulf Oil[3]	10%	Chevron[5]	5.7%

Notes:
1 JPDC (Japan Petroleum Development Corp.) changed its name to the current JNOC, in June 1978.
2 Overseas Petroleum Corp.
3 Gulf Oil's 10% share was split proportionally from the shares of the largest Japanese partners.
4 Japan Petroleum Exploration Company Ltd. JNOC is its main shareholder, with 65.7%. Consequently, JNOC's share in SODECO recorded 49.6%.
5 Chevron has now merged with Gulf Oil.
Source: SODECO.

According to a recent report, Japan plans to provide China with its fourth loan worth a total of 700 billion yen (as of 1994, roughly $7 billion) from 1996 for three years.[5]

In contrast, Japan's financial support for Soviet Far East oil and gas development has not been favourable. For example, SODECO has spent some 60 billion yen ($612.84 million) over a decade,[6] but little progress has been made in terms of any real development so far. As shown in Table 6.2, SODECO is virtually under the control of JNOC, which has almost 50% of shares, and as a result the Japanese government can influence any important decision about SODECO's further involvement in development.

[5] *Chosun Ilbo*, 2 Nov. 1994.
[6] *FT International Gas Report*, 22 July 1994, p. 22.

In general, cumulative Japanese aid to Russia reached roughly $4.6 billion in 1993; grant aid such as food and medical supplies, personnel exchange, Chernobyl disaster help, establishment of a nuclear-power technical centre, and the disposal of weapons of mass destruction accounted for $0.5 billion. The remaining $4.1 billion was for loans, including trade insurance of $2.9 billion pledged between the aid package announced in October 1991 ($1.8 billion) and the G7 ministerial aid agreement announced in April 1993 ($1.1 billion). However, of the pledged $2.9 billion, only $1.1 billion has actually been provisionally approved.[7]

In March 1993 MITI provided $0.3-billion worth of insurance covering 350,000 tonnes of steel pipe and construction machinery for Gazprom (see Chapter 2, section 1). This constituted the first portion of the $1.8-billion trade insurance promised in October 1991. In the same month, a trade-insurance application for another $0.4 billion to cover 0.3 mt of steel pipe and construction machinery for Gazprom was submitted, but not fully implemented. The credit-based business negotiation between Gazprom and four Japanese steelmakers was settled in September 1994, with the Japanese price discount for steel pipes at 2–3%, and the following month negotiations for another 203,000 tonnes of steel pipes began. Consequently, the promised trade insurance for Gazprom will not be realized until after the credit-based contract is accomplished. The delay is caused by Russia's failure to pay debts of $330 million to nine Japanese trading companies.[8] Japan has not yet committed itself to another contract for delivery of $700-million worth of Japanese machinery and equipment for Lukoil.[9]

The scale of its financial support for Russia's oil and gas development is not comparable with that for China's. This could be explained by the stance of three organizations, the Ministry of Foreign Affairs (MFA), MITI and the Ministry of Finance (MOF), which have been the main players in Japanese policy towards the FSU. During the Cold War era, the MFA virtually dictated the terms of Japanese policy

[7] Takashi Murakami, 'Future Outlook for Russo-Japanese Relations', paper prepared for the Friedrich-Elbert-Stiftung, 1994 (unpublished), p. 23 (Table 4).

[8] The details of this Gazprom case are provided by Kunio Okada, Institute for Russian and East European Studies. On 28 November 1994, Russia and Japan agreed to postpone Russia's trade debts. See *Financial Times*, 28 Nov. 1994.

[9] A Russian delegation led by Oleg Soskovets, first deputy prime minister, visiting Tokyo in late November agreed with Japan to restart blocked negotiations on a Russian request for official Japanese export-credit guarantees for Japanese suppliers of equipment to Lukoil. See *Financial Times*, 2 Dec. 1994. According to RPI, Lukoil has obtained the loan from Japan's EximBank. The condition of the loan is that 15% of Russia's equipment purchase must be made in the Japanese market. Other conditions are the same as those agreed with Gasprom (*Russian Petroleum Investor*, June 1993, p. 55; Sept 1994, p. 33). This report appears to be incorrect.

towards the Soviet Union. However, as *seikei fukabun*, the inseparability of politics and economics, has given way to a policy of expanded equilibrium and the business community has raised its hopes for increased opportunities in the FSU, policy coordination has become more important.[10]

The MFA, MITI and MOF, as well as the business community, are generally agreed that Japanese aid to the former Soviet republics should include only technical assistance, i.e. industrial and managerial know-how and emergency food and medical aid. Tokyo's reluctance to extend economic aid is based in part on its sober assessment of political uncertainties and the numerous obstacles to economic reform discussed above and, more importantly, on its disappointment with the lack of progress on the Northern Territories issue.[11]

Japan's unbalanced financial support to Russia, compared with China, seems likely to continue unless the Northern Islands issue is settled. However, Japan has begun to recognize the danger of losing its vested interests in Russian Far East oil and gas development to those major international oil companies that are pursuing opportunities in the Russian Far East, especially Sakhalin offshore. Consequently its financial support for RFE, especially Sakhalin offshore, oil and gas development (not Yakutsk gas development) seems to be less confined by the long-standing territorial dispute.

The Sakhalin-I project compromise between Japan and Russia proves the case. In late September 1993, when Michio Mudaguchi, president of SODECO, visited Moscow, he proposed three conditions for oil and gas development: first, the development area should be expanded beyond the Chaivo and Odoptu structures to assure the economic viability of the project; secondly, joint exploration and development should be undertaken with the Russians; thirdly, Exxon should be allowed to participate.[12] As mentioned in Chapter 2, section 1, the Russians agreed to include Arkutun-Daginskoye field in the SODECO development package, and SODECO decided to write off Russia's $277-million debt.[13] This compromise paved the way for real development.

In September 1993 a private advisory group to the director-generals of the Petroleum Department of MITI's Natural Resources and Energy Agency released a report calling for increased government support for private natural-gas-

---

[10] Tsuneo Akaha and Takashi Murakami, 'Soviet/Russian Economic Relations', in Tsuyoshi Hasegawa, Jonathan Haslam and Andrew C. Kuchins, eds, *Russia and Japan: an unresolved dilemma between distant neighbours*, University of California Press, Berkeley, 1993, pp. 161–86.

[11] Ibid.

[12] *Japan Petroleum and Energy Trends*, 1 Oct. 1993, p. 2.

[13] *Russian Petroleum Investor*, Dec. 1993/Jan 1994, p. 40.

development projects overseas by applying trade insurance and, through JNOC, public financial aid to such projects.[14] If the existing JNOC Law, under which JNOC can provide financial aid to oil and gas exploration projects alone and can only guarantee liabilities related to development projects, is revised as requested, the Sakhalin offshore gas-development project will qualify for JNOC financial aid. China's Tarim Basin and Indonesia's Natuna projects also seem to be possible beneficiaries of JNOC aid.

These developments reflect Japan's new policy of expanded equilibrium, which adroitly exploits a partial divorce of political from economic issues.

6.1.3 Approaches to China's and Russia's frontier oil and gas exploration and development

In the early 1990s all the major frontier oil and gas areas in Northeast Asia became accessible following China's hurried opening up of its previously prohibited frontier onshore and offshore areas in 1992–3. In the 1970s China had succeeded in blocking Japan's massive investments in Soviet Far East oil and gas development by arranging Daqing crude-oil exports to Japan and thereby distracting Japan away from the Soviet Far East. This time China aimed to distract Japan by providing it with a chance to explore its western-frontier oil and gas areas.

In fact, JNOC took the initiative and opened the way for the active participation of Japanese private companies. JNOC signed an agreement with the CNPC (China National Petroleum Corp.) in mid-1991 to invest 8 billion yen ($61.5 million) in a geological survey of the Tarim Basin. The survey started in March 1992 and will last four and a half years, covering 30,000 sq. km of the southwestern part of the Basin.[15]

After the announcement of the opening of the Tarim Basin in early 1993, international bidding for its oil and gas exploration followed. As discussed in Chapter 2, section 2, three consortia comprising eight Japanese companies made exploration contracts with CNPC during December 1993 and March 1994. The first consortium, composed of Esso (US) and Sumitomo and Inpex (Japan), secured Block 3 (Qiemo) covering 14,474 sq. km. The second group, composed of Agip (Italy), Elf (France), Texaco China B.V. (US), and Japex & Japan Energy (Japan), secured Block 1 (Yatongguzi) with 9,814 sq. km. The third, composed of BP (UK), Nippon Oil Exploration Co., Itochu Oil Exploration Co. Ltd, Mitsubishi Co. Ltd and Mitsui

[14] *Japan Petroleum and Energy Trends*, 1 Oct. 1993, p. 3.

[15] *China Daily*, 9 July 1991; *Oil and Gas Journal*, 6 May 1991, p. 143; Qi Daqing and David Fridley, 'Tarim Basin: Hopes and Challenges for China's Oil Industry', Resources Programmes, East-West Centre, Jan. 1992, p. 8.

Co. Ltd (Japan), secured Block 4 (Tulabei) with 14,475 sq. km.[16]

In contrast to onshore development, Japanese companies have not been as aggressive in seeking participation in East China Sea exploration. Only one Japanese consortium, composed of Japex and Teikoku, signed production-sharing contracts with CNOOC for 41/17 and 42/03 blocks in the East China Sea in December 1993[17] (see Map 2.2). The unsettled boundary issue between Japan and China in the East China Sea may be responsible for the cautious approach of Japanese companies to exploration there.

In the case of Yakutsk and Sakhalin offshore oil and gas development, Japan secured an interest in both projects by signing a general agreement for the exploration of Yakutian gas in November 1974 and a general agreement for Sakhalin offshore oil and gas exploration in January 1975 (for details, see Chapter 7, sections 1 and 2). Japan's involvement in the Yakutian gas project was suspended after the invasion of Afghanistan in 1979, but was revived in January 1989, soon after a Korean company, the Hyundai Business Group, proposed a Yakutsk gas-development project. At that time, John Sears, of the US Far Eastern Energy, and Uebayashi Takeshi, of Tokyo Boeki Ltd, a subsidiary company of the Mitsubishi group, visited Moscow to present an idea for building a gas pipeline from Yakutsk to Kita Kyushu, via Khabarovsk, Vladivostok, North Korea and Pusan (South Korea), with a total length of 6,250 km.[18] This proposal has had a low profile.

The year 1992 witnessed some significant initiatives by Japanese businesses to revive the Yakutian gas project. On 8 March both Tokyo Boeki and Far Eastern Energy commissioned a feasibility study for developing the Sakha Republic's oil and gas reserves, and an agreement between Tokyo Gas and the Sakha Republic for the same purpose was made in June 1992[19] (when the Keidanren group was visiting

---

[16] *China OGP* 2: 5 (1 March 1994), pp. 3–4; and 2: 8 (15 April 1994), p. 3; *China Petroleum Investment Guide*, *China OGP* and AP Energy Business Publications, Singapore, 1994, p. 74 (Table 4). There are already five Japanese companies – Japan Xinjiang Oil Co. Ltd, Japan Energy (Tarim) Corp., Japex Tarim Ltd, Inpex Southeast Tarim Ltd, and Sumisho Oil & Gas Exploration (Tarim) Ltd – for Xinjiang province, including Tarim Basin, oil and gas exploration. See JNOC, *Annual Report 1994*, pp. 8–9.

[17] *China Petroleum Investment Guide*, *China OGP* and AP Energy Business Publications, Singapore, 1994, p. 94 (Table 2). Four Japanese companies – Japex Donghai East Ltd, Japex Donghai West Ltd, Teikoku Oil (Donghai East) Co. Ltd and Teikoku Oil (Donghai West) Co. Ltd – were set up for East China Sea oil and gas exploration. See JNOC, *Annual Report 1994*, pp. 8–9.

[18] *Asahi Shimbun*, 13 June 1990.

[19] Lowell Feld, John H. Herbert and Erik Kreil, 'East Siberia and the Russian Far East: The Final Frontier?', *Geopolitics of Energy*, 1 July 1992, pp. 6–8; Keun Wook Paik, 'A Northeast Asian Gas Grid?', *Geopolitics of Energy*, 1 Jan. 1993, pp. 6–10.

Figure 6.1: Gas-transportation costs comparison: pipeline vs LNG

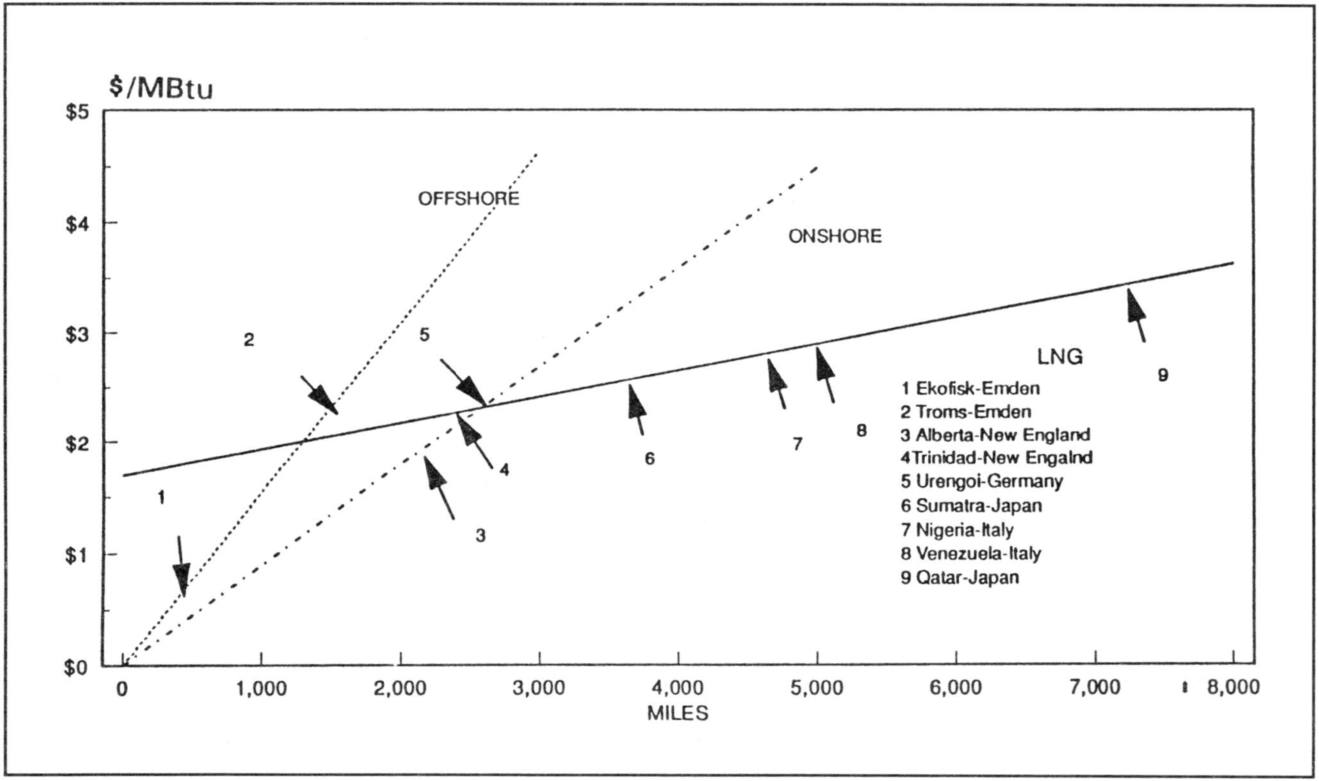

Source: James T. Jensen, 'Gas Supplies for the World Market', *Energy Journal* (IAEE), 1994 Special Issue, p. 248.

the Republic of Sakha). Then, in 1993, the Japan–Russia Economic Committee of Keidanren (Japan Federation of Economic Organizations) established a natural-gas subcommittee to study the development of Yakut gas resources. The subcommittee, chaired by Mikio Nose, director of Tokyo Gas, comprised representatives of JNOC and 13 electric power, utility-gas and trading firms.[20] These developments are concerned with establishing a gas-pipeline grid, but confirm that Japanese business circles are gearing themselves up for Yakutian gas projects.

In early 1994 four Japanese organizations, Keidanren, the National Pipeline Research Society of Japan, JNOC and the Institute of Energy Economics (Japan), were undertaking a feasibility study. Given the economic advantages of Russian gas imports, the Japanese utilities cannot overlook the project. As shown in Figure 6.1, depending on the type of pipeline used, the break-even point for LNG is in the 2,000-km range for offshore pipeline, around 4,200 km for onshore pipeline. The break-even point for Qatar–Japan LNG delivery (the distance is over 10,000 km) is around 6,000 km for onshore pipeline.

RFE gas exports to Japan travel roungly 4,000 km (from Yakutsk to Hokkaido), and so RFE gas seems to be a competitive alternative for the Japanese utilities, in terms of economics. It is worth noting, however, that what has really mattered to them is politics, not economics, which is why they have always been interested in RFE gas projects but never committed a serious investment to development.

Japan must now be taking this option seriously, but unless an advance is made on the Northern Territories issue its expanded-equilibrium policy seems unlikely to be extended to RFE gas development. Japanese businesses could challenge the government's negative stance towards this project by joining it as soon as the region's business environment changes.

As for Sakhalin offshore oil and gas, Japan managed to secure all major fields in the Sakhalin-I and II projects. After the Sakhalin-I compromise, Russia and the Sakhalin Energy Investment Co. – the formal name of the Bermuda-based legal entity created by the MMMSM consortium – signed a production-sharing agreement to develop Sakhalin-II, covering the Piltun-Astokskoye and Lunskoye oil and gas fields on the Sakhalin shelf, in late June 1994. Significantly, Clause 4 of the contract allowed the Sakhalin Energy Investment Co. to abrogate all its financial obligations to Russia within two years of the effective date if the State Duma, Sakhalin authorities or various licensing agencies fail to satisfy the company's requirements as set forth in the agreement.[21] This could provide Sakhalin Energy

[20] *Japan Petroleum and Energy Trends*, 8 Jan. 1993, p. 9. The 13 companies included, Tokyo Gas Co., Tokyo Electric Power Co., Nippon Steel Corp. and JGC Corp.See *RA Report* 14 (Jan. 1993), p. 106.

[21] *Russian Petroleum Investor*, July/Aug. 1994, pp. 53–4.

Investment Co. with a two-year investment moratorium. If the investment is arranged in 1996, then Sakhalin offshore gas production will not begin before the end of this decade (see Chapter 7).

Japan has secured a firm basis in frontier oil and gas exploration and development projects in both China and Russia. It is uncertain so far where Japan's priorities lie, though an ambitious energy plan put forward by Japanese businesses offer some clues.

6.1.4 The Asia-Pacific Energy Community plan

Japanese business circles have promoted a Japan-centred multilateral energy project in the Asia-Pacific region since the early 1990s. This, the 'Asia-Pacific Energy Community (AFEC)' plan, was proposed in an open panel held on 16 December 1991 by Masaru Hirata, professor emeritus of the University of Tokyo and chairman of the National Pipeline Research Society of Japan (NPRSJ), a group whose 51 members are illustrious names in Japanese corporate circles.[22]

AFEC's grand plan aims at laying down a 42,500-km pipeline grid from Yakutsk in the Russian Far East to Dampier in northwestern Australia, through China, Korea, Japan, Taiwan and the six countries of the Association of South East Asian Nations (ASEAN). The NPRSJ saw that the grid could be divided into two sections: the first is the Northeast Asia and northern Pacific section with a length of 28,400 km, comprising the Turkmenistan–West China–Korea–Japan pipeline grid, the Yakutsk–China–Korea–Japan grid and the Alaska–Sakhalin–Japan grid; and the second is the southeast Asian and Oceania section with a length of 14,100 km, comprising the Australia–ASEAN grid, the ASEAN grid and the ASEAN–southern China grid.[23] The NPRSJ did not, however, suggest how the plan would be implemeted and the financing handled.

---

[22] On 11 July 1991 *Yomiuri Shimbun* reported the Asia-Pacific Energy Community plan. The NPRSJ's initial 32 members are broadly divided into six groups: first, from the energy industry, Tokyo Electric Power Co., Kansai Electric Power Co., Tokyo Gas Co., Osaka Gas Co., Toho Gas Co., Showa Shell Sekiyu K.K., NEC Corp.; second, from trading houses, Mitsui & Co., Sumitomo Corp., Mitsubishi Corp., Nissho Iwai Corp., Tomen Corp.; third, from the steel industry, Nippon Steel Corp., Kawasaki Steel Corp., NKK Corp., Sumitomo Metal Industries, Ltd; fourth, from the construction industry, Taisei Corp., Obayashi Corp., Shimizu Corp., Sato Kyogyo Co. Ltd, Kajima Corp., Hazama Corp., Nippon Hodo Co. Ltd, Toa Corp., Toyo Construction Co. Ltd, JCC Corp., Knoike Construction Co. Ltd; fifth, from the machine industry, Chiyoda Corp., Mitsubishi Heavy Industries Ltd; sixth, two others Central Japan Railway Co. and Mitsubishi Research Institute, Inc. See Keun Wook Paik, 'A Northeast Asian Gas Grid?' (op. cit., n. 19), pp. 6–7.

[23] *Proposal on the Trans-Asian Natural Gas Pipeline Project by NPRSJ*, June 1993, pp. 4–5.

The plan overlaps with two mega-projects that could provide the basis of the AFEC grid. One is the Vostok project, envisaging the construction of over 6,000 km of gas pipelines from the Sakhalin and Yakutian gas fields through the Khabarovsk and Maritime Territories and the Amur Region, across the Korean Peninsula and the Tsushima Straits to southern Japan (see Chapter 7).

The other is a 7,830-km Trans-ASEAN Gas Pipeline (TAGP) project which would carry natural gas over land and under water from Indonesia, Malaysia and Brunei to Singapore, Thailand and the Philippines. The TAGP project, divided into seven sections, would have a capacity of 60 bcm/year and cost an estimated $10 billion. Participants at the summit meeting of Asean energy ministers in Singapore on 9 October 1991 agreed to proceed with a feasibility study for the TAGP. An 18-month study has now been initiated. The start of Malaysian gas sales to Singapore in early 1992 was regarded as the first step towards the establishment of the TAGP project.[24] It looks feasible from a longer-term perspective, but only covers a part of the AFEC plan.

The crucial element in the AFEC plan is the proposed establishment of a gas-pipeline grid for Northeast Asia. As the pipeline route for the Northeast Asian sector in the original plan could not satisfy regional countries, NPRSJ revised the route, as shown in Maps 6.2 and 6.3, with a grid connecting Japan, the Korean Peninsula, China's northeastern provinces, the Republic of Sakha, Khabarovsk and Primorskii Krai, and the Sakhalin Islands. The NPRSJ had to proceed carefully for no matter what benefits the AFEC plan might bring, Japanese imperial expansion in East Asia before the Second World War, epitomized by Japan's 'Greater East Asia Co-Prosperity Sphere', had not been forgotten. However, the NPRSJ has found a way to reassure all the countries around the Donghae (Sea of Japan).

In early March 1995 a Northeast Asian Forum of Natural Gas Pipeline (NAFNGP) was proposed at an international conference on the Northeast Asian Natural Gas Pipeline convened by NPRSJ. The results of this Tokyo conference

---

[24] In June 1988 members of ASEAN agreed plans for a gas-pipeline grid to boost the economy of the region. Then ASEAN hired a European consortium led by French and Italian oil companies to prepare a feasibility study. (According to C. Donville, the idea of TAGP emerged at a 1989 meeting in Thailand organized by the International Energy Policy Formation Centre, the Asian Institute of Technology and the European Community.) Reportedly, the gas grid will be expanded to include China and the Middle East. See Christopher Donville, 'Asean Gas Grid gains New Support', *Asian Oil and Gas*, Feb. 1992, pp. 14–15; *International Herald Tribune*, 20 Feb. 1992; George Ives, Jr, *et al.*, 'Activity shows Slight Drop, but Future Plans remain at High Levels', *Pipe Line Industry*, Nov. 1992, pp. 34–6; William Scholes, 'ASEAN Gas Grid under Study', *Petroleum Review*, Nov. 1991, pp. 538–9; *FT International Gas Report*, 27 Nov. 1992, p. 20; 5 Sept. 1991, pp. 15–16; *Oil and Gas Journal*, 24 Feb. 1992, p. 36; *OPEC Bulletin*, May 1990, p. 62.

Map 6.1: The Asia-Pacific Energy Community plan for a natural-gas pipeline grid

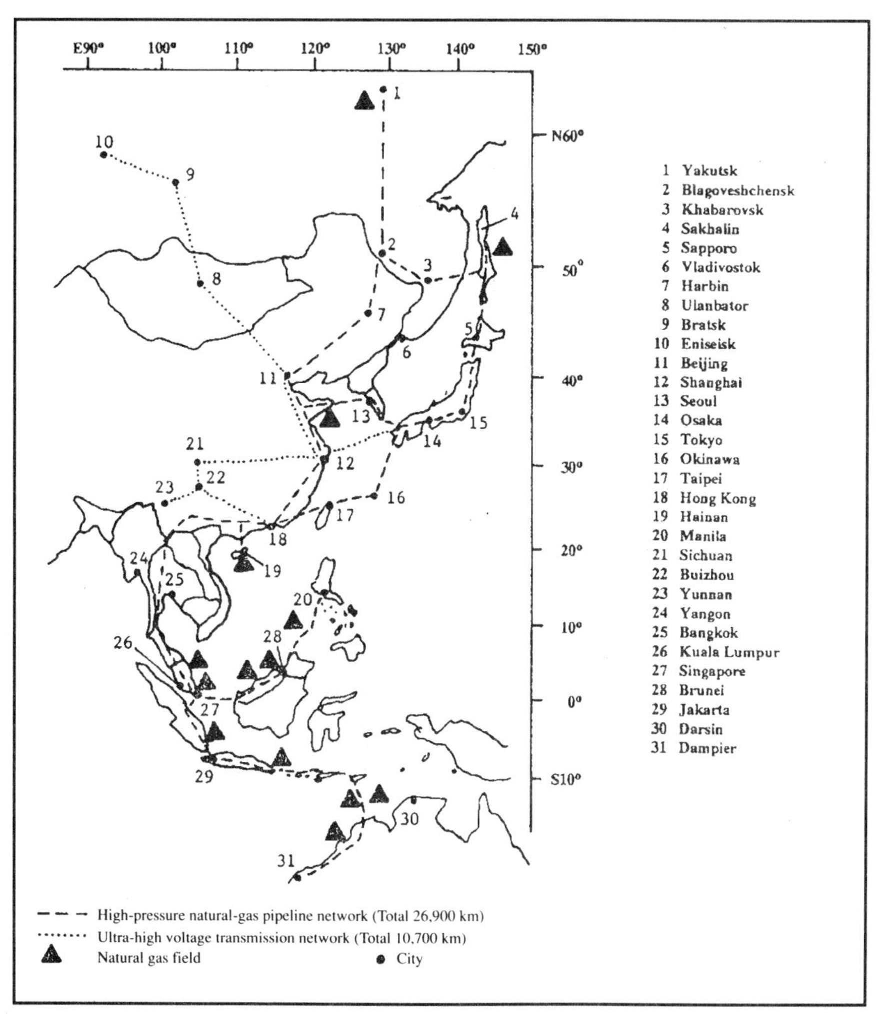

Source: Proposal by Professor Masaru Hirata, University of Tokyo, July 1991

Map 6.2: The revised Asia-Pacific Energy Community plan for a natural-gas pipeline grid

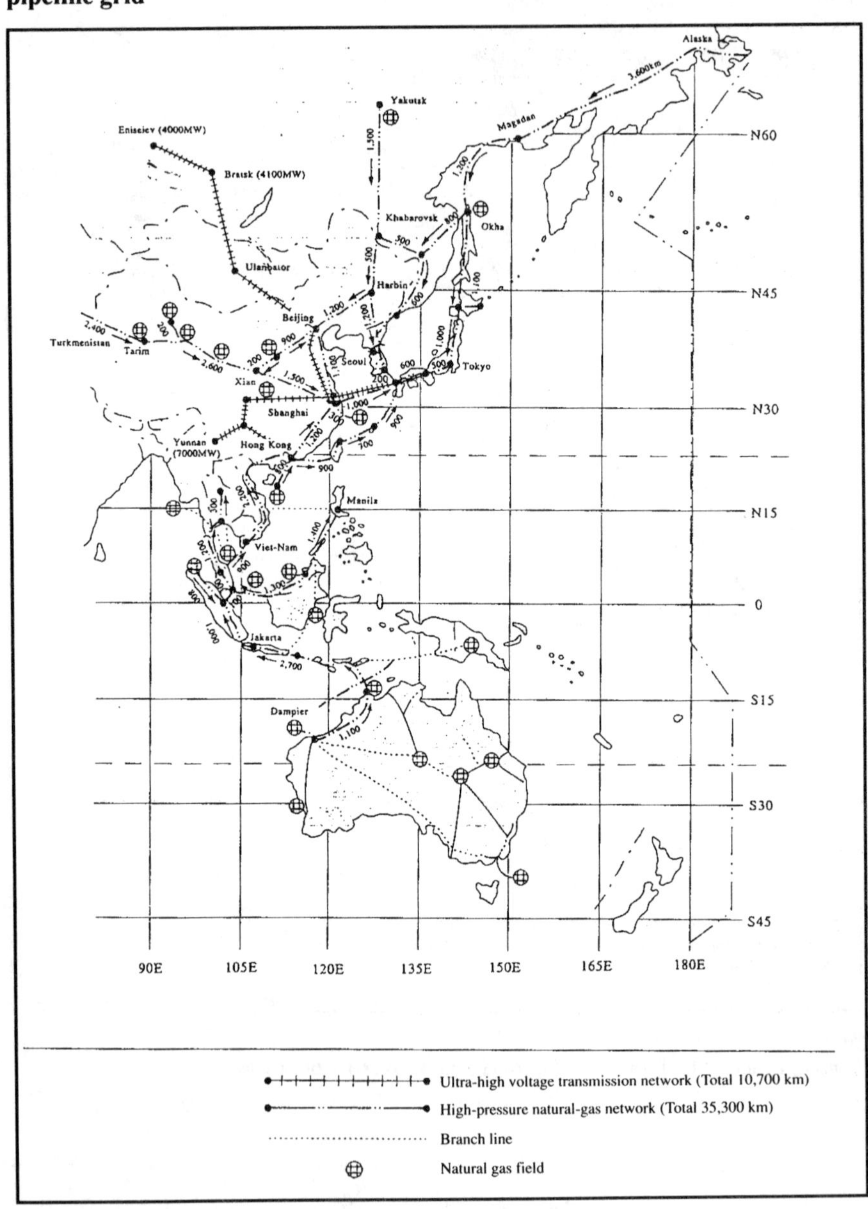

Source: Proposal by Professor Masaru Hirata, National Pipeline Research Society of Japan, June 1993

were mixed. The NAFNGP is intended to accelerate the region's gas development, but it is not proposed that it should have the status of an international organization whose resolutions are binding or official. The question then arises as to whether the NAFNGP could provide a basis for the early realization of RFE gas development based on multilateral cooperation.

The appearance of a Japanese scheme for multilateral energy cooperation is in itself a very positive development in the move towards the formation of a multilateral energy framework in Northeast Asia. Despite the NPRSJ's revision of the Northeast Asian pipeline route, however, it introduced the idea of an 'Energy Silk Route', which raises questions as to where Japan places its priorities in the Northeast Asian sector of the pipeline grid[25] (see the box overleaf and Map 6.3). If the Japanese government supports the implementation of the Energy Silk Route project, connecting the rich gas fields of Central Asia with end-users in Northeast Asia by early next decade, the decision will affect the Northeast Asian gas market fundamentally and will block any serious development of the Republic of Sakha's gas project in the 2000s.

6.1.5 The options for Japan

In the mid-1990s Japan's policy towards China's and Russia's frontier oil and gas development seems to be being tested by the Energy Silk Route project and the Yakutsk gas project. Its decision here will significantly affect the development of the Asia-Pacific region's grassroots LNG projects. It is worth briefly discussing the realities of Japan's LNG demand and supply.

Japan has dominated LNG use in the Asia-Pacific region since it first received LNG from Alaska in 1969. Although Korea and Taiwan entered the market in 1986 and 1990 respectively, Japan continues to take the lion's share of supplies. In 1993 around 87% of the region's LNG was consumed in Japan, with Korea accounting for 9% and Taiwan 4%. As shown in Table 6.3, the Japanese utilities have already contracted sufficient supplies until 2000. Considering that Japan's present long-term contracts with seven countries (including Qatar) total roughly 52 mt (Tables 6.4 and 6.5), its estimated demand of 51–3 mt in 2000 would seem to be easily satisfied by existing fields even though demand in 2010 will require the implementation of new grassroots projects.

At present (Table 6.6), some 13 projects from 9 countries are currently being planned or under consideration, and the total output of these planned projects is at best 91 mt (125 bcm), of which 64 mt is based on proven reserves. (The Turkmenistan and Yakutsk projects are excluded from the 13 as both are pipeline

---

[25] Strictly speaking, China's CNPC and Japan's Mitsubishi Co. are the driving forces behind this concept.

The 'Energy Silk Route' project[1]

This project is based on the concept of developing a 'New Silk Road' to connect the rich gas-prone fields of Central Asia with end-users in Northeast Asia. (Turkmenistan's proven gas reserves are 88 tcf, and its potential gas reserves are estimated at 364 tcf.) At the end of 1992, the project proposal was disclosed at a meeting of representatives from the Turkmengaz Association, the Mitsubishi Corp. and the CNPC, held in Ashkhabad, Turkmenistan.

The cost of this project has been estimated by the Mitsubishi Corp. at $12 billion and it will take five years to complete. The $12 billion covers a 1,440-mm-diameter, 6,720-km pipeline (including a sub-sea section between Lianyungang, Jiangsu province, and Japan), with a total capacity of 30 bcm/y, from Turkmenistan through Uzbekistan and Kazakhstan to China, and a 10-mt/y liquefaction plant on the shores of the Yellow Sea. The facilities would provide gas for domestic use in China as well as export to Japan. In 1993 CNPC set up a company named Central Asia Corp. for this project, and in 1995 CNPC and Mitsubishi decided to undertake a preliminary feasibility study. In the summer of 1995, the US oil giant, Exxon joined in the study. Besides this, the World Bank, having carried out a fairly extensive survey of oil and gas resources in the Central Asian countries by its energy missions since 1992, was planning to undertake a study on oil and gas export options from Central Asia, from mid-1995, with two years working period. The third phase of the bank study will focus on a pre-investment study for gas export to China.[2]

[1]Keun Wook Paik, 'Pipeline Politics: Turkmenistan vs. Russian Far East Gas Development', *Geopolitics of Energy*, 1 Sept. 1994, pp. 1–8; *China OGP*, 1 July 1995, p. 5.
[2]In early May 1995, it was confirmed by Shigeru Kubota, Oil and Gas Division, Industry and Energy Department, the World Bank, in an interview with the author.

projects.) Mega-size grassroots projects such as the Natuna and Alaska projects cannot be developed at the same time, as the Asia-Pacific gas market in 2010 will not be big enough to absorb the additional volume.

According to BP's study, for example, by 2010 LNG demand in Japan, Korea and Taiwan is expected to reach 94 mt/y, from 46 mt/y in 1993.[26] (The forecast for LNG demand in 2010 ranges from 84 to 108 mt: see Table 6.4.) Assuming that demand in 2010 is 90–100 mt/y, contract shortfall will be roughly 28–38 mt as at least 62 mt is already committed under long-term contract to Japan, Korea and Taiwan.

If the Sakhalin offshore (6 mt) and Energy Silk Route (10 mt) projects start LNG and pipeline gas exports to the Northeast Asian market between 2000 and 2005, Japan, Korea and Taiwan's long-term LNG contract shortfall in 2010 will be scaled

[26] Andrew R. Flower, 'LNG – Is There a Way out of the Cost/Price Dilemma?', paper presented at GasTrade 94, Hong Kong, 16–18 March 1994.

Map 6.3: Energy silk route: original plan

down to 12–22 mt. In view of other smaller projects (the Oman project with 6 mt[27] and Australia's Gorgon project with 5–6 mt[28] are also aiming at entering the North-east Asian gas market in 2000–2002) and the possibility of a somewhat smaller LNG demand in 2010 than has been expected, development of only one mega-size project looks possible.

It is extremely difficult to predict which mega-size LNG project can survive, but the following considerations will provide some pointers. First of all, the Sakhalin LNG project will go ahead. Preparations for imports from Sakhalin are already being made, according to two reports in October 1992. The prefectural government

[27] On 10 Aug. 1994, the proposed $9 billion Oman LNG project, with the establishment of Oman LNG LLC (51% owned by Oman, 34% by Shell, 6% by Total, 2% by Partex, 3% each by Mitsubishi and Mitsui, and 15% by Itochu), moved forward with the signing of a memorandum on gas supply. The project is aiming at its first LNG export in early 2000. See *Financial Times*, 27 May 1994, p. 2; 2 Sept. 1994, pp. 4–5.

[28] *Financial Times*, 2 Sept. 1994, pp. 16–19.

Table 6.3: Japan's long-term LNG contracts

Country	Project/ capacity	Contract period	Contracting company	Remarks
Indonesia (sub-total: 17.64 mt)	Badak 1-2 & Arun 1-3/8.2 mt	1977–99	KE, CE, KYE, OG, THG, NS	
	Badak 3-4/3.6 mt	1983–2003	KE, CE, THG, OG	
	Arun 4-5/3.55 mt	1984–2004	THE,TE	
	Badak 6/2 mt	1994–2013	OG, TG, THG	Supply from 1994.
	?/0.29 mt	1996–2015	HG,NG	Supply from 1996. (1st year, 0.07 mt)
Malaysia (sub-total: 10.36 mt)	Bintulu/7.4 mt	1983–2003	TE, TG	
	Bintulu/0.36 mt	1993–2013	SG	Supply from 1993. (1st year, 0.15 mt)
	Bintulu/2.1 mt	1994–2014	TG, OG, THG, KE	Supply from 1994.
	Bintulu/0.5 mt	1996–2016	THE	Letter of Intent signed; supply from 1996.
Brunei (sub-total: 5.54 mt)	Lumut/5.54 mt	1973–2013	TE, TG, OG	Renewed contract in 1993 increased volume 10% from 5.1 mt.
Abu Dhabi (sub-total: 4.3 mt)	Das Island/4.3 mt	1977–2019	TE	Initial contract volume in 1977–93: 2.6 mt.
Alaska (sub-total: 1.09 mt)	Kenai/1.09 mt	1969–2009	TE, TG	Until 1993, volume: 0.99 mt.
Australia (sub-total: 6.82 mt)	Karratha/5.84 mt	1989–2007	TE, CE, KE, CGE, KSE, TG, OG, THG	
	Karratha/0.98 mt	1995–2008	Same as above	Letter of Intent signed; supply from 1995.
Qatar (sub-total: 6 mt)	Qatargas/4 mt	1997–2010	CE	Supply from 1997.
	Qatargas/2 mt	1998–2022	THE, TE, KE, TG, CGE, OG, THG	Supply from 1998.
Total: 51.75 mt				

Key: CE = Chubu ElectricNS = Nippon Steel
CGE = Chugoku ElectricOG = Osaka Gas
HG = Hiroshima GasSG = Seibu Gas
KE = Kansai ElectricTE = Tokyo Electric
KSE = Kyushu ElectricTG = Tokyo Gas
KYE = Kyushu ElectricTHE = Tohoku Electric
NG = Nippon GasTHG = Toho Gas

Source: Hiroki Mizumachi, 'Long Term Forecast for LNG Imports into Japan', paper presented at the MPM-PEC Seminar, Tokyo, 26 Jan. 1994; Shiva Pezeshki and Fereidun Fesharaki, 'Outlook for the Asia-Pacific LNG Market', *Energy Advisory* 116 (1 Dec. 1993); Babak Kiani, 'LNG Trade in the Asia-Pacific region: current status and future prospects', *Energy Policy*, Jan./Feb. 1991, pp. 63–75; *FT International Gas Report*, 27 May 1994, p. 15; 8 July 1994, p. 4; 5 Aug. 1994, p. 16.

---

of Aomori, the northernmost prefecture of Japan's main island, Honshu, has revealed plans to invite stockpiling facilities for Sakhalin and Yakut LNG, and was planning to send its officials to Sakhalin and Khabarovsk for preliminary studies in 1993. (In fact, Aomori prefecture wants to use its industrial-plant-siting area totaling 2,500 hectares, of which 60% remains unsold, in Mutsu-Ogawara.[29]) Next, Japan's Ministry of Transport was drafting plans to turn Niigata, a port city on the west coast, into Japan's largest LNG terminal for Russian gas, presumably from Sakhalin and East Siberia. The ten-year project costing over $8 billion is earmarked for inclusion in the 1996–2000 port-building plan.[30]

As for the starting point of three trains of Sakhalin LNG exports, Japan would prefer to keep to 2003 as planned since the Japanese utilities have already secured enough volume until the end of this decade. If a portion of Sakhalin LNG is allocated to Korea or Taiwan for early export, the pressure on Japan to commit itself to Yakutsk gas development will be strengthened. Japan would not want to invite such pressure.

Secondly, as Japan's business circles are currently giving more support to the Energy Silk Route project than to the Yakutsk project, the likelihood of the former's being implemented is greater if Korea and Taiwan join in. If it becomes a reality, the chance that Russia's Yakutsk project will be developed without Japanese support is extremely slight as other mega-size LNG projects (with a volume of over 10 mt), such as the Natuna and Alaska projects, are also competing for early entry into the Northeast Asian gas market.

---

[29] FBIS, EAS 92: 205 (22 Oct. 1992), p. 5; *Japan Petroleum and Energy Trends*, 19 March 1993, p. 8.

[30] *Oil and Gas Journal*, 12 Oct. 1992, newsletter; *FT International Gas Report*, 2 Oct. 1992, p. 13.

Table 6.4: LNG supply and demand forecast (Far East) (mt/y)

	1993		2000		2010
Demand	45.2		68–71		84–108
Japan	39.3		51–53		63–75
		[MITI	53	MITI	58]
		[BP	53	BP	63]
		[IEEJ	53	IEEJ	66]
		[Mitsubishi	52	Mitsubishi	67–71]
				[EWC	70]
		[MEEI	51	MEEI	75]
		[NPRSJ	71	NPRSJ	95]
Korea	4.3		10–12		13–19
Taiwan	1.6		5–6		8–14
Supply (committed)	45.2		62.1		62.1
Japan	39.3		52		52
Korea	4.3		6.3*		6.3*
Taiwan	1.6		3.8*		3.8*
Contract Shortfall	–		6–9		22–46

Key: IEEJ = The Institute of Energy Economics, Japan; MEEI = The Middle East Economics Institute; NPRSJ = National Pipeline Research Society of Japan; EWC = East-West Center.
Note: Korea and Taiwan each signed letters of intent for 2 mt/y of LNG from Qatar's Ras Lafflan project.
[Here, the detailed figures on Japan's LNG demand in 2000 and 2010 show the range of projections by well-known organizations.]
Sources: *BP Review of World Gas 1994*; National Pipeline Research Society of Japan (*Report*, June 1993); Ichiro Yokose, 'Natural Gas Situation in the Far East', paper presented at the IEA and OECD Second Energy Experts Meeting, Paris, November 1993; Tsutomu Toichi, 'LNG development at the turning point and policy issues for Japan', *Energy Policy*, May 1994, p. 372; Shiva Pezeshki and Fereidun Fesharaki, 'Outlook for the Asia-Pacific LNG Market', *Energy Advisory* 116 (1 Dec. 1993); *FT International Gas Report*, 27 May 1994, p. 15; 11 Nov. 1994, p. 21.

In fact, Indonesia's Natuna sea gas project, equivalent in size to Norway's Troll gas field, the largest in Western Europe, is gaining momentum after many twists and turns. In November 1994 the Indonesian government, Indonesia's state-owned oil company Pertamina and the US Exxon unit, Esso Exploration & Production

Table 6.5: LNG liquefaction capacity held by existing sources supplying to Japan/Korea/Taiwan, as of 1993

Country	Terminal	No. of trains[1]	Liquefaction capacity[2] (mt/y)		
			Name plate	Existing	After expansion
US Alaska	Kenai	2	1.1	1.23	1.23
Brunei	Lumut	5	5.3	6	6
UAE (Abu Dhabi)	Das Island	2 (3)	2.3	2.3	4.3
Indonesia	Arun	6[3]	9	12	12
	Badak	5 (6)	10.9	11.5	13.8
Malaysia	Bintulu	3 (6)	7.5	7.8	15.6
Australia	Karratha	3 (4)	6	6	8.9
Total (6 countries & 7 terminals)		26 (32)	42.1	46.83	62.13

Notes:
1 Number of units after expansion.
2 Liquefaction capacities, both existing and after expansion, are estimated.
3 Indonesia is planning to reduce Arun's 6 trains to 4 in 2000, and to 2 in 2007–2008, with complete closure in 2014 unless new reserves are found.
Source: Koji Morita, 'Will Expanding Natural Gas Use Continue?: Supply Security and Japan's Choice', *Energy in Japan* 122 (July 1993), p. 2 (Table 1); *FT International Gas Report*, 24 June 1994, p. 16.

Natuna Inc., agreed to develop the $35–40 billion Natuna project. This project, whose gas reserves are estimated at 210 tcf (its LNG production seems to be more than 14 mt/year), is targeting the Asia Pacific gas market in 2000–2010.[31]

Reportedly, the Japanese companies Mitsubishi and Mitsui, with Mobil Oil, are negotiating with Pertamina for participation in the project, but China's claims to the Spratlys are giving the negotiating parties cause for concern.[32] If the Japanese

[31] The project could involve as many as 200 wells and 18 fixed steel-jacketed platforms producing and processing about 2 billion cubic feet/day of gas for more than 30 years. See *Financial Times*, 17 Nov. 1994; *Oil & Gas Journal*, 21 Nov. 1994, pp. 30–1; *Far Eastern Economic Review*, 24–31 Dec. 1992, pp. 60–1; 22 April 1993, pp. 52–4; 17 Nov. 1994, p. 69.
[32] Pertamina is currently negotiating with various oil companies to dispose of 39% of its 50% stake in the Natuna gas field. See *Financial Times*, 26 May 1995.

Table 6.6: New projects under study

Country	Capacity (mt)	Production year	Participants	Reserves (p = proven)	Cost ($bn) (A/B)[1]
Qatar:					
Ras Laffan	10	2000	QGPC/Mobil	Total:	6.3/1.55
Ras Laffan	4	2000	QGPC/Elf/Sumitomo	4.25 tcm (p)	5/1.53
Oman	6	2000	Oman Gov't/Shell/ Total/Mitsui/C. Ito Mitsubishi	8 tcf	9
Yemen	5	after 2000	Exxon/Hunt/Yukong		
Indonesia: Natuna	14	after 2000	Pertamina/Exxon	1.28 tcm (p) /127 tcf	17–35/ 1.95
Malaysia: SK 8 & 10	5	2000	Petronas/Occidental Nippon Oil	0.14 tcm	
Australia:					
Petrel, Tern	2–4	after 2000	Santos/Teikoku/ Sumitomo/Osaka Gas	0.07 tcm (p) 0.09–0.24 tcm	0.9–1.6
Gorgon	5–6	after 2000	Shell/Texaco/ Chevron/Ampolex	0.43 tcm	10/3.78
PNG:					
Pandora (off)	5	after 2000	Mobil/Nippon Oil/ Japex/Nissho Iwai	0.09 tcm	20/4.98
Hides (on)	6	after 2000	Mitsubishi/Chevron BP/BHP/Ampolex	0.22 tcm	7.4/5.4
US Alaska	7–14	after 2000	Arco/BP/Exxon	1.05 tcm (p) 2.61 tcm	10.6/2.56
Russia:					
Sakhalin-I	5–6	after 2000	Sodeco/Exxon	0.17 tcm (p)	
Sakhalin-II	6	1999	Marathon/Shell/ McDermott/Mitsui Mitsubishi	0.35 tcm (p)	10/5.77
Sub-total (13 projects): 78–91 mt					
Yakutsk	7.5	after 2000	Russia/Korean group	0.85 tcm (p)	20
Turkmenistan/ China	10	2000	CNPC/Mitsubishi		
Total (15 projects): 95.5–108.5 mt					

Note:
1 A = estimated project cost; B = amounts of credits (investment loans) approved by the EXIMBank of Japan.
Sources: Hiroki Mizumachi, 'Long Term Forecast for LNG Imports into Japan', paper presented at the MPM-PEC Seminar, Tokyo, 26 Jan. 1994; Ichiro Yokose, 'Natural Gas Situation in the Far East toward 2010', paper presented at the EA and OECD Second Energy Specialist Meeting, Paris, 30 Nov. 1993; Koji Morita, 'Will Expanding Natural Gas Use Continue?: Supply Security and Japan's Choice', *Energy in Japan* 122 (July 1993), p. 5 (Fig. 3); *FT International Gas Report*, 24 June 1994, p. 16; 2 Sept. 1994, pp. 4–5.

---

buyers decide to join in the project, most of the major grassroot LNG projects aiming at entering the Northeast Asian gas market would be fundamentally affected.

A significant change has occurred in the Alaska project as well. The TAGS project was originally proposed by the Yukon-Pacific Corp. (YPC), which called for the construction of a 1,350-km pipeline parallel to the Trans-Alaska Pipeline and a natural-gas liquefaction facility in Anderson Bay, Valdez, in 1983.[33] To make it more competitive, in 1991 YPC revised its conceptual design capacity, increasing the pipeline diameter from 36 inches to 42 inches and the scale of LNG supply from 14 mt to 1–6 mt/year.[34]

However, YPC owned no gas, and had limited financial resources, even though it had acquired all necessary permits and export licences. The company had little success in marketing the TAGS project to Asian buyers and the North Slope equity producers Exxon, British Petroleum and Arco, from which it needed gas.[35]

Then, in 1994, things changed. First, Japan's MITI said that it would welcome a definite proposal. Reportedly, a Japanese official stated that 'it [North Slope LNG] is right there as a definite candidate, along with Natuna, Sakhalin, and Qatar', after mentioning that 'Recent Japanese sessions were marked by a dramatic change in their tone.' Secondly, with upstream-oil prospects growing dim and forecasts for

---

[33] When the TAGS project was proposed, a three-stage plan was envisaged over a nine-year period, with 6.5 bcm being delivered to Japan (and other markets) at the end of the fifth year, 12 bcm two years later and 19 bcm by the ninth year and annually thereafter. YPC is a business unit of CSX Corp., a Virginia-based international transportation-services company. See Jonathan P. Stern, *Natural Gas Trade in North America and Asia*, Gower Publishing, Aldershot, 1985, p. 18; John Choon Kim, 'Alaska Energy Resource Potential: Opportunities and Constraints', *Resources Economics Study* 1: 2 (Summer 1989), p. 110; Yukon Pacific Corp., 'TAGS 1991 Project Evaluation: Executive Summary', p. ES-5.

[34] A report (unpublished) prepared in 1991 by the Korea Gas Corp.

[35] In fact, Japan was not committed to the project, and North Slope producers did not foresee the project coming on line until after 2005, whereas YPC was in favour of an early start. See *World Gas Intelligence*, 14 Oct. 1994, pp. 1–2.

Prudhoe Bay's crude production not much brighter, North Slope producers began to make a serious evaluation of markets for the field's sizable 20 to 25 tcf of gas reserves.[36]

If North Slope producers can find a way to reduce the project's hefty price tag, the Alaska option could be realistic due to some favourable political factors. First, the project would attract the support of state officials, who are searching for new revenue sources as crude production begins to fade. Secondly, and more importantly, it can surely find considerable political and financial support among Asian trading partners such as Japan, which might be willing to favour the scheme, even if it is somewhat less competitive than alternative supplies, as shipments from Alaska to Japan would make a sizable dent in Japan's massive and troublesome trade surplus with the United States.[37]

In short, fierce competition to enter the Northeast Asian gas market among gas producers in the Asia-Pacific region puts pressure on Japan to come to a decision on Russia's frontier gas development. It could provide an excuse for Japan not to commit itself to an earlier realization of Yakutsk gas. However, while the opening of giant grassroots LNG projects to Japanese buyers including trading houses and utilities could affect Japan's stance towards RFE gas development, it would not alter the priority given to the Sakhalin offshore project.

Furthermore Japanese buyers have enough capital and markets to change the order of grassroots projects awaiting development to supply the Northeast Asian market. For example, Japan's decision to support the Natuna gas project would delay or suspend the development of most of the major grassroots LNG projects, except Sakhalin offshore.

It remains to be seen whether Japan will favour China again by supporting the Energy Silk Route project, whose implementation could cause a considerable delay to Yakutsk gas development, or strengthen the policy of expanded equilibrium by committing itself to Yakutsk gas development regardless of settlement of the territorial dispute.

6.2 South Korea

6.2.1 South Korea's exploration and production policy

South Korea's energy-supply position is worse even than Japan's. Demand for energy is increasing very fast. In fact, in the period 1984–93 South Korea's total primary energy consumption expanded 2.37 times, from 53.38 mtoe in 1984 to

[36] *World Gas Intelligence*, 14 Oct. 1994, p. 2.
[37] Ibid.

126.88 mtoe in 1993. On the supply side, during the same period the country's dependence on imported energy resources increased significantly, from 75% to 95%. South Korea's dependence on oil reached 61% in 1993 from 44% in 1987, and the Middle East remained its main oil supplier (in 1993 total crude-oil imports were 561 million barrels, of which 431 million barrels came from the Middle East).[38] As a result, the country's oil industry is extremely vulnerable to any future oil crisis.

It was in the late 1970s that South Korea recognized the urgent need to diversify its oil-import sources and secure its supply sources by the participation of Korean companies in overseas exploration and production. The Korea Petroleum Development Corp. (PEDCO) was established in 1979, and the first Korean involvement in overseas activities came in 1981, when Kodeco Energy Co. took part in Indonesia's West Madura oil-development project. In 1979–93, a total of $264 million was invested in South Korea's continental offshore exploration. However, 54% ($143 million) of the total investment was covered by foreign companies. The results of seismic acquisition of 91,170 km of lines and 28 exploratory wells confirm 149 oil-bearing structures and discoveries of small gas fields in Block VI-I. (The estimated recoverable gas reserves are only 200–80 bcf.)

Overseas, Korean companies have promoted 43 projects in 26 countries since 1981. Table 6.7 lists 25 projects in 17 countries as of March 1994, of which 6 are producing in Indonesia, Yemen, Egypt, Argentina and Venezuela.[39] Total investment for 40 overseas E & P projects undertaken between 1981 and 1993 recorded $1.21 billion, of which $0.56 billion went to exploration. (The figures for Japan until 1990 were $31.7 billion and $18 billion respectively.) The investment figure of $1.21 billion is divided as follows: $0.76 billion for the Marib (Yemen) and Madura (Indonesia) projects; $0.45 billion for the remaining 38 projects. The discovery of Marib oil field, rating 175,000 b/d, owed more to luck, therefore, than investment.

Currently, crude-oil imports by Korean companies are only 20,000 b/d, accounting for 1.2% of South Korean oil consumption. The government reduced the target for crude-oil imports by Korean companies from 20% to 10% in 2000, but even that looks ambitious in the present circumstances. In 1994, some $1.54 billion was allocated to the Petroleum Business Fund, whose aim is to stabilize the supply and demand of petroleum, maintain moderate prices, and undertake petroleum

---

[38] *Hydrocarbon Asia Business Report*, 16–30 Sept. 1994, pp. 6–16; *Yearbook of Energy Statistics 1993*, Ministry of Trade, Industry and Energy (MTIE) and Korea Energy Economics Institute (KEEI), Seoul.

[39] *Korea Petroleum Association Journal*, March 1994, pp. 72–3 (Table 3), and June 1994, pp. 67–79.

Table 6.7: South Korea's overseas exploration and production activities, as of 1993

Production projects

Country	Block	Korean share (%)	Participating Korean companies	Operator
Indonesia	W. Madura	50	KD, PD	Kodeco
Yemen	Marib	24.5	PD, YK, HD, SH	Hunt
Egypt	Khalda	10	PD, SS, HO, LG	Repsol
Argentina	Palma-Largo	14	PD, D-W, KH, DB, HB	Pluspetrol
Egypt	Zaaparana	25	YK	British Gas
Argentina	Hojjin, Tonono	70	D-W	Dongwon
Evaluation Projects				
Malaysia	SK-7	29.75	PD, YK, SS	OPIC
Indonesia	Warim	15	KI, YK, LG, PD	Conoco
Myanmar	BLK-C	100	YK, SK	Yukong
Ecuador	BLK-13	25	KI, PD	Unocal
US	On/Offshore	2.1–15	HD	Phillips
UAE	RAK	35	LG, YK, HD, PD	IPL
Libya	NC 173/4	50	PD, DW, HD, MK, DS	Lasmo
Malaysia	SK-17	20	LG, HD	Idemitsu
US	Alaska	50	SR	?
Syria	Al-Nabk	25	YK	Damascus
Algeria	Issaouane	30	SS, KI	?
Australia	ZOCA 91-10	25	HD, PD, KI, DS, DW LG, MK	Marathon
Australia	ZOCA 91-11	15	HD, PD, KI, DS, DW LG, MK	Marathon
Papua New Guinea	PPL-123	20	HL	Trend
Vietnam	11-2	70	PD, DS, HD, DW, LG SH, SR, SS	Pedco
Jordan	Risha/Sarhan	100	HB	Hanbo
Libya	NC 170-2	20	YK, HO, LG	Petrofina
Angola	2-92	15	DW, PD	Total
China offshore	26/23	100	PD, YK, DW, SH, HHI KH, HS, HD, DW	
Venezuela	Palkon?	75	HHI	?

Key:	
DB = Dongbang	KH = Kohap
DS = Daesung	KI = Kyung In
DW = Daewoo	LG = Lucky-Goldstar
D-W = Dongwon	MK = Mazuko
HB = Hanbo	PD = Pedco
HD = Hyundai	SH = Samwhan
HHI = Hyundai Heavy Industry	SK = Sunkyong
HL = Halla	SR = Ssangyong Refinery
HO = Hyundai Oil	SS = Samsung
KD = Kodeco	YK = Yukong

Source: Korea Petroleum Association Journal, March 1994, pp. 70–1.

development projects more effectively. However, overseas oil exploration and development took only $0.08 billion, representing 5.2% of the total fund.[40] This poor investment scale confirms that the government has not recognized the importance of oil and gas exploration and development.

South Korea is pursuing an oil and gas development policy that hopes to land a windfall with minimum investment. This policy exactly reflects Korean business style, which expects a quick return rather than settling for a long-term investment. To achieve the target of 10% in 2000 with this scale of governmental support could be possible if another lucky discovery is made. It remains to be seen, however, whether approaches by Korean companies to frontier oil and gas areas will get the government's full financial support.

6.2.2 Approaches to China's and Russia's frontier oil and gas exploration and development

So far as both Russia's and China's frontier oil and gas exploration and development are concerned, South Korea is one of the main beneficiaries of the collapse of the Cold War. The establishment of diplomatic relations with the FSU and China opened the way for its participation in both countries' frontier development. The Korea–Russia relationship also provided Russia with freedom of movement in Far East oil and gas development.

Korean companies began to show an interest in Soviet frontier oil and gas before diplomatic relations were established in 1990. Among 26 South Korean companies (as members of the Overseas Petroleum Development Association of Korea) directly or indirectly involved in oil and gas exploration and production, it was the Hyundai Group that took the initiative in Soviet Far East oil and gas development. After Mr Chung Ju-Yung's Moscow visit in January 1989, an agreement in

[40] *Korea Petroleum Association Journal*, June 1994, pp. 67–79.

principle to develop natural resources in the Yakut ASSR was made between the Hyundai Group and a Soviet delegation headed by Mr R.D. Margulov, first deputy chairman of the Council of Ministers' Bureau for the Fuel and Energy Complex, in June 1990.[41]

Soon after Mr Gorbachev's visit to the Cheju Island in April 1991, it was reported that the Ministry of Energy and Resources (now Ministry of Trade, Industry and Energy) planned to develop the Lunskoye field.[42] The following month, international bidding for the feasibility study for Lunskoye and Piltun-Astokskoye oil and gas fields development was announced, and a consortium composed of the Hyundai Co., Broken Hill Proprietary Co. Ltd and Amoco participated (it became one of five losers).

Earlier another approach had been made by Palmco Corp., a Korean company based in California, and working in association with the US engineering company Ralph M Parsons. In mid-1990 the partnership submitted a proposal to the Sakhalin parliament under which it would develop the Lunskoye field, construct offshore platforms and onshore pipelines, and build a gas-liquefaction plant. Palmco's classic buy/sell arrangement, whereby the Korean side would purchase natural gas at prevailing market prices for a 30-year period, was an unusual one for the Soviets. The LNG plants would be owned by Palmco, while the other facilities would be owned by the Russians. In return, Palmco would be granted export rights for LNG and condensate. Subsequently pledges were secured from the Korean Gas Corporation to purchase the gas, which would be shipped as LNG to Korea.[43] The project cost (as of 1991) was estimated at a total of $3.2 billion, of which $2.2 billion was for gas production and transmission facilities, and $1 billion for a gas-liquefaction plant.[44]

Palmco's approach was ideal for early development of the Lunskoye gas project, and it was strongly supported by the Sakhalin parliament. (It is my belief, however, that the consideration of Piltun-Astokskoye and Lunskoye oil and gas fields was not right for the early realization of Sakhalin offshore gas because of their location. As shown in Map 6.4, the Piltun-Astokskoye field in Sakhalin Block 1 should have been included in the Sakhalin-I project comprising Odoptu, Chaivo and Arkutun-

---

[41] *Korea Times*, 3 June 1990.

[42] *Korea Herald*, 21 April 1991.

[43] For details, see Keun Wook Paik, 'Japan, Korea, and the Development of Russian Far Eastern Energy Resources', *Journal of Energy and Development* 16: 2 (1992), pp. 227–45; Keun Wook Paik, 'Towards a Northeast Asian Energy Charter,' *Energy Policy*, May 1992, p. 434; Keun Wook Paik, 'A Northeast Asian Gas Grid?' (op. cit., n. 19), p. 9.

[44] For details, see *Korea Times*, 12 July 1991; a press release by Palmco Corp. in preparation for a briefing session held in Seoul on 11 July 1991.

Map 6.4: Sakhalin offshore fields: tender blocks

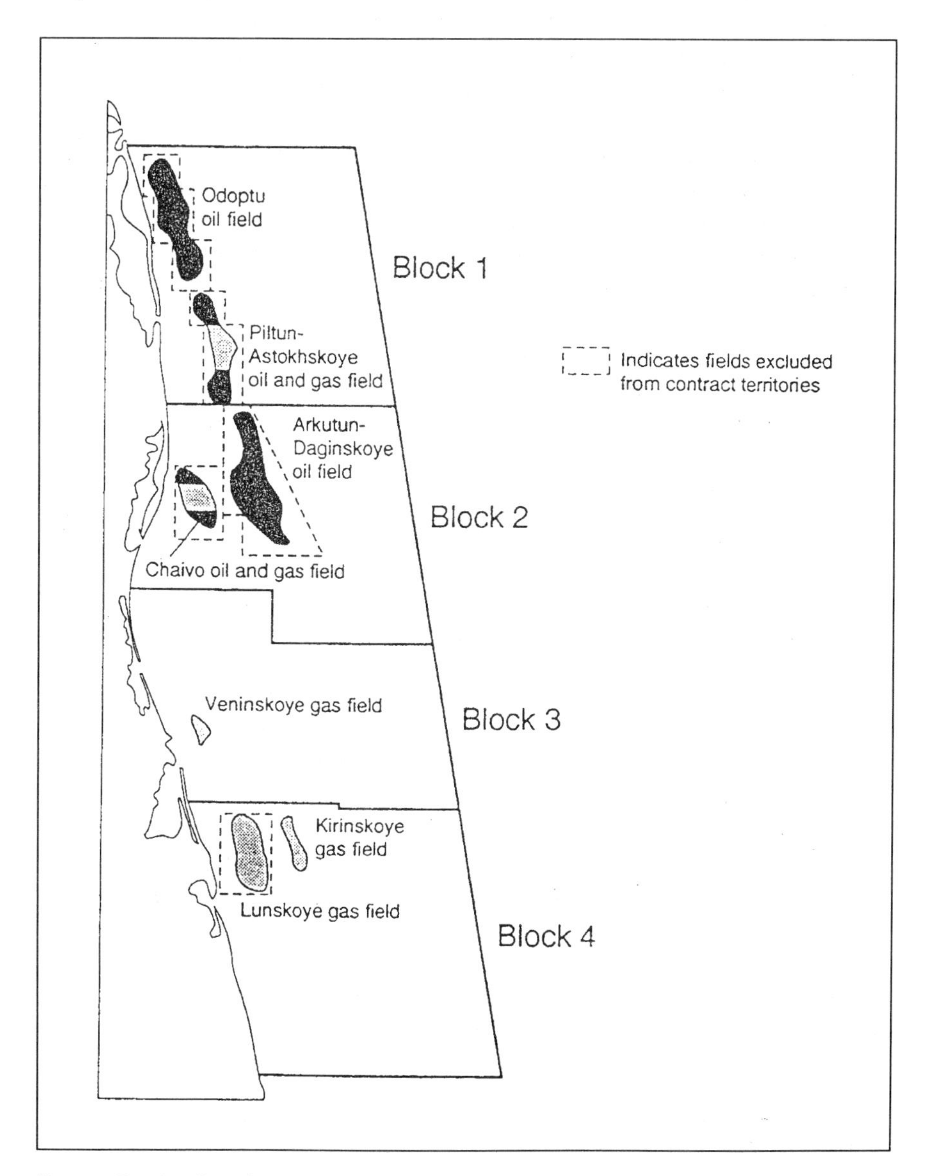

Source: Russian Petroleum Investor, July 1993, p. 43

Daginskoye fields.) But Palmco's approach was frustrated by its partnership with Samsung Co. and then Enron LNG (a division of Enron International Inc.) had failed to convince the Moscow authorities. Had Palmco succeeded in finding a reliable partner with an international reputation, the outcome would have been different.

In July 1992 a Korean consortium originally composed of nine companies was established to develop the Sakha Republic's gas.[45] In the power transfer from the Soviet president Gorbachev to the Russian president Yeltsin, however, the Daewoo group took the initiative over Yakutsk gas development from the Hyundai group. As a result the Hyundai group decided not to join the Korean consortium in silent protest against the government's support for Daewoo's leadership in the consortium.

Regardless of such competition among Korean companies over Yakutsk gas development, an important step was taken in November 1992, when Boris Yeltsin visited Seoul. According to Clause 16 in the ROK–Russia Joint Statement:

> They welcomed the signing of agreement between consortia of the two countries on the preparation of feasibility studies for joint development of the natural gas field in the Republic of Sakha (Yakutia) and construction of pipelines for transport of natural gas to the Republic of Korea. They agreed that two Governments would make joint efforts for the development of several Sakhalin offshore gas fields in order to supply gas from Sakhalin to the Republic of Korea.[46]

The statement did not specify the gas field's name, and the Ministry of Energy and Resources decided to promote Korean participation in the Lunskoye development.[47] In July 1993 a Korean evaluation group composed of PEDCO, Hyundai Co., Kohap Ltd, Daesung Co., Daewoo Corp., Dongbu Corp., Lucky-Goldstar International Corp., Samhwan Corp., Kolon International Co., POSCO and Hanbo Energy Co. Ltd was formed to study the Sakhalin-II project. The group was established at the Hyundai group's initiative[48] and is studying Marathon's offer to purchase its 50% share as a way of taking part in Piltun-Astokskoye and Lunskoye oil and gas development.

One month after the statement, the first Yakut gas project joint-committee meeting was held in Seoul, but the Russian-Sakha delegation, with 16 members, failed

[45] As of 1994, it has twelve members: PEDCO; KGC (Korea Gas Corp.); Daewoo Corp.; Yukong Ltd; LG International Corp.; Samsung Co.; Samhwan Corp.; POSCO (Pohang Iron and Steel Co. Ltd); Kohap Ltd; Ssangyong Corp.; Hanbo Energy Co. Ltd; and Dongbu Corp.
[46] *Korea Times*, 21 Nov. 1992.
[47] *Hankook Ilbo*, 19 Nov. 1992.
[48] Daewoo felt they had nothing to lose by joining the group despite Hyundai's leadership.

to agree the details of the preliminary feasibility study, especially the budget scale. The Korean consortium was willing to cover $8 million, while the Russians argued for a budget of $25 million.

Two further meetings, a working-level meeting to discuss the preliminary feasibility study of Yakutsk gas development in July 1993 and a high-ranking officers' meeting for the same purpose in February 1994, could not produce a compromise on the budget issue. Disappointed with the delay in a budget compromise, the Yakut president Mikhail Nikolayev visited Tokyo in February 1994 for a briefing on Yakutia's oil and gas prospects. Even though the briefing attracted more than 70 Japanese companies, the response of Japanese businesses was not very positive as Yakutia then had nothing concrete to offer oil companies.[49] This attempt to attract Japanese interest could be interpreted as a tactic on the part of the Republic of Sakha to obtain a generous budget offer from the Korean consortium.

Eventually, a compromise was arrived at in June 1994, when South Korea's president Kim Yong-Sam visited Moscow. South Korea and the Russian Federation agreed to implement the preliminary feasibility study with a budget of $20 million – each side contributing $10 million. (Strictly speaking, only the Koreans will pay. The Russians will provide a bundle of study data, including some that is old, which was regarded as worth $10 million.) The second joint-committee meeting was scheduled to be held in Seoul in late September 1994, and the preliminary study seemed set to begin in late 1994 with a one-year timetable to begin as soon as details are finalized.[50] If the results are positive, a two-year full feasibility study with an estimated budget of $100 million will follow.

This agreement was the only tangible result of Korea's move towards involvement in RFE oil and gas development. Strictly speaking it was not the first. In April 1991 Tongwon Consolidated Coal Mine Development Co. agreed with Sameco (Sakhalin Oil Company) to set up a joint venture for exploration of Okruzhnoye oil field (Sakhalin onshore). However, the agreement was not implemented due to problems such as Sameco's recontract with Smith Energy Co. (US) without Tongwon's permission, profits remittance and exchange-rate applications.[51]

As for China's onshore and offshore oil and gas development, South Korea

---

[49] *Russian Petroleum Investor*, July/August 1994, p. 48.

[50] After the Moscow agreement in June 1994, a joint venture named 'Takt' and composed of OMV (Austria), Lenaneftegas Geologiya and Goskomnedra, having secured two blocks in the Republic of Sakha, decided to join the Russian consortium. As a result, the JV 'Takt' will take part in the preliminary feasibility study.

[51] *Chosun Ilbo*, 26 Sept. 1990; *Kookmin Ilbo*, 24 June 1991; a report prepared by the Ministry of Energy and Resources on the Korean Delegate's visit to the Russian Federation and Mongolia in May 1992.

responded immediately to China's hurried opening of its frontier areas in 1992–3. No South Korean consortium has tried to secure a block of the Tarim Basin's contract area as the scale of the project is beyond Korea's capacity, but a joint-study agreement for Qian-Nan block with a contract area of 41,136 sq. km in Guizhou province was made between China National Oil and Gas Development Corp. (CNODC) and a Korean consortium composed of Hanbo Energy Co., Hyundai Corp., Halla Resources Corp. and PEDCO in 1993.[52] However, this joint study seems unlikely to lead to joint exploration work as a Korean delegation to Guizhou province in March 1994 found no merit in undertaking further work after the data study.

Korean companies have secured an offshore block, however, in the East China Sea. In December 1993 a Korean consortium composed of eight companies, PEDCO, Yukong Co., Daewoo Co., Samhwan Co., Hyundai Co., Hyundai Heavy Industry Co., Kohap Co. and Hyosung Co., signed a geophysical agreement with CNOOC for exploration of block 26/23, consisting of 3,700 sq. km in southern acreage off Wenzhou. The consortium will decide on test drilling after running 2,000 km of seismic lines during the contract period of 18 months.[53]

So far the results of moves by South Korean companies to participate in Russia's and China's oil and gas development have not been very impressive. But the frontier areas seem likely to continue to attract the interest of Korean companies in the foreseeable future because of geographical proximity and South Korea's strengthened relations with both countries.

6.2.3 The options for South Korea

South Korea's options are quite limited as its gas market is not big enough to make a mega-size grassroots project fully viable. But it is big enough to give vitality to a new project. As shown in Table 6.4, as of 1993 South Korea was importing 4.3 mt/year of LNG, and the total long-term-contract volume was 6.3 mt including 2 mt from Malaysia in 1995 onwards. The Korea Gas Corp. (KGC) signed a letter of intent for 2.4 mt of LNG from Qatar, but the deal is not yet finalized.

In 1993 the KGC revised its forecast for LNG demand to 11.6 mt (from 10 mt) in 2000 and 15.5 mt in 2006, and so Korea needs to secure another 5.3 mt of LNG by 2000 or another 2.9 mt if Qatar's 2.4 mt is finalized).[54] In short, the Korean gas

[52] *Meil Kyungje* (*Economic Daily*), 16 Dec. 1994; *China Petroleum Investment Guide*, *China OGP* and AP Energy Business Publications, Singapore, 1994, p. 74 (Table 4).

[53] *Korea Petroleum Association Journal*, June 1994, pp. 69–70.

[54] The Korea Gas Union thought the figure could rise to 14 mt. See *FT International Gas Report*, 4 March 1994, p. 18; 11 Nov. 1994, p. 21; David Hayes, 'Korean LNG Demand to soar to 10 MT by 2000', *Asian Oil ad Gas*, May 1992, pp. 25–30.

market in 2000 can accommodate roughly 3.5 mt of LNG import, and a number of potential suppliers, such as the Energy Silk Route project (10 mt), the Sakhalin project (6 mt), the Oman project (6 mt) and Australia's Gorgon project (5–6 mt), aim to supply that market in 2000.[55]

The final decision on LNG imports is to be made in the mid-1990s, along with the government decision on the Yakutsk gas project's full feasibility study with a two-year timetable. At present, the project's development economics is not encouraging at all. If North Korea's oil and gas industries after unification are considered, however, the Yakutsk gas project would be an ideal solution to North Korea's energy-supply problem. In this context, the possibility that South Korea will promote the development of Yakutsk gas regardless of its poor economics cannot be ruled out. (This possibility could be seriously affected by South Korea's recent approach on Irkutsk gas development for imports to the South Korean gas market. For further discussion, see Chapter 7.)

One scenario would allow South Korea to promote an early realization of Yakutsk gas, along with Sakhalin offshore gas, as follows: first, the development rights for the Lunskoye gas field is awarded to a Russian entity, like Gasprom; secondly, a gas pipeline grid between northern Sakhalin and the Greater Vladivostok Zone, via Okha, Komsomolsk, Khabarovsk and Primorskii region is established; and thirdly, LNG and power plants are constructed in the Greater Vladivostok Zone. Such an approach would solve the RFE energy shortage at a stroke, and enable Russia to export its surplus electricity to the adjacent Tumen River Economic Development Area and its gas to the Northeast Asian market. My rough calculation suggests that RFE oriented gas development could be initiated with a $5–6 billion investment, roughly half that of the generally quoted Sakhalin II project cost of $10–12 billion.[56]

This approach parallels Dr Eugene Khartukov's argument:

> a more plausible case of securing gas exports from the Russian Far East is the projected construction of an export pipeline to transport gas produced in Sakhalin. Under our base scenario, exports of about 10 billion cubic metres/year will be handled by 2005 along the route Lunskoye to Komsomolsk-on-Amur to Khabarovsk to Daknerechensk to Russia's state border with North Korea.[57]

[55] In March 1995, the KGC signed a letter of intent with Oman LNG for the supply of 3 mt/y of LNG for 25 years commencing in 2000. Its finalization remains to be seen. See *Korea Times*, 24 Feb. 1995; *FT International Gas Report*, 2 Sept. 1994, pp. 4–5 and 16, 19.

[56] Keun Wook Paik, 'Pipeline Politics' (op. cit.), p. 5.

[57] Eugene Khartukov, 'Potential of Pacific Frontiers of Former Soviet Oil, Gas Empire', *Oil and Gas Journal*, 25 April 1994, p. 73.

Had the South Korean government decided to allocate a part of the promised $3 billion loan (suspended after $1.5 billion had been provided because of Russia's failure to pay interest) for RFE gas development, it would not have left the Yakutsk project in open competition for its entry to the Northeast Asian gas market. If Korean companies manage to join Sakhalin-I by securing a portion of the Russian companies' share (Sakhalinmorneftegas and Rosenefte have a 40% share), then this approach is still viable.

Sakhalin-II provides the second-best alternative. As mentioned above, the offer is being studied by a Korean evaluation group, which has no reason to reject the offer so long as early export of Sakhalin-II LNG, and participation in pipeline and LNG construction projects, are guaranteed. For South Korea, the advantage of Sakhalin-offshore gas imports is that they would provide a very useful stopgap until implementation of the Yakutian project. However, it remains to be seen whether Japan would accept Korea's participation in Sakahlin-II.

If Japan's response is positive, it will accelerate not only Sakhalin-offshore gas and oil development, but also Yakutsk gas and oil development. Eventually, it will pave the way for an era of multilateral cooperation in RFE oil and gas development. But if Japan sticks to Japan-oriented development of Sakhalin offshore, it will delay Korean and Japanese cooperation in RFE development and dampen the enthusiasm of the Korean consortium for Yakutsk gas development.

As regards the Energy Silk Route project, South Korea could obtain virtually a free ride here by opening its gas market with minimum investment. South Korea has no reason to reject this project so long as a stable gas supply is guaranteed and the delivered gas is acceptable. However, serious questions arise concerning the economics and security of the project's supply. The delivered gas will not be cheap, and consequently the project will be hard-pressed to compete with any other source of gas or LNG. To complicate matters further, China has the potential to consume a large portion of gas from Central Asia and for South Korea the real problem lies in the fact that development of the Energy Silk Route project would delay Yakutian gas development considerably.

6.3 Conclusion

This study confirms both Japan's and South Korea's deep interest in Russia's and China's frontier oil and gas development, but it also suggests that their priorities when it comes to actual development can be quite different. A clear finding is that Japan's stance towards the frontier oil and gas development of both countries will be a decisive factor in accelerating or delaying development.

Japan's policy seems to favour China's frontier oil and gas development, whereas its stance towards the Russian Far East, especially Yakutsk gas development, is unlikely to be flexible unless the territorial issue is settled. As far as Sakhalin offshore development is concerned, however, both Japanese companies and the government seem to have no choice but to support it as a result of the rapidly changing business environment.

South Korea's policy seems to be positive so long as development of Russia's and China's frontier oil remains manageable. However, its attitude towards gas development seems to be limited by its financing capacity and the scale of its market. Unification of North and South Korea is an issue that could produce an unexpected result in South Korean policy towards Russia's East Siberian gas development.

Japan and South Korea will either cooperate or compete over Russia's and China's frontier oil and gas. In the second half of the 1990s RFE gas development will test the policies of both countries, and Northeast Asia will know whether multilateral oil and gas development can be realized or remains a dream.

Chapter 7

The frontier projects: Sakhalin, Sakha and Tarim

Three giant oil and gas projects, which could fundamentally affect the region's oil and gas supply structure in the next decade, are currently under preparation or in the early stages of development in the frontier areas of Northeast Asia. Due to their remote location, a harsh environment and the lack of a regional infrastructure, these projects require a huge investment if their long-waited exploration and development is to be realized.

As well as Sakhalin, Sakha and Tarim, the development of the Irkutsk gas project is now also under active investigation. Irkutsk is bound to be linked to Sakha because of the projects' geographical proximity. Information is limited, but this chapter will look briefly at the Irkutsk project in the section on Sakha gas.

The region's frontier projects have attracted foreign investment ever since their simultaneous opening. Now that the Irkutsk project has joined the race, the fierce competition for early development among these frontier projects seems to have been intensified. At present Sakhalin is the front runner in this race.

The development of Sakhalin-I and II projects, with a respective estimated cost of $13–15 and $10–12 billion, seems likely to begin in the late 1990s. The projected peak oil and gas production from Sakhalin I and II at the end of the next decade is 30 mt and 20 bcm respectively, and export timing is around 2003–2005.

The estimated development cost of the Sakha gas project, currently undergoing a preliminary feasibility study, is around $20 billion. According to the most optimistic forecast, Sakha would start development in the late 1990s and reach a peak in gas production of around 30 bcm in 2010.

The development economics of the Irkutsk project, whose development cost is estimated at $10 billion, look better than for the Sakha project, and the possibility of its development prior to Sakha, presumably in the second half of this decade, cannot be ruled out (both projects would be linked eventually, however). If that is the case, export could start early in the next decade, and around 20–30 bcm would seem to be available for export.

The Tarim project is somewhat different. Some areas in the Basin have been explored and a couple of fields are being developed by the CNPC, but it is virtually untapped. No reliable projection will be available until exploration work is finished in the areas opened to foreign investors in early 1993 and June 1995.

This chapter will examine the development programmes of each project, after a brief historical review.

7.1 The Sakhalin offshore projects

The Sakhalin projects are based mainly in the north Sakhalin basin, one of the nine basins belonging to the waters of the Russian Far East. The north Sakhalin basin, with a combined off and on shore area of 24,000 sq. km, is the most explored region in Far Eastern waters and contains 50 oil and gas fields. Besides the north Sakhalin basin, the Pogranichnoye Graben, Terpeniye Gulf basin, Aniva Gulf basin and Tatar Strait basin are also located along Sakhalin Island.[1] Major oil and gas discoveries in Sakhalin offshore so far include the Odoptu, Chaivo, Lunskoye, Piltun-Astokskoye, Arkutun-Daginskoye, Veninskoye and Kirinskoye fields.

7.1.1 Historical review

The first proposal for a Sakhalin natural-gas project appeared in 1965. The plan called for Japanese interests to participate in the construction of an 850-km, large-diameter gas pipeline from Okha to Nevelsk, and a gas liquefaction plant at Nevelsk. As shown in Map 7.1, a second plan proposed by the Soviets in 1968 called for Japanese assistance in the construction of a 1,880-km gas pipeline from Okha to Nakhodka, through Primorsky Krai after crossing the Tatarsky Strait. The Japanese response, made in December 1968, was to propose the construction of a 66-cm-diameter gas pipeline from Okha to Gornozavodsk, and then to Wakkanai after crossing the Soya Strait.[2]

Difficult negotiations continued during the first half of the 1970s, and the way lay open for Sakhalin offshore oil and gas exploration with a general agreement between the USSR Ministry of Foreign Trade and Sodeco (Sakhalin Oil Develop-

---

[1] Arthur A. Meyerhoff, 'Soviet Petroleum: History, Technology, Geology, Reserves, Potential and Policy', in Robert G. Jensen, Theodore Shabad and Arthur W. Wright, eds, *Soviet Natural Resources in the World Economy*, University of Chicago Press, Chicago, 1983, pp. 339–41; A.A. Meyerhoff, *The Oil and Gas Potential of the Soviet Far East*, Scientific Press, Beaconsfield, 1981, pp. 96–128.

[2] Peter Egyed, *Western Participation in the Development of Siberian Energy Resources: Case Studies*, East-West Commercial Relations Series, Research Report 22, Institute of Soviet and East European Studies, Carleton University, Ottawa, 1983, pp. 27–59; Jeremy Russell, *Energy as a Factor in Soviet Foreign Policy*, Saxon House, Westmead, 1976, pp. 155–66; Arthur Jay Klinghoffer, *The Soviet Union and International Oil Politics*, Columbia University Press, New York, 1977, pp. 243–53.

Map 7.1: Sakhalin gas-pipeline proposals: 1965–8

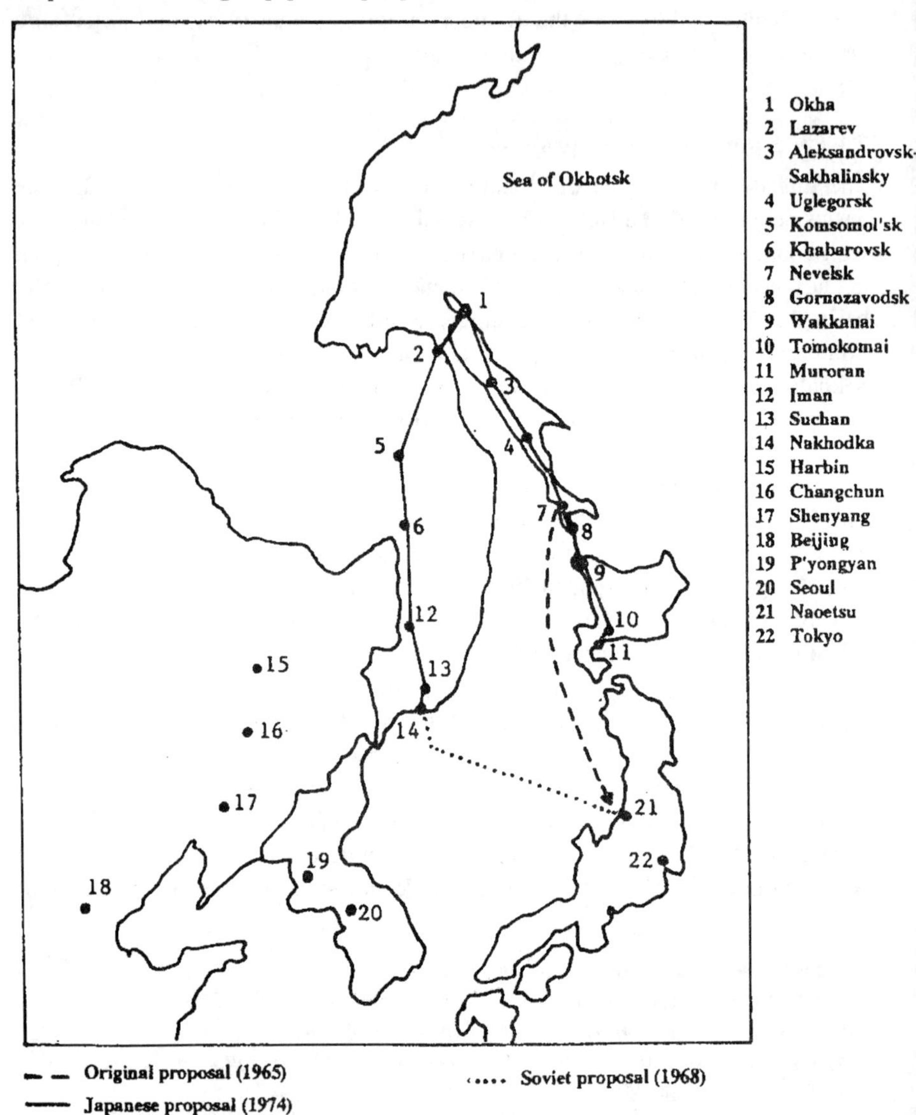

Source: Peter Egyed, *Western Participation in the Development of Siberian Energy Resources: Case Studies*, East–West Commercial Relations Series Report 20, Institute of Soviet and East European Studies, May 1983, p. 34

ment Corp.) signed on 28 January 1975.[3] During May–November 1976 geophysical surveys off the northeast and southwest coasts of Sakhalin Island were conducted.[4] In the summer of 1977 the *Borgsten-Dolphin*, a jack-up owned and operated by a US company, Dolphin International, was used to spud the first offshore well by a foreign company in the history of the Soviet Union.[5]

Exploration of the northeastern Sakhalin shelf in 1976–82 resulted in discovery of two oil, condensate and gas fields, Odoptu (1977) and Chaivo (1979), with total reserves of 67 mt of oil and condensate and 172 bcm of gas.[6] Sodeco was responsible for discovering these two fields, and a Soviet production programme, utilizing its self-made 'Shelf' series offshore rigs, was not applied to the discoveries. This fact reflects the stage Soviet offshore development had reached in the 1970s.

During 1980–2 Sakhalin offshore development was hampered by the US embargo on the transfer of advanced energy technology and equipment to the Soviet Union.[7] As a way round the ban, the Soviets purchased the Japanese-built jack-up *Okha* in 1982 and despatched an Arctic-class drillship the *Mikhail Mirchink* to the area in 1983.[8] As soon as the sanction was lifted, an agreement on the joint Soviet–Japanese development of the Chaivo field was made, in August 1984.[9] However, the oil-price

---

[3] Egyed, *Western Participation in the Development of Siberian Energy Resources* (op. cit., n. 2), pp. 27–59; S. Lewarne, *Soviet Oil: The Move Offshore*, Westview Press, Boulder, 1988, pp. 81–90.

[4] Egyed, *Western Participation in the Development of Siberian Energy Resources* (op. cit., n. 2), p. 50.

[5] The rig was capable of drilling 8,000 m in water depths of 90 m. Ibid., p. 51; A.A. Meyerhoff, 'The USSR Northern and Far Eastern Coasts: Petroleum Geology and Technology, Mining Activities, and Environmental Factors', working draft prepared for Dept of Indian and Northern Affairs, Ottawa, p. 173.

[6] Geological/geophysical surveys and exploratory drilling were financed through a Japanese risk-venture credit of $181.5 million at a 6% per year rate. As of 1 January 1987, the Soviet Union's outstanding debt on that credit amounted to $276.6 million. See *Oil and Gas Journal*, 23 March 1992, p. 129.

[7] It was not until after the imposition of martial law in Poland on 13 December 1981 that the United States actually imposed sanctions agianst the Siberian gas pipeline. See Bruce W. Jentleson, *Pipeline Politics: The Complex Political Economy of East–West Energy Trade*, Cornell University Press, Ithaca, 1986, pp. 172–214.

[8] *Offshore*, 20 June 1982, p. 145.

[9] The development plans included the installation of 4 ice-resistant platforms (each with 49 production/injection wells and accommodation for personnel) at the field which will be linked by 6 pipelines with the Soviet mainland town of De Kastries, site of two new 1.5-million-tonnes/year LNG plants. In return, Japan would receive 25,000 barrels per day, plus 3 mt of LNG over a 20-year period starting in 1990. Total cost was estimated at $3.8 billion. See *World Oil*, Aug. 1985, p. 92; *Petroleum Economist*, Oct. 1984, p. 387; *Oil and Gas Journal*, 27 Aug. 1984, p. 128.

Table 7.1: Characteristics of the main oil and gas fields off Sakhalin

		Odoptu	Chaivo	Piltun-Astokskoye	Lunskoye	Daginskoye
1 Number of drilled wells/ maximum well depth (m)		15/ 2,500	5/ 3,379	14/ 2,500	6/ 3,036	3/ 3,066
2 Field type, O/G/C		O, G, C	O, G, C	O, G, C	G, C	O, G, C
3 Water depth		2–35	18–32	25–35	42–47	55
4 Distance from shore		6–8 km	12 km	15–20 km	12–15 km	42 km
5 Ice-free period (months)		4.5–5	4.5–5	4.5–5	4.5	4.5–5.5
6 Reserves (mt/bcm) (1 Jan. 1992)						
Geological gas:	C1	58.1	113.9	52	298.2	18.2
	C2	26.2	26.6	13.4	93.4	39.8
Recoverable oil:	C1	38.1	18.2	62.1	2.4	8.8
	C2	4.4	1.3	18.1	5.2	92.3
Re-condensate:	C1	1.7	8.5	4.3	24.5	0.9
	C2	0.5	1.6	0.4	7.6	2.8
7 Max. annual production		Oil: 2.7 Gas: 2	Oil: 1.5 Gas: 4.5	Oil: 5–6 Gas: 3–5	Con: 1.4–2 Gas: 15–20	Oil: 2–5
8 Comment		Approved by SCR	Approved by SCR		Approved by SCR	Tentative estimate

Key: O/G/C = Oil/Gas/Condensate; SCR = State Committee for Reserves.
Source: Igor B. Dubin, 'Offshore Production Areas: The Barents and Kara Seas, The Sea of Okhotsk', paper presented at the Conference on 'Opening Up the Post-Soviet Gas Industry', London, 14–15 April 1992.

decline, and the Japanese refusal to guarantee purchases of LNG, and its withdrawal from an agreement extending a low-interest dedicated credit line for the construction of surface facilities, led the Soviets in June 1987 to postpone Chaivo development.[10]

[10] *Oil and Gas Journal*, 23 March 1992, p. 129. In November 1987 both sides unofficially agreed to develop natural gas at Chaivo field and crude oil at Odoptu field simultaneously, on the condition that the Soviets would purchase all Sakhalin-produced natural gas, while the Japanese would buy the crude oil. See *Platt's Oilgram News*, 30 June 1987, pp. 2–3; *Japan Economic Journal*, 21 Nov. 1987, p. 12.

One view argues that it was the Soviet Union that forced a slowdown in cooperation. According to Stephen Lewarne, production was not a priority for the Soviets as most of the exploratory work had already been done to their satisfaction.[11] During 1984–9, without foreign participation, there were some major discoveries, including the Piltun-Astokhskoye, Lunskoye and Arkutun-Daginskoye fields, confirming the potential of oil and gas reserves off Sakhalin Island (see Table 7.1).

In April 1989, Intershelf, a joint venture between J.P. Kenny, a UK engineering company, and the Moscow Institute of Civil Engineering and the Industrial Construction Bank, planned to introduce a sub-sea early-production system for the Piltun-Astokskoye field, but it was later suspended.[12]

7.1.2 Sakhalin-I

The Sakhalin-I project originated in the 1975 general agreement, under which the $100-million credit offered by the Japan Petroleum Development Corp. (later JNOC) and Sodeco was arranged on a no-success, no-repayment basis. Sodeco proceeded to drill 26 exploration wells over 10 years, even though the agreement stipulated 56 wells. The first oil crisis in the early 1970s had driven Sodeco to undertake the exploration work in Sakhalin offshore, and it is not certain why it stopped. The Russians speculate that Sodeco feared it would never be paid for its work, despite the discoveries of the Odoptu and Chaivo fields whose crude oil reserves were far bigger than were expected. Sodeco was not pushed to undertake further exploration.[13]

Its spending was not enormous. It provided credits totalling $185 million, of which 70% originated from JNOC for use in exploration on a 'success and repay' risk-taking basis, and a syndicate of Japanese commercial banks provided bank loans totalling 6,740 million yen ($33.7 million, based on the then current exchange rate $1 = 200 yen) to cover purchases of equipment. The bank loans were repaid by October 1983.[14]

---

[11] Stephen Lewarne, *Soviet Oil* (op. cit., n. 3), p. 98.

[12] The planned work was an instalment of 4 sub-sea wells and a control system tied back via two 10-mile pipelines to onshore processing facilities. See *Oil and Gas Journal*, 24 April 1989, p. 22; *Petroleum Economist*, Sept. 1990, p. 27.

[13] *Russian Petroleum Investor*, Sept. 1993, pp. 32–3.

[14] Sodeco was established on 1 October 1974 to provide Japan's financial and technical cooperation with the Soviet Union in Sakhalin offshore oil and gas exploration and development. It was based upon an agreement reached in February 1972 between Japan and the Soviet Union at the fifth Japan–USSR Joint Economic Committee meeting. See *Japan Petroleum and Energy Trends*, 1 Oct. 1993, p. 2.

The development of the two major discoveries, the Odoptu and Chaivo oil and gas fields, failed to proceed in the 1980s. The territorial dispute between the Soviet Union and Japan was a major obstacle, but the failure of the two sides to agree on the approach for evaluating the likely profitability of the project was also responsible for the delay. With progress in the Sakhalin-II tender, settlement of the Sodeco case became a matter of urgency, prior to the Sakhalin-III tender, covering eastern offshore areas excluding the Odoptu, Chaivo, Lunskoye, Piltun-Astokskoye oil and gas fields. If the Odoptu and Chaivo fields were to be put to tender, Sodeco's spending had to be reimbursed, as Russia's Law on Underground Resources required that all new fields be allocated for development only through competitive bidding. Russia was unable to repay Sodeco's spending for exploration work, but at the same time could not break its own law. A compromise had to be found. In 1992 a joint Russian–Japanese commission headed by the deputy minister of fuel and energy, Anatoly Shatalov, set to work to resolve the issue.[15]

The solution lay in the inclusion of the Arkutun-Daginskoye field in the deal, with estimated reserves of 122 mt of oil and gas condensate, and 84 bcm of gas. The field was explored by Sakhalinmorneftegas using a floating drilling-rig, initially owned by Sodeco, but given to Sakhalinmorneftegas after Sodeco's work at Chaivo and Odoptu.[16] With the addition of the Arkutun-Daginskoye field, Sodeco's project was certain to be viable, and it had no reason to reject the compromise.

This breakthrough was confirmed by the Russian premier Chernomyrdin's signing of Resolution No. 1560-p, dated 30 August 1993. The decree enabled the Russian Federation Ministry of Fuel and Energy and the Sakhalin regional administration to conduct negotiations with Sodeco for joint development of the Chaivo, Odoptu and Arkutun-Daginskoye fields as a single complex (Sakhalin-I).[17]

On the basis of this preliminary arrangement, as discussed in Chapter 6, Michio Mudaguchi, president of SODECO, visited Moscow in late September 1993, and submitted a formal proposal elaborating three conditions for oil and gas development: the expansion of the development area in addition to the Chaivo and Odoptu structures; joint exploration and development with the Russians; and the participation of Exxon in the project.[18] The Russians agreed to include the Arkutun-Daginskoye field in the Sodeco development package, and Sodeco decided to write off Russia's $277-million debt.[19]

---

[15] *Russian Petroleum Investor*, Sept. 1993, p. 33.

[16] Ibid.

[17] Ibid., pp. 33–4.

[18] *Japan Petroleum and Energy Trends*, 1 Oct. 1993, p. 2.

[19] *Russian Petroleum Investor*, Dec. 1993/Jan. 1994, p. 40. Sodeco shareholders may decide to scrap the consortium and form a new company to clear away old debts. If the new

This compromise on the Sakhalin-I project paved the way for real development. On 24 November 1993 Sodeco, joined by Exxon, signed a memorandum with the Russian government that guaranteed its right to participate in developing the Odoptu, Chaivo and Arkutun-Daginskoye fields, containing 290 mt of oil, 33 mt of condensate and 425 bcm of gas at depths of 1,200 to 2,850 m.[20]

The development concept proposed by Sodeco and Exxon included the construction of six ice-resistant offshore platforms and eight sub-sea templates, the installation of underwater equipment, drilling of 611 wells, laying pipelines between the platforms and the shore, and finally the construction of a 683-km trunk pipeline for exporting the crude oil. The plan envisages that Sakhalin-I will supply the Russian domestic market with 3 mt of crude and 5.5 bcm of gas, starting in 2003. Peak annual production of oil and condensate totalling 23 mt is expected to be reached in 2011.[21] The plan confirms that the economics of Sakhalin-I will depend on oil development rather than gas development, and suggests that Sakhalin-I will not be developed ahead of Sakhalin-II, whose development economics will be dominated by gas development.

In September 1994 the Expert Council of the Russian Federation government approved a preliminary feasibility study presented by Sodeco and Exxon on the proposed Sakhalin-I project. Just before, however, a committee of the State Ecological Expert Commission at the Ministry of Environmental Protection and Natural Resources had rejected the same proposal and returned it to Sodeco and Exxon.[22]

Two main reasons account for the rejection of Sakhalin-I on ecological grounds. The first is that Sodeco and Exxon's environmental impact studies failed to acknowledge the existence of the Sakhalin-II project, even though all five deposits on the island shelf constitute a combined oil- and gas-producing zone, being geographically very close. The second is an increased likelihood of ecological disaster near the island because of Sodeco and Exxon's plan to build a complete pipeline network for Sakhalin-I in virtually the same area as the infrastructure already planned for Sakhalin-II.[23]

---

company is set up, Sodeco's shareholders will swap their stake for shares in the new firm, while the Japanese government may take some losses. See *Russian Petroleum Investor*, July/Aug. 1994, pp. 36–7.

[20] *Russian Petroleum Investor*, Nov. 1994, pp. 57–8.

[21] Ibid., p. 58.

[22] Ibid., p. 57.

[23] The Expert Council requests that the Sodeco and Exxon proposal should be consistent with plans for Sakhalin-II, and should also conform with Russian environmental requirements outlined by the State Ecological Expert Commission, before plans to develop the Sakhalin-I deposit can be implemented. Ibid., pp. 58–9.

In spring 1995 Sodeco and Exxon were said to have completed a year of negotiations and a feasibility study for Sakhalin-I, and submitted a production-sharing contract (PSC) to federal and local governments for approval. Sodeco and Exxon will each have a 30% interest while that of their Russian partners will be 40%, of which Roseneft's share will be 17% and Sakhalinmorneftegaz's 23%.[24]

It is too early to predict the shape of any future development, but some important possibilities are worth mentioning. Cooperation between Sakhalin-I and II cannot be ruled out as their geographical proximity could prevent overlapping investments. Also, the project consortium could expand if Russia farms out its shares. In fact, a group of South Korean companies has explored the possibility of joining the project in this way.

7.1.3 Sakhalin-II

The Sakhalin-II project originated in a protocol signed in December 1988 between McDermott, a US company, and the Ministry of the Oil and Gas Industry for a development study of the Lunskoye and Piltun-Astokskoye fields. (At the US–Soviet summit meeting in May 1987, the Soviet president had requested US cooperation in this development.) In 1990 the Soviets invited Mitsui to join the study, and in December an agreement on the feasibility study for these two fields was made between the Soviet Union and McDermott/Mitsui.[25] Separately, late in the same year, a proposal by Palmco Corp. in association with Ralph M. Parsons, to develop the Lunskoye field on a compensation-deal basis with commitments to transport gas to the Sakhalin area and export a portion of that gas, was submitted to Moscow.[26]

The Sakhalin-tender saga then began. On 20 May 1991 Sakhalinmorneftegaz on behalf of the USSR Ministry of the Oil and Gas Industry, and the Russian Federation's State Committee for Geology, announced the tender for a joint feasibility study for the development of the Lunskoye and Piltun-Astokskoye fields off north-eastern Sakhalin, and on 30 March 1992, the MMM consortium, composed of McDermott, Marathon and Mitsui, won the bidding.[27]

---

[24] *Nefte Compass*, 13 April 1995, p. 5; *Oil and Gas Journal*, 17 April 1995, newsletter; interview conducted by the author with a Korean company.

[25] Soren Touou Geizai Gengkyu Sho (The Institute for Soviet and East European Economic Studies), *Kokusai Sekyu Ichiba ni ogeru Soren no Purezence* (The FSU's Presence in the International Oil Market), ISEEES, Tokyo, 1991, p. 90.

[26] *Oil and Gas Journal*, 23 March 1992, p. 129.

[27] Ibid. pp. 129–30; Evgueni Khartukov and Fereidun Fesharaki, 'Russian Far East: Energy Review and Outlook to 2000', *Energy Advisory* 105, East-West Center, 15 Sept. 1992, pp. 8–12; *Oil and Gas Journal*, 30 March 1992, pp. 34–6; 20 April 1992, pp. 124–6; Keun Wook Paik, 'Japan, Korea, and the Development of Russian Far Eastern Energy Resources', *Journal of Energy and Development* 16: 2 (1992), pp. 227–45.

As shown in Annex 7.1, however, there were many twists and turns before the MMMSM consortium (Mitsubishi and Shell joined the MMM consortium in late 1992, and a 6,075-page report on the feasibility study was submitted at the end of 1992[28]) could secure the development rights from the Russian government in June 1994. The problem lay in the Law on the Surface, often referred to as the Law on Underground Resources and adopted on 21 February 1992, which stipulated that an exploration licence did not give the holder a priority in obtaining rights to production.[29]

The long-drawn-out procedure meant a delay in development. The Sakhalin region expressed its dissatisfaction in two resolutions.[30] The first was a decision by the Sakhalin Regional Soviet of People's Deputies (chairman, A.P. Aksenov) on 27 February 1993, which resolved to propose to the government of Russia, State Experts Commission and regional experts groups to make a comparative analysis of the feasibility study of the MMMSM consortium and the feasibility proposal from Palmco (the Korean consortium).

The second was the request by the Sakhalin Regional Council of People's Deputies on 16 June 1993 that simultaneous negotiations be held with other foreign companies for development rights to the Lunskoye and Piltun-Astokskoye fields, even though the regional parliament approved the Sakhalin regional administration's final draft of the production-sharing contract for the development of the two fields with MMMSM.

Then, on 30 August 1993, Chernomyrdin's decree obliged the Russian Federation Ministry of Fuel and Energy and the Sakhalin regional administration to conduct negotiations with MMMSM for a production-sharing contract on the development of the Sakhalin-II project.[31]

On 23 February 1994 mutual concessions allowed the virtual completion of negotiations on the project. The MMMSM consortium agreed to transfer simultaneous bonus payments to the Russian budget and the Sakhalin budget, to begin the early supply of gas to the Far East, and to place 70% of all orders for work and

---

[28] *International Gas Report*, 2 Oct. 1992, pp. 8–9; *Petroleum Intelligence Weekly*, 5 Oct. 1992, p. 5. The study estimates that production could begin in late 1995, rising eventually to nearly 0.2 mb/d of crude and around 44 mcm/day of gas. It also calls for construction of an LNG export plant with a capacity of up to 6 mt/y, and of a 15,000 b/d domestic refinery in Sakhalin. See *Nefte Compass*, 5 Feb. 1993, p. 6.

[29] William E. Holland and Alexander Buyevitch, 'Foreign Rights in Russian Oil: Fundamentals, Licenses and Security Interests', paper presented at the 2nd Annual Russian Oil Conference held in London, 11–12 Feb. 1993.

[30] *Russian Petroleum Investor*, May 1993, p. 40; July 1993, p. 20.

[31] *Russian Petroleum Investor*, Sept. 1993, p. 34.

equipment manufacturing with Russian enterprises (most of them in the defence industry). MMMSM also agreed to shorten the additional exploration period from 3–5 years to 2–3 years, but it stood firm on its demand that the Project Supervisory Council be empowered to extend this period if necessary. In return, the Russian side accepted MMMSM demands concerning the basic production-sharing agreements and amounts for royalties. Most importantly, Moscow agreed to grant MMMSM an exemption from export tariffs and excise duties.[32]

In March 1994 D. John Kennedy, head of the MMMSM working group, and Vadim Dvurechensky, Russia's deputy minister of fuel and energy, signed a protocol finalizing the terms and conditions of the Sakhalin-II production-sharing contract to develop the Lunskoye and Piltun-Astokskoye offshore deposits.[33] MMMSM then formed an independent company to be the project's licensed operator, because Roskomnedra, the federal geological agency, can issue a sub-oil utilization licence only to a specific legal entity, in accordance with the 1992 Law on Underground Resources. On 18 April 1994 Sakhalin Energy was established, and registered in the Bahamas.[34]

Finally, on 22 June 1994 a production-sharing contract between the Russian Federation, represented by Y. Shafranik, the minister for fuel and energy of the government of the Russian Federation, E. Krasnoyarov, governor of the administration of the Sakhalin oblast, and the Sakhalin Energy Investment Company Limited (referred to as Sakhalin Energy and representing the interests of the five non-Russian companies making up the MMMSM consortium) was signed in the Russian Embassy in Washington, DC.[35]

Sakhalin Energy's greatest success lay with Clause 4 of the contract, which effectively relieves the consortium of any obligations to Russia during the two years that follow the contract's effective date.[36] This was Sakhalin Energy's safety device to protect its interests against Russian bureaucratic delays and legal and fiscal uncertainties. It could prove useful since the production-sharing contract will take effect after licenses to both fields have been issued to the consortium, and the State Duma has issued a document providing a legal framework for production-sharing agreements in Russia.

Currently, however, there are literally dozens of clauses in the contract that violate either existing Russian laws or draft legislation that is expected to be passed

---

[32] *Russian Petroleum Investor*, March 1994, p. 36.

[33] *Russian Petroleum Investor*, April 1994, p. 53.

[34] *Russian Petroleum Investor*, May 1994, p. 58.

[35] *Russian Petroleum Investor*, July/Aug. 1994, pp. 53–5 and 58; *Oil and Gas Journal*, 4 July 1994, p. 32.

[36] *Russian Petroleum Investor*, July/Aug. 1994, pp. 53–5 and 58.

in the near future. Even though a Sakhalin Energy official denied the suggestion that the company is holding Sakhalin-II hostage until passage of the PSC legislation, the company appears determined not to begin operations on Sakhalin-II until the Russian parliament adopts PSC legislation consistent with the Sakhalin-II contract. In late August 1994 Sakhalin Energy presented Moscow with a long list of suggested legislative changes, including new provisions for dispute resolution and modifications in tax law.[37]

Yevgeni Krasnoyarov, governor of the Sakhalin region, suggested that the only way of getting Sakhalin-II off the ground in the near future if the PSA legislation is delayed would be to make the Duma ratify the agreement itself, while postponing the decision on the enabling legislation until 1995. The governor has strong reasons for supporting the early passage of the PSA legislation. If work on the Sakhalin-II contract is stalled, in 1995 Sakhalin region will lose up to $60 million in unpaid bonuses and credits that investors have agreed to grant under a credit line to be opened provided that production-sharing legislation is adopted by April 1995.[38]

According to Frank D. Duffield, president of Sakhalin Energy, many challenges must be overcome before the project moves forward to the development phase. To arrive at a commencement date is the first challenge and will be achieved only after contractual conditions to stabilize the legal, fiscal and commercial environment in Russia have been met. The PSC licences will be valid for 25 years but may be extended by 5-year periods thereafter.[39]

Sakhalin Energy envisages that total production from the Piltun-Astokskoye field will be 750 million barrels of oil and condensate, and 1.9 tcf of associated gas. The oil will flow at a plateau rate of about 6 mt/y. The gas will reach a plateau rate of 1.7–2.1 bcm/y, with a sharp increase to 2.6 bcm/y once oil production begins to fall. The company forecasts Lunskoye's total recoverable gas at 11.1 tcf with 325 million barrels of associated oil and condensate, and gas reserves are big enough to support a 20-year contract for 6 mt/y of LNG. The Lunskoye gas will flow through a 625-km pipeline system to the port of Progordnoye, where an LNG plant and oil-export terminal will be located.[40]

---

[37] *Russian Petroleum Investor*, Dec. 1994/Jan. 1995, p. 60.

[38] The figure of $60 million is around 27% of the annual federal subsidies. Moscow's subsidies to the Sakhalin region in 1994 are expected to total 683.5 billion roubles or about $220 million. Ibid., pp. 60 and 63.

[39] Frank D. Duffield, 'The Sakhalin-II Project', paper presented at the 'Third International Conference on Natural Gas: Trade and Investment Opportunities in Russia and the CIS', convened by the Royal Institute of International Affairs in association with the Centre for Foreign Investment and Privitisation (Moscow), *Petroleum Intelligence Weekly*, and Russian Strategic Services Ltd., London, 13 and 14 Oct. 1994.

[40] Ibid.

Table 7.2: Sakhalin's and Sakha's long-term gas-production and consumption plan (bcm)

	1995	2000	2005	2010	2015
Sakha Republic					
Production	3	12	20	26	26
Vilyui region	3	12	20	20	17.5
Nepsko-Botuobin region				6	8.5
Consumption	2.9	4.2	5.6	7.3	7.3
Export Capacity		7	10	10	10
Sakhalin Region					
Production	4.7	21.9	23.3	23	22.8
Offshore	2.9	20.3	22.2	22.2	22.2
Consumption	4.8	12.7	17.4	21.7	21.5
Amur Krai		0.5	1.5	2.5	2.5
Sakhalin Island	2	3.5	4.4	5	5
Khabarovsk Krai	2.4	4.4	5.7	6.5	6.5
Primorskii Krai		1	2	3	3
Indigenous consumption[1]	0.4	3.3	4.1	4.7	4.7
Export Capacity		10	10	10	10

Note:
1 Includes the Sakha Republic's consumption.
Source: Ministry of Foreign Affairs, 'Russian Far East and East Siberia's Energy Resources', study report, The Economics Bureau (MFA), Tokyo, March 1994, pp. 39–40.

Assuming that the commencement date will be finalized in early 1995, Sakhalin Energy is aiming for a final investment decision in the first quarter of 1997. If the development phase follows immediately, Piltun-Astokskoye's first oil and gas could flow in 2001. As for Lunskoye, a final investment decision will come at the beginning of 1998 at the earliest. The first LNG shipment cannot be expected until late 2002.[41]

In June 1995 the Duma, the lower house of the Russian parliament, approved the production-sharing law, and cleared the way for 12 big oil and gas projects with

[41] Ibid.

Western investors which had been in abeyance due to inadequate legislation.[42] If Sakhalin Energy implements development as projected, there would be no chance of achieving the Sakhalin gas production target of 21.9 bcm (19.7 mtoe), of which 20.3 bcm would come from offshore fields, in 2000 (see Table 7.2). The target could be achieved in 2005. The delay will mean a continuing energy shortage in the Russian Far East region.

7.1.4 Sakhalin-III and IV

In July 1993 a briefing on the Sakhalin-III tender was held in Denver, and nearly 30 of the world's largest oil and gas companies, including Russia's joint-stock company Gazprom, attended. (Another briefing was arranged in Moscow in September 1993.) The offered tender areas covering over 20,000 sq. km are divided into four blocks (each covering 4,300–6,000 sq. km); total hydrocarbon reserves on the four blocks are estimated at over 3.17 bt.[43]

The result of the bids for Sakhalin-III was announced in late December 1993. Exxon won the East Odoptu and Ayashsky blocks (block 1 and 2), and the Kirinsky block (block 4) was awarded to the Mobil/Texaco consortium. However, block 3 went unclaimed in the same bidding.[44] Edward Gendelman, president of Wavetech Geophysical (US), who organized the tender as a partner in JV GeolnterTech, attributed the slackening of interest to the continued slump in world oil prices.[45] A significant development in the Sakhalin-III tender is that Exxon became an important player in the Sakhalin shelf development.

In September 1994 a briefing was given on fourth-round bidding for the Sakhalin offshore. The deadline for submission of bids in the Sakhalin-IV tender, organized by Wavetech Geophysical (US) and GeolnterTech (Russia), has been extended from April to July 1995, and the results of the bidding is expected to be announced in August 1995.[46] According to S. Bogdanchikov, general director of Sakhalinmorneftegaz, almost 30 foreign companies have expressed interest by requesting information and materials on the Sakhalin-IV tender blocks.[47]

As shown in Map 7.2, three blocks were on offer, each covering around 4,500–6,000 sq. km. Shmidt (block 6) and Astrakhan (block 5) lie off the northern tip of

---

[42] *Financial Times*, 15 June 1995.

[43] *Russian Petroleum Investor*, July 1993, p. 42.

[44] *Russian Petroleum Investor*, Dec. 1993/Jan. 1994, p. 42.

[45] Ibid.

[46] *Petroleum Economist*, March 1995, p. 42.

[47] S. Bogdanchikov, 'Sakhalin 1, 2, 3, 4', paper presented at the 'Fourth International Conference on Trade and Investment Opportunities in the Russian Oil Industry', convened by the *Royal Institute of International Affairs*, 23–24 March 1995, London.

Map 7.2: Sakhalin tender III and IV blocks

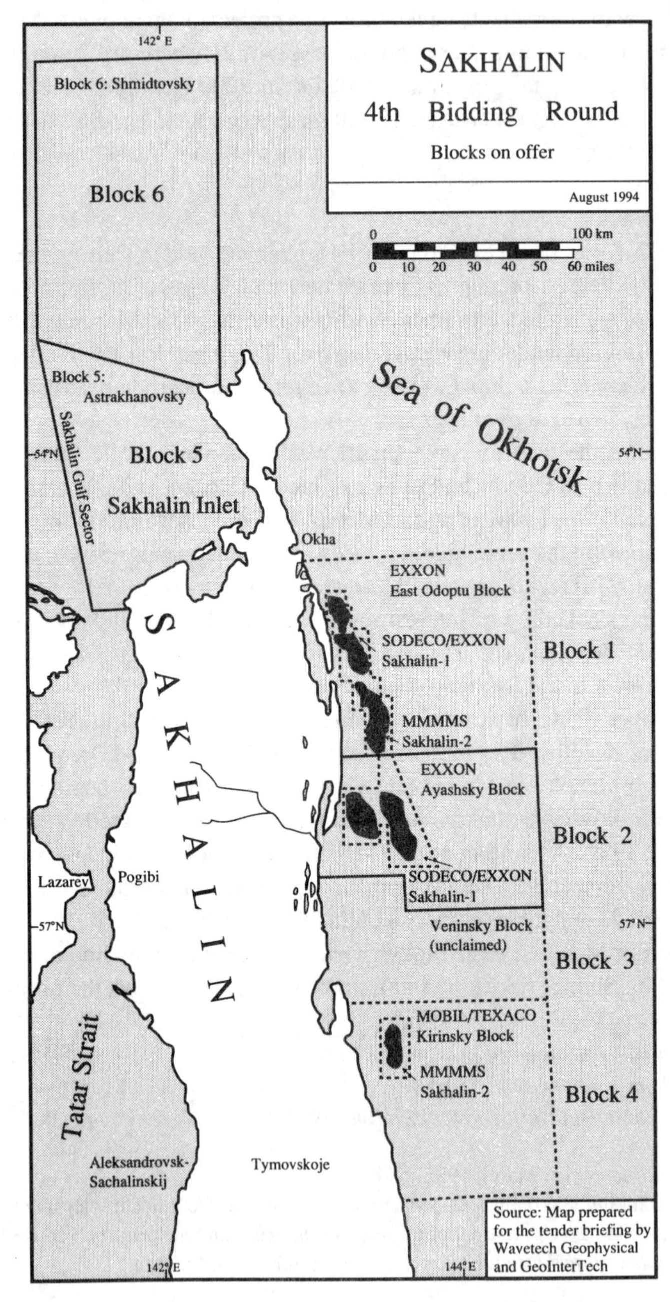

Source: Map prepared for the tender briefing by Wavetech Geophysical and GeoInterTech

the island, and Veninsky (block 3), which was earlier included in the third round, is located off the east coast.[48] No oil or gas fields have been discovered in these three blocks, but the acreage is considered to be highly promising. If the exploration of Sakhalin-III and IV tender blocks leads to some significant discoveries comparable to the five fields in Sakhalin-I and II, the development of the Sakhalin shelf alone could make a significant contribution to Northeast Asia's oil and gas supply balance over the next decade. For the time being, the development of Sakhalin-I and II will still make Sakhalin island a major oil and gas supply source for the region in the coming years.

Northeast Asia's changing environment has brought a golden opportunity to accelerate the long-delayed Sakhalin offshore oil and gas development. Even though major foreign companies have joined this development, their cautious stance towards a huge investment commitment is likely to continue without a substantial improvement in the investment climate, with provision of production-sharing legislation, an end to the struggle between central and local regimes over ownership and management of oil and gas resources, and establishment of a reliable and predictable energy fiscal system. The development of Sakhalin offshore projects will be the test case.

7.2 Sakha Republic (Yakutia) gas project

Sakha, covering one-fifth of the Russian Federation (3.1 million sq. km), is the country's largest autonomous republic but has a population of only 1.3 million. (Sakha is the name of the principal ethnic group, the Yakut; the Sakha Republic was previously named the Yakut ASSR.) The area regarded as likely to contain oil and gas covers 1.64 million sq. km, across which only 0.2 km of seismic data has been shot. In the Soviet era, Yakutian gas resources remained undeveloped because of the region's geographical remoteness and inhospitable climate, as well as the failure to attract foreign investment.

In September 1990 the Yakut ASSR proclaimed the sovereignty of the Yakut-Sakha SSR within the Russian Federation. Demarcation of the powers of the Russian Federation and the Republic of Sakha (Yakutia) was stipulated by the Federal Treaty signed on 31 March 1992, and an agreement 'On Mutual Relations between the Governments of the Russian Federation and the Republic of Sakha' provided the Republic with the right to develop, extract and sell natural resources in its territory.[49]

---

[48] *Petroleum Economist*, Nov. 1994, p. 42.

[49] 'The Differentiation of Powers of the Russian Federation and the Republic of Sakha (Yakutia) regarding the Use of Mineral Resources', paper prepared for presentation in Tokyo by Sakhaneftegaz, Safairg and Intera, March 1994, p. 1.

The Sakha Republic is now exploring all possible ways of accelerating development of its huge energy resources, especially gas, with foreign investment.

7.2.1 Sakha gas development

Hydrocarbon exploration in the Yakut ASSR began in 1935. Real exploration work began in the 1950s, in the Sub-Verkhoyanian region and the Vilyui Basin, and gas-condensate reservoirs were discovered at Ust-Vilyui in 1956. Sredne-Vilyuiskoye and Mastakhskoye gas fields were discovered in 1965 and 1967 respectively. The discovery of the Markovo oil and gas field in the Irkutsk region in 1962 indicated the potential for Cambrian and Proterozoic discoveries across the Nepa-Botuobian region, which was confirmed by the discovery of the Sredne-Botuobian field in 1970.[50] During the 1970s and 1980s, all the major gas fields, such as Verkhne-vilyuchaskoye, Taas-Yuriakhskoye, Talakanskoye and Chayandinskoye, were discovered in the Botuobinsky geological region.

Despite these discoveries, it is still the case that the Republic of Sakha's oil and gas reserves are barely tapped. Initial geological gas reserves are estimated at 9.6 tcm, including 8.3 tcm of recoverable reserves. Almost three-quarters of these reserves are predicted as being located at depths of up to 4 km (4.8 tcm within a depth of 1–3 km, 2.2 tcm within a depth of 3–4 km). Reserves are concentrated in the Vilyuiskaya, Nepsko-Botuobinskaya and Predpatomskaya oil- and gas-bearing regions.[51]

As for oil, the initial geological oil reserves are estimated at 9.7 bt, including 2.9 bt of recoverable reserves. Currently all the republic's discovered oil deposits lie in the Nepsko-Botuobinskaya region, where initial geological oil reserves are estimated at 1.34 bt. Around 86% of these reserves are thought to be at depths of up to 4 km (62% within 1–2 km, and 24% within 3–4 km).[52]

Thirty deposits of hydrocarbons have been discovered so far, of which 19 are located in the southwest Nepsko-Botuobinskaya oil- and gas-bearing region, and 11 in the central Vilyuisk region (9 deposits) and Predpatomsk region (2 deposits). Of these 30 deposits, 10 – Ust-Vilyuiskoye, Verkhnevilyu-Yuchaskoye, Sredne-Vilyuis-

[50] 'The Hydrocarbon Potential and Development Opportunities in the Republic of Sakha (Yakutia)', paper prepared for presentation in Tokyo by Sakhaneftegaz, Safairg and Intera, March 1994, p. 4.

[51] Vladimir Petrovich Larionov, 'Deposits of Natural Gas in the Sakha Republic (Yakutia), Current Situation and Prospects of their Use in the Context of the Republic's Energy Policy (Heat and Energy Industry of the Republic and adjacent Territories)', paper presented at the 'International Conference on the Northeast Asian Natural Gas Pipeline', convened by National Pipeline Research Society of Japan, 3 March 1995, Tokyo.

[52] Ibid.

Table 7.3: Gas reserves in oil- and gas-bearing regions, Sakha Republic, as of Jan. 1995 (bcm)

Regions	G/R	CP	A + B + C1	C2	C3	D1 + D2	Total
1 Anabaro-Khatangskaya	G	0	0	0	0	190	190
	R					160	160
2 Leno-Anabarskaya	G	0	0	0	0	760	760
	R					638	638
3 Predverkhoynskaya	G	1.54	0.76	0	0	665	667.3
	R					565	567.3
4 Vilyuiskaya	G	19.21	451	28.2	3.5	1,943.9	2,445.8
	R				2.9	1,657.9	2,159.2
5 Katangskaya	G	0	0	0	0	70	70
	R					60	60
6 Nepsko-Botuobinskaya	G	1.77	580	234.2	42.8	1,083.9	1,942.7
	R				36.4	887	1,739.4
7 Predpatomskaya	G	0	4.7	7.4	0	1,346.5	1,358.6
	R					1141.5	1,153.6
8 Anabarskaya	G	0	0	0	0	470	470
	R					400	400
9 West-Vilyuiskaya	G	0	0	0	0	260	260
	R					220	220
10 North-Aldanskaya	G	0	0	0	0	260	260
	R					220	220
Total		22.52	1,037	269.8	46.3	7,389.3	8,764.4
					39.3	6,239.4	7,607.5

Key:G/R = geological/recoverable reserves; CP = cumulative production.
Source: V.P. Larionov, 'Deposits of Natural Gas in the Sakha Republic (Yakutia), Current Situation and Propsepcts of their Usage in the Context of the Republic's Energy Policy', paper presented at an International Conference on the Northeast Asian Natural Gas Pipeline, convened by the National Pipeline Research Society of Japan, 3 March 1995, Tokyo.

Table 7.4: Gas reserves in the Sakha Republic, as of Jan. 1995 (bcm)

	Discovery/ production	Gas Reserves A + B + C1	C2
Vilyuisky Geological Region		451.08	28.23
Fields under development:			
1 Sredne-Vilyuiskoye GCF	1965/75	164.59	
2 Mastakhskoye GCF	1967/73	26.8	3.85
3 Ust-Vilyuiskoye GF	1956/68	0.76	
Fields prepared for commercial exploitation:			
4 Sobolokh-Nedzhelinskoye GCF	1966	52.64	0.74
5 Sredne-Tyunskoye GCF	1976	156.18	9.23
6 Tolonskoye GCF	1967/73	33.35	10.63
Fields under conservation:			
7 Badaranskoye GF		6.1	
8 Nizkevilyaiskoye GCF		2.6	
9 Andylakhskoye GCF		7.79	
10 Nizhnetyukyanskoye GF		0.26	3.78
Botuobinsky Geological Region		580.48	234.2
Fields under development:			
11 Severo-Nelbinskoye GCF		0.53	
Fields prepared for commercial exploitation:			
12 Sredne-Botuobinskoye OGCF	1970	152.26	18.56
13 Taas-Yuriakhskoye OGCF	1981	102.73	11.31
14 Irelyakhskoye OGCF	1981	3.59	0.09
Fields under exploration:			
15 Verkhnevilyuchaskoye OGF	1975	74.44	33.05
16 Vilyuisko-Dzherbinskoye GF		18.98	16.43
17 Nizhnekhamakinskoye GCF		13.35	35.68
18 Iktekhskoye OGCF		6.2	10.54
19 Talakanskoye OGCF	1984	27.83	16.78
20 Machobinskoye OGF		3.58	2.15
21 East-Talakanskoye GF		0.4	5.42
22 Nelbinskoye GF		4.3	2.33
23 Tympuchikanskoye OGF	1989	2.19	11.23
24 Chayandinskoye OGCF	1989	164.78	44.72
25 Besyuriakhskoye GF		1.22	9.18
26 Mirninskoye OGF		1.44	
27 Alinskoye GOF		0.72	1.7
Fields under conservation:			
28 Khotogo-Murbaiskoye GF		1	9.6
29 Otradninskoye GCF		0.94	5.4
Predpatomskaya oil- and gas-bearing region			
30 Bysakhtakhskoye GF		4.7	7.41
Total, Sakha Republic		1,036.28	269.8

Key:GCF = gas-condensate field; GF = gas field; GOF = gas and oil field; OGCF = oil and gas-condensate field, OGF = oil and gas field.
Source: V.P. Larinov, 'Deposits of Natural Gas in the Sakha Republic', *FACTS, Oil and Gas in the Russian Far East*, Honolulu, Feb. 1994, pp. 40–1.

koye, Mastakhskoye, Tolonskoye, Sobolkh-Nedzhelinskoye, Sredne-Botuobinskoye, Sredne-Tyungskoye, Irelyakhskoye and Tas-Yuryakskoye – are completely explored.[53]

As shown in Tables 7.3 and 7.4, the explored commercial gas reserves in the Sakha Republic are concentrated in two oil- and gas-bearing regions: Vilyuiskaya (0.451 tcm) and Nepsko-Botuobinskaya (0.58 tcm). The major gas reserves in the Vilyuiskaya region are concentrated in three fields: Sredne-Vilyuiskoye (0.165 tcm), Sredne-Tyungskoye (0.156 tcm) and Sobolokh-Nedzhelinskoye (0.053 tcm). In the case of Nepsko-Botuobinskaya, the major gas reserves are located in four fields: Sredne-Botuobinskoye (0.152 tcm), Taas-Yuryakhskoye (0.103 tcm), Chayandinskoye (0.165 tcm) and Verkhnevilyuchanskoye (0.074 tcm).[54]

In 1994, the Republic's gas production reached 1.634 bcm, of which 1.04 bcm (64%) was produced by the Sredne-Vilyuiskoye field. The gas production of Mastakskoye and Sredne-Botuobinskoye recorded 20.5% and 14.5% respectively. At present, four gas fields are under development: Sredne-Vilyuiskoye, Mastakhskoye, Sredne-Botuobinskoye and Severo-Nelbinskoye. As for oil production, the record in 1994 was a mere 0.05 mt, from Sredne-Botuobinskoye field.[55]

According to the Sakha Republic's long-term gas plan, shown in Table 7.2, gas production will reach 12 bcm in 2000 and 26 bcm in 2010, while demand will be 4.2 bcm in 2000 and 7.3 bcm in 2010. The volume of gas for export is projected at 7 bcm in 2000 and 10 bcm in 2010. Consequently, the expansion of the Republic's domestic pipeline grid is inevitable, and the construction of new pipeline grids not only for domestic use but also for export are requested.

As shown in Map 7.3, at present there are two independent trunk pipelines: one is in the central region, connecting Kysyl-Syr and Yakutsk via Berge, and then

[53] Ibid.
[54] Out of Nepsko-Botuobinskaya region's 0.58 tcm, 83% is located in gas caps and cannot be recovered until main reserves of oil are extracted. The region's oil reserves are estimated at 510 mt in A + B + C1 categories, including 154 mt of recoverable resources. Ibid.
[55] Ibid.; Vladimir Petrovich Larionov, 'Present Situation and Future Trends of Trunk Gas Pipeline Construction from Deposits of the Hydrocarbon Resources in the Sakha Republic (Yakutia)' paper presented at the 'International Conference on the Northeast Asian Natural Gas Pipeline', convened by National Pipeline Research Society of Japan, 3 March 1995, Tokyo.

Map 7.3: The Sakha Republic pipeline grid

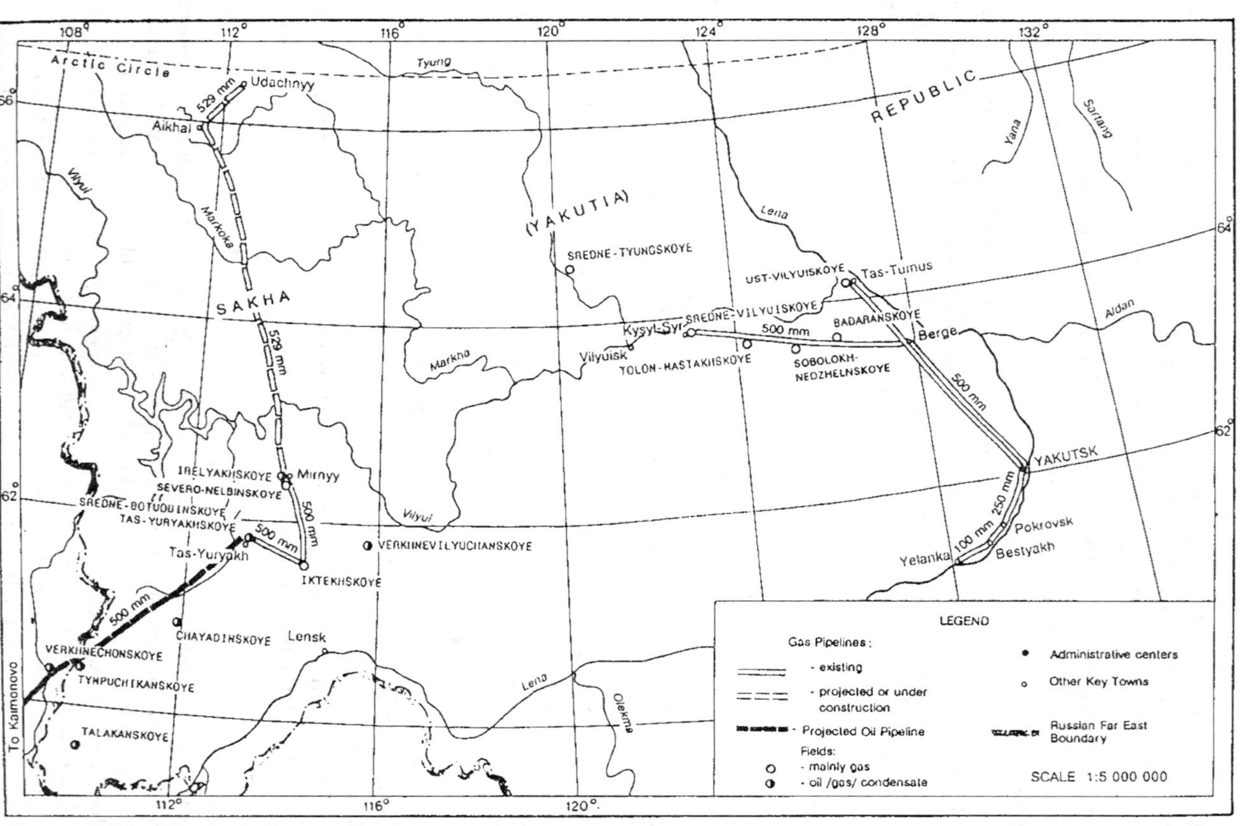

Source: *Oil and Gas in the Russian Far East*, a study report prepared by Fesharaki Associates Consulting and Technical Services, Inc., Honolulu, Feb. 1994, p. 205

extending along the river Lena to Yelanka via Pokrovsk; its total length is 585 km (operating design pressure, 7.5 MPa), and it delivers gas from the Sredne-Viliuiskoye and Tolon-Mastakhskoye fields to Yakutsk and neighbouring towns. The other pipeline, in the southwestern region, connects Tas-Yuryakhskoye with Mirny via Iktekhskoye, runs for 171 km with an operating design pressure of 5.5 MPa, and delivers gas from the Sredne-Botuobinskoye, Tas-Yuryakhskoye and Severo-Nelbinskoye fields to the town of Mirny.

The Sakha Republic envisages the construction of three pipelines before 2005 to meet domestic demand.[56] The first is a trunk pipeline (length 482 km, diameter 500 mm and operating pressure 5.5 MPa) connecting Mirny with Udachny via Chernyshevsk and Aikhal, currently under construction to supply gas to the region's industrial sector, especially the diamond-mining industry. The volume of delivered gas will be 0.38 bcm/y and the estimated cost of the Mirny–Udachny line is 466 billion roubles (October/December 1994 prices).

The second is a trunk pipeline linking Kysyl-Syr with Mirny, which is being designed (length 618.5 km, diameter 700 mm and operating pressure 7.5 MPa). It will run from the Srednevilyuisky gas deposit and create a common gas pipeline grid passing through the central region of the Republic, and could deliver gas from the Vilyuisky deposits to the Aikhal-Udachninsky industrial centre. Projected throughput capacity of this pipeline is 1.4 bcm/y and project cost is estimated at 1,197 billion roubles (October/December 1994 prices).

The third project is the pipeline connecting Mastakh and Yakutsk via Berge (length 383 km, diameter 700 mm and operating pressure 5.5 MPa). This pipeline's transport capacity is expected to be 3 bcm/y, and estimated project cost is 703 billion roubles (October/December 1994 prices).

Plans for these three domestic gas pipelines are closely connected with the Republic's aim to export gas to the Northeast Asian market.

7.2.2 Yakutian gas export proposals in the Soviet era

The first proposal, as shown in Map 7.4, aimed at securing Japanese participation in the construction of a gas pipeline from the Yakutsk gas fields to the Soviet Far East coast, and was made by N.K. Baibakov, Gosplan chairman, in November 1968. The proposal partly overlapped with another made by Baibakov in the same year for Sakhalin offshore gas export to Japan.[57]

On 12 February 1970 the Soviets proposed constructing a 1-m-diameter pipeline tying Yakutian gas reserves into the Sakhalin–Hokkaido system. The line would run

---

[56] Ibid.

[57] Egyed, *Western Participation in the Development of Siberian Energy Resources* (op. cit., n. 2), pp. 60–90.

Map 7.4: Yakutian gas-pipeline proposals, 1968–74

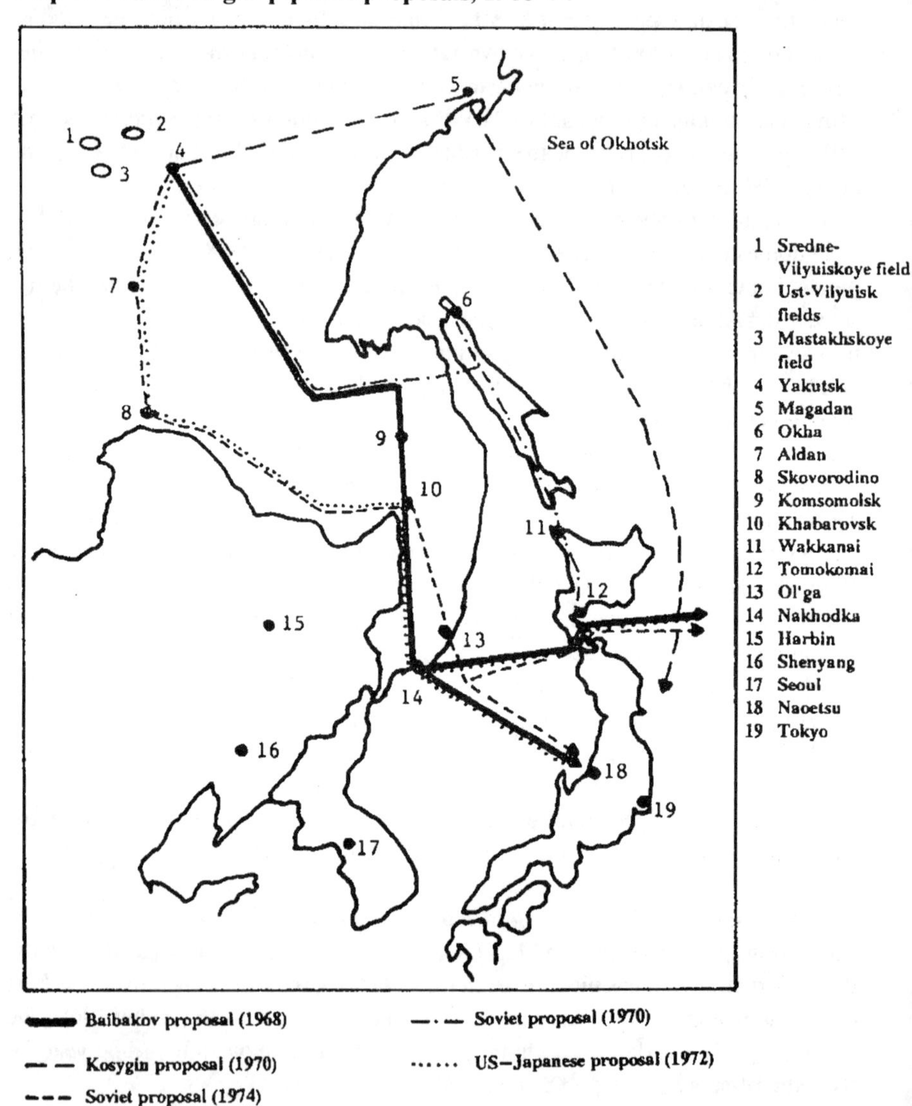

Source: Peter Egyed, *Western Participation in the Development of Siberian Energy Resources: Case Studies*, East–West Commercial Relations Series Report 20, Institute of Soviet and East European Studies, May 1983, pp. 68 and 87

from Yakutsk via Khabarovsk and Sakhalin to Hokkaido. This second proposal is still at the core of what interests the Japanese today. Two other Yakutian gas-export routes were proposed between 1970 and 1972. One was an unexpected proposal by the former Soviet premier Aleksei Kosygin, made soon after the second one above, to construct a pipeline from Yakutsk to Magadan, with a gas-liquefaction plant at Magadan. The other was proposed by El Paso Natural Gas Co. and Bechtel Corp. of the United States and Sumitomo Shoji from Japan in May 1972, and consisted essentially of a 3,600-km-long, 142-cm-diameter pipeline from Yakutsk to Nakhodka.[58]

The Yakutian project lapsed because each of the three parties wanted a different pipeline route. They met in Paris in November 1974 with the purpose of achieving a general agreement on exploration of Yakutian natural gas – but failed to do so. To make matters worse, the Soviet side proposed Ol'ga as the liquefaction-plant site instead of Nakhodka (see Map 7.4). Although in 1979 the Soviets finally agreed to the Yakutsk–Ol'ga pipeline route, the Yakutsk project was suspended in the wake of the Soviet invasion of Afghanistan in December 1979.[59]

In January 1989 an ambitious plan divised by Mr Chung Ju-Yung, founder of the Hyundai Group, to lay down a pipeline grid from Yakutsk to South Korea through North Korea revived the project. At much the same time, the US lawyer John Sears and Uebayashi Takeshi of Tokyo Boeki visited Moscow to present a similar idea.[60] These proposals in effect constituted a revival of the Vostok plan (see below), aiming as they did at the construction of gas pipelines from Sakhalin and Yakutian gas fields through Primorskii Krai and down across the Korean Peninsula and the Tsushima Straits to southern Japan (see Map 7.5).

In October 1990, the Yakut-Sakha Republic invited foreign companies to explore and develop hydrocarbon resources in 17 promising areas of southwestern Yakutia, and in June 1991 the two most prolific structures (Chayandinskaya and Illeginskaya) were granted to OMV, the Austrian state oil company.[61]

At the end of 1991 a consortium composed of Tokyo Boeki Ltd (a subsidiary company of the Mitsubishi group) of Japan and Far East Energy Inc. of the United States reached an accord with the Yakut-Sakha Republic to conduct a feasibility study for the development of Yakutian oil and gas resources within the Vostok

---

[58] Unpublished preliminary project analysis summary, 'Yakutia LNG Project', prepared by American Siberian Natural Gas Company and Occidental LNG Corp., Nov. 1977.

[59] Egyed, *Western Participation in the Development of Siberian Energy Resources* (op. cit., n. 2), pp. 60–90.

[60] *Asahi Shimbun*, 13 July 1990.

[61] *Oil and Gas Journal*, 12 Nov. 1990, pp. 40–2; 8 July 1991, p. 21; Fereidun Fesharaki and Eugene Khartukov, 'Oil and Gas of the Soviet Far East: How Big a Play?', *Petroleum Advisory* 76, East-West Center, 3 Sept. 1991, p. 6.

Map 7.5: The Vostok plan: pipeline route

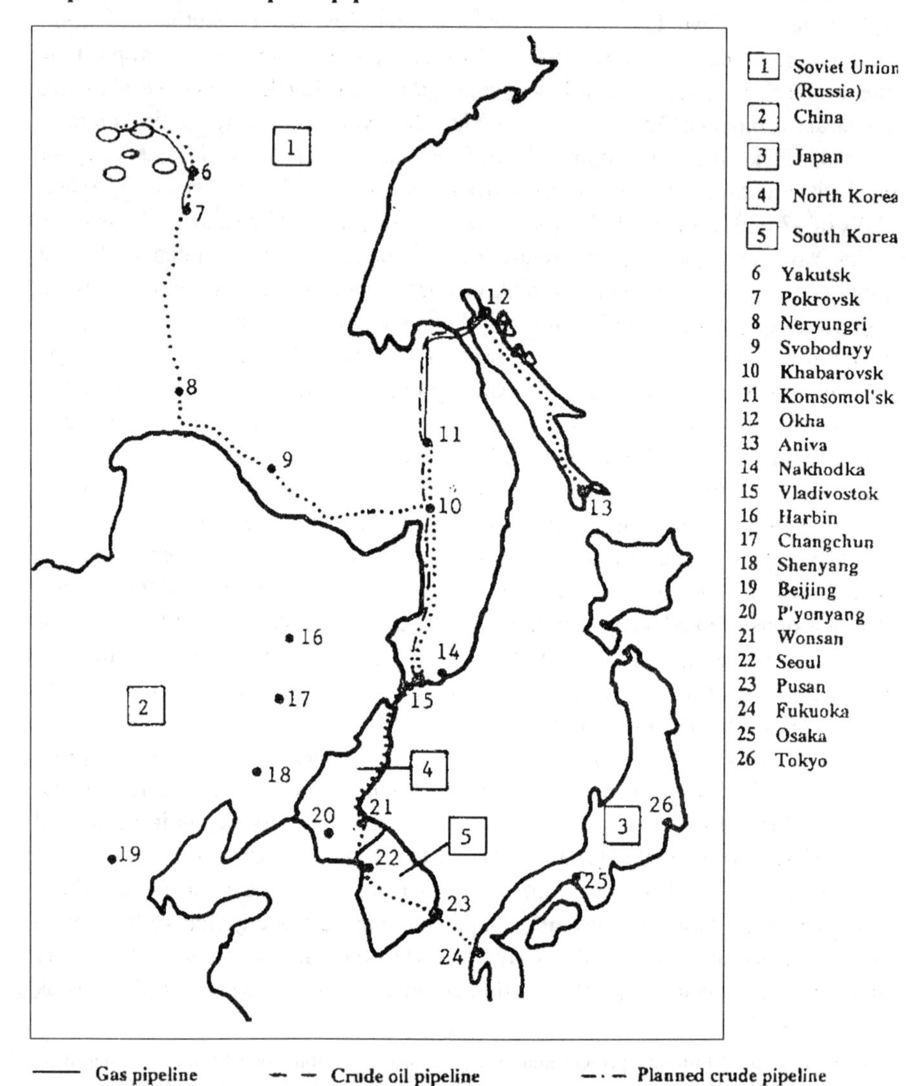

Source: Hyundai Resources Development Co., Ltd

project. The agreement was followed by a related contract signed with the Russian government on 18 March 1992, and envisages appraisal of a 4,000-km gas pipeline from southern Yakutia to Wakkanai (Hokkaido) via Sakhalin, and a 6,300-km trunkline to northern Kyushu via Vladivostok, North and South Korea.[62] The study was to be completed by May 1993, but was suspended.

Other foreign companies have established a presence in the Republic in preparation for its full-fledged gas development. Maxus Energy Corp. (Dallas) and OMV AG (Vienna) both have exploration joint ventures, and Intera Information Technologies (Henley-on-Thames, UK), in partnership with Yakutskgeofisika and Sakhaneftegas, has prepared a geographic exploration database and regional data package for the Republic.[63]

The Vostok plan: At the end of the Soviet era, early in 1991 a very ambitious plan for accelerating Soviet Far East gas development and export was prepared. This was a report entitled the 'Concept of Developing Yakutian and Sakhalin Gas and Mineral Resources of Eastern Siberia and the USSR Far East', commonly known as the 'Vostok (East) plan'. It was prepared by the USSR Ministry of Geology, the Russian Republic's Committee on Geology and Utilization of Energy and Mineral Resources, the USSR Ministry of Oil and Gas Industry, the State Gazprom Concern, the USSR Academy of Sciences and the Russian Technological Academy.[64]

According to the Vostok plan (see Table 7.5), by 2005 the region would produce about 15.7 mt/year of gas for the Russian Far East and 13.3 mt/y for export. Of this, 6.0 mt/y each would go to South Korea and Japan and 1.3 mt/y to North Korea. A key element of the plan would be the construction of a 3,230-km gas pipeline from Sakhalin across Russian territory and North Korea to South Korea by 1995, and a 3,050-km line from Yakutsk to Khabarovsk by 2000. (The line proposed by the Vostok plan is a hybrid of the Yakutian gas pipeline routes proposed diring 1968–74; see Map 7.4.)

The estimated project cost was gigantic. According to the Soviet official calculation (as of 1991), the total cost of Yakutian gas-field development was 23.3 billion roubles plus $5.5 billion.[65] Eugene Khartukov estimated that the capital require-

[62] The contractors were also to study the feasibility of constructing, by mid-1997, a 1,900-mile oil pipeline connecting Yakutian oil fields (capable of producing 0.3 mb/d) with Vanino, a deepwater port just to the north of Sovietskaya Gavan (the Tatar Straits). See Khartukov and Fesharaki, 'Russian Far East' (op. cit., n. 27), p. 4.

[63] *Oil and Gas Journal*, 8 Aug. 1994, p. 71.

[64] *Oil and Gas Journal*, 23 March 1992, p. 121.

[65] The unpublished report 'Concept of Developing Yakutian and Sakhalin Gas and Mineral Resources of East Siberia and the USSR Far East' was produced at the beginning of 1991.

Table 7.5: The RFE balance: 1995–2010 (the Vostok plan) (mt)

	1995	2000	2005	2010
Production	3.34	22.5	29	32
Sakhalin	3.34	14.9	15.7	14.7
Yakutsk		7.6	13.3	17.3
Consumption (domestic)	2.34	10.9	15.7	18.7
Sakhalin	0.93	1.3	1.5	1.7
Yakutsk		2	2.3	3.3
Amur		0.6	1.3	1.7
Komsomolsk	1.34	2	2	2
Khabarovsk		1.5	3	3
Primorskii		1	2.3	3
Other requirement	0.07	2.5	3.3	3.5
Export	1	11.6	13.3	13.3
N. Korea		1.3	1.3	1.3
S. Korea	1	6	6	6
Japan		4.3	6	6

Source: Report entitled 'Concept of developing Yakutian and Sakhalin Gas and Mineral Resources of Eastern Siberia and the USSR Far East' (the so-called Vostok plan), 1991.

ment for additional geophysical work and exploratory drilling, necessary to secure a required increase of exploitable gas reserves from 1.6 tcm in 1991 to 3.1 tcm in 2006, would be 10.5 billion roubles. The capital outlays for construction of a 6,700-km trunkline system from Yakutia and Sakhalin to Japan is estimated at 25.3 billion roubles plus $6.6 billion.[66] (Based on the official exchange rate, the total is $20.7 billion, and on the commercial rate, $7.4 billion.)

As the Sakhalin tender went to the Japanese without significant Korean participation, the first phase of the Vostok plan, aimed at supplying 1 mt of Sakhalin offshore gas to South Korea, evaporated. In other words, the Vostok plan is dead at present. The plan can be revived only when the results of the preliminary and full feasibility studies for the Sakha gas project prove positive.

[66] As of 1991, the official commercial exchange rate of the US dollar was 1.8 roubles, while the market rate was 30 roubles. See Fesharaki and Khartukov, 'Oil and Gas of the Soviet Far East' (op. cit., n. 61), pp. 5–6. According to Hyundai Resources Development Co. Ltd., the construction cost of the Yakutia–Khabarovsk–Vladivostok–Seoul pipeline is estimated at $5.1 billion (interview conducted by the author with Hyundai).

7.2.3 Korean initiatives and Japan's role

In November 1992 Russia and South Korea agreed to undertake a preliminary feasibility study for the joint development of Sakha Republic gas resources, and construction of a gas pipeline grid connecting the Sakha Republic with South Korea.[67] Differences on both sides especially with regard to financing meant that no progress was made with the feasibility study until June 1994, when South Korea and Russia agreed to invest $20 million in the study, with a 12-month working period.[68]

Meanwhile the Sakha Republic was anxious to make an early start on its gas development and explored another possibility to this end. In February 1994 the Yakut president Mikhail Nikolayev visited Japan to attract Japanese interest in the Republic's oil and gas projects. Even though more than 70 Japanese companies attended the briefing, their interest was largely theoretical, focused on future cooperation rather than on current projects.[69] In the following month a first licensing round for Yakutia was announced, with the related presentation made in Tokyo.

The Sakha Republic recognizes the importance of Japanese investment, as V.P. Larionov, chairman of the Yakut Research Centre, Siberian Division of the Russian Academy of Sciences, has commented: 'It would be desirable to use Japanese credits under the condition of their liquidation by gas supply. Such credits in the form of equipment for gas extraction, transportation, and liquefaction will allow us to realise the programme of exploitation of Yakutian gas in the nearest future with the great economic effect'.[70]

South Korea's initiative on Sakha gas development embarrassed Japan, which knew only too well the importance of its commitment to the development. Four Japanese organizations – the Ministry of Foreign Affairs, JNOC, Institute of Energy Economics of Japan and Keidanren – have undertaken studies on the Sakha Republic's gas project, and Japan will not become an idle onlooker. It continues to be interested in Sakha gas development and is only waiting for the best moment to become actively involved.

7.2.4 The Sakha gas-export route and East Siberian gas

At present there are two possible eastern routes for Yakutian gas exports to the Russian Far East and the Asian Pacific gas market. The first pipeline (3,300 km) connects Yakutsk with Nakhodka via Bolshoy Never, Khabarovsk and Vladivostok,

---

[67] *Korea Times*, 21 Nov. 1992.

[68] Keun Wook Paik, 'Pipeline Politics: Turkmenistan vs. Russian Far East Gas Development', *Geopolitics of Energy*, 1 Sept. 1994, pp. 5–6.

[69] *Russian Petroleum Investor*, July/Aug. 1994, p. 49.

[70] Larionov, 'Present Situation and Future Trends of Trunk Gas Pipeline Construction from Deposits of the Hydrocarbon Resources in the Sakha Republic' (op. cit., n. 55).

and the second (2,000 km) connects Yakutsk with Magadan. The environment of the latter route is harsher than for the former. Consequently the construction cost for the latter route, though shorter, would not be noticeably cheaper than for the former. The strong point if favour of the first route is that Nahodka's is an all-year-round navigation port, which can reduce the cost of storing and transporting liquified gas.[71]

The Sakha Republic estimated that the throughput capacity of the trunk pipeline connecting Yakutsk with the Korean peninsula, a length of over 4,000 km, should be at least 30 bcm/y (diameter 1,422 mm and 28 compressor stations), and the scale of gas export to the Northeast Asian gas market around 20–2 bcm/y. The Republic is also recognizing the necessity of using Japanese credits in the form of equipment for gas extraction, transportation and liquefaction, under the condition of their liquidation by gas supply.[72]

Here it is worth noting that the possibility of a western export route, eventually leading to China and Korea, via Mongolia, is being explored, in parallel with the eastern route aimed mainly at the Japanese and Korean markets. Unlike the Sakha Republic, which has already announced its autonomy within the Russian Federation, the Irkutsk region has much less political independence, and gas development there is directly under the control of Moscow. Consequently the Moscow authorities are positive about the export of Irkutsk gas to the Northeast Asian market for it gives them a useful leverage in relation to the Sakha Republic's exports to the region.

The signs are that the Sakha Republic is seeking Moscow's cooperation in its gas exports to the Northeast Asian market by allocating a part of its gas to the Irkutsk region. According to Larionov, the Republic is exploring the possibility of developing a series of the Botuobinsky condensed-gas deposits and constructing a new gas pipeline to satisfy West Yakutia and the Irkutsk region's gas demand. Both regions' estimated annual gas consumption of 3.7 bcm could be met if the already explored Nepsko-Botuobinsky oil- and gas-bearing region in West Yakutia and Baikitsky oil and gas region in Krasnoyarsky territory are developed at an opportune moment.[73] The seriousness of the Sakha Republic's intentions is confirmed by the president's visit in April 1995 to Irkutsk to discuss this possibility.[74]

The Sakha Republic approach on Irkutsk gas development is in line with Sidanco's concept of constructing a pipeline linking Kovyktinskoye with gas fields

---

[71] Ibid.

[72] Ibid.

[73] Ibid.

[74] It was confirmed also by Mr Anatoly Golovin, vice-president of Sidanco, in an interview with the author.

in the neighbouring Sakha region that would tie into a planned 25 bcm/y pipeline to South Korea.[75] Since Sidanco aims at building a gas pipeline from the Irkutsk region across Mongolia and into northern China, Moscow can promote its two gas export routes simultaneously.

Sidanco's concept of establishing an Irkutsk–Beijing gas pipeline grid is shared by CNPC. Shi Xunzhi, assistant president of CNPC, said that the optimum scheme to transmit gas into China would use East Siberian gas. If gas from East Siberia, the Far East and West Siberia can be brought together, and several large-size gas pipelines with a capacity of 100–50 bcm/y built (in other words, an oil and gas corridor to the ports of China, via the Irkutsk region and Mongolia), Northeast Asian countries including China would benefit.[76]

This CNPC concept is based on the following analysis: the current international oil market provides China with a favourable opportunity to exploit and share the world's oil and gas resources in the coming decade. It is unwise to boost oil production in the eastern oilfields, and is much too costly to depend only on development in its western regions. It would be too late to look for oil elsewhere when international prices will go up and declining oil reserves in East China become exhausted in ten years time.[77]

China, it seems, has already begun to think of its energy-supply problem in the next decade, and the Irkutsk region's oil and gas could be an ideal option for CNPC. Irkutsk's gas export to the Northeast Asian market could be even faster than Yakutian gas exports because of its relative proximity to the market and the ease with which a gas pipeline grid could be constructed.

The ideal way to promote East Siberian gas exports to China seems to lie in combining Irkutsk with Sakha gas for export to the Northeast Asian market. Given that Sakhalin-shelf gas can cover the Russian Far East's demand and export, and can be exported to Korea and southern Japan after passing through Mongolia and China and then through a sub-sea pipeline extension, the Moscow authorities and the Sakha Republic have no reason to reject this option so long as development and export materializes soon.

---

[75] *World Gas Intelligence,* 10 March 1995, p. 12.

[76] Shi Xunzhi, 'Present Situation and Forecast of Natural Gas Exploitation and Utilization in China', paper presented at the 'International Conference on the Northeast Asian Natural Gas Pipeline', convened by National Pipeline Research Society of Japan, 3 March 1995, Tokyo.

[77] *China OGP* 1: 10 (15 Oct. 1993), p. 1.

The Irkutsk region's gas project

The Irkutsk region has two major oil and gas fields. The estimated reserves of the Verkhnechonskoye oil field, discovered in 1978 and located in the Katangsky district, are 600–50 mt. The Kovyktinskoye gas-condensate field, discovered in 1987 and located in the Zhigalovsky region (240 km from Irkutsk), has estimated total reserves of 600–800 bcm (21.2–28.2 tcf) of gas (Sidanco put them at 1 tcm).

The possibility of East Siberian oil and gas development and their export to China was initially mentioned in July 1992 by Zhang Yongyi, vice-president of the China National Petroleum Corp. (CNPC), who proposed to Russia and Japan the development of oil in East Siberia. Zhang added that the oil pipeline could be extended to Japan via Korea, if Japan got involved in the project.[1] However, in late 1992, BP and Statoil having undertaken a rough feasibility study during 1990–91 on the Irkutsk region's oil and gas development, and put the figure of the Kovytinskoye field at 570 bcm, decided not to sign a joint venture with Irkutsk Province Executive Committee to develop oil, gas and condensate reserves in the region, presumably because they concluded that there would be no export market for them for the time being. Canada's Bitech Corp. attempted to set up a JV with Russia Petroleum, a subsidiary of Sidanco (Siberian Far East Oil Company), but the field development costs were too high for the company.

In September 1993 Daqing Oilfield Company, in partnership with Canada's MacDonald Petroleum, was negotiating with Russia for exploration rights to the Mapkob and Yarokotan oil and gas fields in the Irkutsk region, East Siberia. To negotiate mutually acceptable terms of cooperation with the Daqing Oilfield Company (a subsidiary of CNPC), Irkutsk's Petroleum and Gas Geological Company and Geophysical Research Institute, together with 14 other local companies and organizations, have formed a company named Bend. The Daqing Company has gained approval from Irkutsk to set up a branch office there, and two drilling rigs have already sunk exploratory wells in the two virgin fields.[2]

The Irkutsk province authority has promoted plans to develop the Kovyktinskoye gas field and to export electricity to China. An American company, Quality Steel Ltd, has already

7.3 The Tarim Basin project

7.3.1 Historical review

The Tarim Basin, located in the south-central part of the remote Xinjiang Uygur Autonomous Region, is the largest onshore basin in the world, covering 560,000 sq. km, an area a little larger than France. The famous Taklamakan Desert at the centre makes up almost 60% of the Basin covering an area of 330,000 sq. km. The climate is so harsh that the temperature is as high as 47°C in summer and as low as -34°C in winter, with a five-month frost season. A very strong wind, sometimes measuring as high as force 10–12, dominates the period from March to June.[78] These inhospitable conditions form the reason why the Basin remained virtually untouched until the end of the 1980s.

The start of hydrocarbon prospecting in the Tarim Basin dates back to the early

[78] *China Oil and Gas* 1: 2 (1994), p. 41.

offered to invest in a 500-kv line from Irkutsk to the Chinese border over a distance of 1,250 km, and it was claimed that the Russian government approved the plan.[3]

The possibility of Irkutsk gas development was more seriously explored by Sidanco (Siberian Far East Oil Company), established by ordinance 452 of the Russian Federation, dated 5 May 1994, and one of the most ambitious of the country's new integrated oil corporations.[4] Reportedly Sidanco has set its sights on developing East Siberian gas reserves for eventual supply to the Far East. In early November 1994, CNPC and Sidanco signed a memorandum of understanding for the construction of a gas pipeline from Irkutsk region to China across Mongolia. The result of CNPC and Sidanco's feasibility study seems to be announced in the Spring of 1996. Besides this, the Russian Ministry of Fuels and Power has started to negotiate with Chinese Partners about building an oil pipeline from Irkutsk to China. In 1995, two Korean proposals for the construction of long distance gas pipeline connecting Irkutsk region with South Korea via Mongolia and China were made, but no further steps were taken. Between 1996 and 1997 work is expected to begin at the Kovyktinskoye gas-condensate field, located just north of Lake Baikal in the region of Irkutsk, with ambitious plans to export up to 30 bcm/y of gas into China and South Korea.[5]

Kovyktinskoye is licensed to Sidanco's subsidiary, Russia Petroleum. The field's start-up is scheduled for 1997. Local markets could absorb up to 9 bcm, as industry and power plants switch from oil to gas. The liquids that are produced would go to Sidanko's 0.49 mb/d Angarsk refinery.

[1] *RA Report* (previously *Supar Report*) 14 (Jan. 1993), p. 102.
[2] *Russian Petroleum Investor*, Sept. 1992, p. 25; *Oil and Gas Journal*, 4 Jan. 1993, pp. 30–1; *China OGP* 1: 12 (15 Nov. 1993), p. 3.
[3] *Eastern Bloc Energy* 6: 6 (Aug. 1993), p. 6.
[4] Under the ordinance, Sidanco incorporates the following companies: Varyegan-neftegaz, Kondpetroleum, Chernogorneft, Purneftegaz, Udmurtneft, the Angarsky Petrochemical Company, the Saratovsky Refinery and Sakhalinnefteprodukt. See MIG and Inkombank, *Russian Petroleum Encyclopedia*, 1995, p. 154. In January 1995 Purneftegaz rejoined Roseneft. See *Petroleum Economist*, March 1995, p. 42.
[5] *Russian Petroleum Investor* (Mar. 1996), pp. 68–72; *China OGP* 3:22 (15 Nov. 1995), p. 8; Keun-Wook Paik, 'Energy Cooperation in Sino-Russian Relations', *Pacific Review* 9:1, pp. 77–95.

1950s, when Soviet technical staff conducted a regional geological reconnaissance, with a detailed surface-structure survey and measurement and a gravitational/magnetic survey and electric sounding based on the analogies between the Tarim Basin and the Fergana or Targik Basin in the Soviet Union. Seven wells were drilled in the three structures, but no commercial oil flow was discovered. In 1958, however, the first commercial oil flow was confirmed after drilling of the Yiqikelike No. 1 well.[79]

No more oil was obtained until 1975, when a prospecting team looking for sulphur accidently found oil sands in Tarim. In May 1977 the Kekeya oil field was discovered, but no further discovery followed.[80] In 1982 the US Geophysical

[79] Zhang Jiyi, 'Review and Prospect for Petroleum Exploration in Tarim Basin', *China Oil and Gas* 1: 1 (1994), p. 35.
[80] *China Daily*, 5 June 1990.

Service Co. signed a contract to conduct seismic surveys in the Basin. About 100 exploration wells have been drilled outside the desert zone, with the first discovery – of Shacan 2 – testing 6,300 b/d of crude oil and 70 mcf of gas in 1984.[81]

From 1984 to the beginning of 1989, three more discoveries were made, all in the Tabei Uplift: the Yakela gas field (centre), the Lunnan oilfield (east) and the Yingmaili oil/gas field (west).[82] During this period, China made its first attempt at desert drilling – the Manxiyi 1 wildcat well, drilled by CNPC in early 1988.[83]

The first significant discovery in the Tarim Basin was made in November 1988, when the Lunnan buried-hill structure, located in Luntai county, 360 km southwest of Urumqi, tested a flow of 4,290 b/d of crude oil from 30 feet of pay layer.[84] In April 1989 CNPC established the Tarim Oil Exploration and Development Bureau (TOEDB).

Then, in October 1989, the Tazhong 1 anticline was discovered in the heart of the Taklamakan Desert. The first wildcat drilled by CNPC on the structure flowed at rates of 3,623 b/d of light, sweet crude and 12.7 mmcf/d of gas during an interim test at a depth of 12,139 feet. This discovery led Chinese geologists to re-evaluate their estimates of Tarim's potential, as Tazhong 1 is three times as large as the Daqing producing area.[85]

7.3.2 Geological setting and potential reserves

The Tarim Basin is a large cratonic basin developed on a continental-crust basement. In terms of structural framework it can be classified into three uplifts and four depressions. The three uplifts, the Tabei (north), Tazhong (central) and Tanan (south) lifts, occupy a total area of 180,000 sq. km, and the four depressions, comprising the Kuche, north, southwest and southeast depressions, cover 350,000 sq. km.[86] Seismic surveys have found 48 structures, of which Tazhong 1 and 2 anticlines, Luobuzhuang buried hill and the Xuetannan structures are each larger than 386 sq. miles, heralding the possibility of super-large fields.[87]

As discussed in Chapter 4, the huge potential of Tarim's oil and gas reserves is

---

[81] Bruce Vernor and Richard E. Gillespie, 'China's Northwest: The Final Oil Frontier', *China Business Review*, March–April 1990, p. 14.

[82] *China Oil and Gas* 1: 2 (1994), p. 42.

[83] Vernor and Gillespie, 'China's Northwest' (op. cit., n. 81), p. 14.

[84] Qi Daqing and David Fridley, 'Tarim Basin: Hopes and Challenges for China's Oil Industry', Resources Programs, East-West Center, Jan. 1992, pp. 4–5.

[85] Ibid., pp. 5–6.

[86] *China Oil and Gas* 1: 2 (1994), p. 41.

[87] Shi Xunzhi, 'Present Situation and Forecast of Natural Gas Exploitation and Utilization in China' (op. cit., n. 76); Daging and Fridley, 'Tarim Basin' (op. cit., n. 84), p. 4.

very well known. A Chinese newsletter published by the Xinhua News Agency reported that the Basin's oil and gas reserves are estimated at 19.8 bt and 8.4 tcm, accounting for 12% and 20% respectively of China's total.[88] In a paper contributed to the *Oil and Gas Journal*, K.J. Hsu, of Tarim Associates for Oil and Mineral Exploration AG (Zurich), argued that there might be 50 bt of hydrocarbons under the desert sands of Tarim (this figure looks too optimistic). In his view the best prospects lie in the anticlinal traps of the Central Tarim Uplift, where a 230-km long anticline has been described with a closure of more than 2,000 m. (Eight domes have been identified on the anticline, and the total area of those closures is 724 sq. km.)[89]

7.3.3 The Tarim Basin opening

According to David Fridley, three factors drove CNPC to take an aggressive stance towards Tarim's exploration and development. First of all, a string of major discoveries have made CNPC very confident about the oil potential of the Basin. Secondly, it felt it could hardly afford to proceed slowly and allow production to stagnate. Finally, it is poised to reap financial benefits from early development. According to an agreement between CNPC and the central government, output from Tarim can be sold at much higher than standard prices and CNPC can retain the profits to reinvest in its exploration and development programme in the Basin.[90]

In July 1991 CNPC signed an agreement with JNOC to explore a 30,000 sq.-km area in southwestern Tarim. With an investment of 8 billion yen ($58 million) from JNOC, the geological survey begun soon after the 1991 agreement will be finished in 1996, and the results shared with China.[91] And late in 1992, CNPC signed an agreement with Exxon of the United States to act as technical contractor for exploration work.[92]

Two demonstration oil wells (the first near Kuqu, and the second near Aksu) were drilled in January and May 1992 respectively with UNDP grants of $5.8 million, and 82 million yuan ($15 million) put in by the Chinese. This project is the largest UN-assisted energy development in China.[93]

On 17 February 1993 China announced the opening of the southern sector of the Tarim Basin to foreign oil companies. The five blocks on offer for international bidding cover 72,730 sq. km, slightly more than the combined size of the Netherlands

---

[88] *China OGP* 3: 1 (1 Jan. 1995), p. 3.
[89] *Oil and Gas Journal*, 28 Nov. 1994, pp. 51–60.
[90] Daqing and Fridley, 'Tarim Basin' (op. cit., n. 84), p. 7.
[91] *China Daily*, 6 July 1991.
[92] *Far Eastern Economic Review*, 4 March 1993, p. 44.
[93] *China Daily*, 9 June 1992.

Map 7.6: China's bidding areas: Tarim Basin

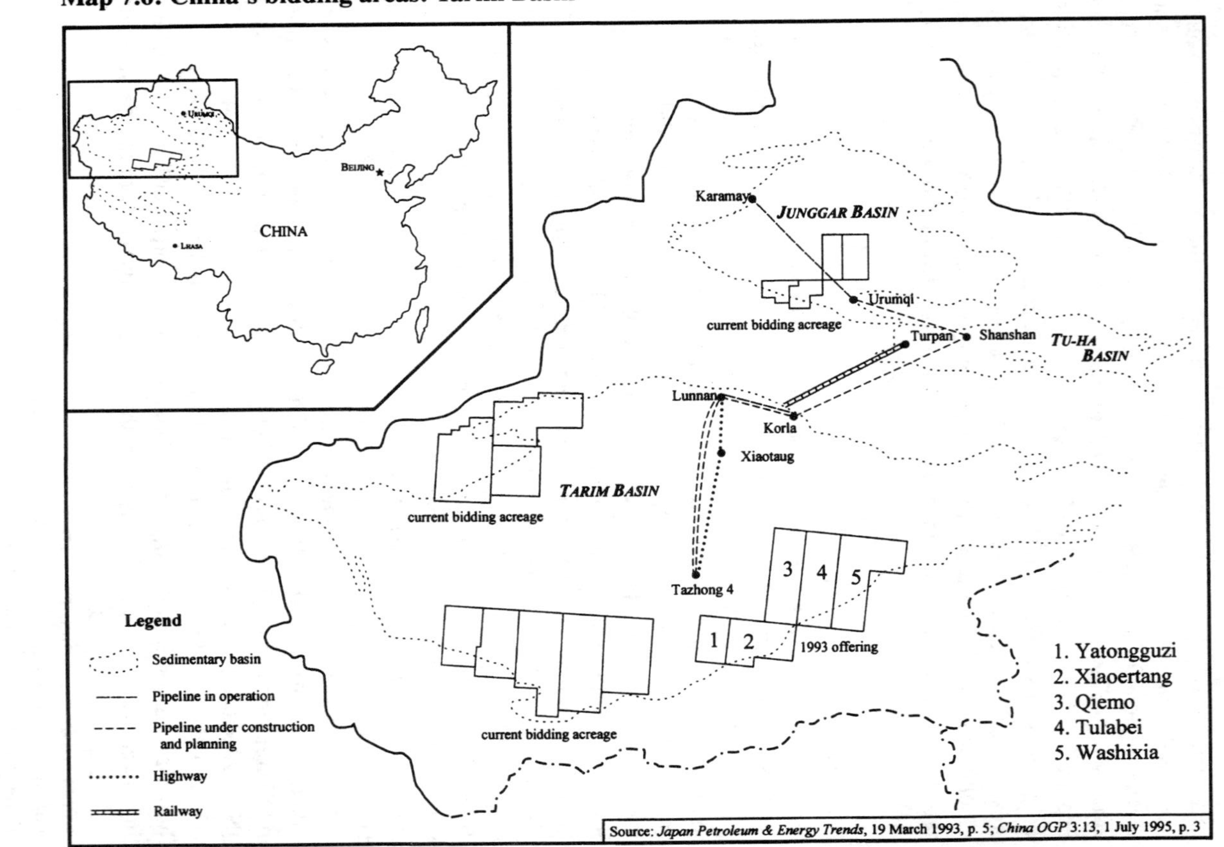

Source: *Japan Petroleum & Energy Trends*, 19 March 1993, p. 5; *China OGP* 3:13, 1 July 1995, p. 3

and Belgium. The blocks make up about one-eighth of the basin's total area.[94] On 1 March 1993 the China National Oil and Gas Exploration and Development Corp. (CNODC), authorized by CNPC to handle the bidding, announced the commencement of the first round, for the exploitation of onshore oil and gas resources.[95]

By 31 May 1993 CNODC had delivered its model contract to foreign applicants. The contract contained a series of uniquely favourable terms, such as the extension of the exploration period to 8–9 years, instead of the internationally accepted 7, and permission for a development delay after discovery in any block of a commercial flow, for the domestic marketing of oil shares by foreign companies, and for foreign companies to embark on downstream projects.[96]

Even though 68 companies from 17 countries registered for the bidding and 54 companies sent their experts to China for data review and investigation, the result of the bidding was disappointing.[97] Only two production-sharing contracts have been signed. Block 1, the 9,800-sq.-km Yatongguzi block, was awarded to an Agip, Elf, Texaco, Japex and Japan Energy consortium, and block 3, the 15,000-sq.-km Qiemo block, was awarded to the Exxon, Sumitomo, and Inpex consortium. A BP-led consortium, including Nippon Oil, Itochu, Mitsubishi and Mitsui, has signed a seismic commitment for block 4, the 14,475-sq.-km Tulabei block, with an option to switch to a production sharing contract if the seismic results are positive (see Map 7.6).[98]

The poor result was a reflection of foreign companies' wariness after the disappointments many suffered in their search for oil offshore. For example, BP spent about $200 million drilling dry well after dry well in the 1980s in the Yellow Sea and Pearl River delta.[99] When it was realized that the blocks opened to foreign investors were located in the most inaccessible part of an already remote region, the initial excitement at the opening subsided.

Foreign companies that did decide to participate in the Tarim Basin's exploration are complaining that most of the blocks on offer are difficult to handle and reserves

---

[94] *Japan Petroleum and Energy Trends*, 19 March 1993, p. 4.

[95] Wang Shali, 'China's Model Contracts: Onshore and Offshore Comparisons', paper presented at PSC '93 (Oil and Gas Production Sharing Contracts, Concessions & New Petroleum Ventures in the Asia Pacific Region), convened by the Institute for International Research, Singapore, 15–17 Sept. 1993.

[96] *Japan Petroleum and Energy Trends*, 25 June 1993, p. 3; *Oil and Gas Journal*, 12 April 1993, p. 37.

[97] *China Oil and Gas* 1: 2 (1994), p. 4.

[98] *China OGP* 2: 1 (1 Jan. 1994), p. 6; *China OGP* 2: 8 (15 April 1994), p. 3; *Petroleum Economist*, June 1994, p. 10.

[99] *Finanacial Times*, 31 March 1993.

Map 7.7: Tarim Basin's oil and gas fields

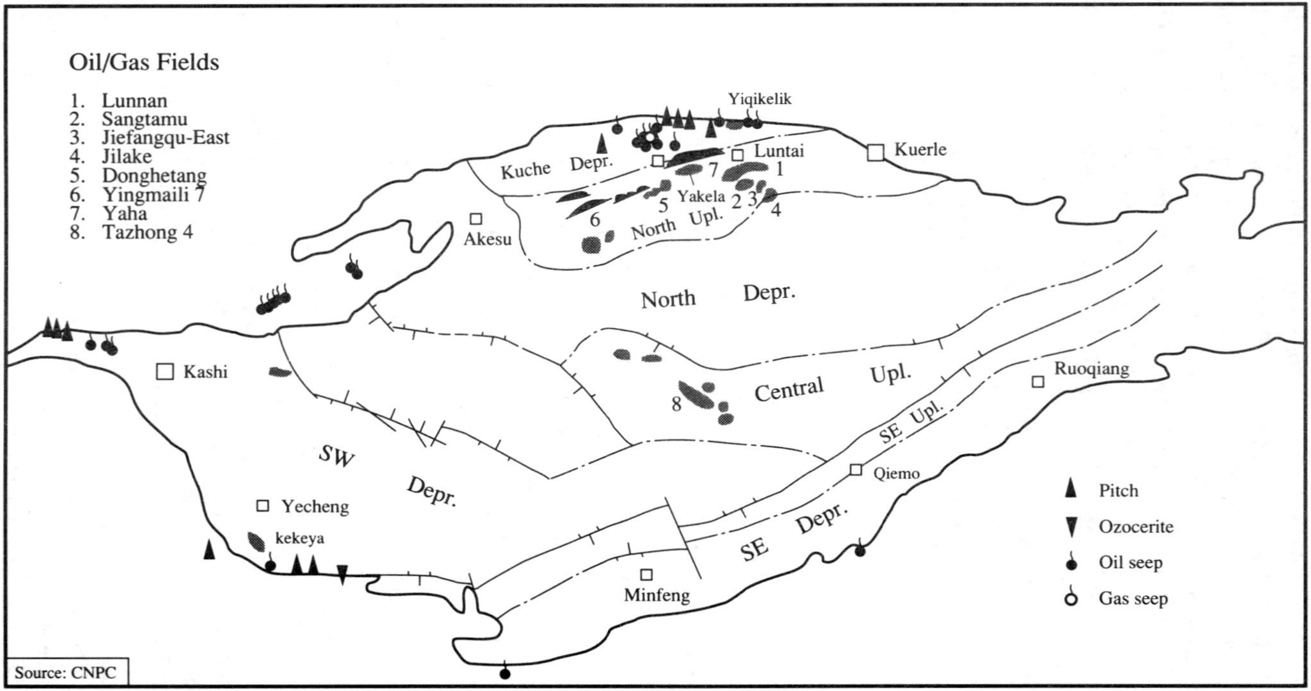

are not as great as those offered elsewhere in Asia, given the high cost of exploration. China, it seems, decided to let the foreigners in, but gave them the least desirable tracts. This approach was confirmed by the second-round bidding for Tarim exploration in June 1995. As shown in Map 7.6, of the 12 blocks offered by CNPC, 8 are in remote tracts of the Basin (though four blocks offered in the Junggar Basin can use existing pipeline between Karamay and Urumqi). In these circumstances, China is going to find it difficult to attract foreign interest in Tarim's exploration.

The important question is: to what extent is CNPC willing to share its better acreages with foreign companies? *China OGP* reported that the Chinese government is uncertain as to how much and in which direction it should open up its energy sector without causing consequent unrest. Although the country needs both foreign capital and expertise, the policy of self-reliance will continue to influence events for at least the next few years.[100]

7.3.4 Recent achievements in the Tarim

CNPC's five-year exploration and development in the Tarim Basin, beginning in 1989, led to the identification of 23 oil- and gas-bearing structures. By the end of 1994 verified oil and gas reserves amounted to 270 mt and over 100 bcm respectively.[101] During 1989–93 a total of 167 exploratory wells were drilled to an average depth of 5,232 m, with 76 wells producing a high volume of industrial oil and gas. The success rate for exploratory wells stands at 45.4%, and the average oil and gas reserves for each exploratory well are three times the national average.[102]

Significant discoveries have been made at the Sangtamu, Jiefangqu-dong, Donghetang and Tazhong oil fields, and the Jilake condensate gas field (see Map 7.7). The biggest discovery so far is the Tazhong 4 oil field with an estimated 100 mt in place reserves. Tazhong 4, discovered in 1992, tested commercial oil and gas flows from 13 pay zones, of which 11 produced more than 629 b/d of oil, with a maximum production of 3711 b/d. In 1993 Tazhong 6, testing 100,000 cm/d of gas and 132 b/d of condensate oil, and Tazhong 10, testing 1447 b/d of oil, were discovered.[103]

In 1994 the Yaha field, north of the producing Lunnan field, was discovered. Initial exploration here has put estimated reserves at 86 mt. The first wildcat, drilled on 15 November 1994 through a 7.140-mm choke, provided 203 cm of crude oil

---

[100] *China OGP* 2: 18 (15 Sept. 1994), p. 2.

[101] *China OGP* 3: 1 (1 Jan. 1995), p. 3; *China OGP* 3: 3 (1 Feb. 1995), p. 3.

[102] *Beijing Review*, 24–30 April 1995, p. 11–13.

[103] *China Oil and Gas* 1: 2 (1994), pp. 44–8. Sangtamu oil field, discovered in early 1990, had an initial flow of 250 t/d from a layer 4.2 km deep. See *Far Eastern Economic Review*, 10 June 1993, p. 56.

and 53,656 cm of gas at a depth of 5,227 m.[104] The same year, CNPC started exploration at two virgin basins, Yanqi, covering 13,000 sq. km, and Santanghu, covering 12,000 sq. km, in southern and eastern Xinjiang. Drilling at a depth of 2,632 m, the Yanqi basin showed an initial commercial flow of 104 cm of light crude and 50,000 cm of gas at a pay zone of 180 m.[105]

Tarim's oil production is gradually increasing. In 1992 the five fields in operation, Lunnan, Donghetang, Sangtamu, Jilake and Jiefang Qu Dong, produced 0.8 mt of oil.[106] Strictly speaking, the Donghetang field, located in Kuche county, came on stream in June 1994. The field, with a design capacity of 1 mt/y, will produce 0.6 mt/y of oil.[107]

By the end of 1994, roughly 170 wildcat and appraisal wells had been sunk, with a total drilling footage of 935,000 m. Another 102 development wells were completed, whose total footage measured some 510,000 m.[108] In the same year, oil production at Tarim recorded 2 mt, up from 1.6 mt in 1993. If not for the shut-down of producing wells due to transportation constraints, it could have reached 2.4 mt. With the development of Tazhong 4, whose estimated annual production is 2.5 mt, the Tarim Basin is expected to produce 5 mt by the end of 1995.[109] It is likely to become China's sixth largest production base in 1996, and could be placed fourth early in the next decade.

Tazhong 4, about 36 km west of Tazhong 1 and believed to contain around 130 mt of crude oil, initially flowed 1,804 b/d of high-gravity crude and 18.4 mmcf/d of gas through an 11.1-mm choke from pay zones at 3,600 m. The field was scheduled to come on stream in June 1994. It is the largest and most important find so far in the Tarim, with 13 strata promising rich commercial oil and gas flows.[110] Geologist Wang Zhaoming says Tazhong's proven reserves already total 100 mt.[111]

The combined crude-oil production from the Tarim, Junggar and Turpan-Hami basins in 1994 was expected to reach over 10 mt, and is expected to reach 20 mt by 2000, a substantially scaled-down projection compared with the previous 30 mt.

---

[104] *China OGP* 3: 1 (1 Jan. 1995), p. 3.

[105] *China OGP* 3: 1 (1 Jan 1995), p. 2.

[106] *Japan Petroleum and Energy Trends*, 25 June 1993, p. 3. In 1991 the figure was 0.55 mt. See *Oil and Gas Journal*, 28 Sept, 1992, p. 25.

[107] In mid-1990 the first well of Donghetang field, 70 km west of Lunnan, was completed. The crude oil's specific gravity is 0.8572 and its pour point is -13°C. See *China Oil and Gas* 1: 4 (1994), p. 32; *Far Eastern Economic Review*, 10 June 1993, p. 56.

[108] *China OGP* 2: 8 (15 April 1994), p. 4.

[109] *China OGP* 3: 1 (1 Jan. 1995), p. 2; *China OGP* 3: 3 (1 Feb. 1995), p. 3.

[110] *China Petroleum Investment Guide 1994*, pp. 89–90; *Oil and Gas Journal*, 28 Sept. 1992, p. 25; *Japan Petroleum and Energy Trends*, 19 Feb. 1993, p. 4.

[111] *Far Eastern Economic Review*, 10 June 1993, p. 55.

Most of the increase will come from the Tarim fields.[112] According to the TOEDB's target for the ninth five-year plan (1996–2000), by 2000 annual oil production will rise to 8.8 mt and gas production will reach 2 bcm.[113]

7.3.5 The burden of investment

CNPC is facing mounting problems in tackling Tarim's exploration and development: deep pay zones, high drilling costs, complex geology, high sub-surface pressures and temperatures, a harsh climate and lack of infrastructure. For example, the Donghetang field's oil-bearing layers are extremely deep at 5.7 km, which will add to the cost of extracting the oil. To drill a single well 5 km deep costs 35 million yuan, and and total drilling costs alone so far stand at 2.8 billion yuan. The solutions to many of these problems lie in adequate financing.[114]

The TOEDB is spending about 2 billion yuan per year, of which 450 million yuan comes from CNPC, a similar amount comes from oil sales (Beijing buys oil at international prices rather than China's low and subsidized price), and the remainder comes from a $1.2-billion loan from the Bank of China.[115] A proportion of the loan ($0.7 billion) was provided at the end of 1991 for the laying of a second track on the rail route into the Tarim Basin and a 20,000 b/d refinery at Korla. The remaining $0.5 billion was provided at the end of 1993 for the purchase of specialized oil-field equipment, including precision instruments and desert transport vehicles.[116]

Reportedly, in 1993 investment earmarked for wells with oil and gas reserves of 100 mt equalled the national average for the period,[117] which confirms the scale of investment requested for Tarim's exploration. In the early 1990s China earmarked $20 billion (1,000 billion yuan) for oil exploration in the Tarim Basin during 1991–5.[118] It is not certain whether the real investment figure reached that level as China drastically cut back its budget for exploration due to its large fiscal deficit. In fact, the exploration budget for Tarim was slashed to $0.3 billion for 1991–2, down

[112] *China OGP* 2: 20 (15 Oct. 1994), p. 4.
[113] *Beijing Review*, 24–30 April 1995, p. 12.
[114] *Far Eastern Economic Review*, 10 June 1993, p. 56. The cost of the Tazhong discovery well amounted to $20 million. See Daqing and Fridley, 'Tarim Basin' (op. cit., n. 84), p. 8.
[115] *Far Eastern Economic Review*, 10 June 1993, p. 56. During 1990–94, CNPC invested a total of 15 billion yuan. The $1.2 billion loan from the Bank of China is included in this total. See *China OGP*, 1 July 1995, p. 1.
[116] *China Petroleum Investment Guide 1994*, p. 90; *China OGP* 2: 1 (1 Jan. 1994), p. 7; *China Daily*, 29 June 1991.
[117] *Beijing Review*, 24–30 April 1995, p. 13.
[118] *China Daily*, 18 Feb. 1991.

from the $0.6 billion allocated in 1989–90.[119]

Such a dire capital shortage seems unlikely to be much improved during the second half of the 1990s. Had China made its decision on the opening of the Tarim Basin before the breakup of the Soviet Union in 1991, it would have seemed a lot more attractive. Recently China announced new foreign investment guidelines, aiming at channelling funds into agriculture and infrastructure such as energy and transportation. Under these new guidelines, China was intent on 'shifting its method of attracting foreign investment from simply giving favourable conditions to that of mutual benefit and long-term cooperation'.[120] It remains to be seen whether this new policy will also be applied to the Tarim Basin's exploration and development.

7.3.6 Poor infrastructure

According to Chinese geologists, the northwest frontier including the Tarim Basin may hold as much as 40% of the nation's undiscovered oil resources and half its undiscovered gas resources. Less than 10% of the postulated hydrocarbon resources, however, have been identified.[121] These figures could increase substantially once comprehensive infrastructure is provided in the northwest frontier region, and this is China's top priority.

In July 1995 CNPC began construction of a 310-km Tazhong 4–Lunnan oil and gas pipeline, with a delivery capacity of 3 mt/y of oil and 400 mcm/y of gas. This, China's first, desert oil and gas pipeline is scheduled to be completed in July 1996 at an investment cost of 5 billion yuan ($588 million).[122] It will help to accelerate development of a group of Tazhong fields, and is a small step towards China's aim to construct a long-distance pipeline. As shown in Map 7.8, China hopes to build a 4,200-km (20 mt delivery capacity) oil-pipeline system extending from Xinjiang to southwestern and eastern China.[123] As the planned trunk pipeline was unlikely to pass the state assessment due to a high construction cost of over $1.2 billion, CNPC proposed to build the pipeline section by section, which was regarded as a workable alternative.[124]

The first section of China's long-distance crude-oil pipeline is awaiting final approval from the State Planning Commission (SPC). This 491-km pipeline from

---

[119] Keun Wook Paik, 'Tarim Opening: Geopolitics of Chinese Oil', *Geopolitics of Energy*, 1 April 1993, p. 9.

[120] *Financial Times*, 20 April 1995.

[121] *Oil and Gas Journal*, 28 Sept. 1992, p. 24.

[122] *China OGP*, 15 July 1995, p. 5.

[123] *Pipeline Industry*, Nov. 1994, p. 48.

[124] *China OGP* 2: 20 (15 Oct. 1994), p. 4.

Map 7.8: China's oil, gas and products pipelines

Source: Pipe Line Industry, Nov. 1994, p. 45

Korla to Shanshan, costing 1.5 billion yuan ($178 million), was initially projected to be in operation by August 1996. Designed by Snamprogetti of Italy, the Xinjiang pipeline (diameter 610mm) will have a maximum annual conveying capacity of 10 mt/y. It is the first leg of an extensive system which will run 4,200 km from Korla to Pengxian in Sichuan province. The proposed Sichuan refinery, located in Pengzhou county near Chengdu, will have an annual refining capacity of 5 mt. The pipeline is expected to cost 7–8 billion yuan ($805–920 million).[125]

[125] Snamprogetti won the design contract in March 1994. Three other oil and gas pipelines, including the Shanshan-Urumqi oil line (310 km), Tazhong 4-Lunnan oil and gas line (330 km), are under planning or construction at the Tarim and Turfan-Hami basins. See *China OGP* 2: 7 (1 April 1994), p. 4; 1 May 1994, p. 3; 15 Oct. 1994, p. 4; 1 July 1995, p. 2; *Petromin*, Aug. 1994, p. 50.

To make the project economically viable, proven reserves of the basin will have to total at least 650 mt.[126] Initially, CNPC aimed at proving 800 mt of reserves by 1995, but the figure seems unlikely to be achieved. As of early 1995, less than 270 mt of reserves were confirmed throughout this huge desert. According to TOEDB's target for the ninth five-year plan, Tarim's proven crude-oil reserves will be over 1 bt by 2000, with 300 bcm of proven gas reserves.[127]

The CNPC's original idea was to pipe Tarim's oil to Luoyang in central China, where the pipeline was to be connected with an existing one leading to Lianyungang, a port city in east China. Tarim oil was to be exported to earn foreign currency.[128] Due to China's rapidly growing oil consumption, the proposed crude-oil pipeline from Tarim to Luoyang, Henan province, had to be rerouted through Baoji in Shannxi province en route to southwest Sichuan.

The SPC initially thought of feeding refineries along the Yangtze (Changjiang) River. Two factors forced it to revise the route. The first is that current refining capacity in southwest China, especially in Sichuan province, is far too small to support the region's growing economy. At present, Sichuan's Nanchong and Chongqing refineries can refine only 0.2 mt/y. The second is that many refineries along China's east coast are designed to process imported crude rather than domestically recovered reserves.[129]

Clearly, China is giving top priority to satisfying the central region's oil demand with Tarim oil. CNPC is also interested in delivering Xinjiang's natural gas to eastern and southern China. This is why CNPC in association with Mitsubishi Corp. is promoting the concept of a Silk Route gas pipeline in parallel with the crude pipeline. (Turkmenistan's proven gas reserves are 88.1 tcf and potential reserves are estimated at 364 tcf.[130] Turkmenistan gas could prove an important energy source for China's economic development.)

Until this long-distance trunk pipeline is established, China will have to improvise in coping with the problem of oil delivery to its main consuming areas. Since the beginning of 1994 Tarim has twice been forced to close down wells because of inadequate storage and transportation facilities. Tarim Petroleum E & D Headquarters has decided to build six 50,000-tonne storage tanks for the Lunnan–Korla pipeline, four at Lunnan and two at Korla. As of 1994, daily production capacity in

---

[126] *China OGP* 2: 3 (1 Feb. 1994), p. 2.

[127] *China OGP* 2: 20 (15 Oct. 1994), p. 2; 3: 7 (1 April 1995), p. 4; *Beijing Review*, 24–30 April 1995, p. 12.

[128] *China, OGP* 1: 1 (1 June 1993), p. 1.

[129] *China OGP* 2: 3 (1 Feb. 1994), p. 2; 1: 3 (1 July 1993), p. 2.

[130] Paik, 'Pipeline Politics' (op. cit., n. 68), pp. 1–8. Both CNPC and Mitsubishi have recently decided to undertake the preliminary feasibility study. See *China OGP*, 1 July 1995, p. 5.

Tarim is around 6,000 tonnes, and daily railway-transportation capacity is only 5,000 tonnes.[131] This is reason why the Xinjiang–Lanzhou railway is being double-tracked at a cost of 3 billion yuan ($525 million), a project that seems unlikely to be finished until 1995.[132]

Currently a 476-km railway from Korla to Turphan with an annual capacity of 5 mt/y delivers crude from Tarim to the single-track line at Urumqi. The actual volume of crude and products carried by the Tarim line is only a fifth of the designed capacity (1.1 mt/y). Oil transportation to other provinces is mainly by way of the 3,000-km trunkline from Urumqi to Lanzhou, which has the capacity to handle 15 mt/y.[133]

The second transportation option on which China can depend is the motorway network. The first phase of the Tarim Desert Road Network in the Taklamakan Desert was finished at the end of June 1994. The 295-km highway consists of two sections: the first, 76 km long, extending from Lunnan to Xiaotang on the northern tip of the Taklamakan; the second, 219 km long, running southwards from Xiaotang to Tazhong 4, in the middle of Taklamakan.[134]

This development dates back to March 1990, when a 380-km route survey from Tazhong 1 well to Lunnan 16 well was conducted by the Desert Highway Reconnaissance. The project was listed as the National Scientific and Technological Key Project during the eighth FYP, and to complete it severe natural conditions and geological features had to be overcome. Along the highway, annual rainfall amounts to only 20–40 mm, with annual evaporation as high as 2,100–3,400 mm, relative humidity less than 10% and the drying index in excess of 20. Temperatures at the sand surface can reach as high as 60–70° Celsius in summer and fall to minus 30° Celsius in winter.[135]

The scale of the Basin's infrastructure development will be greatly affected by the size and number of oil and gas fields discovered during the second half of the 1990s: hence the SPC's hesitation in approving CNPC's proposals for pipeline construction in the Tarim until the Basin's proven reserves reach a level that can justify the investment. CNPC must urgently secure big proven reserves if it is to convince the SPC. Thus CNPC has decided to offer another 12 blocks in the Tarim and Junggar basins for further exploration.

---

[131] *China OGP* 2: 9 (1 May 1994), pp. 2–3. In the summer of 1994, the four tanks were erected and increased Tarim's annual production capacity to 5 mt. See *China OGP* 2: 15 (1 Aug. 1994), p. 5.

[132] *Japan Petroleum and Energy Trends*, 26 Nov. 1993, p. 8; *China OGP* 1: 9 (1 Oct. 1993), pp. 2–3.

[133] *China OGP* 2: 6 (15 March 1994), p. 6.

[134] *China Oil and Gas* 1: 4 (1994), pp. 50–1; *China OGP* 2: 15 (1 Aug. 1994), p. 5.

[135] *China Oil and Gas* 1: 4 (1994), pp. 50–1.

7.4 Conclusion

The development of Northeast Asia's four major frontier oil and gas projects will bring about a significant change in the energy structure of the region. No regional country would challenge the urgent need to accelerate development of these projects, which would help ease the energy shortage and alleviate the burden of energy imports. Frontier energy development would guarantee Northeast Asia a major and stable energy source.

However, many obstacles stand in the way. All the region's frontier oil and gas resources are located in remote and environmentally harsh areas where no infrastructure exists. To extract oil and gas from these forbidding places needs new technology, equipment and especially a very long-distance pipeline network. (In the case of Sakhalin, in fact, a relatively short-distance pipeline is required.) Money is needed if these obstacles are to be overcome.

Russia and China are currently suffering from capital shortages, and neither country is in a position to commit a huge investment to these frontier energy projects. Major Western energy companies are also cautious about the massive investment needed. In the case of China, the remote location of oil and gas areas coupled with uncertain prospects are seen as serious hindrances. And the disappointing results in the Chinese offshore are surely exerting a negative effect. With Russia, despite the country's huge proven oil and gas reserves, investment is seen as a risk because of political instability and lack of an adequate fiscal system.

Consequently, only a couple of major Western energy companies can afford to secure a position in Russia's and China's frontier oil and gas areas. Japanese and Korean companies could also be important players in financing these projects, but only if their respective governments give full support.

At present, investors are interested mainly in Russia's Sakhalin offshore projects, though development of the Tarim Basin project is in some respects more advanced. However, some of Tarim's developed areas are mainly based on a string of discoveries by CNPC, not by foreign investors. CNPC's target for Tarim oil and gas production in 2000 is roughly 9 mt and 2 bcm respectively. Figures for future plans are not available at the moment. The existence of massive new reserves of oil and gas in the Basin is still a matter of debate and only serious exploratory effort will reveal their true magnitude.

Even if there is a discovery in the Tarim comparable to the Daqing field (which, as we have seen, has produced 50 mt a year for almost 20 years), no substantial allocation for export can be expected in the next decade because of China's own demand. But major foreign investors are still interested in Tarim's development because of China's lucrative domestic market, which will absorb all its developed oil and gas. Tarim does not involve transboundary transport, and only one government has to be

The Junggar and Turpan-Hami basins

There are two other oil-producing basins in Xinjiang province. The first is the Junggar basin, covering 141,000 sq. km and located in the north-central part of the province. The basin's oil and gas reserves are estimated at 8.9 bt and 4.1 tcm respectively.[1] The Karamay oil field, in the northwest and accounting for 39% of China's total oil production in 1960, was once thought to be nearly depleted but has steadily expanded. Karamay's oil reserves are estimated at 1.23 bt.[2] In 1991 the Cainan oil field, with estimated reserves of 60 mt, was discovered in the Mahu area.[3]

As of 1993, nine oil fields have been completed or are under construction in the Junggar Basin, where existing fields have a combined production capacity of 8 mt/y, including Karamay.[4] In May 1994 the first geophysical exploration team from Xinjiang Petroleum Administrative Bureau entered Fuhai, a marginal depression in the Junggar Basin. Another two marginal depressions, Hetuo and Kupu, are also included in the Bureau's 1994 exploration plan. The three depressions cover 30,000 sq. km.[5]

The Turpan-Hami Basin, covering 48,000 sq. km, is located 170 km southeast of the regional capital Urumqi. Its oil and gas reserves are estimated at 1.6 bt and 380 bcm. At the end of 1993 some 11 oil fields had been discovered in the Basin and production capacity rose to 1.15 mt.[6] The Shanshan oil field is built, and construction of the Wenjisang and Mideng fields was expected to be completed by the end of 1993. By then construction of the Qiuling field, the biggest in Turpan-Hami, was under way and preparations for Baka field were being made. Oil reserves confirmed in Turpan-Hami are capable of supporting 3 mt/y of production.[7]

Even if the combined oil production of the Tarim, Junggar and Turpan-Hami basins reaches 20 mt in 2000, it would only be slightly over 8% of China's total oil production. (The target total in 2000 is 175 mt.) Given its fast-growing economy and rising oil demand, China needs a breakthrough in the Tarim Basin – the discovery of a giant field comparable to Daqing, where annual production has surpassed 50 mt in the past 17 years.

[1] *China Oil and Gas* 1: 1 (1994), p. 6.
[2] *China Petroleum Investment Guide 1994*, p. 58; *Japan Petroleum and Energy Trends*, 26 Nov. 1993, p. 8; David Fridley, 'China's Xinjiang Looks West: The Central Asian Oil Connection', *Energy Advisory* 107 (16 Oct. 1992), p. 2.
[3] *China Oil and Gas* 1: 1 (1994), p. 6.
[4] China OGP 1: 10 (15 Oct. 1993), p. 4.
[5] *China OGP* 2: 12 (15 June 1994), p. 5.
[6] *China Oil and Gas* 1: 1 (1994), pp. 6 and 52.
[7] *Japan Petroleum and Energy Trends*, 26 Nov. 1993, p. 7; *China Daily*, 2 Feb. 1991.

dealt with. Presumably, though, more uncertainty exists over value, but in terms of the region's dependence, Tarim is important as it frees oil and gas that China would otherwise import.

The Sakhalin offshore projects are under preparation. Sakhalin-II is the most

Table 7.6: Comparison of Northeast Asia's frontier projects

	Sakhalin-I	Sakhalin-II	Sakha	Irkutsk	Tarim
Location:	Sakhalin	Sakhalin	Sakha Rep.	RF	Xinjiang province
Stage:	Waiting devl.	Waiting devl.	Under PFS	Under PFS	Expl./Devl.
Field/Region:	Odoptu, Chaivo/ Arkutun	Piltun/ Lunskoye	Vilyuiskaya/ Nepsko-Botuobinskaya	Kovyktinskoye/ Verkhnechon-skoye	Tazhong-4 & bidding areas
Reserves (proven):	O/C: 323 mt G: 425 bcm	O/C: 146 mt G: 364 bcm	O: 438 mt G: 1 tcm	O: 650 mt G: 1 tcm	O: 270 mt G: 100 bcm[8]
Companies:	Sodeco: 30% Exxon: 30% Sakhalinmor-neftegas: 23% Roseneft: 17%	Marathon: 30% McDermott: 20% Mitsui: 20% Mitsubishi: 10% Shell: 20%	Sakhaneftegas RF Korean (C)[4]	Sidanco CNPC Korean (G)[7]	CNPC Esso/Agip BP (C)[9]
Cost:	$13–15 bn	$10–12 bn	$20 bn	$10 bn	?
Pipeline:	700 km/ 1,500 km[1]	700 km	5,500 km	3,800 km	4,300 km
Planned I-P	3 mt/5.5 bcm	?/10 bcm	(12 bcm)	?	9 mt/2 bcm[10]
P-P	23 mt/-	6 mt/(23 bcm)[3]	(26 bcm)[5]	25 bcm	
Start[2]: Devl.	1997/8	1996/7	1998/9	1997/8	early 1990s
Expl.	2005/6	2003/4	2005/6[6]	2004/5	?

Key: O/C = oil and condensate; G = gas; I-P = initial production; P-P = peak production.

Notes:

1 As Sakhalin-I's 700-km pipeline will overlap with that of Sakhalin-II, a 1,500-km pipeline connecting northern Sakhalin with Vladivostok is conceivable.
2 Development and export starting time is the earliest possible.
3 This is the projected total Sakhalin gas production in 2010.
4 Composed of 14 companies.
5 Projected gas production in 2000 and 2010.
6 Based on an assumption that the Sakha project will be linked with the Irkutsk project.
7 A group of 4 companies.
8 Tarim's proven reserves seem to increase. The estimated oil and gas reserves are 19.8 bt and 8.4 tcm respectively.
9 These 3 consortia are for exploration.
10 CNPC's production target for 2000.

Source: Author

advanced among the Russian Far East oil and gas projects. The formidable hurdle in the form of the final investment decision is now removed with the Duma's approval of the production-sharing law in June 1995, but it remains to be seen whether real development will start in 1996, with export of the developed oil and gas between 2002 and 2003, or whether another excuse for delay will be found. (Table 7.6 suggests that 2003–2004 is the earliest time possible date for start-up.)

Sakhalin-I, awaiting the signing of a production-sharing deal in late June 1995, is following in the tracks of Sakhalin-II. According to the development plan, Sakhalin-I is expected to supply oil and gas to the Russian domestic market around 2003. Even though a recent Sakhalin quake measuring 7.5 on the Richter scale has flattened the oil town of Neftegorsk and affected Sakhalinmorneftegas very seriously,[136] in the long term it seems unlikely to affect the development plans of either Sakhalin-I or II very much. So far as Sakhalin-III and IV are concerned, both still need expensive and risky exploration work, and investment can only be long-term.

Many people also regard investment in the Sakha Republic gas project as only of interest in the long term, but early development could become possible if the current preliminary feasibility study projects the development economics positively. Given the Republic's gas potential, proving 2 tcm of reserves, up from the previous 1 tcm of reserves, would not be a problem. The issue will be the availability of the region's gas markets and finance. If South Korea is sufficiently determined, development will go ahead. But the project would not come cheap, and the ideal way forward is simultaneous commitment from Japan and Korea.

Unexpected movement could also come in the Irkutsk region's gas development. South Korean companies are exploring the possibility of joining Sidanco and CNPC in developing the Kovyktinskoye gas field. It remains to be seen whether an agreement among the three parties to cooperate in the field's development and in the construction of a pipeline grid will come about in the near future. According to the most optimistic scenario, the development timescale of this project could parallel that of Sakhalin-I and II.

The factors that will determine the ranking and sequence of these projects include the scale of proven reserves, export availability of the developed oil and gas, contractual stage, pricing, internal political stability in Russia and China, the value of the energy, governmental support for funding of transport infrastructure and the degree of cohesion between projects.

---

[136] One of the rigs belonging to Sakhalinmorneftegas was destroyed, while 27 of its oil and gas wells were set ablaze. Its gas pipeline was not damaged, allowing it to deliver 3 mcm/d of gas to the area, but the crude-oil pipeline was shut after the discovery of 17 leaks. See *Nefte Compass*, 1 June 1995, pp. 1–2.

Sakhalin-I and II are at the top of the rank. Their advantages are export availability with geographical proximity to the export market, and their development is only a matter of time. Any serious delay seems unlikely. If CNPC development is included in the calculation, Tarim is the most advanced among Northeast Asia's frontier projects in terms of development stage. As far as the export possibility is concerned, however, Tarim has severe limitations as only a few major companies can afford to participate in the hugely expensive exploration work.

Tarim, therefore, ranks alongside Sakhalin-III and IV, despite the development achieved in specific areas of the Basin. However, if the Energy Silk Route project, envisaging the export of gas from central Asian Republics to the Northeast Asian market, goes ahead despite its burdensome development economics, it will greatly help the acceleration of the Tarim Basin development.

The Sakha and Irkutsk projects seem among the least promising for early development – though, as noted, Irkutsk could prove a surprise. Due to their remote locations, both are regarded as the last frontier projects. However, the Irkutsk project is somewhat better positioned than the Sakha, as the latter will not be developed with the current proven gas reserves, while the former is ready to be so long as project partners are found.

This ranking could easily be challenged if other factors are taken into account. However, indisputably, full-fledged development of both the Tarim Basin project and Sakhalin offshore projects will materialize in the next decade, but it will make a limited contribution to the region's oil and gas supply structure as most of the supplies from Tarim will be allocated to China's domestic demand.

It should also be emphasized that the current approach to development of the three frontier projects will not fully benefit the countries of Northeast Asia. To achieve an energy supply balance in the next decade, the region needs to promote a package development of Russian Far East gas projects, eventually leading to multilateral cooperation. The merit of such a package concept lies in the fact that the countries of the region will be participants as well as beneficiaries of development. The final chapter will explain why this sort of new thinking is necessary for the region's long-term oil and gas security.

Annex 7.1: Chronology of Sakhalin Tenders

(1) May 1991

Sakhalinmoneftegas (Sakhalin Offshore Oil and Gas) Association revealed that the Soviet Ministry of Oil and Gas decided to set up a joint venture involving the Association, and announced an international tender, in lieu of the joint sponsors, the Soviet Oil and Gas Ministry, and the Russian Republic's State Committee on Geology and Utilization of Fuel, Energy, and Mineral Resources, for development of the Lunskoye and Piltun-Astokskoye fields.

The tender covered a total offshore area of 17,000 sq. km, or about 10% of the explorable Sakhalin shelf.

(2) 10 August 1991: Deadline for proposal submission

After the announcement of an international tender, six groups took part in the bidding. MMM: McDermott, Marathon, and Mitsui; Exxon and Sodeco; BHP, Amoco and Hyundai; Mobil; Idemitsu Kosan; Shell, Mitsubishi, Nisso Iwai, Showa Shell Sekiyu and Shoseki Oil Development Co.

Palmco and Ralph M. Parsons did not join in the tender.

Examination of the proposals was based on the following criteria:

(a) Time schedule for commercialization.
(b) Time schedule for delivery of gas to consumers in Russia's Far Eastern Economic Region.
(c) Exploration and surveys in the tender zone.
(d) Evaluation of promising new areas in terms of time and the size of deposit.
(e) Reasoning behind the engineering and technological solutions and their reliability and environmental safety.
(f) Preparedness to capitalize authorized funds.

(3) 20 September 20 1991

Sakhalinmorneftegaz made a proposal to the Tender Organizing Committee (TOC) to recognize the MMM group as the tender winner and recommended that a feasibility study be jointly drafted.

(4) 5 October 1991

Sakhalin Deputy Governors Viktor Sirenco and Valery Mozolevsky declared the summer tender void.

(5) 18 October 1991

The Sakhalin government imposed new conditions, the so-called 'Social Development Programme'. These additional requirements involved $10 billion in investment and loans for development of transport systems, telecommunications, agriculture, and other industries. However, financing of the programme would come from the proposed reduction in royalties from 12.5% under the tender terms to 1.5% and from granting the foreign partner a seven-year tax holiday for the repatriated profit.

The government asked the foreign companies to submit their respective proposals by 10 November 1991, including the following provisions:

(a) Delivery of gas to the Sakhalin region was to increase to 3 bcm in 1995, 5 bcm in 1997 and 8 bcm in 2005.
(b) The amount of gas for export was to ensure minimal profitability of the project, with remaining gas to be delivered to Khabarovsk Territory.
(c) Cooperation options to be provided were to include – apart from joint ventures – concessions, production-sharing contracts and service contracts.

The government suggested that the following constructions should be begun simultaneously with the Sakhalin offshore project:

(a) Reconstruction of the road between Okha and Yuzhno-Sakhalinsk, a distance of 800 km; 2 lanes, with branches to Poronaisk, Uglegorsk and Aleksandrovsk-Sakhalinskii.
(b) Railway from Nogliki to Okha (provide an analysis of necessity and estimate of costs).
(c) Maritime ports in Ilinskii with ferry terminal or in Prigorodnyi for ships with a capacity of 100,000 tonnes or with a 150,000-tonnes-a-day turnover with a container terminal.
(d) Development and reconstruction of the maritime port of Korsakov for ships of 30,000 tonnes with a container terminal.
(e) Expansion of the Okha TETs with 2 power blocks and a capacity of 80 megawatts.
(f) LEP 220 kilovolts from Okha to Dagi, a distance of 180 km.
(g) Reconstruction of the airports in Okha, Nogliki, and Zonalnoe.
(h) Oblast communications link with international circuits.
(i) Water supply to Yuzhno-Sakhalinsk.

(6) 12 November 1991

The Russian president Boris Yeltsin approved the Sakhalin authority's annulment of the decision on the summer bidding. However, Yegor Gaidar, deputy chairman of the Russian Council of Ministers, challenged Yeltsin's decision.

The same day, by decision of the Sakhalin govenor Fedorov, the Sakhalin Tender Committee (STC) was set up, and seven groups of experts representing the subcommittees of the Executive Committee on energy, environmental protection, economics, construction, transport, communications, food, social issues and public relations were constituted. STC was to submit to the Sakhalin governor its proposal on the tender winner by 30 November 1991.

(7) 18 November 1991

Four days of presentations by the bidders were held in the oblast executive committee meeting hall.

MMM (McDermott, Marathon, and Mitsui) offered to rebuild the Yuzhno-Sakhalinsk and Okha airports if it won, and offered $115 million as a development fund after contract signing.

Mobil Oil flew in 30 tonnes of medical supplies and powdered milk from Anchorage (16 November 1991).

(8) 28 November 1991

The Sakhalin administration put forward additional requirements to foreign companies, asking them to submit draft contracts for a feasibility study by 7 December 1991 to determine the economic viability of the fields on the assumption that the foreign partner and the domestic partner would select a mode of cooperation calling for a production-sharing contract.

(9) 3 December 1991: The Salmanov Commission

A panel of experts was constituted by decision of the Examining Council under the chairman of the Russian government, headed by F. Salmanov, first deputy minister of geology of the USSR.

The Salmanov Commission ruled that the tender area should be divided into several blocks.

The panel of experts proposed dividing the zone as follows:

(a) *Block 1*, about 5,800 sq. km, including Arkutun-Daginskoye oil and gas fields and two conditioned structures, East Kaiginskaya and East Odoptinskaya. The panel included Chaivo and Odoptu fields in the block. However, the tender organizers excluded two fields from the tender zones because those fall within the general agreement with Japan. The panel slated the block for transfer to the Exxon-Sodeco group.

(b) *Block 2*, about 4,500 sq. km, including Piltun-Astokhskoye gas field and the conditioned Lozinskaya and Bautinskaya structures. The block was slated for transfer to the randomly formed group of MMM-Idemitsu.

(c)) *Block 3*, more than 7,500 sq. km, including Lunskoye, Veninskoye and Kirinskoye oil/gas/condensate fields and conditioned Nabilskaya and south Lunskaya structures. The block was slated for transfer to the randomly formed group of BHP, Amoco and Hyundai-Mobil.

(10) 23 December 1991: The Danilov-Danilyan Committee

A committee convened by order of the Russian government, headed by V.I. Danilov-Danilyan, the Russian Federation's minister for ecology and natural resources, reviewed the result of the Sakhalin tender announced in May 1991.

(11) 27 January 1992

Yegor Gaidar, first deputy chairman of the Russian Council of Ministers, announced that MMM had won the Sakhalin tender for a feasibility study into the development of reserves estimated at 730 mbbl of oil and more than 400 bcm of gas. A formal agreement was due to be concluded on 13 March 1992.

Before the announcement, the local officials had asked the Russian Federation to postpone tender results until plans from bidders for investing in the local infrastructure had been evaluated.

After the announcement the Sakhalin governor, Valentin Fedorov, claiming opinions of local government officials had been ignored, resigned from the tender committee. The governor was concerned that if Sodeco were left out of the development, the Japanese government, financing earlier exploration in the area, would demand repayment of loans amounting to $181.5 m at a 6%/y interest rate.

As a result of local opposition, MMM agreed to allow Sodeco and Mobil Oil to participate in the feasibility study.

(12) 4 February 1992: the Shumeiko Commission

S.A. Filatov, first deputy chairman of the Supreme Soviet of the Russian Federation, set up a deputies' commission, chaired by Vladimir K. Shumeiko, also a deputy chairman of the Russian parliament, to reconsider the Sakhalin decision. As a result, the Russian Supreme Council suspended the award again, and original bidders were reconvened. The new committee of experts (Russian Supreme Council) was composed of eight members including officials from Sakhalin.

Until 20 February 1992 the deputies' commission was asked to consider the decision of the Government Commission and Experts Council of the chairman of the Government of the Russian Federation, and submit its conclusion consideration by the Presidium of the Supreme Soviet of the Russian Federation.

(13) 26 March 1992

The Shumeiko Commission concluded that the decision of the Government Commission, dated 27 January 1992, should be annulled.

The Commission recommended that the area of competition should be divided into at least three blocks, and it was envisaged that the winning group in every block would have a 60% share of the rights for exploration and development, while the rights for the remaining 40% would be distributed between winners in other blocks.

(14) 27 March 1992

Based on conclusions by the Shumeiko Commission, S.A. Filatov advised Y. Gaidar to retract his 27 January decision in favour of MMM.

(15) 28 March 1992

Deputy prime minister Yegor Gaidar authorized the negotiations and concluded an agreement with MMM to do a feasibility study for the exploration and development of the Piltun-Astokskoye and Lunskoye fields.

(16) 30 March 1992

MMM signed an agreement with the Russian Ministry of Fuel and Energy pursuant to Yegor Gaidar's decision on 28 March.

(17) December 1992

MMMSM (MMM plus Mitsubishi and Shell, which joined in Autumn 1992) submitted a 6,075-page feasibility study (a 13-volume document) at the end of 1992. The study estimated production could begin in late 1995, rising eventually to nearly 200,000 b/d of crude oil and 44 mcm/d of gas. The study also called for construction of LNG plant with 6 mt/y, and a 15,000 b/d domestic refinery in Sakhalin.

(18) 27 February 1993

The Sakhalin Regional Soviet of People's Deputies (chaired by A.P. Aksenov) passed a resolution asking the Russian government, the State Experts Commission and the regional groups to make a comparative study of the MMMSM's feasibility study and the feasibility proposal of Palmco.

(19) 19 March 1993

The State Evaluation Commission of the Russian Federation Ministry of Economy rejected the feasibility study by MMMSM, and issued an ultimatum on 24 March 1993, instructing MMMSM to either incorporate all of the proposed changes, or risk losing the deal entirely.

While the Russian side was expecting a minimum internal rate of return at 16%, MMMSM projected the rate at 10–14%. (The rate for Lunskoye was a mere 6%.)

(20) 10 June 1993

The Sakhalin Minutes, signed by Yuri Shafranik, minister of fuel and energy of the Russian Federation, Yevgeny Krasnoyarov, Head of the Sakhalin Regional Administration, and Anatoly Aksyonov, chairman of the Council of People's Deputies on 10 June 1993, gave top priority to the fastest possible implementation of the Sakhalin-II project for development of the Lunskoye and Piltun-Astokskoye oil and gas fields in collaboration with the MMMSM consortium

(21) 16 June 1993

The Sakhalin Regional Council of People's Deputies demanded that simultaneous negotiations be held with other foreign companies for development rights to Lunskoye and Piltun-Astokskoye fields, even though the regional parliament approved the Sakhalin regional administration's final draft of the production-sharing contract for the development of the fields with MMMSM.

(22) 30 August 1993

The prime minister Viktor Chernomyrdin signed Resolution No. 1560-p, dated 30 August 1993, making it incumbent upon the Russian Federation Ministry of Fuel and Energy and the Sakhalin Regional Administration to conduct negotiations in September–October 1993 with MMMSM for a production-sharing contract on the development of the Lunskoye and Piltun-Astokskoye fields.

(23) 22 June 1994

The MMMSM contract for development of the Lunskoye and Piltun-Astokskoye fields was finally signed by the Russian prime minister Viktor Chernomyrdin and the US vice-president Al Gore in Washington on 22 June 1994.

However, only when the Duma approve the deal and pass the Law of Concessions legalizing production-sharing deals in Russia for the first time, can any significant investment begin.

Chapter 8

A Northeast Asian energy regime

The 1980s witnessed the rise of Asian-Pacific economic power and with it a growth in energy demand greater than that of any other region in the world. Japan, South Korea, Taiwan and China, in particular, were the driving force behind that growth, and China's energy demand alone will fundamentally affect Northeast Asia's energy balance in the coming decades.

Such an explosive rise in energy demand brings many problems. The main one lies in the balance of oil supply and demand. Northeast Asia's heavy dependence on Middle East oil has already returned to its level before the oil crises in the 1970s, and there is growing concern over China's need for massive oil imports in the next decade which would make the region extremely vulnerable to any future oil crisis. Oil shocks, re-establishment of an effective cartel, import-cost increases, and sea-lane blockage in the South China Sea could all follow on from future Middle East crises and burden the region's economic development.

As Northeast Asia's energy demand grows so do its needs. Even though coal and nuclear power are important energy sources, their roles are restricted by concerns over environmental problems, such as poor local air quality, acid rain, CO_2 emission and safety problems. As for gas, its role has been considerably under-estimated so far. Natural gas would provide the ideal balance for the region's energy-supply structure in the coming decades.

To increase gas use substantially, the early development of Russian Far East resources based on multilateral cooperation must be realized. Even though China boasts of its own frontier oil and gas resources, these cannot form the basis for multilateral energy cooperation. Oil and gas from the Tarim Basin (and elsewhere) will play an important part in reducing the scale of Chinese imports, but supplies are not large enough to help to resolve Northeast Asia's energy problems for the time being. RFE gas could prove to be the solution, rather than oil, which does not exist on the scale needed for multilateral cooperation.

In the past three decades, however, RFE gas resources have not been developed, mainly because of regional power politics but also because of poor development economics. This long delay raises some fundamental questions: Will RFE resources be adequately developed? If so, when, how and by whom? Will development contribute to the region's stability, or could competition over access to the resources and infrastructure actually be a flashpoint for conflict? How can policy minimize the danger of this?

There is no doubt that the development of Northeast Asia's frontier oil and gas resources will be implemented in the coming years. Competition is challenging development, but the changing environment is acting in its favour.

8.1 Competitive forces

As stated in Chapter 7, Sakhalin and Sakha's initial long-term gas-production plan figures in 2000 and 2010 are 34 bcm (Sakhalin 22 bcm, Sakha 12 bcm), and 49 bcm (Sakhalin 23 bcm, Sakha 26 bcm) respectively. Exportable gas volume in 2000 and 2010 was projected at 17 bcm (Sakhalin 10 bcm, Sakha 7 bcm) and 20 bcm (Sakhalin 10 bcm, Sakha 10 bcm) respectively. Since the development programmes of Sakhalin-I and II envisage roughly 10 mt and 10 bcm of oil and gas production early in the next decade and roughly 30 mt and 20 bcm around 2010, and no detailed development programme for the Sakha gas project has yet been established, the above long-term projections seem unlikely to be achieved as planned.

However, the exportable gas volume from Sakhalin and the Sakha Republic during the next decade will, it seems, amount to at least 20 bcm. If gas resources in the Irkutsk region and Turkmenistan republic are also taken into account, volume could reach around 40–60 bcm. The strength of RFE gas development lies in the fact that the region's proved gas reserves are big enough to satisfy regional consumption as well as export to neighbouring countries, such as China, especially its north eastern provinces, North and South Korea, and Japan.

The countries in the region fully recognize the urgency of accelerating frontier gas development, but lack the experience to promote multilateral cooperation so that they are all beneficiaries of development. To make matters worse, potential investors have no confidence in the projects, and the current low energy-price environment does not provide any incentive for gas development. A couple of other frontier oil areas in the world, notably the Caspian and new provinces in offshore Veitnam, are attracting many Western energy companies instead. Unless investors' confidence is built up, they will not be attracted to Northeast Asia's frontier gas development. What countries in the region must do is to arrive at a consensus for the early development of their frontier resources of gas.

Competition comes from two super-giant LNG projects, which could affect RFE gas export to Northeast Asian markets. The two projects are the US Alaska project and Indonesia's Natuna project. The Natuna field is expected to produce 35 mt of LNG for 20 years. Alaska's LNG project is smaller, but could still, on its own, badly affect the entry of RFE gas into Northeast Asian markets.

Both projects need Japanese and South Korean commitment for development. Japan's involvement especially would be decisive, and its political aims would be well served by the Alaska project. At present Japan is not keen to commit itself to RFE energy development, except Sakhalin offshore, and its lukewarm stance threatens to hinder the early realization of RFE oil and gas.

Gas from Natuna and North Alaska could prove significant competition, but the RFE projects have one important advantage: delivery by pipeline, so long as the infrastructure is developed. The scale of investment required for the establishment of a pan-regional gas-pipeline grid would be astronomical, but so, potentially, would be the benefits, not only in terms of development economics but in easing political tensions and accelerating vertical integration. It is true too that the projects could inflame political tensions, but in fact the political environment in Northeast Asia is changing for the better and acting favourably both on investors' confidence and on the attitudes of countries in the region.

8.2 The changing environment

During the past four decades, Northeast Asia has been an arena of East–West confrontation. The break-up of the Soviet Union and the end of the Cold War have changed virtually everything except Russia–Japan relations. Major new uncertainties have arisen in domestic and international economic and political relations. These sweeping changes have not damaged China which, on the contrary, fully utilized the opportunity for economic development. However, it is possible that in the post-Deng era China could face the situation occurring now in the FSU. If China also becomes a casualty of Russian-style chaos, it can only make for further uncertainties in the region's future.

The impact so far of these changes can be considered positive rather than negative. In the international-relations environment new links have been established between states formerly operating in economic isolation. These new connections provide possibilities for reshaping international relations in Northeast Asia to meet the challenges of the post-Cold War world.

In parallel with the geo-political realignment, geo-economic patterns are assuming a much greater importance than in the Cold War period. The countries of Northeast Asia are increasingly interested in regional economic cooperation. Recently China, Russia, South and North Korea, and Mongolia agreed to cooperate in the UN-sponsored Tumen River Area Development Programme.[1] Even though substantial amounts of investment will not necessarily follow from this agreement, none the less it confirms the trend.

Interest in economic cooperation stems from three sources. First, the end of the Cold War has softened bilateral hostilities and nurtured bilateral commercial relations, including those between China and South Korea, China and Japan, and Russia and all its Northeast Asian neighbours. Secondly, the collapse of the Soviet Union abruptly cut off the supply line to the Russian Far East from European Russia. Economic necessity sparked a new Russian openness to trade and investment by Chinese, Korean and Japanese firms and families.

Thirdly, the national economies of the region are characterized by differing and potentially complementary economic capabilities. Japan and South Korea have technological and financial strengths, China has a large and literate labour force, and Mongolia, the Russian Far East and North Korea have a large base of primary resources, including forests and minerals.[2]

Recent dynamic changes in energy relations hint that the energy sector could be an important driving force towards the region's political and economic cooperation. In the past few years, energy relations have undergone their own peculiar brand of perestroika, which provides a chance to readjust the region's energy relations. A total readjustment of regional energy relations is in fact urgently needed to accelerate frontier oil and gas development, and it would be ideal to extend the prevalent bilateral cooperation to multilateral energy development.

The question is whether the changing environment in Northeast Asia can affect the region's frontier energy development favourably and consequently open the way for its early realization despite the competitive challenges.

8.3 From competition to cooperation?

It might be a simplification to say that China's announcement of its decision to open the East China Sea, and the Tarim Basin and other onshore fields, during 1992–3 was aimed at distracting Japanese and Korean interests from RFE oil and gas development, but there is some truth in the claim. Similarly, in the early 1970s, China succeeded in manipulating regional power politics to affect its oil policy

---

[1] The first agreement covers establishment of the Tumen River Area Development Coordination Committee, and the second is on a consultative commission with broader responsibilities for developing trade, infrastructure, finance and banking. The third is on environmental issues. See *Financial Times*, 31 May 1995.

[2] Peter Hayes and Lyuba Zarsky, 'Environmental Issues and Regimes in Northeast Asia', *International Environmental Affairs* 6: 4 (Fall 1994), p. 293.

favourably, blocking Japanese involvement in the region by committing crude-oil exports to Japan.[3]

Thus RFE oil and gas development was a casualty of regional power politics for two decades. Strictly speaking, the delay was caused mainly by the territorial dispute between the Soviet Union and Japan, and only partly by poor field-development economics in the wake of the oil-price collapse. In the 1990s the coincidental and urgent requirement for oil and gas development in the frontier areas of both Russia and China has provided grounds for competition.

As both countries are in dire need of capital, they cannot afford to channel huge amounts of investment to their frontier oil and gas development. Highly advanced technology and equipment from Western countries are also desperately needed to develop oil and gas reserves located in environmentally harsh areas. As a result Russia and China could be driven into competition with one another in the 1990s. For example, as discussed in Chapter 6, if the Energy Silk Route materializes by the end of this decade or at the beginning of the next, a substantial delay in the Sakha Republic's gas development will be inevitable. The possibility of a repeat of the situation in the 1970s cannot be ruled out.

However, there are some fundamental differences between the 1970s and the 1990s. First, the environment for oil and gas development in Northeast Asia in the 1990s is quite favourable to Russia. Geo-political realignments have allowed Russia the manoeuverability it needs for integration into the Asia-Pacific area for the first time. In other words, the new environment signalled a virtual end to Russia's isolation and a new era of multipolarity in the region.

As the long-standing territorial dispute between Russia and Japan remains unresolved, however, the RFE's early integration into the Northeast Asian economy may not be easily achieved. Until this dispute is resolved, it is not certain to what extent the full-fledged development of Sakhalin offshore oil and gas resources will facilitate Russia's integration into the region, or whether Japan will commit itself to the Republic of Sakha's gas development.

Secondly, unlike the 1970s, in the 1990s Japan is not the only potential investor or the only developed oil and gas importer. The end of the Cold War has opened South Korean and Taiwanese investments and markets to RFE oil and gas. South Korea – because of its location – is an essential counterpart in the Russian strategy of keeping Japan nervously guessing about the prospects of economic cooperation,

[3] There were several motives, one being that China genuinely wanted to do things for itself, as well as wanting to embarrass Russia. That is, China's crude-oil export to Japan originated in economic more than political causes. China had been faced with the necessity for hard-currency earnings, and in the 1970s and early 1980s crude oil was its only valuable export commodity. Some may not support this interpretation.

especially in oil and gas development: hence its agreement with South Korea for a feasibility study of the Republic of Sakha's gas project, while allocating the development rights of the five major Sakhalin offshore oil and gas fields to the two multinational consortia comprising three Japanese companies.

Thirdly, there is a strong possibility that China could become a beneficiary of RFE oil and natural-gas development in the next decade, following the Sino-Soviet rapprochement in 1989. In 1991 the Harbin Gas Company (HGC) expressed interest in purchasing Sakha Republic gas, if the Vostok plan was implemented.[4]

China is also exploring the possibility of importing East Siberian oil and gas. As discussed in Chapter 7, both CNPC and Sidanco (Siberian Far East Oil Company) are very serious about this idea, and recently Sidanco decided to develop East Siberian gas reserves for eventual supply to Northeast Asian markets. Sidanco's ambition is to construct a gas pipeline grid connecting the Irkutsk region with northern China via Mongolia. It is also researching a proposal to link the Kovyktinskoye gas field with the neighbouring Sakha fields, which would tie in to a projected 25-bcm/y pipeline to South Korea. In early March 1995, at the 'Conference on the Northeast Asian Natural Gas Pipeline' in Tokyo, Shi Xunzhi, assistant president of CNPC, confirmed that China is also considering this option very seriously. A number of South Korean companies have also expressed interest in the project (see Table 7.6).

In short, despite the danger of competition between Russia and China to attract foreign investment for the acceleration of their long-delayed oil and gas development, the new environment in Northeast Asia suggests that cooperation among regional countries could bring substantial benefits for all concerned.

However, if the current approach of separate development for Sakhalin offshore, the Republic of Sakha and the Irkutsk region is maintained, regional countries cannot all participate in and therefore benefit from development. Only some countries will become beneficiaries, which will not act to raise investors' confidence in the region's multilateral energy-development cooperation.

Northeast Asian countries must calculate the cost of basing current development programmes on bilateral rather than multilateral relations. Even though a number of major international oil and gas companies are participating in these projects, strictly speaking the Sakhalin-I and II projects and the Tarim Basin project are governed by bilateral relations, rather than multilateral cooperation, which is the only way forward if Russia's Far East is to become an important energy-supply source for Northeast Asia.

This emphasis on multilateral cooperation for the region's gas development does

---

[4] Keun Wook Paik, 'Towards a Northeast Asian Energy Charter', *Energy Policy*, May 1992, pp. 438–40.

not necessarily extend to oil development, which is likely to be based mainly on bilateral cooperation. Even if multilateral cooperation in oil development is achieved, it will be after or in parallel with gas development. The biggest need and the biggest opportunities for regional cooperation lie in gas.

8.4 The role of a regional gas grid

Fortunately there is still a chance for the early implementation of RFE gas development on the basis of multilateral cooperation. All three Russian frontier projects, the Sakhalin offshore project, the Sakha Republic gas project and the Irkutsk region gas project, lend themselves to multilateral cooperation in their common need for a pan-regional gas-pipeline grid (see Map 8.1).

Map 8.1: Proposed pipeline routes in Northeast Asia

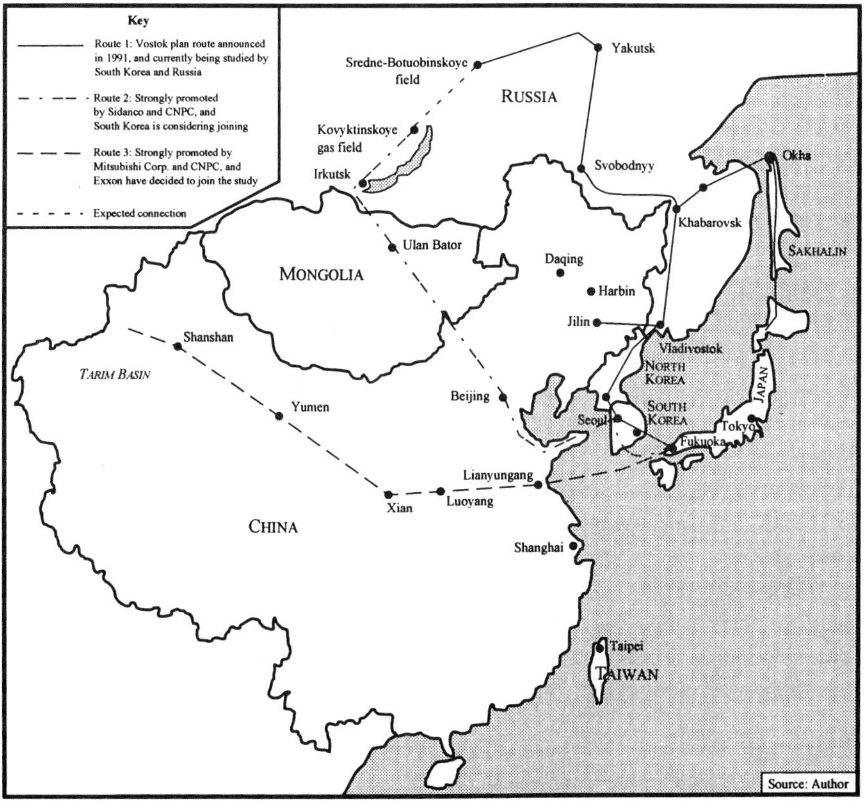

Source: Author

Sakhalin-I and II are very well positioned to take the lead in establishing a North-east Asian gas-pipeline grid. At present, no arrangement has been made for cooperation between the two projects, but combined development based on their geographical proximity is very necessary. Foreign investors involved in the projects have no reason to reject combined development as it will save a substantial amount of overlapping investment in the region's infrastructure. The Russians are in favour of it as it will minimize environmental damage and accelerate the development of both projects, which is badly needed – the sooner the better.

Both Russia and Japan acknowledge that constructing a gas pipeline grid connecting Okha and the greater Vladivostok zone comprising Vladivostok, Nakhodka and Hassan districts, and then passing through the Tatar Strait, Komsomolsk-na-Amur, Khabarovsk and Primorskii Krai is an ideal way to settle the RFE energy problem, but they have no blueprint for its construction. Inclusion of both South Korea and China in the project could solve this problem.

At present South Korean companies are exploring the possibility of participating in Sakhalin-I and II. Their investment will be meaningless, however, if Korean companies participate in the projects in exchange simply for their opening gas market. Given that most of the LNG from Sakhalin-II will be allocated to Japan, South Korea would be better advised to plump for Sakhalin-I. Its participation here would be made meaningful if it contributed to the establishment of the Okha–Vladivostok pipeline grid, a key point in Sakhalin offshore and Sakha Republic gas development.

South Korea's participation in the Sakhalin-I project would pave the way for China to contribute to the grid's establishment. China would be willing to participate in the construction of an Okha–Vladivostok grid as it would be a full beneficiary of the development with an extension from Vladivostok to Jilin province.[5] Even North Korea can be a beneficiary extension from Vladivostok to Najin and Sonbong, which are now open to foreign investment. The importance of early establishment of the Okha–Vladivostok grid lies in the fact that a 3,000-km section connecting Yakutsk and Khabarovsk could follow after a relatively short lead-period.

An alternative plan would also include all regional countries as beneficiaries as well as participants. Ways of exporting Irkutsk gas to China via Mongolia are currently being explored by CNPC and Sidanco. This grid could be extended to South Korea and southern Japan by sub-sea pipeline. If the Irkutsk region's gas

[5] The possibility of electricity export from Vladivostok to Hunchun is also conceivable. It is based on an assumption that a gas-fired power plant will be constructed in Vladivostok once the Okha–Vladivostok grid is established. This concept of electricity export is applicable to Najin and Sonbong as well.

reserves prove to be enormous, then its gas exports to China, South Korea and Japan could be realized even faster than the Sakha Republic's because of the relatively short distance to the market and the ease of construction of a gas-pipeline grid. As a grid connecting Irkutsk and the Sakha Republic is also conceivable, Sakha would get two gas-export outlets, one towards the Khabarovsk region, and the other towards Irkutsk.

Thus Northeast Asia has two options for a pan-regional pipeline grid constructed with multilateral cooperation. The Energy Silk Route project, envisaging gas export from Turkmenistan – passing through Uzbekistan and Khazakstan – to China's east coast and then Japan and South Korea, could be regarded as a multilateral project, but it is not really a third option as it would not make all countries in the region beneficiaries of development.

That all countries should benefit from development is the baseline for multilateral cooperation in Northeast Asia and can be achieved by early development of RFE gas projects. Priority must be given to obtaining a consensus on multilateral cooperation, emphasizing not only the economics of energy development but the enormous benefits to be gained in terms of easing the region's political tensions, and consequently promoting peace and security.

8.5 A Northeast Asian energy regime

In the first half of the 1990s the region failed to hammer out a way of promoting the development of its major frontier oil and gas projects on a multilateral basis. This was partly because countries in the region had relied mainly on bilateral relations until the end of the 1980s and had no experience of developing the concept of multilateral cooperation, and partly because tension between Russia and Japan over their territorial dispute virtually blocked any significant move towards Russia's early integration into the Northeast Asian economy.

The region may fail to achieve multilateral energy cooperation in the second half of the 1990s. The policies of the regional governments will be decisive, especially in the matter of financing. For example, with Sakhalin-I, whose development cost is estimated at $13–15 billion, the Japanese government can exercise its influence through JNOC, which is a main shareholder of SODECO. And the two Japanese companies involved in Sakhalin-II, with a projected development cost of $10–12 billion, will surely apply to JNOC for a loan to cover the LNG project. Likewise, in South Korea, even though private companies have taken the initiative, it is the government that will decide on Korean commitment to the development of the Sakha Republic gas project as South Korean companies do not have the financial capacity to undertake the project alone.

Clearly, the policies of regional governments in Northeast Asia are extremely important in creating multilateral energy cooperation. So too are the roles of international energy companies actively exploring new business opportunities in the region. The advanced technology and equipment necessary for the region's frontier oil and gas projects can only be provided by these companies, and their active participation in multilateral energy-development cooperation is as essential as that of the regional countries.

Energy, especially oil, development is politically, strategically and economically a very sensitive issue; it is also very closely linked with the environmental issue. Natural gas is ideal not only for the region's energy balance and security in the coming decades but also for accommodating its concern over environmental problems. No regional government would be against the introduction of natural gas as a major energy source.

Fortunately, Northeast Asia has natural gas, even though the resources are located in remote and environmentally harsh areas of Russia's Far East. The only way to extract the gas from the frozen land and transport it to Northeast Asian markets is to lay down a long-distance pipeline grid. To see the early establishment of a pan-regional gas grid, the region needs region-wide energy cooperation comparable to that of the European Union. What this has done is not to finance projects but to provide a political underpinning for energy cooperation.

Thus a model for Northeast Asian energy cooperation exists. The aims of the European Energy Charter Treaty were to agree on binding investment protection, transit of energy supplies, environmental protection, development of energy security installations, dispute settlement procedures and increased energy security throughout Western Europe and the new democracies. The real impetus for the treaty lay in the desire to assist in the economic development of Central and Eastern Europe through greater cooperation and foreign investment from Western industrial nations and corporations.[6] However, the European Charter does not finance anything or put projects together, but provides institutional assistance to potential investors in the event of political problems. Of course, the introduction of such institutional arrangements in Northeast Asia, which has no history of bloc cooperation, would be a big undertaking, and the finance and project-development issues would remain. The proposal for a Northeast Asian Energy Forum (NAEF)[7] is of great importance in this context.

---

[6] Julia Dore and Robert De Bauw, *The Energy Charter Treaty: Origins, Aims and Prospects*, Royal Institute of International Affairs, London, 1995.

[7] For the theoretical background of the concept of a resource regime, see Oran R. Young, *International Cooperation: Building Regimes for Natural Resources and the Environment*, Cornell University Press, Ithaca, 1989, pp. 11–30.

At present, there is no official apparatus to handle energy issues in Northeast Asia. If any sort of coordinated official initiative on energy policy in the region should arise, it will come from the Energy Group of the APEC (Asia Pacific Economic Cooperation) Conference (which now has 18 members) as the only government-level organization in the Asia-Pacific area. Since Russia is not a member of the APEC Conference, however, it is questionable whether APEC members can reach a consensus on prioritizing the region's oil and gas development.

Multilateral energy cooperation in Northeast Asia cannot be achieved without Russia. Until Russia – or the RFE – becomes an active member of APEC, and APEC pays attention to the Northeast Asian region, the NAEF, as an inter-government negotiating body for energy in general but focusing on energy development and related disputes, could provide the framework for hammering out multilateral energy cooperation.[8] There are four emerging regional environmental regimes in Northeast Asia,[9] and in February 1995, the Northeast Asian Economic Forum was convened in Niigata for its fifth round of talks. The forum proposed a Northeast Asia Energy consortium, based on Siberia's gas resources, that could analyse the feasability of a gas grid linking all of Northeast Asia.[10] The establishment of the NAEF is not such a remote possibility.

What is really needed for the region is an NAEF whose resolutions are binding or official. The formation of such an energy regime would be possible in the changing environment of the region, as the example of the Tumen River area development shows. As discussed earlier, five regional countries have agreed to cooperate in this development, recognizing the mutual benefits that will accrue. A stable energy supply source needs to be secured without delay, and the development programme has studied ways of utilizing the abundant coal resources in the Tumen River area. But Sakhalin offshore gas could supply the main energy source for the area's development, since the timetables of the two projects, Sakhalin offshore and the Tumen River area development, overlap. Given too that eventually a gas pipeline grid will

---

[8] Paik, 'Towards a Northeast Asian Energy Charter (op. cit., n. 4), pp. 433–43.

[9] Those regimes are the Northwest Pacific Action Plan, the Intergovernmental Oceanographic Commission's WESTPAC, the Economic and Social Commission for Asia and the Pacific/Northeast Asian Environmental Programme, and the Sub-Regional Programme. See Peter Hayes and Lyuba Zarsky, 'Environmental Issues and Regimes in Northeast Asia', *International Environmental Affairs* 6: 4 (Fall 1994), pp. 298–306.

[10] The forum recommended follow-up analysis of a proposal to establish a Northeast Asian Development Bank and a coordination mechanism to identify, evaluate and publicize commercially viable projects for investment. It also proposed an information pooling centre and a Northeast Asia Association of Chambers of Commerce. See *Asia Pacific Observer*, vol. 2, April-June 1995, p. 1.

connect northern Sakhalin with the greater Vladivostok area, Sakhalin offshore gas would be ideal as a main energy source for the Tumen River area development.

Furthermore, this approach will accelerate not only Sakhalin offshore development but also the region's economic development, and involve all the regional countries as participants as well as beneficiaries of the development. Japan, which is not yet committed to the Tumen River area development, can be involved quite naturally if Sakhalin offshore gas is delivered to the Tumen River area. No country will remain an outsider. Finally, the introduction of Sakhalin offshore gas to the Tumen River Area's development will enhance efforts to tackle the region's environmental problems.

The NAEF is necessary not only for the region's multilateral energy-development cooperation but also for dealing with energy-related issues. For example, in the second half of the 1990s another currently dormant territorial dispute, the so-called Senkaku issue, could erupt when the East China Sea's oil and gas development passes from exploration to exploitation. If Northeast Asia achieves the formation of a new regional energy framework, it will be spurred by strengthened bilateral energy relations, and especially by Russia's and China's positive stance towards regional energy cooperation.

8.6 Conclusion

Northeast Asia stands at a crossroads. The relics of the Cold War still linger in the region, but the trend towards multilateral cooperation for economic development is gaining momentum. In the second half of the 1990s the region will be tested by political, strategic, economic, environmental and social issues. One test will be whether the region can develop a common regional framework for frontier energy development despite political and economic diversity at national level.

Before concluding this study, I would like to project three scenarios for oil and gas development in Northeast Asia until 2010.

8.6.1 A realistic scenario

In the years 1996–2000 Northeast Asia will attempt multilateral cooperation in the region's gas development, but cooperation will be half-baked as Japan will not join in because of its uneasy relations with Russia. Development of Sakhalin-II will start first, and the Irkutsk and Sakhalin-I projects will follow. South Korea's participation in both Irkutsk and Sakhalin-I will constitute a degree of multilateral energy cooperation, for the first time in the region. Sakha gas development will follow on through its connection with the Irkutsk project.

Between 2001 and 2005, by extending the pipeline grid, Japan will participate in

Irkutsk gas development. This will open the way for the establishment of the NAEF. The NAEF will contribute greatly to the settlement of the Yellow Sea and East China Sea boundary issues. Sakhalin-LNG export to Japan will be realized before 2005 (if any delay occurs, it won't amount to much more than 1 or 2 years). As far as the Tarim Basin is concerned, the results of foreign companies' exploration work during 1996–2000 will accelerate development. The results will not be very good, but good enough to complete construction of the long-distance crude-oil pipeline.

Between 2006 and 2010, the full-fledged oil and gas development of Sakhalin offshore, Irkutsk and Sakha combined will have been realized and will accelerate the RFE's integration into the Northeast Asian economy. Improved relations between Russia and Japan will enable both sides to compromise on the territorial dispute. However, a pan-regional gas-pipeline grid connecting Japan, Russia's Sakhalin Island, the Sakha Republic, the Irkutsk region, Mongolia and China will be established between 2010 and 2015, not before 2010.

8.6.2 A pessimistic scenario

In the years 1996–2000 no significant step for the development of the Irkutsk and Sakha projects will be taken, except for Sakhalin-I and II. The development of the Energy Silk Route project supported by CNPC and Mitsubishi will start. As a result relations between Japan and Russia will deteriorate. Multilateral oil and gas development cooperation will not materialize; only bilateral relations will be strengthened.

Between 2001 and 2005, the production of Sakhalin offshore gas will start, but not LNG export to Japan. Meanwhile, Turkmenistan gas export to China and Japan will sour Japan–Russia relations but will not seriously affect Sino–Russian relations as China will appease Russia by the aggressive promotion of Irkutsk gas development with the participation of South Korea.

Between 2006 and 2010 Irkutsk gas export to China and South Korea, and Sakhalin LNG export to Japan, will start. The dominance of the bilateral Sino–Japanese energy relations will prevent the region's multilateral energy-development cooperation, and the NAEF will not be established. This will confirm how seriously uneasy Japan–Russia relations can affect regional cooperation in frontier energy development.

8.6.3 An optimistic scenario

In the years 1996–2000 the development of Sakhalin-I and II and the Irkutsk project will start simultaneously. South Korea's participation in Sakhalin-I will facilitate construction of a 1500-km pipeline grid connecting northern Sakhalin and Vladivostok. The regional countries begin to discuss the establishment of a pan-regional pipeline grid, which will lead to the establishment of the NAEF.

Between 2001 and 2005 Sakhalin-LNG export to Japan, and Irkutsk gas export to China and South Korea, will start. Sakha gas development will be combined with Sakhalin offshore development because of both Japan's and South Korea's decision to promote construction of a 3000-km pipeline grid between Yakutsk and Khabarovsk. It will prepare the ground for the establishment of the pipeline grid projected by the Vostok plan.

Between 2006 and 2010, the fully-fledged development of Sakhalin offshore will make the island the energy hub in Northeast Asia. A pan-regional gas-pipeline grid connecting Japan, Russia's Sakhalin Island, the Sakha Republic, the Irkutsk region, Mongolia and China will be established and presumably extended to North Korea. As a result a substantial proportion of increased natural-gas demand in Northeast Asia will be met by the import of pipeline gas rather than LNG.

In summary, this study has found that the region's energy resources, and particularly gas resources, offer huge potential benefits, but many political and economic obstacles stand in the way of their realization. A strong possibility exists for multilateral cooperation in RFE gas development, making all regional countries full beneficiaries of development. If the regional countries recognize the mutual benefits of multilateral cooperation, establishment of a multilateral government–industry forum could clarify and hasten the way forward. If the greatest possible attention is paid to achieving an energy balance and security of supply, the frontier energy development of Northeast Asia should take off without further delay.